A WORD TO THE
WISE

PRACTICAL ADVICE *from*
the BOOK *of* PROVERBS

DEVOTIONAL READINGS FOR
EVERY DAY OF THE YEAR

PAUL CHAPPELL

Striving Together Publications
4020 E. Lancaster Blvd.
Lancaster, CA 93535
800.201.7748

Cover design by Andrew Jones
Layout by Craig Parker
Edited by Robert Byers, Monica Bass, and Rebekah Scott
Special thanks to our proofreaders

The contents of this book are the result of decades of spiritual growth in life and ministry. It is not our intent to claim originality with any quote or thought that could not readily be tied to an original source.

ISBN 978-1-59894-248-4

Printed in the United States of America

Table of Contents

A Word from the Author

Dear Friend,

If there is one asset we need on a daily basis, it is wisdom. Every day we face challenges of life that can only be navigated successfully with God's wisdom. Thankfully, God makes His wisdom incredibly accessible to us through His Word. We have only to open its pages, allow the Holy Spirit to apply its truth to our hearts, and act on its counsel.

The book of Proverbs, in particular, is full of God's wisdom. These thirty-one chapters comprise a concentrated manual of wisdom for Christian living. For many years, I've enjoyed reading a chapter from Proverbs each day, reading through the entire book every month. *A Word to the Wise* is designed to lead you on a journey through Proverbs. The text for each day's reading corresponds to the chapter in Proverbs that matches the day of the month. (For instance, the devotion for January 1 comes from Proverbs 1, the devotion for July 16 comes from Proverbs 16, etc.)

Although Proverbs' focus is on gaining and applying wisdom, its counsel intertwines with the rest of Scripture. You'll find passages from many other books of the Bible interwoven throughout this book. (See pages 412–419 for a complete Scripture index.) Additionally, you'll find a Bible reading schedule at the bottom of each page that will lead you through the entire Bible in one year, as well as through the book of Proverbs monthly.

A Word to the Wise is written for the practically-minded Christian. The emphasis in these devotions is on application, and each reading concludes with a distilled truth that you can apply immediately to your life. I encourage you to read these devotions with your Bible open and a heart prepared to respond to God's truth and to walk in His wisdom.

I pray that each devotion in *A Word to the Wise* will help you in your spiritual growth and encourage you to apply God's wisdom to your life.

Sincerely in Christ,
Paul Chappell

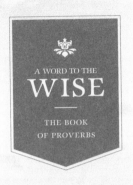

A WORD TO THE

WISE

THE BOOK
OF PROVERBS

PRACTICES OF
EFFECTIVE CHRISTIANS

The Effective Christian Memorizes Scripture

The following principles for effective Scripture memory are taken from *Homiletics from the Heart*, written by Dr. John Goetsch.

1. **Choose a specific time and a quiet place.**
   What gets scheduled gets accomplished. When memorizing the Word of God, you want to free yourself from all distractions.

2. **Organize by topic.**
   Many people attempt to learn the "Golden Chapters" or whole books of the Bible. While this is a noble attempt, it is not the way the Word of God will be used while teaching or preaching. Choose a topic you would like to study and then memorize every verse that deals with it. The next time you are speaking on that particular subject, your mind will be able to tie these verses together to truly allow you to "preach the Word..."

3. **Work out loud.**
   Even though it may sound odd, your mind memorizes better and faster that which it audibly hears. This is why you should choose a specific time and a quiet place!

4. **Walk while you memorize.**
   Your body has a natural sense of rhythm. This is why we memorize the words of songs so quickly. We will memorize much more quickly (and retain it longer) if we are walking around.

5. **Review, review, review.**
   Repetition is the key to learning. The one who is serious about memorizing Scripture cannot simply keep learning new passages weekly. Rather, he must also make the time to review the previous passages already committed to memory. It becomes readily apparent that memorization will take work, but the rewards are worth it!

6. **Set goals of time.**

   If you are not careful, you may ask for disappointment by setting goals of verses per week. The reason why is that some verses are more difficult to learn than others. If you set goals of time spent in memorization, God will honor that.

On the following pages you will find many major Bible doctrines and key verses to memorize. It is time to put into practice these six principles.

The Bible

Psalm 119:160—*Thy word is true from the beginning: and every one of thy righteous judgments endureth for ever.*

Isaiah 40:8—*The grass withereth, the flower fadeth: but the word of our God shall stand for ever.*

2 Timothy 3:16–17—*All scripture is given by inspiration of God, and is profitable for doctrine, for reproof, for correction, for instruction in righteousness: That the man of God may be perfect, throughly furnished unto all good works.*

Hebrews 4:12—*For the word of God is quick, and powerful, and sharper than any twoedged sword, piercing even to the dividing asunder of soul and spirit, and of the joints and marrow, and is a discerner of the thoughts and intents of the heart.*

John 17:17—*Sanctify them through thy truth: thy word is truth.*

Matthew 24:35—*Heaven and earth shall pass away, but my words shall not pass away.*

1 Thessalonians 2:13—*For this cause also thank we God without ceasing, because, when ye received the word of God which ye heard of us, ye received it not as the word of men, but as it is in truth, the word of God, which effectually worketh also in you that believe.*

God

Psalm 111:9—*He sent redemption unto his people: he hath commanded his covenant for ever: holy and reverend is his name.*

Isaiah 57:15—*For thus saith the high and lofty One that inhabiteth eternity, whose name is Holy; I dwell in the high and holy place, with him also that is of a contrite and humble spirit, to revive the spirit of the humble, and to revive the heart of the contrite ones.*

Lamentations 3:22–23—*It is of the LORD's mercies that we are not consumed, because his compassions fail not. They are new every morning: great is thy faithfulness.*

Deuteronomy 32:4—*He is the Rock, his work is perfect: for all his ways are judgment: a God of truth and without iniquity, just and right is he.*

Psalm 138:2—*I will worship toward thy holy temple, and praise thy name for thy lovingkindness and for thy truth: for thou hast magnified thy word above all thy name.*

John 4:24—*God is a Spirit: and they that worship him must worship him in spirit and in truth.*

Psalm 90:2—*Before the mountains were brought forth, or ever thou hadst formed the earth and the world, even from everlasting to everlasting, thou art God.*

Jesus Christ

John 1:1, 14—*In the beginning was the Word, and the Word was with God, and the Word was God. And the Word was made flesh, and dwelt among us, (and we beheld his glory, the glory as of the only begotten of the Father,) full of grace and truth.*

Philippians 2:6–8—*Who, being in the form of God, thought it not robbery to be equal with God: But made himself of no reputation, and took upon him the form of a servant, and was made in the likeness of men: And being found in fashion as a man, he humbled himself, and became obedient unto death, even the death of the cross.*

Colossians 1:16–17—*For by him were all things created, that are in heaven, and that are in earth, visible and invisible, whether they be thrones, or dominions, or principalities, or powers: all things were created by him, and for him: And he is before all things, and by him all things consist.*

1 Timothy 2:5–6—*For there is one God, and one mediator between God and men, the man Christ Jesus; Who gave himself a ransom for all, to be testified in due time.*

Hebrews 1:8—*But unto the Son he saith, Thy throne, O God, is for ever and ever: a sceptre of righteousness is the sceptre of thy kingdom.*

Luke 19:10—*For the Son of man is come to seek and to save that which was lost.*

Holy Spirit

John 14:16—*And I will pray the Father, and he shall give you another Comforter, that he may abide with you for ever;*

John 14:26—*But the Comforter, which is the Holy Ghost, whom the Father will send in my name, he shall teach you all things, and bring all things to your remembrance, whatsoever I have said unto you.*

John 15:26—*But when the Comforter is come, whom I will send unto you from the Father, even the Spirit of truth, which proceedeth from the Father, he shall testify of me:*

John 16:13–14—*Howbeit when he, the Spirit of truth, is come, he will guide you into all truth: for he shall not speak of himself; but whatsoever he shall hear, that shall he speak: and he will shew you things to come. He shall glorify me: for he shall receive of mine, and shall shew it unto you.*

1 Corinthians 3:16—*Know ye not that ye are the temple of God, and that the Spirit of God dwelleth in you?*

Ephesians 4:30—*And grieve not the holy Spirit of God, whereby ye are sealed unto the day of redemption.*

Ephesians 5:18—*And be not drunk with wine, wherein is excess; but be filled with the Spirit;*

Mankind

Genesis 1:26–27—*And God said, Let us make man in our image, after our likeness: and let them have dominion over the fish of the sea, and over the fowl of the air, and over the cattle, and over all the earth, and over every creeping* thing that creepeth upon the earth. So God created man in his own image, in the image of God created he him; male and female created he them.

Job 14:1, 14—Man that is born of a woman is of few days, and full of trouble. If a man die, shall he live again? all the days of my appointed time will I wait, till my change come.

Psalm 8:4–5—What is man, that thou art mindful of him? and the son of man, that thou visitest him? For thou hast made him a little lower than the angels, and hast crowned him with glory and honour.

Isaiah 64:6—But we are all as an unclean thing, and all our righteousnesses are as filthy rags; and we all do fade as a leaf; and our iniquities, like the wind, have taken us away.

Romans 3:10–11—As it is written, There is none righteous, no, not one: There is none that understandeth, there is none that seeketh after God.

Romans 3:23—For all have sinned, and come short of the glory of God.

Sin

Numbers 32:23—But if ye will not do so, behold, ye have sinned against the LORD: and be sure your sin will find you out.

Ezekiel 18:20—The soul that sinneth, it shall die. The son shall not bear the iniquity of the father, neither shall the father bear the iniquity of the son: the righteousness of the righteous shall be upon him, and the wickedness of the wicked shall be upon him.

Romans 6:23—For the wages of sin is death; but the gift of God is eternal life through Jesus Christ our Lord.

James 1:15—Then when lust hath conceived, it bringeth forth sin: and sin, when it is finished, bringeth forth death.

1 John 1:8–10—If we say that we have no sin, we deceive ourselves, and the truth is not in us. If we confess our sins, he is faithful and just to forgive us our sins, and to cleanse us from all unrighteousness. If we say that we have not sinned, we make him a liar, and his word is not in us.

1 John 3:4—*Whosoever committeth sin transgresseth also the law: for sin is the transgression of the law.*

Jeremiah 17:9—*The heart is deceitful above all things, and desperately wicked: who can know it?*

Salvation

Isaiah 45:22—*Look unto me, and be ye saved, all the ends of the earth: for I am God, and there is none else.*

Isaiah 43:11–12—*I, even I, am the LORD; and beside me there is no saviour. I have declared, and have saved, and I have shewed, when there was no strange god among you: therefore ye are my witnesses, saith the LORD, that I am God.*

John 14:6—*Jesus saith unto him, I am the way, the truth, and the life: no man cometh unto the Father, but by me.*

Acts 4:12—*Neither is there salvation in any other: for there is none other name under heaven given among men, whereby we must be saved.*

Romans 10:9–10—*That if thou shalt confess with thy mouth the Lord Jesus, and shalt believe in thine heart that God hath raised him from the dead, thou shalt be saved. For with the heart man believeth unto righteousness; and with the mouth confession is made unto salvation.*

Ephesians 2:8–9—*For by grace are ye saved through faith; and that not of yourselves: it is the gift of God: Not of works, lest any man should boast.*

Titus 3:5—*Not by works of righteousness which we have done, but according to his mercy he saved us, by the washing of regeneration, and renewing of the Holy Ghost;*

Church

Matthew 16:18—*And I say also unto thee, That thou art Peter, and upon this rock I will build my church; and the gates of hell shall not prevail against it.*

Colossians 1:18—*And he is the head of the body, the church: who is the beginning, the firstborn from the dead; that in all things he might have the preeminence.*

Ephesians 5:25–27—*Husbands, love your wives, even as Christ also loved the church, and gave himself for it; That he might sanctify and cleanse it with the washing of water by the word, That he might present it to himself a glorious church, not having spot, or wrinkle, or any such thing; but that it should be holy and without blemish.*

Acts 2:46–47—*And they, continuing daily with one accord in the temple, and breaking bread from house to house, did eat their meat with gladness and singleness of heart, Praising God, and having favour with all the people. And the Lord added to the church daily such as should be saved.*

1 Corinthians 12:13—*For by one Spirit are we all baptized into one body, whether we be Jews or Gentiles, whether we be bond or free; and have been all made to drink into one Spirit.*

1 Timothy 3:15—*But if I tarry long, that thou mayest know how thou oughtest to behave thyself in the house of God, which is the church of the living God, the pillar and ground of the truth.*

Angels

Genesis 3:24—*So he drove out the man; and he placed at the east of the garden of Eden Cherubims, and a flaming sword which turned every way, to keep the way of the tree of life.*

Psalm 148:2, 5—*Praise ye him, all his angels: praise ye him, all his hosts. Let them praise the name of the LORD: for he commanded, and they were created.*

Isaiah 6:1–3—*In the year that king Uzziah died I saw also the Lord sitting upon a throne, high and lifted up, and his train filled the temple. Above it stood the seraphims: each one had six wings; with twain he covered his face, and with twain he covered his feet, and with twain he did fly. And one cried unto another, and said, Holy, holy, holy, is the LORD of hosts: the whole earth is full of his glory.*

Mark 13:32—*But of that day and that hour knoweth no man, no, not the angels which are in heaven, neither the Son, but the Father.*

Hebrews 1:5–6—*For unto which of the angels said he at any time, Thou art my Son, this day have I begotten thee? And again, I will be to him a Father, and he shall be to me a Son? And again, when he bringeth in the firstbegotten into the world, he saith, And let all the angels of God worship him.*

1 Thessalonians 4:16—*For the Lord himself shall descend from heaven with a shout, with the voice of the archangel, and with the trump of God: and the dead in Christ shall rise first:*

End Times

1 Thessalonians 4:13–18—*But I would not have you to be ignorant, brethren, concerning them which are asleep, that ye sorrow not, even as others which have no hope. For if we believe that Jesus died and rose again, even so them also which sleep in Jesus will God bring with him. For this we say unto you by the word of the Lord, that we which are alive and remain unto the coming of the Lord shall not prevent them which are asleep. For the Lord himself shall descend from heaven with a shout, with the voice of the archangel, and with the trump of God: and the dead in Christ shall rise first: Then we which are alive and remain shall be caught up together with them in the clouds, to meet the Lord in the air: and so shall we ever be with the Lord. Wherefore comfort one another with these words.*

John 14:1–3—*Let not your heart be troubled: ye believe in God, believe also in me. In my Father's house are many mansions: if it were not so, I would have told you. I go to prepare a place for you. And if I go and prepare a place for you, I will come again, and receive you unto myself; that where I am, there ye may be also.*

Acts 1:10–11—*And while they looked stedfastly toward heaven as he went up, behold, two men stood by them in white apparel; Which also said, Ye men of Galilee, why stand ye gazing up into heaven? this same Jesus, which is taken up from you into heaven, shall so come in like manner as ye have seen him go into heaven.*

Revelation 22:20—*He which testifieth these things saith, Surely I come quickly. Amen. Even so, come, Lord Jesus.*

How to Lead a Person to Christ

Someone once said: "The fruit of a Christian is another Christian." There is a lot of truth in that statement. The Christian leader will influence people to be more soul-conscious. Yet, sometimes a person will be very active in sharing the gospel, but will not see much fruit. It is the responsibility of the Christian leader to "Train Every Available Member" to not only be available, but effective. Here are some truths that every soulwinner must remember as he prepares to help another soul spend an eternity with Christ.

1. **A soulwinner should start with the truth of God's love for every individual.**
   John 3:16 is perhaps the most familiar verse in all the New Testament. *"For God so loved the world…."* There are sinners living today who actually believe that God hates them and wants them to go to Hell because of their sin. A sinner will never accept a Saviour who he believes will never love him.

2. **A soulwinner must emphasize the fact that we are all sinners— there are no exceptions.**
   There have been some who understand the "love" of God and feel that He would never send anyone to Hell. These sinners must also understand that the God of "love" is also first, and foremost, holy. All men fall short of the holy standard He has set. As a result of this "falling short," we are condemned to an eternity in Hell. Romans 3:23 includes all men everywhere.

3. **A soulwinner must teach the sinner that his sin carries with it an expensive price tag.**
   According to Romans 6:23, *"the wages of sin is death…."* In Ezekiel 18:20, the Israelites learned that the soul that sinned would die. As a soulwinner, the person you are dealing with has the wrath of God already abiding on him (John 3:36).

4. **A soulwinner should demonstrate the good news that Jesus has already paid this price.**
   Not only does Romans 6:23 deal with the penalty of sin, it also deals with the promise of salvation. Romans 5:8 continues with this theme by showing the sinner that Christ died for us while we were yet sinners.

5. **A soulwinner must remember that a sinner must personally accept Christ as Saviour.**
   This promise is given in Romans 10:13—*"For whosoever shall call upon the name of the Lord shall be saved."* A sinner may believe that God loves him, may understand the fact that he is a sinner, and may further understand that Jesus died to pay his sin debt and still be lost. The soulwinner is not after a simple mental assent to a list of subscribed facts. He is looking for a sinner to repent, to confess, and to know the joy of being a Christian.

6. **Ask the sinner, "Is there anything that would hinder you from trusting Christ right now, today, as your Saviour?"**
   This question will show the soulwinner if there are still any "obstacles" that must be removed before a sinner trusts Christ. It will also serve as a good transition into drawing the gospel net. After a sinner is saved, the Great Commission is still unfulfilled. We are commanded to go, to win, to baptize, and to teach (disciple). An effective soulwinner will determine to see each aspect of the Great Commission come to fruition with those he leads to Christ.

Verses Remembered by Effective Christians

When you lose sight of His greatness:
Jeremiah 32:17; Jeremiah 33:3; Psalm 147:5; Romans 11:33–36; and 1 Chronicles 29:11–14

When you have needs:
Matthew 6:33; Philippians 4:19; Psalm 37:3; Psalm 37:25; and Deuteronomy 2:7

When you are overwhelmed:
Psalm 55:5; Psalm 55:18; Psalm 107:6–8; and 2 Corinthians 4:16

When problems seem insurmountable:
2 Corinthians 4:15–18; Romans 8:18; Psalm 32:7; Psalm 60:12; Psalm 61:2; and Psalm 62:6–8

When you need purpose:
1 Corinthians 10:31; Ephesians 3:16–21; John 10:10; and Psalm 139:14

When you have stress:
Philippians 4:4–7; Deuteronomy 20:1–4; and Jeremiah 32:27

When you are under pressure:
Psalm 27:1–2; Psalm 27:13–14; Psalm 46:1–2; and 2 Corinthians 12:9–10

When you worry:
Philippians 4:6–7; 1 Peter 5:7; Psalm 55:22; and Psalm 46:10

When you are afraid:
Psalm 56:3; Genesis 15:1; Psalm 27:1; 2 Timothy 1:7; and John 14:27

When you have a big decision to make:
Psalm 32:8; Psalm 143:10; Psalm 40:8; Proverbs 3:5–6; and Psalm 37:3–6

When you are discouraged:
1 Samuel 30:6; Joshua 1:9; Isaiah 41:10; Isaiah 40:26–28; and 2 Corinthians 4:15–16

When you are disheartened:
Joshua 1:5–9; Psalm 73:17; and Psalm 73:23–26

When you are facing opposition:
2 Timothy 3:12; 2 Timothy 2:3; 1 Peter 4:12–13; 1 John 4:4; and Romans 8:31–32

When friends seem to let you down:
2 Timothy 4:16–17; Hebrews 12:2–3; Hebrews 13:5–6; and Deuteronomy 32:27

When you are lonely:
Isaiah 41:10; Hebrews 13:5–6; Acts 18:9–10; and Isaiah 43:2

When you ask if it is worth it:
Matthew 25:21; 1 Corinthians 15:58; Galatians 6:9; and 2 Corinthians 4:17

The Effective Christian's Daily Bible Reading

Christians used by God have one thing in common: a daily walk with God. A Christian's daily walk is based upon the foundation of Bible reading and prayer. It has often been said, "The Book will keep you from sin, or sin will keep you from the Book."

Printed at the bottom of the page for each day is a segmented reading calendar that will allow you to read through the Old and New Testaments during the course of a year.

When considering whether or not to spend time in the Word of God, it is advisable to listen to the words of David, a man after God's own heart, who under the inspiration of the Holy Spirit wrote:

Psalm 119:105
"Thy word is a lamp unto my feet, and a light unto my path."

Psalm 119:9
"Wherewithal shall a young man cleanse his way? by taking heed thereto according to thy word."

May God's Word draw you closer to Him, and help you be the Christian He saved you to be.

One-Year Bible Reading Schedule

January

❑	1	Gen. 1–3	Matt. 1
❑	2	Gen. 4–6	Matt. 2
❑	3	Gen. 7–9	Matt. 3
❑	4	Gen. 10–12	Matt. 4
❑	5	Gen. 13–15	Matt. 5:1–26
❑	6	Gen. 16–17	Matt. 5:27–48
❑	7	Gen. 18–19	Matt. 6:1–18
❑	8	Gen. 20–22	Matt. 6:19–34
❑	9	Gen. 23–24	Matt. 7
❑	10	Gen. 25–26	Matt. 8:1–17
❑	11	Gen. 27–28	Matt. 8:18–34
❑	12	Gen. 29–30	Matt. 9:1–17
❑	13	Gen. 31–32	Matt. 9:18–38
❑	14	Gen. 33–35	Matt. 10:1–20
❑	15	Gen. 36–38	Matt. 10:21–42
❑	16	Gen. 39–40	Matt. 11
❑	17	Gen. 41–42	Matt. 12:1–23
❑	18	Gen. 43–45	Matt. 12:24–50
❑	19	Gen. 46–48	Matt. 13:1–30
❑	20	Gen. 49–50	Matt. 13:31–58
❑	21	Ex. 1–3	Matt. 14:1–21
❑	22	Ex. 4–6	Matt. 14:22–36
❑	23	Ex. 7–8	Matt. 15:1–20
❑	24	Ex. 9–11	Matt. 15:21–39
❑	25	Ex. 12–13	Matt. 16
❑	26	Ex. 14–15	Matt. 17
❑	27	Ex. 16–18	Matt. 18:1–20
❑	28	Ex. 19–20	Matt. 18:21–35
❑	29	Ex. 21–22	Matt. 19
❑	30	Ex. 23–24	Matt. 20:1–16
❑	31	Ex. 25–26	Matt. 20:17–34

February

❑	1	Ex. 27–28	Matt. 21:1–22
❑	2	Ex. 29–30	Matt. 21:23–46
❑	3	Ex. 31–33	Matt. 22:1–22
❑	4	Ex. 34–35	Matt. 22:23–46
❑	5	Ex. 36–38	Matt. 23:1–22
❑	6	Ex. 39–40	Matt. 23:23–39
❑	7	Lev. 1–3	Matt. 24:1–28
❑	8	Lev. 4–5	Matt. 24:29–51
❑	9	Lev. 6–7	Matt. 25:1–30
❑	10	Lev. 8–10	Matt. 25:31–46
❑	11	Lev. 11–12	Matt. 26:1–25
❑	12	Lev. 13	Matt. 26:26–50
❑	13	Lev. 14	Matt. 26:51–75
❑	14	Lev. 15–16	Matt. 27:1–26
❑	15	Lev. 17–18	Matt. 27:27–50
❑	16	Lev. 19–20	Matt. 27:51–66
❑	17	Lev. 21–22	Matt. 28
❑	18	Lev. 23–24	Mark 1:1–22
❑	19	Lev. 25	Mark 1:23–45
❑	20	Lev. 26–27	Mark 2
❑	21	Num. 1–2	Mark 3:1–19
❑	22	Num. 3–4	Mark 3:20–35
❑	23	Num. 5–6	Mark 4:1–20
❑	24	Num. 7–8	Mark 4:21–41
❑	25	Num. 9–11	Mark 5:1–20
❑	26	Num. 12–14	Mark 5:21–43
❑	27	Num. 15–16	Mark 6:1–29
❑	28	Num. 17–19	Mark 6:30–56

March

❑	1	Num. 20–22	Mark 7:1–13
❑	2	Num. 23–25	Mark 7:14–37
❑	3	Num. 26–28	Mark 8
❑	4	Num. 29–31	Mark 9:1–29
❑	5	Num. 32–34	Mark 9:30–50
❑	6	Num. 35–36	Mark 10:1–31
❑	7	Deut. 1–3	Mark 10:32–52
❑	8	Deut. 4–6	Mark 11:1–18
❑	9	Deut. 7–9	Mark 11:19–33
❑	10	Deut. 10–12	Mark 12:1–27
❑	11	Deut. 13–15	Mark 12:28–44
❑	12	Deut. 16–18	Mark 13:1–20
❑	13	Deut. 19–21	Mark 13:21–37
❑	14	Deut. 22–24	Mark 14:1–26
❑	15	Deut. 25–27	Mark 14:27–53
❑	16	Deut. 28–29	Mark 14:54–72
❑	17	Deut. 30–31	Mark 15:1–25
❑	18	Deut. 32–34	Mark 15:26–47
❑	19	Josh. 1–3	Mark 16
❑	20	Josh. 4–6	Luke 1:1–20
❑	21	Josh. 7–9	Luke 1:21–38
❑	22	Josh. 10–12	Luke 1:39–56
❑	23	Josh. 13–15	Luke 1:57–80
❑	24	Josh. 16–18	Luke 2:1–24
❑	25	Josh. 19–21	Luke 2:25–52
❑	26	Josh. 22–24	Luke 3
❑	27	Judges 1–3	Luke 4:1–30
❑	28	Judges 4–6	Luke 4:31–44
❑	29	Judges 7–8	Luke 5:1–16
❑	30	Judges 9–10	Luke 5:17–39
❑	31	Judges 11–12	Luke 6:1–26

April

❑	1	Judges 13–15	Luke 6:27–49
❑	2	Judges 16–18	Luke 7:1–30
❑	3	Judges 19–21	Luke 7:31–50
❑	4	Ruth 1–4	Luke 8:1–25
❑	5	1 Sam. 1–3	Luke 8:26–56
❑	6	1 Sam. 4–6	Luke 9:1–17
❑	7	1 Sam. 7–9	Luke 9:18–36
❑	8	1 Sam. 10–12	Luke 9:37–62
❑	9	1 Sam. 13–14	Luke 10:1–24
❑	10	1 Sam. 15–16	Luke 10:25–42
❑	11	1 Sam. 17–18	Luke 11:1–28
❑	12	1 Sam. 19–21	Luke 11:29–54
❑	13	1 Sam. 22–24	Luke 12:1–31
❑	14	1 Sam. 25–26	Luke 12:32–59
❑	15	1 Sam. 27–29	Luke 13:1–22
❑	16	1 Sam. 30–31	Luke 13:23–35
❑	17	2 Sam. 1–2	Luke 14:1–24
❑	18	2 Sam. 3–5	Luke 14:25–35
❑	19	2 Sam. 6–8	Luke 15:1–10
❑	20	2 Sam. 9–11	Luke 15:11–32
❑	21	2 Sam. 12–13	Luke 16
❑	22	2 Sam. 14–15	Luke 17:1–19
❑	23	2 Sam. 16–18	Luke 17:20–37
❑	24	2 Sam. 19–20	Luke 18:1–23
❑	25	2 Sam. 21–22	Luke 18:24–43
❑	26	2 Sam. 23–24	Luke 19:1–27
❑	27	1 Kings 1–2	Luke 19:28–48
❑	28	1 Kings 3–5	Luke 20:1–26
❑	29	1 Kings 6–7	Luke 20:27–47
❑	30	1 Kings 8–9	Luke 21:1–19

May

❑	1	1 Kings 10–11	Luke 21:20–38
❑	2	1 Kings 12–13	Luke 22:1–30
❑	3	1 Kings 14–15	Luke 22:31–46
❑	4	1 Kings 16–18	Luke 22:47–71
❑	5	1 Kings 19–20	Luke 23:1–25
❑	6	1 Kings 21–22	Luke 23:26–56
❑	7	2 Kings 1–3	Luke 24:1–35
❑	8	2 Kings 4–6	Luke 24:36–53
❑	9	2 Kings 7–9	John 1:1–28
❑	10	2 Kings 10–12	John 1:29–51
❑	11	2 Kings 13–14	John 2
❑	12	2 Kings 15–16	John 3:1–18
❑	13	2 Kings 17–18	John 3:19–36
❑	14	2 Kings 19–21	John 4:1–30
❑	15	2 Kings 22–23	John 4:31–54
❑	16	2 Kings 24–25	John 5:1–24
❑	17	1 Chr. 1–3	John 5:25–47
❑	18	1 Chr. 4–6	John 6:1–21
❑	19	1 Chr. 7–9	John 6:22–44
❑	20	1 Chr. 10–12	John 6:45–71
❑	21	1 Chr. 13–15	John 7:1–27
❑	22	1 Chr. 16–18	John 7:28–53
❑	23	1 Chr. 19–21	John 8:1–27
❑	24	1 Chr. 22–24	John 8:28–59
❑	25	1 Chr. 25–27	John 9:1–23
❑	26	1 Chr. 28–29	John 9:24–41
❑	27	2 Chr. 1–3	John 10:1–23
❑	28	2 Chr. 4–6	John 10:24–42
❑	29	2 Chr. 7–9	John 11:1–29
❑	30	2 Chr. 10–12	John 11:30–57
❑	31	2 Chr. 13–14	John 12:1–26

June

❑	1	2 Chr. 15–16	John 12:27–50
❑	2	2 Chr. 17–18	John 13:1–20
❑	3	2 Chr. 19–20	John 13:21–38
❑	4	2 Chr. 21–22	John 14
❑	5	2 Chr. 23–24	John 15
❑	6	2 Chr. 25–27	John 16
❑	7	2 Chr. 28–29	John 17
❑	8	2 Chr. 30–31	John 18:1–18
❑	9	2 Chr. 32–33	John 18:19–40
❑	10	2 Chr. 34–36	John 19:1–22
❑	11	Ezra 1–2	John 19:23–42
❑	12	Ezra 3–5	John 20
❑	13	Ezra 6–8	John 21
❑	14	Ezra 9–10	Acts 1
❑	15	Neh. 1–3	Acts 2:1–21
❑	16	Neh. 4–6	Acts 2:22–47
❑	17	Neh. 7–9	Acts 3
❑	18	Neh. 10–11	Acts 4:1–22
❑	19	Neh. 12–13	Acts 4:23–37
❑	20	Esther 1–2	Acts 5:1–21
❑	21	Esther 3–5	Acts 5:22–42
❑	22	Esther 6–8	Acts 6
❑	23	Esther 9–10	Acts 7:1–21
❑	24	Job 1–2	Acts 7:22–43
❑	25	Job 3–4	Acts 7:44–60
❑	26	Job 5–7	Acts 8:1–25
❑	27	Job 8–10	Acts 8:26–40
❑	28	Job 11–13	Acts 9:1–21
❑	29	Job 14–16	Acts 9:22–43
❑	30	Job 17–19	Acts 10:1–23

July

❏	1	Job 20–21	Acts 10:24–48
❏	2	Job 22–24	Acts 11
❏	3	Job 25–27	Acts 12
❏	4	Job 28–29	Acts 13:1–25
❏	5	Job 30–31	Acts 13:26–52
❏	6	Job 32–33	Acts 14
❏	7	Job 34–35	Acts 15:1–21
❏	8	Job 36–37	Acts 15:22–41
❏	9	Job 38–40	Acts 16:1–21
❏	10	Job 41–42	Acts 16:22–40
❏	11	Ps. 1–3	Acts 17:1–15
❏	12	Ps. 4–6	Acts 17:16–34
❏	13	Ps. 7–9	Acts 18
❏	14	Ps. 10–12	Acts 19:1–20
❏	15	Ps. 13–15	Acts 19:21–41
❏	16	Ps. 16–17	Acts 20:1–16
❏	17	Ps. 18–19	Acts 20:17–38
❏	18	Ps. 20–22	Acts 21:1–17
❏	19	Ps. 23–25	Acts 21:18–40
❏	20	Ps. 26–28	Acts 22
❏	21	Ps. 29–30	Acts 23:1–15
❏	22	Ps. 31–32	Acts 23:16–35
❏	23	Ps. 33–34	Acts 24
❏	24	Ps. 35–36	Acts 25
❏	25	Ps. 37–39	Acts 26
❏	26	Ps. 40–42	Acts 27:1–26
❏	27	Ps. 43–45	Acts 27:27–44
❏	28	Ps. 46–48	Acts 28
❏	29	Ps. 49–50	Rom. 1
❏	30	Ps. 51–53	Rom. 2
❏	31	Ps. 54–56	Rom. 3

August

❏	1	Ps. 57–59	Rom. 4
❏	2	Ps. 60–62	Rom. 5
❏	3	Ps. 63–65	Rom. 6
❏	4	Ps. 66–67	Rom. 7
❏	5	Ps. 68–69	Rom. 8:1–21
❏	6	Ps. 70–71	Rom. 8:22–39
❏	7	Ps. 72–73	Rom. 9:1–15
❏	8	Ps. 74–76	Rom. 9:16–33
❏	9	Ps. 77–78	Rom. 10
❏	10	Ps. 79–80	Rom. 11:1–18
❏	11	Ps. 81–83	Rom. 11:19–36
❏	12	Ps. 84–86	Rom. 12
❏	13	Ps. 87–88	Rom. 13
❏	14	Ps. 89–90	Rom. 14
❏	15	Ps. 91–93	Rom. 15:1–13
❏	16	Ps. 94–96	Rom. 15:14–33
❏	17	Ps. 97–99	Rom. 16
❏	18	Ps. 100–102	1 Cor. 1
❏	19	Ps. 103–104	1 Cor. 2
❏	20	Ps. 105–106	1 Cor. 3
❏	21	Ps. 107–109	1 Cor. 4
❏	22	Ps. 110–112	1 Cor. 5
❏	23	Ps. 113–115	1 Cor. 6
❏	24	Ps. 116–118	1 Cor. 7:1–19
❏	25	Ps. 119:1–88	1 Cor. 7:20–40
❏	26	Ps. 119:89–176	1 Cor. 8
❏	27	Ps. 120–122	1 Cor. 9
❏	28	Ps.123–125	1 Cor. 10:1–18
❏	29	Ps. 126–128	1 Cor. 10:19–33
❏	30	Ps. 129–131	1 Cor. 11:1–16
❏	31	Ps. 132–134	1 Cor. 11:17–34

September

❏	1	Ps. 135–136	1 Cor. 12
❏	2	Ps. 137–139	1 Cor. 13
❏	3	Ps. 140–142	1 Cor. 14:1–20
❏	4	Ps. 143–145	1 Cor. 14:21–40
❏	5	Ps. 146–147	1 Cor. 15:1–28
❏	6	Ps. 148–150	1 Cor. 15:29–58
❏	7	Prov. 1–2	1 Cor. 16
❏	8	Prov. 3–5	2 Cor. 1
❏	9	Prov. 6–7	2 Cor. 2
❏	10	Prov. 8–9	2 Cor. 3
❏	11	Prov. 10–12	2 Cor. 4
❏	12	Prov. 13–15	2 Cor. 5
❏	13	Prov. 16–18	2 Cor. 6
❏	14	Prov. 19–21	2 Cor. 7
❏	15	Prov. 22–24	2 Cor. 8
❏	16	Prov. 25–26	2 Cor. 9
❏	17	Prov. 27–29	2 Cor. 10
❏	18	Prov. 30–31	2 Cor. 11:1–15
❏	19	Eccl. 1–3	2 Cor. 11:16–33
❏	20	Eccl. 4–6	2 Cor. 12
❏	21	Eccl. 7–9	2 Cor. 13
❏	22	Eccl. 10–12	Gal. 1
❏	23	Song 1–3	Gal. 2
❏	24	Song 4–5	Gal. 3
❏	25	Song 6–8	Gal. 4
❏	26	Isa. 1–2	Gal. 5
❏	27	Isa. 3–4	Gal. 6
❏	28	Isa. 5–6	Eph. 1
❏	29	Isa. 7–8	Eph. 2
❏	30	Isa. 9–10	Eph. 3

October

❏	1	Isa. 11–13	Eph. 4
❏	2	Isa. 14–16	Eph. 5:1–16
❏	3	Isa. 17–19	Eph. 5:17–33
❏	4	Isa. 20–22	Eph. 6
❏	5	Isa. 23–25	Phil. 1
❏	6	Isa. 26–27	Phil. 2
❏	7	Isa. 28–29	Phil. 3
❏	8	Isa. 30–31	Phil. 4
❏	9	Isa. 32–33	Col. 1
❏	10	Isa. 34–36	Col. 2
❏	11	Isa. 37–38	Col. 3
❏	12	Isa. 39–40	Col. 4
❏	13	Isa. 41–42	1 Thess. 1
❏	14	Isa. 43–44	1 Thess. 2
❏	15	Isa. 45–46	1 Thess. 3
❏	16	Isa. 47–49	1 Thess. 4
❏	17	Isa. 50–52	1 Thess. 5
❏	18	Isa. 53–55	2 Thess. 1
❏	19	Isa. 56–58	2 Thess. 2
❏	20	Isa. 59–61	2 Thess. 3
❏	21	Isa. 62–64	1 Tim. 1
❏	22	Isa. 65–66	1 Tim. 2
❏	23	Jer. 1–2	1 Tim. 3
❏	24	Jer. 3–5	1 Tim. 4
❏	25	Jer. 6–8	1 Tim. 5
❏	26	Jer. 9–11	1 Tim. 6
❏	27	Jer. 12–14	2 Tim. 1
❏	28	Jer. 15–17	2 Tim. 2
❏	29	Jer. 18–19	2 Tim. 3
❏	30	Jer. 20–21	2 Tim. 4
❏	31	Jer. 22–23	Titus 1

November

❏	1	Jer. 24–26	Titus 2
❏	2	Jer. 27–29	Titus 3
❏	3	Jer. 30–31	Philemon
❏	4	Jer. 32–33	Heb. 1
❏	5	Jer. 34–36	Heb. 2
❏	6	Jer. 37–39	Heb. 3
❏	7	Jer. 40–42	Heb. 4
❏	8	Jer. 43–45	Heb. 5
❏	9	Jer. 46–47	Heb. 6
❏	10	Jer. 48–49	Heb. 7
❏	11	Jer. 50	Heb. 8
❏	12	Jer. 51–52	Heb. 9
❏	13	Lam. 1–2	Heb. 10:1–18
❏	14	Lam. 3–5	Heb. 10:19–39
❏	15	Ezek. 1–2	Heb. 11:1–19
❏	16	Ezek. 3–4	Heb. 11:20–40
❏	17	Ezek. 5–7	Heb. 12
❏	18	Ezek. 8–10	Heb. 13
❏	19	Ezek. 11–13	James 1
❏	20	Ezek. 14–15	James 2
❏	21	Ezek. 16–17	James 3
❏	22	Ezek. 18–19	James 4
❏	23	Ezek. 20–21	James 5
❏	24	Ezek. 22–23	1 Peter 1
❏	25	Ezek. 24–26	1 Peter 2
❏	26	Ezek. 27–29	1 Peter 3
❏	27	Ezek. 30–32	1 Peter 4
❏	28	Ezek. 33–34	1 Peter 5
❏	29	Ezek. 35–36	2 Peter 1
❏	30	Ezek. 37–39	2 Peter 2

December

❏	1	Ezek. 40–41	2 Peter 3
❏	2	Ezek. 42–44	1 John 1
❏	3	Ezek. 45–46	1 John 2
❏	4	Ezek. 47–48	1 John 3
❏	5	Dan. 1–2	1 John 4
❏	6	Dan. 3–4	1 John 5
❏	7	Dan. 5–7	2 John
❏	8	Dan. 8–10	3 John
❏	9	Dan. 11–12	Jude
❏	10	Hos. 1–4	Rev. 1
❏	11	Hos. 5–8	Rev. 2
❏	12	Hos. 9–11	Rev. 3
❏	13	Hos. 12–14	Rev. 4
❏	14	Joel	Rev. 5
❏	15	Amos 1–3	Rev. 6
❏	16	Amos 4–6	Rev. 7
❏	17	Amos 7–9	Rev. 8
❏	18	Obad.	Rev. 9
❏	19	Jonah	Rev. 10
❏	20	Micah 1–3	Rev. 11
❏	21	Micah 4–5	Rev. 12
❏	22	Micah 6–7	Rev. 13
❏	23	Nahum	Rev. 14
❏	24	Hab.	Rev. 15
❏	25	Zeph.	Rev. 16
❏	26	Hag.	Rev. 17
❏	27	Zech. 1–4	Rev. 18
❏	28	Zech. 5–8	Rev. 19
❏	29	Zech. 9–12	Rev. 20
❏	30	Zech. 13–14	Rev. 21
❏	31	Mal.	Rev. 22

90-Day Bible Reading Schedule

Day	Start	End	✔
1	Genesis 1:1	Genesis 16:16	❏
2	Genesis 17:1	Genesis 28:19	❏
3	Genesis 28:20	Genesis 40:11	❏
4	Genesis 40:12	Genesis 50:26	❏
5	Exodus 1:1	Exodus 15:18	❏
6	Exodus 15:19	Exodus 28:43	❏
7	Exodus 29:1	Exodus 40:38	❏
8	Leviticus 1:1	Leviticus 14:32	❏
9	Leviticus 14:33	Leviticus 26:26	❏
10	Leviticus 26:27	Numbers 8:14	❏
11	Numbers 8:15	Numbers 21:7	❏
12	Numbers 21:8	Numbers 32:19	❏
13	Numbers 32:20	Deuteronomy 7:26	❏
14	Deuteronomy 8:1	Deuteronomy 23:11	❏
15	Deuteronomy 23:12	Deuteronomy 34:12	❏
16	Joshua 1:1	Joshua 14:15	❏
17	Joshua 15:1	Judges 3:27	❏
18	Judges 3:28	Judges 15:12	❏
19	Judges 15:13	1 Samuel 2:29	❏
20	1 Samuel 2:30	1 Samuel 15:35	❏
21	1 Samuel 16:1	1 Samuel 28:19	❏
22	1 Samuel 28:20	2 Samuel 12:10	❏
23	2 Samuel 12:11	2 Samuel 22:18	❏
24	2 Samuel 22:19	1 Kings 7:37	❏
25	1 Kings 7:38	1 Kings 16:20	❏
26	1 Kings 16:21	2 Kings 4:37	❏
27	2 Kings 4:38	2 Kings 15:26	❏
28	2 Kings 15:27	2 Kings 25:30	❏
29	1 Chronicles 1:1	1 Chronicles 9:44	❏
30	1 Chronicles 10:1	1 Chronicles 23:32	❏
31	1 Chronicles 24:1	2 Chronicles 7:10	❏
32	2 Chronicles 7:11	2 Chronicles 23:15	❏
33	2 Chronicles 23:16	2 Chronicles 35:15	❏
34	2 Chronicles 35:16	Ezra 10:44	❏
35	Nehemiah 1:1	Nehemiah 13:14	❏
36	Nehemiah 13:15	Job 7:21	❏
37	Job 8:1	Job 24:25	❏
38	Job 25:1	Job 41:34	❏
39	Job 42:1	Psalm 24:10	❏
40	Psalm 25:1	Psalm 45:14	❏
41	Psalm 45:15	Psalm 69:21	❏
42	Psalm 69:22	Psalm 89:13	❏
43	Psalm 89:14	Psalm 108:13	❏
44	Psalm 109:1	Psalm 134:3	❏
45	Psalm 135:1	Proverbs 6:35	❏

Day	Start	End	✔
46	Proverbs 7:1	Proverbs 20:21	❏
47	Proverbs 20:22	Ecclesiastes 2:26	❏
48	Ecclesiastes 3:1	Song 8:14	❏
49	Isaiah 1:1	Isaiah 13:22	❏
50	Isaiah 14:1	Isaiah 28:29	❏
51	Isaiah 29:1	Isaiah 41:18	❏
52	Isaiah 41:19	Isaiah 52:12	❏
53	Isaiah 52:13	Isaiah 66:18	❏
54	Isaiah 66:19	Jeremiah 10:13	❏
55	Jeremiah 10:14	Jeremiah 23:8	❏
56	Jeremiah 23:9	Jeremiah 33:22	❏
57	Jeremiah 33:23	Jeremiah 47:7	❏
58	Jeremiah 48:1	Lamentations 1:22	❏
59	Lamentations 2:1	Ezekiel 12:20	❏
60	Ezekiel 12:21	Ezekiel 23:39	❏
61	Ezekiel 23:40	Ezekiel 35:15	❏
62	Ezekiel 36:1	Ezekiel 47:12	❏
63	Ezekiel 47:13	Daniel 8:27	❏
64	Daniel 9:1	Hosea 13:6	❏
65	Hosea 13:7	Amos 9:10	❏
66	Amos 9:11	Nahum 3:19	❏
67	Habakkuk 1:1	Zechariah 10:12	❏
68	Zechariah 11:1	Matthew 4:25	❏
69	Matthew 5:1	Matthew 15:39	❏
70	Matthew 16:1	Matthew 26:56	❏
71	Matthew 26:57	Mark 9:13	❏
72	Mark 9:14	Luke 1:80	❏
73	Luke 2:1	Luke 9:62	❏
74	Luke 10:1	Luke 20:19	❏
75	Luke 20:20	John 5:47	❏
76	John 6:1	John 15:17	❏
77	John 15:18	Acts 6:7	❏
78	Acts 6:8	Acts 16:37	❏
79	Acts 16:38	Acts 28:16	❏
80	Acts 28:17	Romans 14:23	❏
81	Romans 15:1	1 Corinthians 14:40	❏
82	1 Corinthians 15:1	Galatians 3:25	❏
83	Galatians 3:26	Colossians 4:18	❏
84	1 Thessalonians 1:1	Philemon 25	❏
85	Hebrews 1:1	James 3:12	❏
86	James 3:13	3 John 14	❏
87	Jude 1	Revelation 17:18	❏
88	Revelation 18:1	Revelation 22:21	❏
89	Grace Day	Grace Day	❏
90	Grace Day	Grace Day	❏

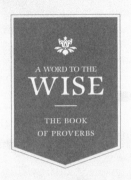

A WORD TO THE

WISE

THE BOOK
OF PROVERBS

JANUARY

A Fresh Quest for a New Year

*The proverbs of Solomon the son of David, king of Israel; To know wisdom and instruction; to perceive the words of understanding;—***Proverbs 1:1–2**

Industrialist Charles Schwab was a key figure in Andrew Carnegie's steel empire. Frustrated with his inability to get everything done, he reluctantly agreed to meet with a consultant named Ivy Lee, who was recommended to him by John D. Rockefeller. Schwab had little use for consultants, but since Rockefeller recommended Lee so highly, he scheduled the meeting. Lee's proposal was elegantly simple.

He told Schwab to make a list of the six most important things he could do the next day to further the overall health and function of U.S. Steel. At the end of the day, Schwab was to review the list, move anything that had not been finished to the top of the next day's list, and then add enough items to make a total of six again. Within fifteen minutes the meeting concluded. Lee told Schwab to follow this practice for thirty days and then send him a payment based on how much Schwab thought the advice was worth. In thirty days, Schwab sent Lee a check for $25,000!

This story illustrates the great value of receiving instruction in wisdom. Wisdom can be defined as "skillfulness in the use of knowledge." It is more than just education and the accumulation of facts. Wisdom is being instructed in God's views and values and then living accordingly. Wisdom is so important, in fact, that God has given us an entire book of Scripture designed to instruct us to live wisely.

Throughout this year, we will be studying in these devotions the wisdom recorded in Proverbs. This book is the written advice that Solomon, under the direct inspiration of the Holy Spirit, wrote and compiled for his son Rehoboam to help prepare him for life. May we apply our hearts to wisdom today and throughout our lives.

Today's Word to the Wise: Allow God's Word to guide the development of your values and live by its principles, and you will receive the benefits of wisdom.

The Treasure Hunt

My son, if thou wilt receive my words, and hide my commandments with thee; So that thou incline thine ear unto wisdom, and apply thine heart to understanding; Yea, if thou criest after knowledge, and liftest up thy voice for understanding; If thou seekest her as silver, and searchest for her as for hid treasures; Then shalt thou understand the fear of the LORD, and find the knowledge of God.—**Proverbs 2:1–5**

For more than thirty years, archaeologist Howard Carter searched the deserts of Egypt for something that most people thought didn't exist—the tomb of King Tutankhamen. Most experts believed that everything in the Valley of the Kings had already been discovered, but Carter continued his search. After five more years without result, Carter's sponsor, Lord Carnarvon of England, indicated that he would stop funding the search.

In November of 1922, during his final season of work, Carter uncovered a hidden staircase near the tomb of Ramses VI. He sent a cable to England which said, "At last have made wonderful discovery in Valley; a magnificent tomb with seals intact." Carter had indeed located the tomb of King Tut, one of the greatest archaeological treasures ever discovered. After months of careful work, the golden treasures of the tomb were cataloged, and the first intact royal mummy ever found was removed from the place where it had rested for more than three thousand years.

Carter's search was driven by his firm belief that there was treasure to be found, even though he could not be certain that he was correct. We have an even better opportunity—a treasure hunt with guaranteed success. If we seek the wisdom of God, the reward is ours! Notice the certainty of the promise—if we receive God's Word, if we cry out for it and seek it as treasure hunters do for precious metals, we will surely find what we seek.

Today's Word to the Wise: If you prioritize the Scripture in your thinking and actions, you will discover the greatest treasure you can possibly find.

The Key to Peace

My son, forget not my law; but let thine heart keep my commandments:
For length of days, and long life, and peace, shall they add to thee.
—Proverbs 3:1–2

Thousands of people each year visit the Winchester Mansion in San Jose, California. This massive structure was built by Sarah Winchester, the widow of the gun company owner. For thirty-eight years, from 1884 until her death in 1922, the house was under constant construction. Teams of carpenters, masons, and other workers were employed around the clock. Various stories have been told about the reason for this unusual practice. Most center on Mrs. Winchester's belief that she was haunted or would be haunted by the ghosts of those killed by her husband's weapons unless she kept building her house. Others claim that she thought she would not die as long as building continued.

Whatever the reason, she continued ordering more renovations and construction as long as she lived. There are more than 10,000 windows in the Winchester Mansion, doorways and stairs that lead to blank walls, and some 160 rooms in total. It is estimated that she spent more than $70,000,000 in today's money on largely pointless construction—all in a desperate search for peace that was ultimately doomed to fail.

Many people today are seeking peace through equally fruitless means. They turn to pleasure, drugs, alcohol, immorality, wealth, and other dead end avenues. Like the staircases that lead nowhere in the Winchester Mansion, pursuing such paths will never bring peace. Instead we find peace when we follow the path that God has given us in His Word. Those who keep the law of God in their hearts and obey it in their actions add peace to their lives. Rather than seeking peace as an end, we should seek to follow Christ. When we do we will find that peace comes as a by product.

Today's Word to the Wise: There is no true and lasting peace apart from remembering and keeping the commandments of God.

Powerful Teaching

Hear, ye children, the instruction of a father, and attend to know
understanding. For I give you good doctrine, forsake ye not my law.
—**Proverbs 4:1–2**

The only pastor among the fifty-six men who signed the Declaration of Independence was John Witherspoon. After pastoring for a number of years in Scotland, he came to America to become president of the College of New Jersey (now Princeton University). In addition to pushing for independence from England and signing the Declaration of Independence, Witherspoon would go on to serve as a member of Congress for a number of years.

But his most lasting contribution to our nation may well have been the impact he had on the lives of his students. Witherspoon was not just an administrator; he proved to be one of the school's most popular teachers. His class, Moral Philosophy, emphasized the Christian foundation of all truth in every sphere of life. Among Witherspoon's pupils were three Supreme Court justices, more than seventy-five senators and congressmen, ten cabinet officials, one vice president, and one president. As an educator, his focus on the foundational role of scriptural truth profoundly impacted his students who would influence the nation.

In our day it is common to find people downplaying the importance of good doctrine, both in the church and in society. Doctrine is simply teaching, and all sound teaching has its foundation in God's truth. There is no substitute for the truth if we want to have a positive impact on our world. It is important to remember that teaching is not limited to classrooms and formal settings. Each of us has an influence on others, often far beyond what we realize. We must make sure that we are giving others good and true doctrine.

Today's Word to the Wise: Since each of us are teachers in some way— to family, friends, co-workers—it is vital that our teaching lines up with Scripture.

Reading Between the Lines

My son, attend unto my wisdom, and bow thine ear to my understanding:
That thou mayest regard discretion, and that thy lips may keep knowledge.
—Proverbs 5:1–2

Operation Fortitude was one of the most important parts of the Allied war effort against Germany during the Second World War. Despite its importance, almost no one outside of what was called the London Controlling Section even knew of its existence. That's because the purpose of Operation Fortitude was to deceive the Germans so they would not reinforce their defense at Normandy, which would be the site of the Allied invasion of Europe.

They intentionally leaked false information, planted misleading news stories, fed detailed copies of supposed invasion plans to known German spies, and created elaborate phantom armies to confuse the German military about their true intentions. When the attack was actually launched in June of 1944, they continued their efforts, releasing stories to suggest it was only a diversion with the real invasion to follow later. The success of this secret operation contributed greatly to the victory over Germany.

Discretion is the ability to sort out truth from error. Someone defined *discretion* as "the ability to read between the lines." God knows that we are facing a stream of temptation from Satan who is a great deceiver. To help protect us, He has given us His Word to teach us discretion. By becoming familiar with the truth, we find it easier to recognize and reject error. This is why the acquisition of wisdom is so important—it goes hand in hand with developing discretion. As we grow in grace, we should be strengthening our skill at reading between the lines and avoiding the deception of the enemy.

Today's Word to the Wise: Reading, studying, and memorizing Scripture will equip you to see through the lies of the enemy.

People Who Don't Need a Boss

Go to the ant, thou sluggard; consider her ways, and be wise: Which having no guide, overseer, or ruler, Provideth her meat in the summer, and gathereth her food in the harvest.—**Proverbs 6:6–8**

It is said that when John Wesley was in his eighties, he complained in his diary that he was struggling with being tempted to stay in bed until 5:30 in the morning! One of the most active and productive evangelists in history, Wesley is said to have traveled more than a quarter of a million miles on horseback and to have preached over four thousand sermons. One thing is for sure, Wesley knew how to work. In spite of difficulties throughout his lifetime, he simply took the initiative to do what God had called him to do.

One of the most difficult things to find in our day is people who are willing to work hard without waiting for someone else to decide what needs to be done and issue instructions. Our culture and society no longer regards work as it once did. Instead of being seen as a way to honor God and provide for our needs, work is often viewed as something to be avoided as much as possible.

Work is not part of the curse that came upon the world with sin. (God had already assigned tasks to Adam prior to the fall. The curse was that work became more difficult.) Work is important because it helps build strength of character. When a society makes it easy for people who are able to work to survive without working, that society is undermining its very foundations. Paul laid out God's plan by inspiration when he wrote, "If any would not work, neither should he eat" (2 Thessalonians 3:10). God's plan is for us to get up, look around, find what needs to be done, and do it.

Today's Word to the Wise: Accomplishing God's plan for your life— even His plan for your day—will require initiative and diligence.

Power to Shape Your Life and Future

My son, keep my words, and lay up my commandments with thee. Keep my commandments, and live; and my law as the apple of thine eye. Bind them upon thy fingers, write them upon the table of thine heart.
—**Proverbs 7:1–3**

Jonathan Goforth was one of the great missionary heroes of the past. For decades he labored among the people of China, and many thousands were saved as a result of his work. He was known for his powerful praying, his love for the lost, and his love for Scripture. He spent prolonged hours reading and studying God's Word.

Late in his life, disease robbed Goforth of his eyesight. Since he could no longer read the Bible for himself, he would have some of the young men who were training for the ministry come in and read to him in Chinese. In her biography, *Goforth of China,* written after her husband's death, Rosalind Goforth described how each time one of the readers would skip a verse or read one incorrectly, Goforth would correct him. Goforth had spent so much time in the Scriptures that he knew virtually the entire Bible by heart. The effectiveness of his ministry was based in the power of the Word of God.

I have learned much from good books, and I am thankful for them and for those who write them. Nothing, however, can take the place of the Bible. It should be our primary source of instruction and education regarding the things of God. There is a reason that when Paul was imprisoned in Rome he asked Timothy to bring him "the parchments" (2 Timothy 4:13). Even the great apostle who, under the inspiration of the Holy Spirit, penned much of the New Testament wanted to have the Word of God to read and study.

Today's Word to the Wise: The time you spend reading, studying, and meditating on the Word of God will shape the future of your life.

An Invitation You Don't Want to Miss

She crieth at the gates, at the entry of the city, at the coming in at the doors. Unto you, O men, I call; and my voice is to the sons of man. O ye simple, understand wisdom: and, ye fools, be ye of an understanding heart. Hear; for I will speak of excellent things; and the opening of my lips shall be right things.—**Proverbs 8:3–6**

One of the grandest and most lavish weddings the world has ever seen was held in April of 2011 as Prince William married Catherine Middleton. Millions of people around the world watched on television as the future ruler of England was married. In contrast to the great number watching electronically, only about 1,900 people were invited to attend the wedding. The royal wedding invitations alone cost an estimated $32,000. Those who received these invitations were the only ones who were allowed to enter the cathedral and observe the wedding in person.

You may never be selected to receive an invitation to a royal wedding, but the King of kings has offered an open invitation to all of His children. He invites us to enter the pages of His Word and find the principles of wisdom that lead to success in every area of life. This invitation is not only for the famous, rich, or well connected. It's not only for the people we look up to as "super Christians." It is extended to all who are willing to hear the call and respond. It is for me, and it is for you.

It's hard to picture someone being invited to a special event like the royal wedding and declining to attend, yet each day many people refuse to listen to the voice of wisdom. When we seek God's wisdom through His Word, we are guaranteed to find it. God has not hidden or restricted His truths. They are displayed for us in His Word, which we understand through the work of His Spirit. No one can be truly wise apart from the knowledge and application of the principles and precepts of Scripture.

Today's Word to the Wise: Respond to God's invitation to seek wisdom, and you will benefit from it for the rest of your life.

Home Building

Wisdom hath builded her house, she hath hewn out her seven pillars:
—Proverbs 9:1

William Levitt headed his family's successful construction company, carefully guiding it through the Great Depression. Following World War II, the company began developing suburbs to meet the housing needs of tens of thousands of soldiers returning to America. These early suburbs, which came to be known as Levittowns, featured homes built according to the principles of an assembly line model. From the assembly line, the homes were shipped to the suburb where they would be permanently located. Because of this production method, Levitt's homes were economical to purchase and therefore attractive to these young men beginning homes of their own. The company eventually built more than 180,000 homes. At the height of its production, the company claimed to be producing a finished home every sixteen minutes. Even now, decades later, thousands of people are living in homes built by Levitt & Sons. Although they were built quickly, they were built to last.

Far more important than the buildings that house our families are the homes that we create inside those buildings. Strong and lasting families are built on the principles of wisdom found in the Word of God. There is no shortage of dangers and threats facing our homes today. Satan knows that by destroying families he undermines both the church and society. Against these threats we must be constantly on guard.

There is a great deal of truth in the simple statement, "The family that prays together stays together." Families who put God first—who focus on pleasing and obeying Him and developing Christ-honoring relationships with one another—find that they are building on a solid foundation. Just as Levitt homes were constructed by following the master plan designed by the architect, God has given us a blueprint to wisely build our homes.

Today's Word to the Wise: If you build your family according to wisdom, you experience and enjoy a lasting and happy home.

How to Honor Your Parents

The proverbs of Solomon. A wise son maketh a glad father: but a foolish son is the heaviness of his mother.—**Proverbs 10:1**

Abraham Lincoln was well known for total abstinence from alcohol. According to one well-known story, he was once offered a drink by a military officer. Lincoln responded by telling the man that when his mother was on her deathbed, she had summoned him as a nine-year-old boy and asked for his promise that he would never take a drink. He then said, "I promised my mother that I never would, and up to this hour, I've kept this promise! Would you advise me to break that promise?" Lincoln honored his mother by keeping his promise to her.

We most commonly think of honoring our parents in terms of obedience. For children in the home, obedience is definitely an important aspect of honor. However, there are two separate commands given in Ephesians 6:1–2. First, children are instructed to obey. Despite the fact that it may be out of style to say so, God holds young people accountable for obedience. While the obligation to obey ends with adulthood and the assumption of responsibility, there is another obligation that does not. The command to honor our parents is open-ended and remains in effect for all of our lives.

This command is also "the first commandment with promise" (Ephesians 6:2). While we are to obey every command of God, there are some commandments which carry particular rewards and blessings for obedience. The very first of those given by God is the command to honor our parents. One of the best ways in which we can do that is to live according to the principles of Scripture. Becoming wise through seeking God's wisdom brings us blessings, but it also delivers our parents from the grief and heartbreak that comes when a child goes astray.

Today's Word to the Wise: When you walk in wisdom, you are bringing honor to your parents and placing yourself in position to receive God's blessings.

The Hidden Snare

When pride cometh, then cometh shame: but with the lowly is wisdom.
—**Proverbs 11:2**

J. Hudson Taylor was one of the great missionary heroes in history. His work in the China Inland Mission saw thousands come to Christ, and the stories of his faith and prayers have inspired the generations that have followed. His work was driven by his passion to see the salvation of the lost. He once said, "If I had a thousand lives, China should have them. No! Not China, but Christ. Can we do enough for such a precious Saviour?" Taylor had another outstanding characteristic—humility.

The story is told of two women in Shanghai who were discussing the topic of pride and began to wonder if the famous missionary was ever tempted to be prideful because of his many accomplishments. One of the women decided to ask Taylor's wife, Maria, about it. When Maria asked her husband if he was ever tempted to be proud, he was surprised. "Proud about what?" he asked. "About all of the things you have done," his wife explained. Taylor responded, "I never knew I had done anything."

One of the great truths we must remember is that it is God who does the work and deserves all of the credit. Paul put it this way: "So then neither is he that planteth any thing, neither he that watereth; but God that giveth the increase" (1 Corinthians 3:7). If we remain focused on this truth, we avoid the snare of pride because we realize that we have done nothing for which we can take credit.

Satan uses pride especially effectively against those who are busy working for the Lord. Many mighty men and women who have done much for God have been brought to shameful sin through the snare of pride. Remember, we deserve no praise or recognition for what God has graciously done through us, but we do enjoy getting to be part of the process when we remain humble!

Today's Word to the Wise: The subtle snare of pride leads to the awful pit of shame; the delightful blessings of humility allow us to rejoice in serving God.

A Stable Legacy

A good man obtaineth favour of the LORD: but a man of wicked devices will he condemn. A man shall not be established by wickedness: but the root of the righteous shall not be moved.—**Proverbs 12:2–3**

The tallest building in the world, the Burj Khalifa in Dubai, rises more than 2,700 feet—over half a mile tall. It has 160 floors and is twice as tall as the Empire State Building in New York City. It is home to the world's fastest elevator which travels at 40 miles per hour. The Burj Khalifa also hosts the world's highest outdoor observation deck (on the 124th floor) and the world's highest swimming pool (on the 76th floor).

The secret to the stability of this massive building is found underground. Before construction began to rise up, workers spent a year digging and pouring the massive foundation that supports the building. The foundation contains some 58,900 cubic yards of concrete weighing more than 120,000 tons. The building is safe because the foundation is solid.

Godly and righteous living is important as a matter of obedience, but there are also many wonderful benefits that follow as a result. When we live according to God's principles of wisdom, we receive His blessing, but we also establish a firm foundation for our lives and our families.

Ever since our children were small, I wanted to be sure that I left a godly legacy for them. Now that I'm a grandparent, I'm even more reminded of the effect of my testimony on young lives.

I want my grandchildren to grow up knowing that their parents and grandparents follow God. I want them to see as well as hear that we honor Him and obey His Word. I want them to be able to follow in my footsteps and serve the Lord. To see that happen, I must continue to lay the foundation of obedience that will give them that sense of stability and purpose.

Today's Word to the Wise: When we live according to the Word, we establish firm foundations, not just for our lives, but for generations to come.

A Refused Source of Wisdom

A wise son heareth his father's instruction: but a scorner heareth not rebuke.—**Proverbs 13:1**

I heard about a couple who bought one of the first automobiles many years ago. They decided to take their prize possession out for a drive to show off to their neighbors. As they made their way along the road, the engine suddenly stopped. The man got out to look at the car, but to his great annoyance and frustration, he didn't have any idea what to do to get it running again. An older man passed by and offered to help with the car, but the driver didn't seem interested. So Henry Ford went on his way, and the wise advice and help he could easily have given was never heard.

While it is not usually pleasant to receive correction or rebuke, it is vitally important that we listen to and heed the warnings of wisdom. God has graciously given us people—parents, a spouse, teachers, pastors, mentors, and friends—to help us avoid the pitfalls of life and the snares of sin. His intention is that we will listen to what they have to tell us and shape our lives accordingly. The modern American glorification of the self-made man is foreign to God's plan for living. His plan is for us to learn from the teachers of wisdom He places in our lives.

It is much less painful to learn from the experiences of others than to refuse correction and experience the pain and trouble firsthand. Those who insist on continuing in their own way are living in folly. Benjamin Franklin put it this way, "Experience keeps a dear school, but fools will learn in no other." If our pride and stubbornness prevent us from listening, we are on the path to danger. When we are willing to humble ourselves and receive instruction, we are on the path to wisdom.

Today's Word to the Wise: Resolve to, with a right spirit, receive and heed the rebukes and warnings that come your way, and you will save yourself much heartbreak.

The Fear of the Lord

He that walketh in his uprightness feareth the LORD: but he that is perverse in his ways despiseth him.—**Proverbs 14:2**

Gunther Gebel-Williams was one of the most famous animal trainers and circus performers of his generation. He began his career in the circus as a teenager. He was so highly regarded that Ringling Brothers bought the entire circus for which he worked just so they could have him as one of their star attractions. His work with wild animals, especially lions and tigers, was stunning and drew record-breaking crowds to see the circus. He was also featured on a number of television broadcasts and specials.

When he announced his retirement from the ring, Gebel-Williams told an interviewer why he knew it was time to quit: he realized that he was no longer afraid of the animals.

The fear of the Lord is vitally important, but it is often misunderstood. Many teach that fearing God means to be in reverence and awe of Him. While we should approach God with respect, that is not what it means to fear Him. Fearing the Lord means that we display a healthy fear of His holiness and hatred of sin.

When first Ananias and then his wife Sapphira fell down dead at Peter's feet after lying about their giving, the Bible says, "And great fear came upon all the church" (Acts 5:11). The fear of the Lord gave the church great power. Acts 9:31 says these first churches "walking in the fear of the Lord, and in the comfort of the Holy Ghost, were multiplied."

Knowing the holiness of God has a profound impact on our own behavior, but it also has a great impact on others. As they see us walking in the fear of the Lord, they realize that there is a God to whom they must also one day answer. Fearing God improves our evangelism as well as our conduct. A Christian without the fear of the Lord will be declining in his walk with God and ineffective in his witness.

Today's Word to the Wise: When we truly and rightly fear God, it will impact every part of our lives.

Soft Answers

A soft answer turneth away wrath: but grievous words stir up anger. The tongue of the wise useth knowledge aright: but the mouth of fools poureth out foolishness.—**Proverbs 15:1–2**

I read about a study that researchers at Kenyon College conducted among naval personnel. They wanted to evaluate how the tone in which orders were given impacted the response those orders received. What the study showed was that the way in which the orders were given had a greater impact on the response than the content of those orders. The tone of the order went a long way toward determining the response.

When someone received an order in a soft voice, the answer tended to be given softly, but when the order was shouted, the response tended to be sharp as well. Interestingly enough, these findings held true whether the communication was in person or on the phone. It was not so much the facial expression or body language as the tone and volume of the voice that drove the response.

The same principle holds true in our lives, just as we find spelled out in the Scripture. When we speak to those around us with harsh, loud, or angry words, we should expect a negative response. Wisdom guides us to govern and control the way in which we speak to others. This is an especially important lesson for those in leadership positions—pastors, teachers, parents—as the manner of our speech often determines the response as much or more than the content.

We should never shrink from a necessary confrontation or correction. If some behavior needs to be changed or stopped, it should be plainly stated. However, this should be done in kindness and love rather than harshness. Jesus was never soft when confronting sin, yet those who heard Him speak were astonished by the "gracious words which proceeded out of his mouth" (Luke 4:22).

Today's Word to the Wise: Much of the conflict that we have to deal with can be avoided by controlling our words and our tone in speaking.

Excuses

All the ways of a man are clean in his own eyes; but the LORD *weigheth the spirits.*—**Proverbs 16:2**

One of America's leading political figures and constitutional experts in the early 1800s was Daniel Webster. Known for his powerful speeches, he worked to hold the country together in the years leading up to the Civil War. One story from his childhood shows his quick wit and way with words.

Daniel and his brother Ezekiel had been given careful instructions about a task they were to perform while their father was gone during the day. Yet when Ebenezer Webster returned home, he found the work had not even been started. He queried his older son, "Ezekiel, what have you been doing today?" "Nothing, sir," came the honest reply. "Well Daniel, what have you been doing?" "Helping Zeke," the boy responded.

We can always find excuses to justify what we have done or not done, but such responses will never change the nature of our actions.

The old Latin expression *mundus vult decipi,* meaning "the world wants to be deceived," is too often true when it comes to the way we view our own behavior. Rather than deal with the sins and failures, we struggle for ways to rationalize our conduct or to blame what we have done on someone else. This temptation is not new. Following the very first sin, Adam blamed Eve, and Eve blamed the serpent.

Jesus told the story of the Good Samaritan, perhaps the most famous of His parables, in response to a lawyer who questioned Jesus because he was "willing to justify himself" (Luke 10:29). Until we stop trying to find ways to justify ourselves, we can never begin to change our behavior for the better. Right and wrong are not determined by what we think or by what we can excuse, but by what God declares in His Word.

Today's Word to the Wise: When we accept responsibility rather than making excuses for what we have done or failed to do, we can grow and mature.

Genesis 39–40 » Matthew 11 » Proverbs 16

Contentment

Better is a dry morsel, and quietness therewith, than an house full of sacrifices with strife.—**Proverbs 17:1**

There is an old parable about a king who had fallen ill. The doctors could not cure his disease, but one of them told him that if he put on the clothing of a truly contented man, he would be healed. The king immediately dispatched his servants throughout the land to seek a contented man so that he could be cured. One by one they went out and returned without success. Finally the last servant returned, and he also was empty-handed.

"Could you not find a single contented man in my kingdom?" the monarch asked." "We found only one, Sire," the servant replied. "Then where is his shirt? I must have that to be cured." "The contented man we found was so poor that he had no shirt," the answer came.

Often we fall prey to the trap of thinking that if we just had a little bit more than we already have, then we would be happy. Satan has been using this lie effectively throughout all of human history. Getting more never works because getting more things creates more obligations and appetites rather than producing satisfaction. As Solomon pointed out, "When goods increase, they are increased that eat them" (Ecclesiastes 5:11).

Instead of looking for more and better things, we should be thankful to God for what we already have. The Hebrew word for "morsel" in Proverbs 17:1 literally means a crumb or a tiny piece. Gratitude does not come from the size and scope of our blessings, though we indeed have received so much. Gratitude comes when we realize that every good thing we have is a gift from God and is a result of His grace rather than our merit. Such thinking produces great benefits for our lives. First Timothy 6:6 says, "But godliness with contentment is great gain."

Today's Word to the Wise: When we are happy with what we have, even a little is enough to produce contentment.

Commitment

Through desire a man, having separated himself, seeketh and intermeddleth with all wisdom.—**Proverbs 18:1**

It took less than ten seconds for Jamaican sprinter Usain Bolt to cover the one hundred meter distance on the Olympic track and win the gold medal in London. Those few seconds cemented his status as the "fastest man alive" and placed him on the winner's podium once again. But the race was not won in those seconds—it was won by hours and hours of practice, workouts, weightlifting, special diet, and coaching.

The race was not won in the performance but in the preparation. It is our desire for something greater that causes us to sacrifice some things, even some good things, for the sake of things that are better. The famous football coach Bear Bryant said, "The difference between success and failure is not the will to win. Everyone has the will to win. Not everyone has the will to do what it takes to prepare to win." The level of commitment that we make beforehand determines the success of our efforts.

Think of Daniel, a teenage boy taken hundreds of miles from home and subjected to a brainwashing program designed to break down his allegiance to his homeland and his God. Long before the temptations came, however, Daniel had "purposed in his heart that he would not defile himself" (Daniel 1:8). Because of Daniel's preparation, no amount of persuasion, threat, or pressure could override his commitment to God. His dedication was unshakeable. For example, when Daniel's enemies got the decree passed that outlawed prayers to anyone other than the king of Persia, Daniel still prayed three times a day to God. He did not start praying when the law was passed, instead he continued his habit of prayer "as he did aforetime" (Daniel 6:10).

Our character is not made when we are put to the test; it is simply revealed then. Character is made before the test ever comes.

Today's Word to the Wise: Make the commitment to follow and please God in everything you do.

Integrity

Better is the poor that walketh in his integrity, than he that is perverse in his lips, and is a fool.—**Proverbs 19:1**

When Carlo Ponzi arrived in Boston from Italy in 1903, he had just $2.51 in his pocket. He quickly became involved in a number of shady deals and served several years in prison, first for forgery and later for his involvement in a smuggling ring. When he returned to society, he determined to make a fortune, and he began encouraging people to invest in a plan that was "guaranteed" to pay them a handsome rate of interest.

Ponzi was selling international reply coupons—a form of postage payment designed for international mail. Since few people had ever seen one and almost no one understood how they worked, it was easy for Ponzi to convince people that buying them in different countries could produce vast profits. Though there was never any real way to make money in the project, Ponzi used the new money coming in to pay off his early investors, and publicity encouraged still more people to "invest." When the plan collapsed, those who had trusted Ponzi lost everything. In less than a year, he had swindled some $250 million in today's money from those who trusted him. To this day, his very name is synonymous with swindles and schemes.

Though God may choose to bless us with financial riches, the presence of wealth is certainly not proof that a person is doing what is right. In fact, there are cases when riches are part of God's judgment on someone's life. Proverbs 1:32 notes, "The prosperity of fools shall destroy them."

Instead of placing our focus on accumulating material possessions, we should focus on being people of integrity. Though that kind of wealth cannot be measured in dollars, stocks, or assets, it is a true wealth that can never be taken away or lost.

Today's Word to the Wise: A man or woman of integrity is far richer than the wealthiest person who has dishonestly accumulated riches.

The Bondage of Alcohol

Wine is a mocker, strong drink is raging: and whosoever is deceived thereby is not wise.—**Proverbs 20:1**

Have you heard the story of Waylon Prendergast? The Tampa, Florida, man had been out drinking when he decided to rob a house on his way home. The drunken man forced his way into the house, filled a suitcase he found there with the valuables he discovered, and made his way to the living room. In his stupor he decided it would be a good idea to set a fire to cover his tracks, so he ignited a blaze before making his way out the back door. Thinking he was home free, he continued on to his house—only to find three fire trucks parked outside fighting the blaze he had set to cover his theft from his own home.

There is a reason the Bible describes alcoholic drinks as being deceitful. According to a study published in *The Washington Post* a few years ago, almost one-third of adults in America admit they either have now or have had in the past a problem with drinking. None of these people started out intending to become alcoholics or dependent on their next drink to make it through the day. But that is where the path they set out on leads.

It has become popular in some Christian circles today to downplay the warnings in Scripture regarding alcoholic beverages in the name of Christian liberty and grace. God's grace, however, never leads to bondage. Those who think they are in control of their drinking often take a long time to realize the awful truth. By the time they understand the strength of the chains of addiction that hold them, they are heavily bound. By listening to the voice of wisdom and the warnings from the Word of God, we will be guarded from the shame and distress that comes from drinking.

Today's Word to the Wise: Just as you would not trust a raging human tempter, refuse to trust the deceitful lures of alcohol.

God Is in Control

The king's heart is in the hand of the Lord, as the rivers of water: he turneth it whithersoever he will.—**Proverbs 21:1**

Cyrus was a heathen king, the ruler of the Medes and Persians. Yet years before Cyrus was born, Isaiah spoke of him by name and prophesied that God would use him to restore the people of Israel to their home and help them rebuild the temple. This prophecy is particularly significant considering that Cyrus hadn't been born, and the temple seemed to be under no threat. Yet God instructed Isaiah to prophesy of Cyrus, "He is my shepherd, and shall perform all my pleasure: even saying to Jerusalem, Thou shalt be built; and to the temple, Thy foundation shall be laid" (Isaiah 44:28).

This wonderful story from the Word of God emphasizes for us the truth that God is in control of our world. Nothing ever takes Him by surprise or causes Him to change His plans. As the poet Henry Wadsworth Longfellow wrote, "At first laying down as a fact fundamental, That nothing with God can be accidental." If we understand that God is in control, there is no reason for us to fear, regardless of how bad our circumstances may appear. Even death for a Christian is not a tragedy but merely the entrance to something far better and more wonderful.

This truth also gives us confidence as we pray. The God to whom we present our petitions has the power to respond, shaping events and moving the hearts of people to help us far beyond our power to influence or persuade. We are not alone as we face the challenges of this world. It is a tragedy when God's children live like orphans rather than children of the King. We have been given His invitation to "come boldly unto the throne of grace" (Hebrews 4:16), and we should do so, praying to God and believing that He will hear and answer our prayers.

Today's Word to the Wise: When we properly understand the sovereignty of God, we have confidence in God to control the future and to answer our prayers.

The Value of a Good Name

A good name is rather to be chosen than great riches, and loving favour rather than silver and gold.—**Proverbs 22:1**

Henry Heinz, born in 1844, to German immigrants in Pittsburg, PA, helped support his family as a teenager by growing and selling vegetables from the family garden. After graduating from college and getting married, he started a business selling horseradish. In 1875, a national financial collapse drove the young company into bankruptcy. Despite the legal freedom bankruptcy gave him, Heinz regarded each of the company's outstanding debts as a moral obligation and personally paid back every penny.

Heinz went on to found the H.J. Heinz Company with its 57 varieties and became a leading American businessman. A devout Christian, he was known for the generous treatment of his employees and his generosity to Christian causes. Throughout his life, Heinz conducted his business and personal dealings with the same integrity that led him to pay back hundreds of thousands of dollars he technically did not owe. He began his will with these words: "I desire to set forth at the very beginning of this will as the most important item in it a confession of my faith in Jesus Christ as my Saviour."

The value of maintaining integrity is beyond any financial price. When people are tempted to cut corners, they often do so without realizing the lasting impact that it will have. Like all things genuine, the foundations of integrity can be undermined in small ways that are almost imperceptible.

Each time we do what is required to uphold and protect our testimony we are making a lasting investment in building a good name. There is no more important or permanent inheritance we can leave behind, than the legacy of a good name.

Today's Word to the Wise: Guard your integrity with great care; no other possession means as much or lasts as long.

Wasted Efforts

Labour not to be rich: cease from thine own wisdom.—**Proverbs 23:4**

According to the Guinness Book of World Records, Hetty Green may have been the biggest miser who ever lived. Her father died when she was thirty leaving her an inheritance of more than $100 million in today's money. Though at the time it was unusual for a woman to be involved with banking and investments, she concentrated all her efforts and attention on growing the family fortune.

Hetty's obsession with money drove a wedge between her and her husband and their two children. Known for eating cold oatmeal to save money for heating and washing only the hem of her dress to save money on soap, she was sometimes called the "Witch of Wall Street." When her son, Ned, broke his leg as a boy, she tried to have him treated in a free clinic for the poor, before treating him at home. His leg would later have to be amputated. When she died, Hetty Green was worth the equivalent of some $4 billion today, but she was alone and miserable.

Each of us have a choice in how we will invest our lives and what goals we will pursue. True joy comes from serving others and investing in the work of the Lord. While this may not result in the same level of possessions and wealth, in light of the eternal dividends that come when we lay up treasures in Heaven, we are wise to pursue eternal goals.

Wealth and riches are not inherently evil, but the pursuit of them has led many people away from following God and into a life of sin and misery. First Timothy 6:10 says it plainly: "For the love of money is the root of all evil: which while some coveted after, they have erred from the faith, and pierced themselves through with many sorrows." The missionary Jim Elliot wisely wrote, "He is no fool who gives what he cannot keep to gain what he cannot lose."

Today's Word to the Wise: Focus your love and effort on the things that provide eternal riches.

How Faith Is Destroyed

Be not thou envious against evil men, neither desire to be with them. For their heart studieth destruction, and their lips talk of mischief.
—**Proverbs 24:1–2**

Samuel Clemens, more commonly known by his pen name, Mark Twain was a gifted writer. Yet Twain held a deep contempt for Christianity, and he often turned his ridicule on those who believed the Bible. He met and fell in love with Olivia Langdon, a young woman from a good Christian family. While they were courting, he downplayed his lack of faith, and she agreed to marry him.

After their marriage, Twain began to openly mock Christianity once again. Before too much time passed, Olivia stopped attending church. Twain and his family suffered many reversals, including a complete financial collapse and the death of a beloved daughter. At one point, Twain attempting to comfort his grieving wife said, "Livy, if it comforts you to lean on your faith, do so." She replied sadly, "I cannot. I do not have any faith left."

The people with whom we spend most of our time and the cultural influences—including books, music, social media, and television—we allow into our hearts and minds have a dramatic influence on us. This is why Proverbs warns of the dangers of wanting to spend time with those who are evil. No matter how charming, enjoyable, or intellectually stimulating those who oppose God and the truths of His Word may be, spending significant amounts of time with them will always have an impact on our thinking and conduct.

Ungodly people can exert a faulty attraction that believers sometimes envy and wish to copy. Remembering the end of the wicked and the destruction of faith that time spent in their company brings will help us guard against this temptation.

Today's Word to the Wise: Guard most carefully who you allow to influence your mind and heart.

Finding the Truth

It is the glory of God to conceal a thing: but the honour of kings is to search out a matter.—**Proverbs 25:2**

George Washington Carver became one of the most honored and respected scientists of his generation by focusing on the very simple peanut. Eventually he would discover some three hundred uses for this most basic and seemingly insignificant common food. Carver attributed all of his scientific discoveries to God.

He once said that he asked God to explain the universe to him, but that he felt God saying that was too large a task. When he asked for something he could handle, God directed his attention to the peanut. Carver's focused research for value from the peanut produced amazing results. Carver never doubted that God was rewarding his faith and effort. He commented, "Without God to draw aside the curtain I would be helpless."

In a day when many people deny that truth even exists as an absolute reality, those of us who know God need to be more focused than ever on seeking it. Truth is not an abstract concept that varies with time and place and can never be fully known. Truth is part of the very nature of God. As we grow and develop in our Christian walk and learn more about Him, we will also learn more about the truth. Scripture tells us that honor comes when we diligently investigate to find the truth.

Winston Churchill once said, "Men occasionally stumble over the truth, but most of them pick themselves up and hurry off as if nothing ever happened." Instead of running away from truth, we should diligently pursue it. Through the pages of God's Word and the principles God provides, we should seek God's wisdom. His truth applies to every aspect of our lives. When we apply it, we will live as people of honor and integrity.

Today's Word to the Wise: Focus on finding the truth about God and the situations you face, and He will reward and honor you.

Unfit Honor

As snow in summer, and as rain in harvest, so honour is not seemly for a fool.—**Proverbs 26:1**

On April 21, 1980, the record time for a female winner of the Boston Marathon was smashed when a twenty-seven year old Cuban-born runner named Rosie Ruiz crossed the finish line in just over two and half hours—more than three minutes ahead of the second place finisher. Onlookers were surprised that she was not soaked with sweat and did not even appear to be out of breath, as is normal for someone who finishes the grueling twenty-six mile race.

Soon, however, evidence began to surface that Ruiz had not actually run the entire event. Photos taken at various checkpoints and stations along the course did not show her, and she could not remember any details of the various landmarks passed along the route. Two witnesses came forward to report they had seen Ruiz break out of the crowd just a half a mile from the finish line and run only that distance to "complete" the race. The evidence of cheating mounted, and after three days Ruiz was stripped of the title and disqualified from the competition. She was found unworthy of the honor she had received. Since then, races have instituted stringent tracking systems to ensure that such a scheme cannot succeed again.

There are many people who are not worthy of honor but still receive it. Our society esteems those who are famous for athletic, financial, or musical achievements without regard to whether or not they have attained their success through honesty and character. Often those who are held up as role models prove to be poor examples for others to follow. It is important for us to ensure that our heroes are not simply famous fools but rather men and women of godly character who are worthy of applause and emulation.

Today's Word to the Wise: Make your heroes those who are wise in God's eyes, and you will not endow fools with your respect.

Presumption

Boast not thyself of to morrow; for thou knowest not what a day may bring forth.—**Proverbs 27:1**

Major General John Sedgwick was born into a family with a long and honored military tradition. He was named for his grandfather, who served as a general with George Washington in the Revolutionary War. After graduating from West Point, he served with distinction in the Mexican-American War where he received two battlefield promotions. During the Civil War, he was twice wounded in battle. After his recovery, he was placed in charge of the VI Corps of the Army of the Potomac.

In May of 1864, during the Battle of Spotsylvania Court House, Sedgwick was directing artillery placements for his troops when they came under fire from the Confederate lines. The men began ducking for cover, and Sedgwick scolded them. "What? Men dodging this way for single bullets? What will you do when they open fire along the whole line? I am ashamed of you. They couldn't hit an elephant at this distance." Those were the last words Sedgwick ever spoke, as just seconds later he was hit in the head and killed by a bullet. Sedgwick was the highest ranking Union officer to die during the Civil War.

Exerting confidence is to be admired, but presuming that we know the future and can control its outcome is the height of folly. In truth, none of us know what is going to happen tomorrow. We can and should make wise plans for our lives, our families, and our ministries, but behind every plan must be the knowledge that God is ultimately in control of the outcome. Rather than presumptuous boasting, we should humbly remember God's sovereignty. James 4:15 cautions those who would boast of tomorrow, "For that ye ought to say, If the Lord will, we shall live, and do this, or that." Trust God fully, and rely on His wise control of events.

Today's Word to the Wise: All of our plans for the future should be laid in submission to the will of God who determines the outcomes.

Courageous in Fear

The wicked flee when no man pursueth: but the righteous are bold as a lion.—**Proverbs 28:1**

Eddie Rickenbacker was already a famous race car driver when he enlisted to fight in World War I. The same quick thinking and reflexes that served him so well on the track made him one of the best fighter pilots the world had ever seen. He received the Congressional Medal of Honor for shooting down at least twenty-six enemy aircraft. After the war, Rickenbacker enjoyed great success in the business world, becoming the owner of the Indianapolis Motor Speedway and head of Eastern Airlines.

During World War II, Rickenbacker was on a mission to encourage the troops in the Pacific and deliver messages from President Roosevelt to General MacArthur when his plane was forced to make a crash landing in the ocean. With six other survivors, he endured more than three weeks adrift before finally reaching land. One day when their food had run out and hope seemed lost, Rickenbacker read Matthew 6:33 and prayed. A few moments later a seagull landed on his head. He caught the seagull, and the men ate most of it and used the rest as bait to catch fish. Rickenbacker believed God had saved him for a life of service. Regarding courage, Rickenbacker said, "Courage is doing what you're afraid to do. There can be no courage unless you're scared."

When we are doing what is right, there is no need to be afraid, regardless of what circumstances we face. God does not guarantee our comfort or even our lives. (Many righteous believers have perished because they would not recant their faith.) What God guarantees is better. He promises to deliver us. Whether that is in life or by death, we have nothing to fear. God is always in control, and we can fully rely on Him to do what is best for us in every situation.

Today's Word to the Wise: Do not allow fear to keep you from doing what you know God wants you to do.

The Best Way to Avoid Destruction

He, that being often reproved hardeneth his neck, shall suddenly be destroyed, and that without remedy.—**Proverbs 29:1**

Bernard Madoff seemed to have it all. He lived the life of the fabulously wealthy in New York City. The securities trading company he founded when he graduated from college produced amazing returns for investors. He was tapped to serve as Chairman of the NASDAQ stock trading company, and he rubbed elbows with the elite of the financial, political, and entertainment worlds. Maddoff enjoyed the best of everything that money could buy.

Yet all of Madoff's apparent success was built on the foundation of a lie. His investment firm was nothing more than a giant Ponzi scheme that for decades depended on getting new investors to pay off the old ones while money was being siphoned off for the personal use of Madoff and his family. With shocking suddenness Madoff was arrested, tried, and convicted to serve a 150-year sentence in federal prison.

One of the most effective lies of Satan is that we will get away with wrongdoing. He convinces us that we will be the exception and can escape the consequences of sin. If we had an accurate assessment of the devastating results of sin in advance, we would be far more hesitant to cross the line that God has drawn in His Word. Often we mistake the grace and forbearance of God as His permission to continue in sin. Yet that forbearance is extended as an opportunity to change our ways. Romans 2:4 tells us, "The goodness of God leadeth thee to repentance."

The only cure for sin is confession and repentance. No cover up will hide sin from the eyes of God, and if we continue stiff necked in doing wrong, eventually judgment will fall.

Today's Word to the Wise: Avoid sudden destruction by responding to the first warnings of reproof.

You Can Trust the Bible

Every word of God is pure: he is a shield unto them that put their trust in him.—**Proverbs 30:5**

In 1985, for the first time in more than fifty years, Congress authorized the issue of official United States government gold coins. Beginning in 1986 these new coins came on the market. Each of these American Eagles, as they are known, is guaranteed by the United States Mint to contain the stated amount of pure twenty-two karat gold. They come in one-tenth, one-fourth, one-half, and one ounce sizes. Buyers from around the world trust that these coins are what they are reported to be because they trust the promises of the United States government.

When it comes to Scripture, we have something far more reliable than the guarantee of a government. We have the promises of Almighty God that His Word is perfect and pure. Psalm 12:7 affirms, "Thou shalt keep them, O Lord, thou shalt preserve them from this generation for ever." God promised to preserve His Word for us. We can have complete faith that every word in the Bible is there on purpose.

The very first temptation in human history began with Satan asking Eve, "Yea hath God said?" This challenge to the authenticity of Scripture continues in our day. If God promised to keep His Word—and He did—we can confidently trust the Bible. God has seen to the preserving of His Word, and the Bible that we hold in our hands today is fully reliable. Instead of evaluating the Word of God, continually trying to decide if it is trustworthy, we should use it to evaluate our thoughts and actions. Trust with complete faith and confidence in the Bible you hold. It is guaranteed by God Himself.

Today's Word to the Wise: Never let anyone shake your confidence and faith in the Bible for it is the very Word of God.

The Danger of Drinking

It is not for kings, O Lemuel, it is not for kings to drink wine; nor for princes strong drink: Lest they drink, and forget the law, and pervert the judgment of any of the afflicted.—**Proverbs 31:4–5**

There is no question that consuming alcohol affects a person's judgment in a negative way. The National Highway Traffic Safety Administration reports that seventy percent of speeding drivers who have fatal accidents between midnight and 3:00 AM are legally drunk. Intoxicated drivers are half as likely to wear seat belts, and alcohol is involved in more than four out of every five crashes involving drivers who are driving on suspended or revoked licenses or with no license at all.

Alcohol abuse is the fifth leading cause of death in the United States. Nearly half of trauma patients in emergency rooms are there because of alcohol. Those who have been drinking are three times more likely to die in a fire than those who have not. More than one-third of adult drownings involve the use of alcohol. Yet people continue to insist that they can "handle it" and know when they have had too much to drink. This is folly because from the first drink alcohol begins to impair judgment.

Every day we are involved in a very real spiritual war. We have a committed enemy who "as a roaring lion, walketh about, seeking whom he may devour" (1 Peter 5:8). The dangers we face day after day require that we must be diligent and on guard. That is one of the reasons the Bible—especially the book of Proverbs, the book devoted to teaching principles for wise living—contains so many warnings about the dangers of drinking and drunkenness. Alcohol affects our senses, dulls our judgment, and keeps us from fulfilling our duty to God. We should reject it in all of its forms.

Today's Word to the Wise: The dangers of spiritual warfare are too great for us to risk allowing our senses and judgment to be dulled by alcoholic drinks.

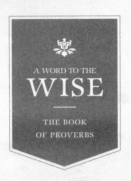

A WORD TO THE

WISE

THE BOOK
OF PROVERBS

FEBRUARY

The Importance of Listening

*A wise man will hear, and will increase learning; and a man of understanding shall attain unto wise counsels:—***Proverbs 1:5**

The story goes that after several years in office as president, Franklin Roosevelt grew tired of the long receiving lines where he would have to greet the guests at White House functions. He felt the people weren't really interested but were just going through the formal motions. To test his theory, he began greeting guests by quietly saying something outrageous. His favorite line was, "I murdered my grandmother this morning." The guests would respond with things like, "Wonderful, keep up the good work!" which indicated that they truly were not listening. Finally the one ambassador came through the line and actually heard Roosevelt's remark. He leaned down and whispered back, "I'm sure she had it coming."

One of the primary indicators of wisdom in a person's life is that he is willing to listen rather than assuming he knows everything. There is much information missed and much pain and damage incurred simply because people do not listen. God has given us in His Word "all things that pertain unto life and godliness" (2 Peter 1:3). Yet He also sadly says, "My people are destroyed for lack of knowledge" (Hosea 4:6).

There are countries where copies of the Word of God are hard to come by and churches are few and far between. But here in the United States, most of us have multiple Bibles in our homes and on our electronic devices, and most of us have a good church within driving distance. The problem is not a lack of instructional sources, but rather a lack of hearing instruction. Because we are not willing to hear and heed the Scriptures, our churches, families, and lives suffer. If you desire God's wisdom, commit yourself to listening to His Word.

Today's Word to the Wise: Focus on listening to the voice of God through the pages of Scripture, and you will obtain the wisdom you need for your life.

Priceless Gifts

For the Lord giveth wisdom: out of his mouth cometh knowledge and understanding.—**Proverbs 2:6**

There are many factors that contribute to the worth of a gift. Some gifts are valuable because of the monetary expense that went into their purchase. For instance, last Christmas the Faber-Castell pen company unveiled a $97,000 gold and diamond fountain pen. I can't imagine how someone would be willing to actually use a pen like that for fear something would happen to it! Other gifts are worth a great deal, not because of their monetary value, but because of the giver. For instance, every parent treasures gifts from their children even though those gifts may have no inherent value.

The combination of a gift of great value from a person of great value produces the most valuable gift. Wisdom is one of the greatest of these gifts. Divine wisdom is a treasure because it offers protection from the dangers and damages of sin. The wisdom of God helps us see through the deceptions of Satan and respond properly to the temptations he brings across our paths. Wisdom helps us deal with the people in our lives in a way that honors God and shows them His mercy and truth. Wisdom provides the insight and understanding to live skillfully according to the precepts of Scripture.

We need wisdom, and in His Word, God revealed clearly how we can obtain it. Wisdom is not produced by our ingenuity or learning; it is given by the grace of God. James 1:5 says, "If any of you lack wisdom, let him ask of God, that giveth to all men liberally, and upbraideth not; and it shall be given him." Wisdom is not reserved for a special class of believers. The promise of wisdom is available to anyone who is willing to ask for it. God gives it freely without restraint or condemnation because it is His nature to give.

Today's Word to the Wise: If you are not daily asking God for wisdom, you are missing one of His greatest gifts for you.

Staying in Balance

Let not mercy and truth forsake thee: bind them about thy neck; write them upon the table of thine heart: So shalt thou find favour and good understanding in the sight of God and man.—**Proverbs 3:3–4**

Archimedes of Syracuse was one of the most highly regarded inventors and mathematicians of ancient times. He devised an ingenious test to satisfy the demand of King Hiero II. The king had given gold to be made into a crown, but he suspected that a dishonest workman had mixed it with silver. He commissioned Archimedes to determine if the crown was pure. Archimedes was not allowed to melt the crown to do the test, so he used the principle of buoyancy to construct a scale placed in water to test the authenticity of the crown. The test confirmed the king's suspicion and revealed the fraud.

Balance is a vital need in our lives. Perhaps no balance is more important than the balance between mercy and truth. Mercy without truth leads to sinful living. Truth without mercy leads to harsh judgment.

An illustration of this balance is found in the story of the woman taken in adultery in John 8. The leaders brought this woman to Jesus in an attempt to trap Him. They thought He would be forced to violate either the law of Moses or the law of the Romans. Jesus saw through their scheme and responded in a way that convicted them so greatly that they walked away without a word. Then Jesus turned to the woman and said, "Neither do I condemn thee: go, and sin no more" (John 8:11). In mercy He offered her freedom from condemnation, and in truth He instructed her to change her ways.

As we grow in Christlikeness, we will also grow in developing both mercy and truth. With this balance, our relationships are strengthened as we "find favour" with others.

Today's Word to the Wise: Be intentional in balancing mercy and truth in all of your relationships.

Why Solomon Asked for Wisdom

For I was my father's son, tender and only beloved in the sight of my mother. He taught me also, and said unto me, Let thine heart retain my words: keep my commandments, and live. Get wisdom, get understanding: forget it not; neither decline from the words of my mouth.—**Proverbs 4:3–5**

According to Bloomberg News, the richest man in the world is Carlos Slim of Mexico. His ownership of vast telecommunications companies added more than $15 billion to his net worth in 2012 alone. Suppose this immensely wealthy man invited you to meet him and told you that he would give you anything you asked to receive. Knowing his resources would be able to back up his promise, what would you request?

Solomon was presented with that decision. But in Solomon's case, the offer was backed by the promise of One who owns far more than the world's richest man. "In Gibeon the LORD appeared to Solomon in a dream by night: and God said, Ask what I shall give thee" (1 Kings 3:5). Solomon was a young man, about twenty years of age, when his father David died and he became king. Presented with the vast array of possibilities he could request, Solomon could have been tempted in many different directions. Yet, he simply asked God for the most important thing he could think of—wisdom. God answered His prayer, "Lo, I have given thee a wise and an understanding heart" (1 Kings 3:12).

Why did Solomon ask for wisdom? Because as part of preparing Solomon to follow him on the throne, David had taken the time to instill an appreciation of wisdom in his son's heart. Although you and I do not run empires, we need the wisdom of God to navigate successfully through life. Like Solomon, we should ask God for wisdom. And like David, we should be teaching our families the value of this commodity.

Today's Word to the Wise: Teach your children and grandchildren the importance of wisdom, and you have fulfilled one of your most important duties.

The Bitter End of Sin

For the lips of a strange woman drop as an honeycomb, and her mouth is smoother than oil: But her end is bitter as wormwood, sharp as a twoedged sword.—**Proverbs 5:3–4**

Mel Trotter, the famous rescue mission worker, wrote that his father was a bartender who "drank as much as he served." Trotter followed in his father's footsteps, losing job after job because of his addiction to drinking and gambling. Each time he lost a job, he promised to reform and start doing better, but each time he failed. After the death of his baby son, Trotter made his way to Chicago where he intended to drown himself in Lake Michigan. He had sold his shoes to get money for another drink and was walking barefoot through the snow toward his death when he went inside the Pacific Garden Mission. After hearing the gospel message, he was miraculously saved. For the next forty years, Trotter did everything he could to help those who, like himself, had fallen prey to the deceptively alluring temptations of sin.

Satan's advertising is never realistic. He paints beautiful pictures of immediate pleasure while ignoring the real consequences that its participants must endure. If the beer companies ran ads filled with crashed cars, paralyzed drinkers, and the tiny caskets of babies killed by drunk drivers, it would not help them sell their products. So they focus on the beginning rather than the ending. Every sin is sold with this tactic.

Satan knows that if we look on the pleasurable part of sin, we are vulnerable. But no matter how beautiful the temptation appears, it is only a cloak for the reality that sin always ends in pain, heartbreak, and judgment. As James 1:15 says, "…sin, when it is finished, bringeth forth death." It is far better to see through Satan's gimmicks to sin's ruinous end than to swallow the short-sighted advertisements of the devil.

Today's Word to the Wise: Focusing on the bitter end of sin is one of the best protections against falling prey to its temptations.

Wake Up!

How long wilt thou sleep, O sluggard? when wilt thou arise out of thy sleep? Yet a little sleep, a little slumber, a little folding of the hands to sleep: So shall thy poverty come as one that travelleth, and thy want as an armed man.—**Proverbs 6:9–11**

Washington Irving was the first American writer to become internationally known. His best known works were written just after the War of 1812 and published in both America and England. One of the stories for which he is most famous, "Rip Van Winkle," tells of a lazy man who does almost anything to avoid work. Eventually Van Winkle wanders into the mountains and falls asleep for twenty years. When he returns, he gets into trouble because he does not know that the American Revolution has taken place and that King George III has been replaced by President George Washington. Ironically, this famous story about laziness and sleep was produced by Irving in a marathon, all-night writing session.

Today we have an epidemic of laziness. The values of hard work and diligence that are so commonly praised and commanded in Scripture are often avoided in society. People search for the shortcut to success and are ever searching for an easier way to make it in the world. Even the government promotes laziness by providing money to many people who have the strength and ability to work but would prefer not to do so.

It is a shame for anyone to be lazy, but it is especially shameful for a child of God. Jesus left a pattern of diligent labor for us to follow. He said, "I must work the works of him that sent me, while it is day: the night cometh, when no man can work" (John 9:4). There will come a day when we will lay down our burdens and cease our labor, but today we should be busy about the Master's work.

Today's Word to the Wise: Laziness may seem attractive in the short run, but it always leads to poverty and lack.

The Danger of Flattery

Say unto wisdom, Thou art my sister; and call understanding thy kinswoman: That they may keep thee from the strange woman, from the stranger which flattereth with her words.—**Proverbs 7:4–5**

King Canute ruled over Denmark, Norway, and England more than one thousand years ago. A wise ruler, he worked diligently to make the lives of his subjects better. As is often the case, he was surrounded by those who sought to gain influence and prominence with him. According to the ancient story, he grew tired of their continual flattery and determined to put an end to it. He ordered that his throne be carried out to the seashore and gathered his courtiers about it.

By the sea, the king asked his courtiers to repeat their flattery concerning his power and might, and they did. Canute then commanded the tide not to come in. Yet soon the waters were lapping around his legs as the tide did not heed him. King Canute rose up from his throne and said, "Let all men know how empty and worthless is the power of kings, for there is none worthy of the name, but He whom Heaven, earth, and sea obey by eternal laws."

Flattery is so effective because it appeals to our pride. We want to believe the wonderful things that are being said about us, even if we know that they are not deserved. False praise has led to the downfall of many Christians. This is especially true in the area of moral purity. Proverbs abounds with warnings about the words of the "strange woman" to help guard those who are committed to remaining pure. Anyone who approaches you with flattery is attempting to get you to do something, and though it is not always the case, most of the time that something is not going to end well. Do not be swayed from following God by flattering lips.

Today's Word to the Wise: Be wary of anyone who attempts to influence you through flattery; they do not have your best interests in mind.

What Is Truly Precious

Receive my instruction, and not silver; and knowledge rather than choice gold.—**Proverbs 8:10**

The Burro Schmidt Tunnel near Garlock, California, is half a mile long, six feet tall, and ten feet wide. It was dug entirely by hand through the solid granite of the El Paso Mountains. William "Burro" Schmidt, a gold miner in the early 1900s, faced a difficult journey over the mountains to get his ore to the smelter at Mojave, so he began constructing a tunnel with a shovel, a pick, and a hammer that would allow him to avoid the dangerous mountain passes—at least that is what he told those who inquired.

Even after a modern road was built in 1920, removing the need for Schmidt's tunnel, he continued to work on his project. He said that he was obsessed with finishing the work he had begun, and continued to dig until he finished the tunnel in 1938. In reality, Schmidt had discovered an incredibly rich vein of gold ore that led back into the mountain. His story of digging a tunnel was just to ensure that no one would try to take his gold claim. No one ever found out exactly how much gold ore Schmidt found during his work.

William Schmidt devoted much of his life to the search for gold. Though gold has great monetary value, its worth is only temporal. In fact, God uses it for pavement! Revelation 21:21 says, "The street of the city was pure gold, as it were transparent glass." Rather than spending our time acquiring things that will perish, we should be focused on those things that are eternal. When the tally of our lives is taken, our net worth will not matter. But whether we acquired and followed God's wisdom will matter. The Christian life is meant to be lived with our affections set on things above for these are truly precious.

Today's Word to the Wise: God's wisdom is the most precious thing you will ever obtain, and it is worthy of diligent and focused effort.

Wrong Way or Right Way?

Forsake the foolish, and live; and go in the way of understanding.
—**Proverbs 9:6**

Even though it occurred more than eighty years ago, the run by Roy Riegels of the California Golden Bears during their game with Georgia Tech in the 1929 Rose Bowl remains one of the most famous football plays in all of history. Georgia Tech had the ball on their own end of the field during the second quarter when a fumble gave Riegels his chance to help his team and win glory. Scooping up the ball, he began a dash for the end zone.

But during the play Riegels had gotten turned around and was heading toward his own end zone. A teammate finally caught up with him after nearly seventy yards and turned him around, but it was too late. The mistake positioned Georgia Tech for a safety that provided the margin in their 8–7 win over California. Roy "Wrong Way" Riegels went down in history, but for the wrong reason.

Many people are focused on their rate of progress without stopping to consider whether or not they are headed in the right direction. Management guru Peter Drucker described this as being more focused on "doing things right" than on "doing the right things." Rather than simply focusing on our speed and output, we would do well to also consider if we are walking according to the truths of Scripture.

The life of Christ gives us an example of continually walking in God's way. Jesus said, "I do always those things that please him" (John 8:29). He never took an action that was contrary to the plan of His Father. Though He was God in the flesh, He always submitted to the will of His Father. As we follow His steps that are revealed in the Word of God, we can be certain we are headed in the right direction.

Today's Word to the Wise: If you are going the wrong way, making good time simply gets you to the wrong place sooner.

Love Covers Sins

Hatred stirreth up strifes: but love coverteth all sins.—**Proverbs 10:12**

Bible teacher Harry Ironside told a stirring story of the power of love to cover sin. One Sunday a group of missionaries and believers in New Guinea were gathered together to observe the Lord's Supper. After a man came in and sat down, a missionary recognized a sudden tremor pass through the young man seated next to him that indicated he was under great nervous strain. Then in a moment all was quiet again. The missionary whispered, "What was it that troubled you?" "Ah," he replied, "The man who just came in killed and ate the body of my father. And now he has come to remember the Lord with us. At first I didn't know whether I could endure it. But it is all right now. He is washed in the same precious blood." Those two men who had so much separating them took the Lord's Supper together in peace.

Love plays a vital role in strengthening and maintaining all of our relationships—and especially those relationships within the body of Christ. Because we are imperfect people, we will at times both give and receive offense. When that happens, we must make a choice. We can opt to hold on to the hurt, nurturing it and allowing it to grow, or we can decide to forgive in love just as we have been forgiven. We do not have to exact vengeance for the wrongs that are done to us; we can choose to forgive.

It is only because of the forgiveness that we have received from God through His grace that we have ability to forgive others in this way. The love of God toward us should be repeated in how we treat others. Jesus said, "By this shall all men know that ye are my disciples, if ye have love one to another" (John 13:35).

Today's Word to the Wise: Every relationship has disappointments—love chooses to see through the eyes of forgiveness and recognize the value of the other person.

The Wisdom of Loving Your Neighbor

He that is void of wisdom despiseth his neighbour: but a man of understanding holdeth his peace.—**Proverbs 11:12**

I read about two neighboring farmers who were embroiled in a bitter dispute. One of them had built a fence between their farms, and the other contended the fence was built on his side of the boundary. After several efforts to resolve the matter, a protracted legal battle ensued. Finally the farmer who had built the fence tired of the dispute and sold his farm. Immediately the aggrieved farmer went to meet with the new owner.

"I want you to know that along with your farm you have bought yourself a lawsuit," he said. The new owner asked about the source of his frustration. "The fence between our two properties was built two feet on my side of the boundary line," the farmer explained. Immediately the new owner said, "Then I will move it four feet back to be sure you are not cheated." "That is more than I ask," the old farmer said. "Yes, but I would rather have peace with my neighbor than a few feet of land," the new owner replied.

The natural tendency is for us to seek only what is best for ourselves and look out for our own rights and interests. God's direction is different— that we seek what is best for others. When we give up our rights for the sake of someone else, we demonstrate love for our neighbors. James said, "If ye fulfil the royal law according to the scripture, Thou shalt love thy neighbour as thyself, ye do well" (James 2:8). When we fail to love our neighbor as we should, we are revealing not just disobedience, but also a lack of wisdom. James calls this the "royal law" because when we truly love our neighbor, we are living like children of the King.

Today's Word to the Wise: Love your neighbor in both thought and action, and your wise living will be pleasing to God.

Love and Honor

A virtuous woman is a crown to her husband: but she that maketh ashamed is as rottenness in his bones.—**Proverbs 12:4**

There is an old story that beautifully illustrates the principle of honor within marriage. A drunkard husband, spending the evening with his jovial companions at a tavern, boasted that if he took a group of his friends home with him at midnight and asked his Christian wife to get up and cook supper for them, she would do it without complaint. The crowd considered it a vain boast and dared him to try it. So the drunken crowd followed him home and watched as he made the unreasonable demands of his wife. She obeyed, dressed, came down, and prepared a very nice supper and served it as cheerfully as if she had been expecting them.

After supper one of the men asked her how she could be so kind when they had been so unreasonable. Her reply was: "Sir, when my husband and I were married, we were both sinners. It has pleased God to call me out of that dangerous condition. My husband continues in it. I tremble for his future state. Were he to die as he is, he would be miserable forever. I think it my duty to render his present existence as comfortable as possible." Not long after, her husband was saved.

The notion of honor seems quaint and outdated to many in the modern world, but it is at the very foundation of any healthy and loving relationship. The Hebrew word for *honor* means "to give something weight—to treat it as valuable or important." When we show disrespect in words or actions, we are revealing a failure of love. Marriages do not usually collapse suddenly. Instead they fall due to a long process of erosion that, continued unchecked, undermines the foundation.

Today's Word to the Wise: It is not possible to love someone as you should without also treating them with honor and respect.

Loving Enough to Correct

He that spareth his rod hateth his son: but he that loveth him chasteneth him betimes.—**Proverbs 13:24**

I read about a wealthy family in England who was taking a trip on the railroad back in the 1800s. They had three children, and the youngest boy was something of a terror. The nanny who was assigned to watch him was trying to keep him quiet, but he saw something that he wanted and would not be quiet until he got it. The nanny tried to distract him with other toys, but his protests became louder and louder.

Finally the boy's exasperated mother called out, "Just give him what he wants." The nanny started to protest, but the mother repeated her command, "Just give it to him!" Seconds later the air was pierced by a shriek of pain from the boy. "What did you do?" the mother demanded. "I let him have the wasp," the nanny replied.

While love always wants what is best for the other person, that does not mean indulging bad behavior and wrong desires. Love overlooks offenses against itself, but it does not allow conduct that is destructive to continue without reproof. The fact that we are willing to speak up and correct someone who is in error is not a demonstration of a lack of love but proof of love's presence. Proverbs 27:6 reminds us, "Faithful are the wounds of a friend; but the kisses of an enemy are deceitful."

Though we think of corrective love most often in the context of the parent-child relationship, the same principle applies in other relationships. While we may not be imposing discipline, we should still be willing to speak boldly to confront sin. Paul exhibited this loving attitude toward Peter when Peter refused to eat with Gentile believers. "…I withstood him to the face…" (Galatians 2:11). We should not allow those we love to continue in sin without speaking up.

Today's Word to the Wise: Sometimes we best show love not by what we allow or overlook, but by what we correct and reprove.

The Focus that Strengthens Love

Where no oxen are, the crib is clean: but much increase is by the strength of the ox.—**Proverbs 14:4**

According to Greek mythology, a sculptor named Pygmalion created an ivory statue of a woman who was so perfect and beautiful that he fell in love with her. In his mind, no living woman could compare to the statue he had crafted. Finally Venus, the goddess of love, brought the statue to life so that Pygmalion could marry the love of his life. Of course we know there is no truth to that ancient fable, yet at the same time it demonstrates a principle that underlies a serious problem in many relationships.

Our society promotes a view of romance that is destructive. The world advises us to find a perfect person and love them. Yet such an effort is doomed to failure before it starts. If we can only love perfect people, we can never love at all. Instead of fruitlessly seeking perfection, we need to adjust our focus. In every human relationship there are problems. Proverbs uses the example of cleaning an ox's stable to show how we should deal with these problems. If you don't have any oxen, you don't have to clean up after them, but pulling a plow yourself isn't much fun, and it isn't very productive.

Each of us has the ability to choose where we place our focus. Are we spending all of our time looking at the problems of the other person, or are we instead focused on the blessings and productivity that they bring to our lives? Dr. Bob Jones, Sr. said, "Behind every tragedy in character lies a long process of wicked thinking." As you make sure that your thoughts about those you love are focused on the good things about them, your love will grow stronger and stronger.

Today's Word to the Wise: Instead of focusing on the problems that are part of every life, focus on the great things that would not be possible without those you love.

The Eyes of the Lord

The eyes of the LORD are in every place, beholding the evil and the good.
—Proverbs 15:3

One of the most prized rights of American citizens is privacy. Even our fourth constitutional amendment reflects this as it guarantees protection from "unreasonable searches and seizures" and promises "no Warrants shall issue, but upon probable cause...." We resist the thought that others, and the government in particular, would pry into our lives, especially in any kind of organized surveillance.

There is a surveillance, however, that we should welcome—that of our Heavenly Father's watchful care. He sees everything about us, within us, around us, and even that which is coming to us in the future.

Some people perceive God's watchful gaze as a threat. It is true that God sees the wrong we do and that His holy hatred of sin is to be feared and avoided. Yet we must never forget that God's great love and mercy toward us mean that He is watching for opportunities to bless and reward us when we do what is right. As the prophet Hanani told King Asa of Judah, "For the eyes of the LORD run to and fro throughout the whole earth, to shew himself strong in the behalf of them whose heart is perfect toward him" (2 Chronicles 16:9).

Sometimes, we forget how much God loves us. We know that He gave His Son to purchase our salvation, yet we do not remember that He delights in receiving and answering our prayers. Too many children of God live as if they were orphans. We need to be reminded that the very God of Heaven takes notice of our situation and that He is looking for opportunities to display His power on our behalf. We should confidently cry out to Him and seek His help because He is watching our lives. As one old preacher put it, "God loves you so much He can't take His eyes off you."

Today's Word to the Wise: Remember that God is watching you, and rejoice that He delights in rewarding all that you do for Him.

A Foundation for Your Thoughts

Commit thy works unto the LORD, and thy thoughts shall be established.
—**Proverbs 16:3**

On October 30, 1938, the CBS radio network broadcasted an adaptation of H. G. Wells' science fiction story *The War of the Worlds*. Though at the beginning and again about two-thirds of the way through the program carried a disclaimer that it was a work of fiction, the broadcast was intentionally produced in a convincing fashion as a series of news updates and bulletins following a breaking news story. "Reporters" gave updates from the scene before "dying" in Martian heat ray attacks and from poison gas. Finally, the Martians were defeated by their lack of immunity to earth germs.

At the end of the broadcast, Orson Wells, who directed the production, went on the air and reminded everyone who was listening that the production was not real. For thousands of listeners, however, the "news" updates were very real. They flooded radio stations and police stations with calls about the danger posed by the invading Martians. Their actions were governed by their thoughts, and their thoughts were filled with fear because of what they had heard on the radio.

Today many people's thoughts are filled with fear. While there are certainly real dangers in the world and things of legitimate concern, often the fears that keep people in bondage are not based on genuine threats. In every situation we face, whether a grave threat or an imagined danger, we can have confidence that God is in control. But such peace only comes as a byproduct of our faith. When we trust God fully with the results and outcomes from our work, we can know His peace as our thoughts are filled with faith rather than fear. Biblical thinking provides us a foundation for godly and successful living.

Today's Word to the Wise: Faith in God provides a solid foundation for our thinking that cannot be shaken by what happens around us.

Dividing Through Gossip

He that covereth a transgression seeketh love; but he that repeateth a matter separateth very friends.—**Proverbs 17:9**

During World War II, the United States government became concerned that a number of German spies were operating in America and sending information back to Germany regarding Allied war plans and specific troop and ship movements. To keep them from impacting the war effort, the Office of War Information launched a national campaign around the slogan "Loose Lips Sink Ships." It was a solemn warning to people not to repeat information that might be damaging or even deadly if it fell into the wrong hands.

In the same way, the Word of God warns us of the dangers of gossip. Repeating stories has a way of dividing the body of Christ. Gossip is even able to separate the closest of friends. Revelation 12:10 refers to Satan as "the accuser of our brethren." Notice that it does not say he makes *false* accusations against us; he doesn't need to. The Bible teaches that he brings our sins to remembrance before God where Jesus serves as our Advocate. When we become sharers of gossip and spreaders of bad reports, even when those reports are true, we are literally doing the devil's work.

There are some problems and sins so severe that they must be reported to church or even civil authorities and dealt with according to the law. In such circumstances, we should not fail to speak the truth regardless of the consequences. There is a vast difference, however, between speaking out in those situations and simply being the first to tell "the latest" to everyone we can reach. No bad report about another should be shared with those who are not in a position of authority to respond to it. God views creating divisions as especially heinous. One of the seven sins on the list of particular abominations to God is "he that soweth discord among brethren" (Proverbs 6:19).

Today's Word to the Wise: Do not cause divisions in the body of Christ by repeating gossip about others.

The Power of Words

Death and life are in the power of the tongue: and they that love it shall eat the fruit thereof.—**Proverbs 18:21**

Sir Walter Scott's tales of chivalry and courage made him one of the most famous authors in the world. It is quite unlikely, however, that he would have become an author at all if not for a meeting with the noted poet Robert Burns. Scott was studying law at the University of Edinburgh when he attended a literary meeting featuring the famous poet. Burns asked a question about an illustration, and the fifteen-year-old Scott was the only one present who knew the answer. Burns is said to have told the young man, "You will be a great man in Scotland, my lad. You have it in you to be a writer."

Words have enormous power for both good and evil. Words can encourage and uplift someone who is struggling or they can tempt or wound. Because of the power of our words, we need to be extremely careful how we speak. We can bring people closer to God and have a positive impact on them, or we can allow our critical and harsh words to discourage people and tear them down.

This is not just true of the impact our words have on others, but also of their impact on our own lives. Many times we carelessly and critically speak of ourselves in very negative ways. While we should never give place to pride and boasting, we should also avoid being overly degrading in our self-description.

We would be wise to follow the instruction of Colossians 4:6: "Let your speech be alway with grace, seasoned with salt…." How would your conversations (in person and online) today be different if you continually remembered the power of your words and chose to speak with grace? You could be a difference-maker in someone's life today!

Today's Word to the Wise: Choose your words carefully; they help shape life both for you and those to whom you speak.

The Folly of Fretting

The foolishness of man perverteth his way: and his heart fretteth against the LORD.—**Proverbs 19:3**

During the darkest days of the Second World War when England was standing almost alone against Hitler's Germany, the German Air Force launched a massive assault against England in preparation for an invasion of the island nation. For fifty-seven straight nights, hundreds of German planes dropped thousands of pounds of bombs on London. At least one million homes were damaged or destroyed, and thousands were killed. Hitler hoped to break the will of England and force them to surrender.

Even in those difficult days, the British people did not give in to fear. One elderly saint was asked by her pastor how she was doing, and she replied that she was sleeping soundly every night, even as the bombs fell. When asked how she was able to sleep in such circumstances she replied, "Well, I give my fears to God, and He never sleeps. I figure there is no reason for us both to stay up all night!"

When we worry, we are in effect saying that we either do not believe that God is able to take care of us or that He does not love us enough to do so even though He could. Either one is an insult on His love and care and a sign that we are living in folly instead of in wisdom. Despite what some popular teachers promote today, Christianity is not a guarantee that things will always go according to our plans. Stephen was stoned to death for preaching the truth; and Paul was shipwrecked, stoned, and arrested many times.

Faith is not the belief that things will be easy, but that everything will work together according to God's plan for our best and His glory. Worry undermines what is meant to be a close and personal relationship with God.

Today's Word to the Wise: Worry is a damaging sin because it is an attack on God's love and care for us.

Be a Peacemaker

It is an honour for a man to cease from strife: but every fool will be meddling.—**Proverbs 20:3**

Several church members commented on how bitter the coffee was that Sunday morning at the Gustaf Adolph Lutheran Church in New Sweden, Maine, in 2003. Soon a number of them became violently ill, and one elderly member died. When a police investigation began, the fifty-three-year-old church member Danny Bondeson killed himself, leaving behind a suicide note apologizing for what he had done.

Bondeson and his family had apparently donated a new table for use in the communion observance, but some of the members of the church objected to replacing the one they had used for so many years. In anger, Bondeson placed arsenic in the church coffee pot. He claimed he only wanted to make people sick to get even for what he felt was his mistreatment. He hadn't intended to kill anyone, but his refusal to make peace and forgive cost two people their lives.

In any situation in which we have been wronged or offended, we face the choice between holding a grudge and forgiving. Peace, however, requires more than forgiveness; it requires that we work at restoring the relationship as much as is possible. Jesus said, "Blessed are the peacemakers: for they shall be called the children of God" (Matthew 5:9). The clear implication here is that peace requires effort and work. Peace does not come naturally in response to the offenses of life.

Part of making peace is putting the past behind us. That is an integral part of ceasing from strife. If we are harboring bitterness in our hearts over what has been done to us in the past, there will be no true peace—in either the relationship or our own minds. The past cannot be changed. The only thing that can be changed is our response, and our response should be to seek peace.

Today's Word to the Wise: When you forgive and do your best to make peace, you receive the blessing of God.

The Rewards of Diligence

The thoughts of the diligent tend only to plenteousness; but of every one that is hasty only to want.—**Proverbs 21:5**

When the Civil War began, one of those who answered the call to fight for the Union was William Scott of Vermont. Along with four of his brothers, the young soldier traveled to Washington to join the Army of the Potomac. On the night of August 31, 1861, Scott, who had volunteered to take the sentry duty of a sick member of his company, was found asleep at his post where he was to have been guarding the bridge that led to the nation's capital. According to military law, the "sleeping sentinel," as he came to be known, was tried and sentenced to be executed on September 9 by firing squad.

The harsh punishment was meant to be a warning to those given positions of responsibility to be diligent and careful in discharging them. Yet it also seemed too harsh for a young man who had volunteered for duty. The case was brought to President Lincoln, who personally issued a pardon to Private Scott. Scott gave his pledge that he would never again fail in his duty to his country. Seven months later during a battle at Lee's Mills, Virginia, Scott, who had already saved several fellow soldiers from drowning, was shot and killed while carrying another wounded soldier to safety. His renewed commitment to diligently do his duty replaced his shame with honor.

In a world where "close enough for government work" is a common excuse for giving less than our best effort, diligence is a vital trait we need to cultivate. In every arena of our lives—work, family, and even worship—we need to be focused on excellence and completing what we are doing to the very best of our ability without allowing anything to distract us. God rewards those who are willing to make this commitment to diligence.

Today's Word to the Wise: If you are careful to do your best in every situation, you will receive both temporal and eternal blessings.

The Destructiveness of Pride

By humility and the fear of the Lord are riches, and honour, and life.
—Proverbs 22:4

The legendary golfer Arnold Palmer described how pride once brought him low on the very brink of great success: "It was the final hole of the 1961 Masters tournament, and I had a one-stroke lead and had just hit a very satisfying tee shot. I felt I was in pretty good shape. As I approached my ball, I saw an old friend standing at the edge of the gallery. He motioned me over, stuck out his hand and said, 'Congratulations.' I took his hand and shook it, but as soon as I did, I knew I had lost my focus. On my next two shots, I hit the ball into a sand trap, then put it over the edge of the green. I missed a putt and lost the Masters. You don't forget a mistake like that; you just learn from it and become determined that you will never do that again. I haven't in the 30 years since."

That brief moment of pride—when he accepted congratulations for a victory not yet won—took certain victory away from Palmer. His story holds a powerful lesson for us. There may be no human attitude more destructive than pride. Though we are tempted to take the credit for our efforts and accomplishments, every good thing that we do is the result of what God has given us. We have no basis for taking credit for ourselves.

Pride places us on a dangerous path, and it harms our relationships with God as well. James 4:6 says, "God resisteth the proud, but giveth grace unto the humble." When we humbly acknowledge Him as the source of all of the good things we have and do, we continue to receive His grace to help us deal with the challenges and temptations of life.

Today's Word to the Wise: Humble yourself before the Lord, and you will receive not only great blessings, but great protection as well.

Keep the Landmarks in Place

Remove not the old landmark; and enter not into the fields of the fatherless:—**Proverbs 23:10**

On June 1, 1796, the "Volunteer State," Tennessee, entered the Union and became the sixteenth state. Formed from land that had once been considered part of North Carolina, the borders of the new state were recognized by Congress as part of the admissions process. It was not long, however, before a dispute arose between Tennessee and Georgia over exactly where the boundary line between the two should have been placed—whether it should be exactly along the 35th parallel or close to it.

The state of Georgia contends that much of the city of Chattanooga and part of the Tennessee River that flows nearby should not be within the boundaries of Tennessee but part of Georgia instead. For nearly two hundred years now, the two states have been unable to resolve the dispute. The boundary between them remains a point of contention.

There is great value in having established, settled, and certain landmarks. It is true in the spiritual realm as well as in the political realm. Though we live in a society where everything is open to challenge and change, there are timeless principles of truth that must never be moved. Though we should always be learning and growing in our walk with God, the things that were true yesterday are still true today and will be true tomorrow.

The ancient landmarks—those things that have been believed and held dear by Christians through the centuries—are not in need of relocation or revision. Today we hear "reasoned" appeals to re-examine our core beliefs. Those are the siren calls of the tempter meant to lure us away from what is right. The old landmarks were placed where they are for a reason, and it is the task of our generation to defend those truths, not change them.

Today's Word to the Wise: Do not allow anything or anyone to persuade you to give up the ancient landmarks of the faith.

Get Up and Try Again

For a just man falleth seven times, and riseth up again: but the wicked shall fall into mischief.—**Proverbs 24:16**

Though he would later be acclaimed as one of the greatest inventors of history, Thomas Edison's school career lasted three months. The teacher believed he was incapable of learning anything and sent him home. Edison's mother taught him, and he was on his way to a lifetime of overcoming what seemed to be insurmountable obstacles. Among his most famous inventions were the commercial incandescent light bulb, the phonograph, and the fluoroscope. Most of his inventions required months if not years of dedication to overcoming obstacles before seeing any results.

In a 1921 interview, Edison described his persistence this way: "After we had conducted thousands of experiments on a certain project without solving the problem, one of my associates, after we had conducted the crowning experiment and it had proved a failure, expressed discouragement and disgust over our having failed to find out anything. I cheerily assured him that we had learned something. For we had learned for a certainty that the thing couldn't be done that way, and that we would have to try some other way."

Very few things of lasting significance and value are achieved without overcoming serious obstacles. The story of almost every "overnight success" is actually the story of someone continuing to persevere in the face of great difficulty and disappointment. If things do not work out the first time we try to accomplish something important, that is not a sign that we should give up and find something easier. No strong family, no strong church, and no strong business is built without the tenacity to overcome obstacles and failures. Completing the work God has given us to do does not come without cost. Those who are willing to pay that cost and continue in spite of setbacks are the ones who reach the goal.

Today's Word to the Wise: You are not defeated when you are knocked down. You are defeated when you stop getting back up.

Removing Bad Influences

Take away the dross from the silver, and there shall come forth a vessel for the finer. Take away the wicked from before the king, and his throne shall be established in righteousness.—**Proverbs 25:4–5**

When silver is mined from the ground it is commonly mixed with a number of other elements. In order to get pure silver that can be used for commercial or industrial purposes, it must be refined. Silver has an extraordinarily high melting point. It must be heated to nearly 2,200 degrees in order to be refined to complete purity. Only when it has been through that process does the silver become useful for its intended function. Beautiful service pieces, high tech equipment, and collectible coins all become possible once the silver has been refined. Without that process, it is largely worthless.

Satan is delighted when we allow wicked influences to remain in our lives, because they keep us from fulfilling the will of God. One of his most effective lies is that such influences won't really have any impact on us. Believing this lie has destroyed many Christians as they fell prey to influences they did not recognize and guard against. As Paul warned the church at Corinth, "Be not deceived: evil communications corrupt good manners" (1 Corinthians 15:33).

Sick people who are contagious don't get well by being around healthy people. Instead they infect the healthy. The same principle holds true in the spiritual realm. The influences we allow to touch our hearts and minds—what we read, what we watch, who we fellowship with—will shape the way we view the world and the way we act. If we want to be established in righteous living, then we must do the hard work of refining our lives and removing the evil influences. Though this may be a painful process, the results are worth the cost.

Today's Word to the Wise: When you remove wicked influences from your life, you are preparing for greater usefulness for God.

Being Responsive

A whip for the horse, a bridle for the ass, and a rod for the fool's back.
—Proverbs 26:3

We get our word *tribulation* from the Latin word *tribulum*. The tribulum was an agricultural instrument designed to help separate the grain from the chaff. It was constructed of several wooden boards nailed together. Pieces of stone, bone, or metal would be attached to the bottom. The tribulum would be weighted with heavy stones, and then pulled by horses or oxen over the grain which would be spread on the threshing floor. The attachments would break apart the hulls holding the grain and allow the kernels to be separated for use.

None of us are eager to endure tribulation or difficulty. And not every difficulty or trial is a chastisement from the Lord. Job, Paul, and others remind us that there are multiple reasons why God may allow suffering into our lives. According to Romans 8:28, regardless of the reason behind our suffering, God's ultimate goal is to make it work for our good and His glory.

Isaiah gives us a fascinating insight into God's chastisement of His children: "For the fitches are not threshed with a threshing instrument, neither is a cart wheel turned about upon the cummin; but the fitches are beaten out with a staff, and the cummin with a rod. Bread corn is bruised; because he will not ever be threshing it, nor break it with the wheel of his cart, nor bruise it with his horsemen" (Isaiah 28:27–28). Delicate plants like fitches (a herb used for seasoning food) were not threshed because the heavy tool would crush them. But the thicker grains used for making bread went under the tribulum.

When our hearts are soft and we quickly listen to God's Word, we do not require judgment to remind us to do right. God calibrates our circumstances based on what is required to draw us to Himself.

Today's Word to the Wise: If we are responsive to the prompting of the Holy Spirit and the instruction of Scripture, we will save ourselves much heartache.

Lift Up Jesus

Let another man praise thee, and not thine own mouth; a stranger, and not thine own lips.—**Proverbs 27:2**

In his day, Charles Spurgeon was probably the most famous preacher in the world. The crowds of people who wanted to hear him preach were so large that before the church was able to erect a building with enough seating, they rented the Royal Surrey Music Hall which seated ten thousand people. For a number of years, tickets were required to get in to hear Spurgeon preach. The story is told that a visitor from America, eager to hear the famous "prince of preachers," convinced a friend to get a ticket for him.

After the message concluded, the American stood in the vestibule of the church talking to his English friend. He did not know that Spurgeon was standing nearby listening. The Englishman asked what his friend thought of the service, and he replied, "What a preacher!" According to the story, Spurgeon began to weep. A church member asked him what was wrong and Spurgeon said, "I wish he had said, 'What a Saviour!'"

Our purpose is not to gain honor, glory, or praise for ourselves, but to bring glory to the Lord. Often we fall into the trap of wanting people to recognize how special, gifted, hard-working, and devoted we are—so we tell them. The temptation to make sure our efforts are recognized by others puts us in a dangerous place. Anyone who is spending time bragging on himself is walking in the pathway of pride, and that path leads to destruction.

Jesus said, "And I, if I be lifted up from the earth, will draw all men unto me" (John 12:32). That is primarily a statement of truth about His work through His death on the cross, but it is also true of our service for Him: when we lift Jesus up rather than ourselves, men and women are attracted to Him.

Today's Word to the Wise: Avoid the snare of promoting yourself, and make sure your words and actions lift up Jesus and bring Him glory.

Fighting for What Is Right

They that forsake the law praise the wicked: but such as keep the law contend with them.—**Proverbs 28:4**

One of the most famous fictional characters ever created, the Lone Ranger, was the brainchild of a desperate radio station executive named Fran Striker. Radio had grown quickly after its introduction, but by the 1930s the Great Depression was making life hard for the entire industry. In an effort to attract listeners and advertisers, Striker created the story of a western lawman who was the only survivor of an ambush and dedicated his life to the cause of what was right. The introduction to the program described him as, "The Lone Ranger...led the fight for law and order in the early western United States."

God has not only given us the truth, but the responsibility to stand for it. If the truth is to be maintained from generation to generation, it must be defended. If we are not willing to confront those who oppose the truth, it is inevitable that it will be obscured. This is why Jude declared, "It was needful for me to write unto you, and exhort you that ye should earnestly contend for the faith which was once delivered unto the saints" (Jude 3).

In our society, the very concept that there is such a thing as settled and absolute truth is under attack. From all sides, we see people devoting their efforts to replacing God's truth with something that is more suited to their whims and desires. We must not make compromises of the truth in order to be liked or acceptable to a culture that has turned its back on God. Much of the history of the church is the story of people suffering for their faith. If such persecution comes in our day, let it be said of us that we were faithful, if necessary even unto death.

Today's Word to the Wise: Loving God properly requires that we be willing to take a stand for the truth even when it is not popular.

The Joy of Obedience

*Where there is no vision, the people perish: but he that keepeth the law,
happy is he.*—**Proverbs 29:18**

Jeremy Taylor pastored in England during the difficult and trying time
of the English Civil War in the 1600s. Because he had served as chaplain
to King Charles I, he was arrested and sent to prison after the king was
overthrown. Taylor continued to be faithful to his work, despite his
circumstances, and eventually he was released. A prolific author, Taylor's
devotional book *Holy Living and Holy Dying* had a profound impact on
John Wesley among many others. Though Taylor suffered for his stand, he
found happiness in obedience even in the midst of trying circumstances.

He wrote: "They have not taken away my merry countenance, my
cheerful spirit, and a good conscience; they have still left me with the
providence of God, and all His promises…my hopes of Heaven, and my
charity to them, too, and still I sleep and digest, eat and drink, I read and
meditate. And he that hath so many causes of joy, and so great should
never choose to sit down upon his little handful of thorns."

Obedience is often viewed as obligation and drudgery. We "must" do
this or "must not" do that. God does not want us to view His law that
way. In fact, those who obey are happy and blessed. Though He was the
Son of God, Jesus "humbled himself, and became obedient unto death"
(Philippians 2:8). He did not view this as an imposition, but rather as a
joy. Jesus, "for the joy that was set before him endured the cross, despising
the shame" (Hebrews 12:2). If our focus is on the things we must give
up or suffer for our obedience, we are looking in the wrong direction.
Instead we should realize that it is out of His great love for us that God
issues His commands.

Today's Word to the Wise: When we recognize that obeying God brings
protection and blessing, we are happy to follow His commands.

A WORD TO THE

WISE

THE BOOK
OF PROVERBS

MARCH

Missing the Foundation

The fear of the LORD is the beginning of knowledge: but fools despise wisdom and instruction.—**Proverbs 1:7**

Dexter Manley was known in the college football world as a fearsome defensive end, capable of wreaking havoc with opposing offenses. Though he stood six feet, three inches and weighed over 250 pounds, his speed and quickness made him a nightmare to block. Following four years of college, he went on to a brilliant career in professional football with the Washington Redskins. After his football career ended, Manley revealed a secret—he was functionally illiterate. Although he played well in football, he was missing a vital part of the foundation for success. Without the sport, he had nothing left to prepare him for life.

In the same way when we lose the meaning of the fear of the Lord, we are not prepared to succeed in the Christian life. This is a basic and foundational truth that underlies the study and acquisition of wisdom and godly knowledge. You cannot properly learn God's principle for living apart from understanding His holiness and hatred of sin. In our day, the fear of the Lord is downplayed or even ignored. This has had devastating consequences for the moral character and power of God's people. His blessing comes as we walk in His fear. His judgment comes when we do not.

The prophet Isaiah and the Apostle John were both given a glimpse into Heaven, and they both recorded what they saw. Both men revealed that constantly circling the throne of God are angelic beings crying out, "Holy, holy, holy." God could have chosen any of His attributes to be proclaimed day and night in His presence, but He selected His holiness. It follows then that we should give priority to this attribute He calls to our attention. When we fear God, realizing that though He loves us greatly His hatred of sin is intense, the foundation is laid for learning wisdom.

Today's Word to the Wise: Fearing God is a vital foundation for all learning regarding Scriptural knowledge and wisdom.

Numbers 20–22   »   Mark 7:1–13   »   Proverbs 1

A Certain Defense

He layeth up sound wisdom for the righteous: he is a buckler to them that walk uprightly.—**Proverbs 2:7**

For many years Robert and Trudie Neighbour were missionaries in South America. God greatly blessed their work, and a number of people were saved. They told the story of how one of their converts, a baker named José, was eager to share his new faith with others. The local priest objected and had José arrested. When the officials asked who authorized him to pass out tracts, José opened his New Testament and read the Great Commission. They threatened to kill José if he continued to tell others about salvation in Jesus.

Forced to flee from his hometown, José was pursued to the next village where another Christian hid him from the soldiers. This dear Christian lady drained the rainwater tank that sat next to her house and José climbed inside with his Bible. He sat there reading the Word and praying for deliverance while the soldiers searched the house. From the roof they could have looked right down into the water tank and seen him, but God blinded their eyes and delivered José from certain death.

God promises in His Word to be a defense to His people. As we walk in His way, we have nothing to fear. Not every child of God is miraculously delivered from danger or death, but everyone is protected until God is ready for them to come to Heaven. Faced with a furnace heated seven times hotter than normal, the three Hebrew children told Nebuchadnezzar that God had the power to deliver them—and that even if He did not, they would still not bow down to the idol Nebuchadnezzar had made. They were confident in their ultimate deliverance by the hand and power of God. When we have that confidence, we will not be swayed by fear into doing wrong.

Today's Word to the Wise: If you are doing right in the eyes of God, you can be confident that He will defend you from evil.

God's Ways Are Not Our Ways

Trust in the LORD with all thine heart; and lean not unto thine own understanding. In all thy ways acknowledge him, and he shall direct thy paths.—**Proverbs 3:5–6**

We were on vacation on a hot June night in 1986 when I preached at the Lancaster Baptist Church. Pastoring in the high desert was not part of my plan for the future. The church was deeply in debt, and only a handful of families were still attending. Their building was in foreclosure, and the church was meeting in an upstairs classroom so they could rent out the lower floor. Yet after a unanimous vote from the twelve adults present to call me pastor, I began to sense that God was leading me to do something that made no logical sense.

I had a young family to support, and of course, this struggling church couldn't pay me a salary. But my wife and I believed that God was calling us to go, so we made the decision to trust Him and follow Him even though we didn't fully understand His plan. We moved to Lancaster and went to work doing what God called us to do. That first week in the Antelope Valley, we started knocking on doors and telling people about Jesus. All these years later, we are still doing the same thing, and God is still blessing the work and building His church.

Often we want everything to make perfect sense and know exactly how each step of a process will go before we start something for God. Instead God wants us to trust His Word and His promises rather than what our understanding is capable of arranging. Just as Abraham left his home and family without a clear understanding of where he was going to end up, we must be willing to walk in obedience to God even when the way ahead is not clear. Only when we put our faith in action do we receive His guidance.

Today's Word to the Wise: If we want God to direct our path we must be willing to trust and follow Him even when we do not understand how things will work out.

Don't Let Down Your Guard

Forsake her not, and she shall preserve thee: love her, and she shall keep thee.—**Proverbs 4:6**

It was a stifling hot morning that August in Hiroshima, Japan. In 1945, citizens feared a pending air strike from the allied forces of World War II. Many people were evacuating belongings from their homes and making preparation for their safety. Hiroshima was one of the largest cities in Japan that had not yet been attacked, and most people expected a raid any day.

When the air raid siren sounded that morning, the city thought the attack had begun, but a few minutes later, the all clear was sounded. Japanese radar operators, seeing only three American planes, decided that this was not a serious attack. A few moments later, the first atomic bomb used in war was dropped on the city, killing tens of thousands of people instantly. They believed that they were safe from attack, not realizing the nature of what was about to happen.

Often Christians make the fatal mistake of underestimating our enemy. He is vicious and determined, and if we let down our guard, he will strike. The Bible warns us not to forsake wisdom. It is not enough to merely know and follow the principles God lays out for us in His Word. We must continue to live them out to be kept safe.

Tragically Solomon himself provides an example of what happens when we forsake wisdom. Though God gave him great wisdom in his youth, Solomon did not continue to walk in wisdom. His heart was turned away from God, and he lost the blessings he had once enjoyed. Following his death the kingdom was divided. When we forsake wisdom, we lose the safety wisdom provides.

Today's Word to the Wise: Continue to walk by God's principles of wisdom, and you will continue to receive the protection of obedience.

Stay Far Away from Sin

Hear me now therefore, O ye children, and depart not from the words of my mouth. Remove thy way far from her, and come not nigh the door of her house:—**Proverbs 5:7–8**

In September of 2012, a twenty-five-year-old New York man horrified onlookers when he jumped from the monorail train touring the Bronx Zoo. Despite two fences, one of them electric, he managed to get into the tiger cage. He later told authorities he "wanted to be one with the tiger." He came very close to getting his wish—being *inside* the tiger. Instead, he only suffered a broken arm, a broken leg, a punctured lung, and serious bite and claw injuries. There were measures to keep him safe from the tiger, but he intentionally placed himself in a position of great danger, and it nearly cost him his life.

Since this story does not have a tragic ending, it is almost funny. We may ask, "What was he thinking?" And yet, though we would never think of climbing into a tiger cage on purpose, far too many Christians intentionally and deliberately walk as close as they can to a roaring lion. They may not want to go completely across the boundaries into serious sin, but they keep walking past the fence and looking longingly to the other side.

The downfall of Lot can be traced to the day when he "pitched his tent toward Sodom" (Genesis 13:12). On that day this "righteous man" (2 Peter 2:8) could never have dreamed of the destruction that was soon to come to him and his family. If he had seen the end result, he would have chosen differently, but Lot was so focused on the fertile land around Sodom that he missed the danger. After many days of looking that direction, he eventually moved his family to that wicked city, and tragedy followed.

If we stand by the door of sin long enough, we will eventually go through it. Don't jump the fences or push against the boundaries God has placed in your life, and you will be safe.

Today's Word to the Wise: Resolve to stay as far away from temptation and sin as you can.

You Are Using It All

A naughty person, a wicked man, walketh with a froward mouth. He winketh with his eyes, he speaketh with his feet, he teacheth with his fingers; Frowardness is in his heart, he deviseth mischief continually; he soweth discord.—**Proverbs 6:12–14**

In 1992, New York Jets defensive lineman Dennis Byrd was paralyzed following a collision with a teammate during a football game. The hit shattered one of the vertebrae in his neck, and even after seven hours of surgery to stabilize him, the powerful football player was left helpless, unable to move. It was not clear whether he would ever be able to walk again. His physical rehabilitation began just two weeks after surgery. At first he was unable to move at all. Therapists began to stretch and flex his arms and legs, and slowly the muscles regained their strength. Byrd progressed to the point where he could stand in a pool and walk with the water supporting most of his weight. After weeks of painstaking effort, straining and using every fiber of his being, Byrd was able to walk again. Eventually he regained the majority of the use of his arms and legs and was able to resume a mostly normal life.

Contrast that level of dedication and commitment to doing something good with the wicked person described in Proverbs. This man is also using every resource at his disposal—his mouth, his eyes, his feet and his hands—but instead of good, his purpose is to do evil and sow discord.

The truth is that whether or not we realize it, all of us are working each day for the cause of right or for the cause of wrong. No one is living a neutral life; everything we do has an impact on others. Paul wrote, "For none of us liveth to himself, and no man dieth to himself" (Romans 14:7). Choose to invest your energy today in advancing the cause of Christ and serving others.

Today's Word to the Wise: The talents and abilities you have are being used today—make sure they are used for good rather than for evil.

The End of Sin

He goeth after her straightway, as an ox goeth to the slaughter, or as a fool to the correction of the stocks; Till a dart strike through his liver; as a bird hasteth to the snare, and knoweth not that it is for his life.
—**Proverbs 7:22–23**

Alcatraz only served as a Federal penitentiary for twenty-nine years, but it became one of the most famous prisons in the nation. Because of its isolated location and the powerful currents that ran through the cold waters separating the island from the mainland, Alcatraz was deemed a place from which it was impossible to escape. "The Rock," as it was known, became home to more than three hundred of the worst prisoners in the entire country including high profile criminals and those who had caused trouble in other prisons. Among its best-known inhabitants were Al Capone and Machine Gun Kelly.

Because the island prison was only a little over a mile from the city of San Francisco and because sound carries well over the water, the inmates at the prison could often hear sounds from major events in the city. Guards said that one of the hardest days of the year for the inmates was New Year's Eve. They could hear the celebrations taking place, but because of what they had done, they were cut off from the happiness others were able to experience.

One of the main protections God has given us to help resist temptation is a careful awareness of the consequences of sin. Though we should do right because it is right, sometimes it is the fear of the Lord and the recognition of what we will lose that keeps us from yielding to temptation. Rather than looking at the allure of sin, we need to look at the end result. When we do, we will be motivated to walk in holiness.

Today's Word to the Wise: Every sin carries the seeds of death and destruction, and if we do not repent and confess our sins, they will find us out.

Better than Rubies

For wisdom is better than rubies; and all the things that may be desired are not to be compared to it.—**Proverbs 8:11**

In May of 2012, a 32-carat Burmese ruby and diamond ring—part of the collection of Lily Safra, one of the richest women in the world—was sold at an auction in New York City. The pre-auction estimate for the sale was $3–5 million, but the final sale price ended up at $6.7 million. It is believed to be the most expensive ruby ever sold at auction.

As valuable as rubies are, the Bible tells us that wisdom is far better and more valuable. No earthly treasure can compare to wisdom because nothing else offers the same protection, benefits, and blessings that wisdom does.

Anything of value is sure to be counterfeited, and such is the case with wisdom. James warns us of wisdom that is not from God. "This wisdom descendeth not from above, but is earthly, sensual, devilish" (James 3:15). Godly wisdom can be discerned by the fruit it produces in our lives. James describes it this way: "But the wisdom that is from above is first pure, then peaceable, gentle, and easy to be intreated, full of mercy and good fruits, without partiality, and without hypocrisy" (James 3:17).

We need to be sure that our definition of wisdom is in line with God's definition. The temptation we face is to make decisions according to our human reasoning of whether or not something is wise. Yet the standard is not our thinking but God's declaration. Godly wisdom may defy logic and reasoning, but it will never defy Scripture. God has given us the principles for successful living in His Word, but they must be applied in our lives to have their intended effect.

Living according to wisdom changes our relationship with God and with those around us for the better—making it more valuable than rubies for our lives.

Today's Word to the Wise: Seek wisdom above all earthly treasures, and God will grant you what you seek.

Receiving Rebuke Rightly

Reprove not a scorner, lest he hate thee: rebuke a wise man, and he will love thee.—**Proverbs 9:8**

When Orel Hershiser was in his first season as a pitcher for the Los Angeles Dodgers, he had great talent but had not been able to translate that into success on the field. Early in the 1984 season, he was struggling with his control. Finally Dodgers manager Tommy Lasorda called the young pitcher into his office for a verbal confrontation that Hershiser later referred to as "The Sermon on the Mound."

Lasorda told Hershiser that he was capable of much better work than he was doing and that he owed it to the team to reach his potential. Hershiser took the rebuke to heart and approached the game with a new attitude. He went on to win the Cy Young award as baseball's best pitcher in 1988 while leading the Dodgers to the World Series title. If Hershiser had not responded properly to his manager's rebuke, it is doubtful that he would ever have achieved such success or helped his team so much.

I have yet to meet anyone who truly enjoys being rebuked and corrected. But the truth is that from time to time all of us need to make changes, and often God uses other people to point out that necessity to us. What happens next is crucial to our future. If we respond in pride and anger, we will miss the instruction and correction that we need. If we respond in humility and wisdom, we can be spared great heartache.

A person standing on the road waving a red flag is not an insult to your driving ability; he may be the only thing standing between you and disaster if you continue full speed ahead. Though a proper response requires us to admit we have been wrong, needed reproof is one of God's great blessings to us.

Today's Word to the Wise: If you respond rightly to rebuke, you protect yourself from danger and prepare yourself for greater service to God.

God's Miraculous Provision

The LORD will not suffer the soul of the righteous to famish: but he casteth away the substance of the wicked.—**Proverbs 10:3**

When Hudson Taylor was preparing to go to China as a missionary, he knew he needed to learn to trust God. He was working for a busy medical doctor who told Taylor to remind him when the salary was due. Hudson Taylor determined instead to ask God to provide for his needs. He told the story that once he had not yet been paid and was down to his last half crown on a Sunday night. A poor man came to ask Taylor to pray for his wife who was desperately sick.

When he arrived at their home Taylor saw they had nothing. He knew he could help, but hesitated to give up his last coin. He knelt to pray with the family and later described what had happened: "But scarcely had I opened my lips with 'Our Father who art in heaven' than conscience said within, 'Dare you mock God? Dare you kneel down and call Him Father with that half-crown in your pocket?'"

Taylor gave the poor man his last coin, with which he was able to purchase food and medicine for his sick wife. Taylor returned home with empty pockets but a full heart. The next day he received an anonymous letter in the mail with a half sovereign coin—worth four times what he had given away the night before.

As children of God, He has given us the privilege to go to Him in prayer for our needs to be met. We can be confident that as we walk in righteousness we can expect His provision. Do not let the fact that you have needs kill your generosity. Instead continue to give as God directs, and believe in faith that He will hear and answer your pleas for help.

Today's Word to the Wise: You can always trust God to meet and supply your needs when you cry out to Him in faith.

The Wisdom of Soulwinning

The fruit of the righteous is a tree of life; and he that winneth souls is wise.—**Proverbs 11:30**

A missionary to Africa told the story of an elderly woman who was reached with the gospel. Though she was blind and could neither read nor write, she wanted to share her new found faith with others. She went to the missionary and asked him for a copy of the Bible in French. When she got it, she asked him to underline John 3:16 in red and mark the page it was on so she could find it. The missionary wanted to see what she would do, so one day he followed her.

In the afternoon, just before school let out, she made her way to the front door. As the boys came out when school was dismissed, she would stop one and ask if he knew how to read French. When he said "Yes" she would ask him to read the verse that was marked in red. Then she would ask, "Do you know what this means?" and tell him about Christ. The missionary said that when he left the field years later there were twenty-four men pastoring churches who had been led to the Lord by that illiterate blind woman when they were school boys.

God's plan for reaching the world is for each of us who have received His gift of salvation to share the good news with others. Soulwinning is not meant to be reserved for pastors or full-time evangelists. It is a command for every Christian. Soulwinning does not require brilliant knowledge, gifted speech, or a charming personality; it requires obedience to tell the message. Each person we meet has a soul that will spend eternity either in Heaven or Hell. Recognizing this truth should motivate us to be faithful to do everything we can to bring people to faith in Christ.

Today's Word to the Wise: Nothing you accomplish in life will have a larger or longer-lasting impact than leading people to Christ.

The Folly of Honoring Ourselves

He that is despised, and hath a servant, is better than he that honoureth himself, and lacketh bread.—**Proverbs 12:9**

Hudson Taylor was scheduled to speak at a large church in Melbourne, Australia. The moderator of the service introduced the missionary in eloquent and glowing terms. He told the large congregation all that Taylor had accomplished in China, and then presented him to the assembled people as "our illustrious guest." Taylor stood quietly for a moment, and then opened his message by saying, "Dear friends, I am the little servant of an illustrious Master."

We live in a day that honors and encourages self-promotion. People are encouraged to "toot their own horns" and let others know how wonderful they are and all that they have accomplished. We see people go to incredible lengths to become famous. In this age of "reality TV" when anyone is willing to allow cameras to broadcast their every move—no matter how embarrassing—we have reached a new level of self-exaltation.

This is the opposite of God's design for our lives. We should be focused on honoring and glorifying Him. John the Baptist had an amazing ministry. He saw huge crowds come to hear him preach, and many believed his message and were baptized. Yet when Jesus came, John willingly stepped into the background. Some of his enemies attempted to discourage John by pointing out that many who had once followed him were now following Jesus. John the Baptist replied, "He must increase, but I must decrease" (John 3:30).

God is looking for servants who are willing to be servants for His glory rather than for recognition and fame. President Ronald Reagan was fond of saying, "There is no limit to what you can do if you don't care who gets the credit." This principle is true in every facet of life.

Today's Word to the Wise: If you are focused on honoring God, He will see to it that you receive the honor that matters most—His approval.

The Source of Conflict

Only by pride cometh contention: but with the well advised is wisdom.
—**Proverbs 13:10**

In 1731 the British ship *Rebecca* was boarded by Spanish sailors who believed the British brig was part of a smuggling operation. During the on-board conflict, Spanish captain, Julio Fandino, cut off the left ear of the British captain, Robert Jenkins. Fandino intended to send a message to England, and he succeeded. Jenkins was called to testify before Parliament about the events aboard the ship, and he brought along his severed ear as a demonstration of the truth of his account.

The incident was declared "an insult to the honour of the nation" and led to war between Spain and England—what came to be known as The War of Jenkins' Ear. The two nations fought for several years, leaving thousands dead, and then the war spread to other countries as well until it involved most of Europe. The War of Austrian Succession and the Seven Years War followed, leaving hundreds of thousands dead. But it all began with an ear.

Today many churches and families are riven with conflict rather than blessed with peace. Proverbs identifies the problem for us—conflict comes from pride. If we are humble and not insistent that we are always right, we will not find it difficult to get along with others. While there are truths that should be held without any compromise, the majority of conflicts come not from such cases but from hurt feelings and wounded pride.

Peter said, "For he that will love life, and see good days…let him seek peace, and ensue it" (1 Peter 3:10–11). To seek and follow peace we must be willing to lay aside our desire to prove we are right or to get our way. We must be willing to extend grace and forgiveness, even to those who have hurt us. We can be certain that if we maintain our pride, we will never know peace.

Today's Word to the Wise: If you want peace, you must abandon pride and listen to the counsels of wisdom.

A Faithful Witness

A faithful witness will not lie: but a false witness will utter lies.
—Proverbs 14:5

Born to a prominent British political family, Jonathan Aitken made a name for himself as a courageous reporter and war correspondent prior to beginning his political career. He rose to the heights of power, serving as Minister of Defense and Chief Secretary of the Treasury. But after he had been twenty years in office, a television news program threatened to expose illegal activity on his part. Aitken took them to court, filing a libel suit. On the stand he testified under oath that the story was false—only to have the media company produce documents which proved beyond any doubt that he was lying. Aitken was sentenced to eighteen months in prison for perjury and lost both his political career and his family as a result.

People will sometimes say, "Honesty is the best policy," but honesty is far more than the *best* policy. It is the *only* policy for those who wish to maintain their character, their integrity, their reputation, and their right standing with God. There is a reason why "a lying tongue" is prominently featured on the list of sins that are an abomination to God (Proverbs 6:16–19). Dishonesty destroys relationships and reputations. It has been a tool of Satan since the beginning of time, and it is one he has used with devastating results.

A lifetime of honesty requires a commitment to tell the truth in every situation. There are no "white lies" because there are no degrees of dishonesty. We are either truth-tellers, or we are deceivers. When we are dishonest, we are doing Satan's work. Jesus said the devil is "a liar, and the father of it" (John 8:44). In contrast, "God…cannot lie" (Titus 1:2). If we are to be like our Heavenly Father we must fully commit ourselves to honesty and integrity in every circumstance and situation.

Today's Word to the Wise: God expects us to be people who will be honest regardless of the potential consequences for telling the truth.

The Power of Encouragement

A wholesome tongue is a tree of life: but perverseness therein is a breach in the spirit.—**Proverbs 15:4**

Dr. George Truett told this story of a dramatic rescue from almost certain death. "There was a fire in the big city, and the firemen flung their ladders together, and went up in their brave fashion to the very topmost story to rescue the people that were trapped. One after another was rescued by the brave firemen.

"All had been rescued, it seemed, but No! As the firemen looked up they saw a face at the most upper window. They wrapped something about one of their firemen, and in the face of the fierce flames, he went again to that window, and put a robe around the little woman and started down. Then they saw him tremble as the fire raged around him, and it seemed that he would fall with his precious burden, but the fire chief cried to his men: 'Cheer him, boys! Cheer him, boys!' They cheered him with words of encouragement as he came down safely with the precious life saved."

There is immense power in our words to either tear people down or build them up. The old playground saying, "Sticks and stones may break my bones but words will never hurt me" is not true. Words of disapproval and discouragement can convince someone to give up. On the other hand, words of encouragement can make all the difference. One vote of confidence, one kind word, one expression of approval may be all a person needs to keep going in the right direction.

Mark Twain famously said, "I can live for two months on a good compliment." A kind word costs us nothing, yet it can mean the world to someone who is struggling. Take the time today to intentionally encourage the people in your life; it will help both you and them.

Today's Word to the Wise: Use your words to encourage and support, and your tongue will be a source of life to you and to others.

The Value of Contentment

Better is a little with righteousness than great revenues without right.
—Proverbs 16:8

At least Mary Butterworth was industrious. Unfortunately, for all her hard work, she was dishonest. When she went into business for herself in colonial Newport, Rhode Island, she did not take up sewing or crafting. Instead Mary Butterworth devised a clever method for counterfeiting currency at home. Since she did not have access to metal plates or printing equipment, she would take a starched cloth and place it on top of a wet genuine bill. She would then use an iron to transfer the outlines of the real currency onto a blank piece of paper and fill in the rest with a quill and ink. The cloth "pattern" could then be burned, destroying the evidence of what had been done.

It is believed that her counterfeiting ring, which included several members of her extended family, was in operation for nearly ten years. They produced so much counterfeit currency that the entire New England economy was negatively affected. Finally the family's purchase of a large and expensive home raised so much suspicion that authorities began an investigation. Mary Butterworth was arrested and tried, but there was not enough evidence to convict her. After her acquittal, Butterworth "retired" from the counterfeiting business.

One of the most effective lies of Satan is that just a little more will make us content. As a result of discontentment with God's provisions, many have abandoned their integrity and been willing to do almost anything for the sake of getting more. It is certainly not wrong to enjoy material blessings from God, but we should be happy regardless of our financial situation. The consequences for dishonesty far outweigh any temporary benefits gained through accumulation of ill-gotten gains. Contentment erects a powerful shield of protection for your integrity.

Today's Word to the Wise: Lack of contentment renders us vulnerable to the temptation to cut corners and be dishonest.

The Wisdom of Silence

Even a fool, when he holdeth his peace, is counted wise: and he that shutteth his lips is esteemed a man of understanding.—**Proverbs 17:28**

One of Aesop's fables concerned a turtle who envied the ducks that swam in the pond where he lived. As he listened to them describe the wonders of the world they had seen, he was filled with a great desire to travel. But being a turtle, he was unable to travel far. Finally two ducks offered to help him. One of the ducks said, "We will each hold an end of a stick in our mouths. You hold the stick in the middle in your mouth, and we will carry you through the air so that you can see what we see when we fly. But be quiet or you will be sorry."

The turtle loved the idea. He took hold of the stick and away into the sky they went. The ducks flew up above the trees and circled around the meadow. The turtle was amazed and overjoyed at his new perspective on the world. He marveled at the flowers on the hillside. Just then a crow flew past. Astonished at the sight of a turtle flying through the air carried by two ducks he said, "Surely this must be the king of all turtles!" "Why certainly…" the turtle began—but as he spoke, he lost his grip on the stick and fell to the ground below.

While there are times when we need to speak out and take a stand, more frequently we find ourselves in trouble because we talk too much. As the old saying goes, "A closed mouth gathers no foot." When we talk much, the tendency to brag and speak of things we should not grows. Instead we should cultivate the wisdom of silence and guard carefully the things we allow to come out of our mouths.

Today's Word to the Wise: Learn the wisdom of silence in situations where what you would say does not edify or enlighten others.

Our Strong Defense

The name of the Lord *is a strong tower: the righteous runneth into it, and is safe.*—**Proverbs 18:10**

During the War of 1812, the British forces that had already captured Washington D.C. turned their focus to Baltimore. Outnumbering the American forces by more than five to one and backed by their powerful navy, the British expected to take control of the key American port city. They were surprised to find their way blocked by an American force stationed in Fort McHenry. British Vice Admiral Alexander Cochrane ordered an extensive bombardment of the fort in preparation for an attack.

Throughout the night of September 13 and into the morning of September 14, nearly two thousand artillery shells were fired at the fort. When the sun came up in the morning, Major George Armistead, the commander, ordered the massive flag to be raised over the walls as a sign that they had not been defeated. This moment was seen by an American lawyer named Francis Scott Key who was on board one of the British ships. The incredible sight led to the writing of "The Star Spangled Banner," which became the American national anthem.

A strong place of defense is not just important to military forces. It is also crucial to those of us who face a spiritual battle on a daily basis. The Bible warns us that Satan is seeking to destroy us and commands us to "resist stedfast in the faith" (1 Peter 5:9). It is vital that we remember that we are not to fight Satan in our own strength. Instead we are offered the mighty protection of God's power through His name.

As believers, we have the right to run to the presence of the Lord and seek His defense when we are attacked. We do not have to fight alone. Like the defenders of Baltimore sheltered by the thick walls of Fort McHenry, we are sheltered by the name of our Saviour.

Today's Word to the Wise: Knowing that we can call on the name of the Lord for defense should give us confidence to face any situation.

Uncertain Friends

Wealth maketh many friends; but the poor is separated from his neighbour.—**Proverbs 19:4**

When Howard Hughes died in 1976, he was worth more than two billion dollars, but his personal life was a miserable wreck. A brilliant engineer even as a teenager, Hughes assumed control of his father's Hughes Tool Company at just nineteen years old, following his father's death from a heart attack. Hughes became a major figure in engineering, aviation, and movie production, and his wealth continued to grow. Despite all his accomplishments, Hughes became a recluse in his later years, living in a hotel he owned and not allowing his staff members to even look at him when they entered his room.

Upon Hughes' death, a variety of people tried to lay claim to his estate. Fake wills began to turn up, and several people claimed they were related to Hughes. At least one woman even claimed a secret marriage gave her rights to his estate. The legal battles dragged on for decades, and the estate was not finally settled until 2010, thirty-four years after Hughes died!

Money does strange things to people. Some abandon their principles in their quest to become rich. They cut corners and do things they know to be wrong in their pursuit of wealth. Even those who come by their resources through honesty and hard work face a dilemma: are their friends true friends, or is the relationship just about the money? The Prodigal Son learned this lesson the hard way. As long as the money he received from his father as his inheritance lasted, he had plenty of friends. When the money ran out and the famine came, "no man gave unto him" (Luke 15:16). We should not be friendly toward others because of what they are able to do for us or give to us, but because they are our friends.

Today's Word to the Wise: Be true to your friends regardless of what you will receive in return.

Being a Blessing to Your Descendants

The just man walketh in his integrity: his children are blessed after him.
—**Proverbs 20:7**

Hudson Taylor was one of the great missionaries of history. When he arrived on the mission field in China, there were only a few hundred believers in the entire nation. By the time of his death, some fifty years later, there were more than 175,000.

Taylor's story, however, cannot be fully appreciated just by studying his own life. Taylor's father was a lay Methodist preacher. His grandfather had been converted under the ministry of John Wesley. These two men established a godly foundation that helped shape the course of Hudson Taylor's life. Though his parents had dedicated him to God before his birth, as a teenager Taylor had little interest in spiritual things. He left home at fifteen to work in a bank, and was surrounded by evil influences. One day his mother set aside a special time of prayer for the salvation of her son. Taylor was at home alone that day without his family and entering his father's study picked up a gospel tract and began to read it. Before he finished, he was convicted of his sin and cried out to God for salvation.

It is unlikely that the great things that Taylor accomplished in his ministry for God would have happened without the investments his parents and grandparents made in his life. Now that Terrie and I have grandchildren, I am becoming ever more focused on touching the future by leaving them a godly heritage. A crucial part of that heritage is that I walk with God in integrity daily. The faithful Christian life is not primarily large decisions, but a series of small ones—doing right day after day. Integrity may be revealed in our response to crisis moments, but it is built and maintained in the small choices we make each day.

Today's Word to the Wise: By following God today, you establish an example that will help shape the lives of your children and grandchildren.

Shortcut to Destruction

The thoughts of the diligent tend only to plenteousness; but of every one that is hasty only to want.—**Proverbs 21:5**

When it was riding high in the 1990s, Enron was one of the most successful and admired companies in America. The energy and commodities conglomerate was one of the best-performing stocks on Wall Street, and *Fortune* magazine named them America's most innovative company six years in a row. Company executives earned millions in bonuses and stock options, and they spent corporate funds on lavish parties and outrageous décor for their offices.

Then suddenly, all of the wealth vanished. In 2001 Enron filed for what was then the largest corporate bankruptcy in history. It was revealed that most of the company's "profits" were actually the result of accounting tricks and even outright fraud rather than from their business operations. Unknown to their investors, they had actually been losing tremendous amounts of money. A number of top executives were charged with insider trading and fraud. The shortcuts they took to achieve success brought about their downfall.

When we are willing to work hard and pursue honesty, God blesses the results of our efforts. Not every child of God will be fabulously wealthy, but everyone who is diligent will see rewards for their efforts. For many people, the thought of the slow route to success through hard work seems too daunting. Instead they look for easy ways to accumulate wealth. They may purchase lottery tickets, bet on sporting events, or "invest" in get-rich-quick schemes that offer a path to prosperity apart from work. In the end, all such efforts are doomed to failure. Many who win lottery prizes are in worse financial condition after a couple of years than they were before. Instead of looking for shortcuts, we need to simply continue to obey God and be diligent—and trust Him for the results.

Today's Word to the Wise: The fastest path to wealth usually leads to destruction. Diligence may pave a longer route, but it is a straight and sure path to provision.

The Slavery of Debt

The rich ruleth over the poor, and the borrower is servant to the lender.
—**Proverbs 22:7**

Today the average American family owes over $8,000 on credit cards, more than $7,000 on automobile loans, and more than $6,500 in student loan debt. When mortgages and other consumer debt are added to the equation, the typical American family owes nearly $150,000. All together, total consumer debt in the United States is more than $11 trillion. Truly we as a society are living in bondage to debt.

Christians are not exempt from this kind of bondage. Many families are struggling with the weight of paying back money long since spent. The culture around us is geared toward instant gratification. Rather than saving money to purchase something, we are enticed with offers of "no money down" and "low monthly payments." But those payments add up over time, and the habit of spending more than we have only adds to the burden of debt.

There are people still paying for the pizza they purchased a year (or longer) ago on credit. That is not the path of wisdom. Instead of reaching for more on credit, we should be cultivating an attitude of contentment. While there are some legitimate reasons for the careful use of debt, the vast majority of debt being accumulated in our society can be traced to our desire for instant gratification.

Many believers find it a struggle to give as they know God wants them to because of their accumulated debt. If you are free from debt, do everything you can to stay that way. If you are currently in bondage to debt, take immediate steps to get out. The freedom you gain, for both your family life and your service to God, will be enormous.

Today's Word to the Wise: Contentment with what God has provided for you will protect you from the bondage of debt.

Dinner with the Boss

When thou sittest to eat with a ruler, consider diligently what is before thee: And put a knife to thy throat, if thou be a man given to appetite. Be not desirous of his dainties: for they are deceitful meat.
—Proverbs 23:1–3

In the early days of Ford Motor Company, Henry Ford's empire stretched far beyond the manufacturing plant where cars were being put together on the assembly line. Ford owned the steel mills where the metal was shaped, the iron mines where the ore was dug out of the ground, and the shipping companies and railroads that moved the materials from one place to another. He was involved in the car making process from start to finish.

With such a vast array of companies to oversee, Ford needed skilled executives who could be trusted to manage the day-to-day operations of their area without constant supervision. After a job candidate had gone through the interview process, the final test was a dinner meeting with Henry Ford. When the food was served, Ford would observe the prospective employee. If he salted his food before tasting it, he failed the test and would not be offered a job. Ford thought that approach to food indicated the man would also be wasteful with money.

God's Word contains not just spiritual truth but also practical advice for daily living—even in areas such as interacting with those in authority over us. The principle of self-control spelled out in the verses above is a vital part of our character as Christians. It makes us more successful in every part of life, it protects us from temptation, and it changes the way we are viewed by those around us. Following the principles of wisdom prepares us to receive blessing and promotion.

Today's Word to the Wise: Learn the principles of wisdom from Scripture, and apply them to your daily life.

The Protection of Wise Counsel

A wise man is strong; yea, a man of knowledge increaseth strength. For by wise counsel thou shalt make thy war: and in multitude of counsellors there is safety.—**Proverbs 24:5–6**

In 1852 a young man wrote the noted Scottish writer and educator, Thomas Carlyle, and asked him for advice on how to better himself. In addition to his advice, he recommended reading good books rather than fluff. Carlyle wrote: "Study to do faithfully whatsoever thing in your actual situation, there and now, you find either expressly or tacitly laid to your charge; that is your post; stand in it like a true soldier. Silently devour the many chagrins of it, as all human situations have many; and see you aim not to quit it without doing all that it, at least, required of you."

It is important to receive wise counsel, but that is only half of the equation. We must also heed and follow it. Being encouraged to study the Word of God or follow the principles of Scripture does not change our conduct. Change only comes about as we purposefully adjust our habits through the power of the Holy Spirit. When we refuse to listen to good advice, we place ourselves in great danger. While there is safety in a multitude of wise counselors, we only benefit from that safety if we heed the wise advice we receive.

We see this truth illustrated in the life of Solomon's son Rehoboam. Upon taking the throne, he consulted his father's advisors (and it is worth noting that the wisest man in history still had advisors to help him) on how he should respond to the people. They counseled a conciliatory approach, but Rehoboam rejected their wise advice. Instead he followed the advice of his young friends and was harsh with the people. Because Rehoboam did not heed the good counsel he received, the kingdom was divided.

Today's Word to the Wise: You only receive the protection offered by wise counsel when you take heed and follow it.

Receiving Honor

Put not forth thyself in the presence of the king, and stand not in the place of great men: For better it is that it be said unto thee, Come up hither; than that thou shouldest be put lower in the presence of the prince whom thine eyes have seen.—**Proverbs 25:6–7**

Lenny Skutnik had no intention of being a hero that day. The staffer at the Congressional Budget Office in Washington was having an ordinary winter day when Air Florida Flight 90 crashed into the 14th Street Bridge over the Potomac River shortly after takeoff. Those who survived the crash faced death as the plane sank in the icy waters.

A helicopter dropped a rescue line to one of the survivors, but she was too weak to hold on. Skutnik saw what was happening and dove into the water. He swam out to her and pulled her back to shore, saving her life. Two weeks later, President Ronald Reagan invited Skutnik to attend the State of the Union address. In describing the accident, President Reagan said: "And we saw the heroism of one of our young Government employees, Lenny Skutnik, who, when he saw a woman lose her grip on the helicopter line, dived into the water and dragged her to safety."

Skutnik was honored by the President of the United States, not because he tried to draw attention to himself, but because he did what was right in a crisis. Our flesh tells us that we need to be sure everything we do is seen and praised, but God reminds us that attempts to promote ourselves eventually backfire. Only the honor that God orchestrates is sure. Psalm 75:6–7 says, "For promotion cometh neither from the east, nor from the west, nor from the south. But God is the judge: he putteth down one, and setteth up another."

We can trust God to see and properly reward all that we do for Him. Better still, when we do "all to the glory of God" (1 Corinthians 10:31), we are free from the being elated or deflated by the finicky approval of men.

Today's Word to the Wise: When we leave our honor in the hands of God, we free ourselves to do all to His glory.

Plotting Evil

Whoso diggeth a pit shall fall therein: and he that rolleth a stone, it will return upon him.—**Proverbs 26:27**

One of the most beautiful stories of God's deliverance of His people is found in the book of Esther. When Haman hatched his plot to destroy the Jews, it seemed foolproof. He had the king on his side, and he had already built the gallows on which he planned to hang his enemy Mordecai. Yet in response to the fervent prayers of His people, God intervened and turned the plot against those who planned it. In the end, Haman was hanged on the same gallows he had intended for Mordecai.

God is able to turn things around even when they seem hopeless. This truth should encourage us even during the bleakest times to trust Him more fully.

More than just providing a way of escape and bringing comfort when we are facing attacks, this truth is also a reminder to us not to plot evil against others. God has decreed that those who attempt such evil will find themselves in the same kind of difficulty they plotted for others. If we are facing a problem with someone, we need to let God handle it rather than trying to take care of things on our own. He is in charge, and He works all things according to His purpose.

There is no greater illustration of this principle than the death and Resurrection of Jesus Christ. Though the cross and the tomb appeared to be a triumph for Satan, they were the beginning of Satan's ultimate defeat. The very acts of evil that put Jesus on the cross were fulfillment of Bible prophecy, and the death of Jesus was essential to the ultimate victory of the Resurrection. God used Satan's plans to bring about the fulfillment of His plan for our redemption.

Today's Word to the Wise: When you have been wronged or when you are tempted to bring calamity to another, remember God's sovereignty, His justice, and His promise to right the scores in the end.

The Honor of Serving

Whoso keepeth the fig tree shall eat the fruit thereof: so he that waiteth on his master shall be honoured.—**Proverbs 27:18**

We live in a society that places little value on serving others. Most people are focused on what they can get others to do for them and how they can receive honor and promotion. The Bible teaches that God honors those who are willing to serve. Jesus Himself was the epitome of a servant as He "made himself of no reputation, and took upon him the form of a servant, and was made in the likeness of men" (Philippians 2:7).

As God, Jesus had every right to be served. But instead of insisting on His prerogatives, He laid aside His rights and became a servant. Jesus' service went far beyond living a life dedicated to helping others. "He humbled himself, and became obedient unto death, even the death of the cross" (Philippians 2:8). Because of love, Jesus was willing to die for those who did not love Him.

Being a servant requires that we focus more on others than we do on ourselves. When we are willing to give up our own preferences and conveniences for the sake of others, we are living as Jesus did. He made the choice to humble Himself, even to the point of death. Most of us are not called on to go to that extreme, but we should be willing to lay aside our selfish desires for the sake of others.

When we make that choice, it does not go unseen by God. The humility and service of Christ produced great honor: "Wherefore God also hath highly exalted him" (Philippians 2:9). If we are willing to serve others and trust God for the reward, we will accomplish what is most important—and we will one day hear the words, "Well done, thou good and faithful servant" (Matthew 25:21).

Today's Word to the Wise: When we devote ourselves to serving others, we are truly following Christ's example.

Faith in Action

He that is of a proud heart stirreth up strife: but he that putteth his trust in the LORD shall be made fat.—**Proverbs 28:25**

Adoniram Judson, the great pioneer missionary to Burma (modern day Myanmar), endured great hardship in his efforts to take the gospel to a country that had never heard it. The sickness of the tropics and the heavy persecution they faced took a heavy toll on the missionary and his family. His first wife and several children died on the mission field, and then Judson had to bury his second wife as well. At one point he wrote back to America, "If I had not felt certain that every additional trial was ordered by infinite love and mercy, I could not have survived my accumulated sufferings."

The Christian life is completely dependent on faith. We are saved by grace through faith. We walk by faith and not by sight. Even when things are not going as we think they should, we can trust that God is in control. Faith is believing that what God says is true and then acting accordingly. Christ demonstrated this kind of faith as He prepared for what He knew was about to happen at the end of His earthly life.

Facing the cross was not easy for Christ. Though He knew that the pain and suffering of the cross would be followed by the triumph of the Resurrection, there was still a great struggle in His spirit. The night before the crucifixion as Jesus prayed alone in the Garden of Gethsemane, He cried out to His Father, "O my Father, if it be possible, let this cup pass from me: nevertheless not as I will, but as thou wilt" (Matthew 26:39). Ultimately He chose to trust that what God had planned was best. That is the choice faith always makes.

Today's Word to the Wise: Determine that you will walk by faith no matter what circumstances come.

A Judge Who Knows Our Lives

Many seek the ruler's favour; but every man's judgment cometh from the LORD.—**Proverbs 29:26**

The fifth Caliph of the ancient Arab Abbasid Empire in what is now Iraq was Harun Al-Rashid. This legendary ruler was noted for his careful and wise dispensing of justice to his subjects. Representatives of rulers from many lands came to his court to hear him speak. One of Al-Rashid's techniques (which later made its way into many of the stories in *1001 Arabian Nights*) was to dress as a commoner and go through the city. When he noticed someone behaving especially well or especially badly, he would note their conduct and have them brought to the palace to stand before his throne. There they were either rewarded or punished as they deserved. Al-Rashid was able to judge well because he understood the daily lives of his subjects since he spent time living as they did.

In Jesus we have not just a righteous and perfect Judge, but one who also understands our lives. "For we have not an high priest which cannot be touched with the feeling of our infirmities; but was in all points tempted like as we are, yet without sin" (Hebrews 4:15). Jesus experienced the temptations we face and overcame them. The righteous and sinless life of Christ, and His death and resurrection allows Him to be both "just, and the justifier of him which believeth" (Romans 3:26).

The justice of God demands that the penalty for sin be paid. The love and mercy of God sent Jesus Christ to be the payment for that debt. Every person will one day face a Judge with perfect understanding of his or her life. Those who have trusted Him as the only acceptable sacrifice for sin face no terror, but those who have not will be without excuse.

Today's Word to the Wise: We can face the future without fear because the Judge has already paid the penalty for our sins.

The Defeated Grave

The horseleach hath two daughters, crying, Give, give. There are three things that are never satisfied, yea, four things say not, It is enough: The grave; and the barren womb; the earth that is not filled with water; and the fire that saith not, It is enough.—**Proverbs 30:15–16**

On May 13, 1864, a twenty-one-year-old private named William Christman from Pennsylvania became the first soldier to be buried in what is now Arlington National Cemetery. The two hundred acre farm and house had belonged to Robert E. Lee, who resigned his commission in the United States Army to lead the Confederate forces. The property had belonged to Lee's wife, the great great granddaughter of Martha Washington.

The decision to place a military cemetery there was intended to ensure Lee would never be able to live there again. In addition to placing the graves as close to the house as possible, the director of the cemetery placed the remains of more than two thousand unknown soldiers in what had been the Lee's rose garden. Today Arlington is home to the Tomb of the Unknowns and the graves of some four hundred thousand men and women who have served their country. Nearly seven thousand funerals per year continue to add to those buried among "the honored dead."

While the grave may never be satisfied as long as sin and death are part of the world, its power has already been defeated. On the first Easter morning, when after three days and three nights in a borrowed tomb the Lord of Heaven and Earth arose in His glorified body, the power of the grave was shattered. We have not yet seen the end, but the outcome of the battle is already assured. Today in faith we can ask with Paul, "O death, where is thy sting? O grave, where is thy victory?" (1 Corinthians 15:55).

Today's Word to the Wise: The Resurrection of Jesus Christ is our hope for the defeat of the grave and the promise of eternal life.

A Risen Saviour

Open thy mouth for the dumb in the cause of all such as are appointed to destruction. Open thy mouth, judge righteously, and plead the cause of the poor and needy.—**Proverbs 31:8–9**

The greatest need of mankind is a Saviour. There are great economical, political, physical, mental, and emotional problems facing people today, but the greatest problem—the eternity deciding problem—is the sin problem. Each person must either accept the payment for sin made through the death of Jesus Christ on the cross or bear the punishment themselves.

The primary reason Christ came into the world was to provide a way of escape from the penalty of sin. Even as His coming was announced, the angel pronounced, "Thou shalt call his name JESUS: for he shall save his people from their sins" (Matthew 1:21). Jesus Himself said, "The Son of man came not to be ministered unto, but to minister, and to give his life a ransom for many" (Matthew 20:28).

The Bible tells us that all of mankind is under condemnation because of sin. In mercy and grace God sent His Son to provide the means of salvation through His death, burial, and resurrection. The empty tomb proves that Jesus has the power to be our Saviour.

Each of us who have received the free gift of salvation has the privilege and responsibility to share the gospel with those around us. Even as the women who first saw the empty tomb were instructed to "go...and tell" (Matthew 28:7), so we should tell others the glad news of a risen Saviour.

Every person we meet today is—as described in the verses above—appointed to destruction. It is our privilege and responsibility to open our mouths to share with them the gladdest tidings they could ever hear: Jesus paid for their sin, rose from the dead, and offers them His salvation.

Today's Word to the Wise: We should share the good news of salvation through Jesus with those who need deliverance from sin.

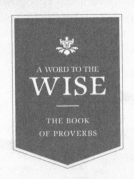

A WORD TO THE

WISE

THE BOOK
OF PROVERBS

APRIL

You Don't Have To Agree

My son, if sinners entice thee, consent thou not.—**Proverbs 1:10**

Konosuke Matsushita, the founder of Panasonic, often told his employees this story to emphasize the vital importance of maintaining integrity: "In China's later Han era, there lived a politician called Yang Zhen, a man known for his upright character. After Yang Zhen was made a provincial governor, one of his earlier patrons, Wang Mi, paid him an unexpected visit. As they talked over old times, Wang Mi brought out a large gold cup and presented it to Yang Zhen. Yang Zhen refused to accept it, but Wang Mi persisted, saying, 'There's no one here tonight but you and me, so no one will know.' 'You say that no one will know,' Yang Zhen replied, 'but that is not true. Heaven will know, and you and I will know too.'"

When we are tempted to sin, we have two choices: will we listen to the enticement and agree to go along with it, or will we stand firm for what is right? There will always be "reasons" we can use to convince ourselves why it is okay for us to do wrong—but any reasons that justify sin are short-sighted. If we allow ourselves to accept them, we will bear the consequences. Instead of trying to justify our sin, we should search for God's means of escape.

Paul wrote, "There hath no temptation taken you but such as is common to man: but God is faithful, who will not suffer you to be tempted above that ye are able; but will with the temptation also make a way to escape, that ye may be able to bear it" (1 Corinthians 10:13). Sin is not an overpowering force. Through grace we have been given the means to resist temptation—but to overcome we must refuse to listen to those who would draw us astray.

Today's Word to the Wise: Temptation to sin never overcomes us without our consent—there is a way to escape.

God's Preservation

He keepeth the paths of judgment, and preserveth the way of his saints.
—Proverbs 2:8

Ira Sankey, who for years led the music for D.L. Moody's evangelistic meetings, was traveling by steamboat on Christmas Eve in 1875. He was recognized by some of the passengers, and they asked him to sing. Sankey agreed, and began singing "Saviour Like a Shepherd Lead Us."

When the song was finished, one of the listeners stepped forward and asked, "Did you serve in the Union Army?" "Yes," Mr. Sankey answered. "Can you remember if you were doing picket duty on a bright, moonlit night in 1862?" "Yes," Mr. Sankey said again. "I was serving in the Confederate army. When I saw you standing at your post, I raised my gun and took aim. I was standing in the shadow, completely concealed, while the full light of the moon was falling upon you. At that instant, you raised your eyes to Heaven and began to sing that same song. 'Let him sing his song to the end,' I said to myself, 'I can shoot him afterwards.' I heard the words perfectly: 'We are Thine; do Thou befriend us. Be the Guardian of our way.' I began to think of my childhood and my God-fearing mother who sang that song to me. When you finished, it was impossible for me to take aim again. I thought, 'The Lord who is able to save that man from certain death must surely be great and mighty.'"

The God who loves us also protects us, often in ways we do not even realize at the time. His promise to keep and preserve His children is one on which we can rely. Every step of our lives is guarded by His mercies which "are new every morning" (Lamentations 3:23). God's preservation does not mean that we are exempt from difficult situations, but it does mean that anything that comes our way must first be filtered through His providence.

Today's Word to the Wise: You can trust God to take care of you no matter what circumstances you face.

The Greatest Return for Your Investment

Honour the LORD with thy substance, and with the firstfruits of all thine increase: So shall thy barns be filled with plenty, and thy presses shall burst out with new wine.—**Proverbs 3:9–10**

August Francke, a Lutheran pastor in Halle, Germany, in the late 1600s was distressed by the needs of the orphan children who roamed the streets. He resolved to establish an orphanage for them, but money was always in short supply to provide for the many needs of more than one hundred children.

One day when Francke was struggling to juggle the funds and pay the bills, a poor widow came to his office begging for help. When he regretfully informed her that he could not help, she began to weep. Moved by her need, Francke went to pray. He believed God was leading him to help, so he returned and gave her a ducat—a single gold coin. Later that week, he received a thank you letter from the widow. In it she expressed her gratitude and told Francke that she had asked God to shower blessings on his work because of his generosity. Before the week was out, Francke received fourteen gold ducats in the mail, and he learned that the estate of a wealthy prince included a bequest of five hundred gold ducats for the orphanage.

It is not popular to teach on giving. The world's philosophy is to hoard everything we can. Although there is wisdom in making provision for the future, there is nothing more significant we can do with our resources than to honor God. Since all we have comes from Him, the least we can do is return to Him what is already His. When we give in this way, He will bless. God does not promise that givers will have anything they want, but He does promise they will have everything they need.

Today's Word to the Wise: When we give generously, God promises a return on our investment beyond anything we could produce on our own.

The Promotion of Wisdom

Wisdom is the principal thing; therefore get wisdom: and with all thy getting get understanding. Exalt her, and she shall promote thee: she shall bring thee to honour, when thou dost embrace her.
—Proverbs 4:7–8

Though David was a hero to the nation of Israel after God gave him victory in the battle with Goliath, his introduction to King Saul's court afterward must have posed some difficult challenges. David was not highly regarded by his family. In fact, when Samuel came and told Jesse that one of his sons would be the next king of Israel, Jesse didn't even bother to invite David to meet the prophet.

Despite the lack of respect he received from his family and his lack of training in political intrigue, David quickly became a favorite around the palace as he found favor and acceptance in the eyes of the people. The Bible tells us the reason for his quick rise: "David behaved himself wisely in all his ways" (1 Samuel 18:14). When we follow the path of wisdom, good things happen in every area of life.

Certainly not everything went exactly as David would have wished. His favor in the eyes of the people made him an enemy in the eyes of Saul. As a result, David spent several years literally running for his life. Yet throughout these unjust events, David lived wisely. When we pursue wisdom, when we "embrace her" as Scripture says, it produces wonderful results in our lives.

Wisdom improves the way we interact with others and changes the way we approach our responsibilities at home, church, work, and school. Wisdom is not something that is limited to spiritual matters; it encompasses every aspect of life and brings promotion and blessing to those who follow it. That is why it is so important that we devote ourselves to acquiring wisdom.

Today's Word to the Wise: Devote yourself to learning and following God's principles for wise living, and your life will be blessed.

The Regret of Sin

Lest thou give thine honour unto others, and thy years unto the cruel:
Lest strangers be filled with thy wealth; and thy labours be in the house
of a stranger; And thou mourn at the last, when thy flesh and thy body
are consumed,—**Proverbs 5:9–11**

John Greenleaf Whittier, in his poem *Maud Muller* describes a couple who are smitten with each other but neither speaks out to let the other know because of the great divide between their wealth, education, and social standing. Instead they each go on with their lives, only to look back in the end with regret for the road not taken:

> God pity them both! and pity us all,
> Who vainly the dreams of youth recall;
> For of all sad words of tongue or pen,
> The saddest are these: "It might have been!"

But there is something far worse than regretting a missed opportunity, and that is regretting sin after it is too late to undo what has been done. Many people sin despite knowing that it is wrong, because they believe the lie that somehow they will escape the consequences. That has not happened in all of human history, for God has written the law of sowing and reaping into the very fabric of His creation. Sin always brings consequences, and the only way to avoid the regret that comes with those consequences is to avoid the sin in the first place.

If you view each temptation to sin through the lens of the end consequences, you will find the allure of sin greatly diminished. The Bible says that Moses was willing to forego "the pleasures of sin for a season" (Hebrews 11:25) to do what was right. When we realize how fleeting those pleasures are and how long the regret and suffering last, we find it easier to do right.

Today's Word to the Wise: Live your life today in such a way that you will not look back with regret tomorrow.

Keeping the Commandments

My son, keep thy father's commandment, and forsake not the law of thy mother: Bind them continually upon thine heart, and tie them about thy neck.—**Proverbs 6:20–21**

There is a wonderful story of the impact godly ancestors can have on their descendants in the Old Testament. In the days when Jehu overthrew the wicked house of Ahab, a godly man named Jonadab fought with him against the Baal worshippers who had invaded Israel. Not content to merely do right himself, Jonadab passed down instructions to his descendants to help future generations do right.

Some three hundred years later, God sent the prophet Jeremiah to test the resolve of the Rechabites (named after Jonadab's father Rechab). When he offered the Rechabites wine to drink, they refused. God noted their obedience, and contrasted it to the disobedience of Israel. "The words of Jonadab the son of Rechab, that he commanded his sons not to drink wine, are performed; for unto this day they drink none, but obey their father's commandment: notwithstanding I have spoken unto you, rising early and speaking; but ye hearkened not unto me" (Jeremiah 35:14).

The commitment to follow the commandments of the past protected the Rechabites from evil, and it will do the same for us. Today it is popular to cast aside the old ways and the ancient landmarks for the sake of keeping up with the times. Many who faithfully followed God for years are leaving the old paths and forsaking the commandments they received from their fathers before them. This is all the more reason why we should remain faithful to the instructions we have received.

God's message to the Rechabites through Jeremiah was one of blessing: "Jonadab the son of Rechab shall not want a man to stand before me for ever" (Jeremiah 35:19). God blessed that family because of their continued obedience to the commandments of their father.

Today's Word to the Wise: Continue to follow the commandments, and you will continue to be blessed by God.

Don't Linger in the Dark

For at the window of my house I looked through my casement, And beheld among the simple ones, I discerned among the youths, a young man void of understanding, Passing through the street near her corner; and he went the way to her house, In the twilight, in the evening, in the black and dark night:—**Proverbs 7:6–9**

If you have ever been inside an operating room, you've probably noticed how bright the lights are. The same is true for the makeup room used by actors getting ready for a performance. Why? Because bright lights reveal things that the darkness conceals and allow a person to make the proper response to what they see. Temptation thrives in dark places. Satan knows that if he can conceal the true nature of what we are being offered, we are more likely to give in.

In contrast, 1 John 1:5 tells us, "God is light, and in him is no darkness at all." Deeds that can only be discussed or done in the shadows are never activities in which we should involve ourselves. Protection from sin requires more than just not doing wrong; it requires that we take steps to avoid the places of temptation as well. If we are spending time where we are likely to do wrong, it should not come as a surprise that we succumb to temptation.

Someone said that the reason people have a hard time resisting temptation is that they don't want to discourage it completely. Folly tempts us to linger and toy with temptation and sin. Wisdom instructs us to "Flee also youthful lusts" (2 Timothy 2:22). If the foolish young man in Solomon's illustration had left the place of temptation in the twilight—instead of lingering there until it was fully dark—he would have kept his purity and escaped great suffering. Keep walking until you reach the light, and then stay there.

Today's Word to the Wise: Don't allow temptation to linger; reject it firmly and remove yourself from its presence.

Hating Sin

*The fear of the LORD is to hate evil: pride, and arrogancy, and the evil way, and the froward mouth, do I hate.—***Proverbs 8:13**

Just days before the start of World War II, Germany and Russia signed a non-aggression treaty known as the Molotov-Ribbentrop Pact. In it the two nations agreed that they would not take military action against each other, despite the animosity of their leaders. The purpose of the plan was to leave the two powers free to divide up the portions of Europe they conquered without having to fear an invasion from the other. Of course Hitler had no intention of honoring the agreement, and in June of 1941 Germany launched a surprise invasion of Russia.

It is not possible to make a deal with Satan that will allow us to sin peacefully. The only hope for avoiding the horrible consequences and judgment that follows sin is to hate and shun it. God does not only *dislike* evil—He *hates* it. We cannot afford to treat sin lightly, not just because of the impact it has on our lives and the lives of those around us, but because of the way it impacts God. William S. Plummer said, "We never see sin aright until we see it as against God. All sin is against God in this sense: that it is His law that is broken, His authority that is despised, His government that is set at naught."

When we recognize sin for what it is—an act of rebellion against a high and holy God—we will begin to hate it as God does. As we join God in His attitude toward sin, we will find that its power and allure is diminished. While we will never reach a point of perfection and sinless living, if we truly fear God we will become more holy in our conduct.

Today's Word to the Wise: If you look at sin through God's eyes, you will hate it just as He does and do everything possible to remove it from your life.

The Growth of Wisdom

Give instruction to a wise man, and he will be yet wiser: teach a just man, and he will increase in learning.—**Proverbs 9:9**

There is an ancient Indian legend of a king who loved chess. He challenged visitors to a game and was usually victorious. One day a traveling sage visited the kingdom and was challenged to a game. To entice him to play, the king offered to give the sage whatever reward he asked if he won. When the king was defeated, to honor his word, he asked the sage what prize he would like. The sage asked for one grain of rice to be placed on the first square of the chessboard, and then that it be doubled on each following square.

The request seemed modest, and the king ordered a bag of rice to be brought. One grain was placed on the first square, two on the second, four on the third, eight on the fourth and so on. But it quickly became apparent the terms of the request were impossible to meet. By the twenty-first square more than one million grains of rice would be required. By the thirty-first square the total would go over one billion—with more than half of the chessboard still left to go.

Small things can have a big impact when they are added together! Albert Einstein said, "Compound interest is the most powerful force in the universe." This is not just true in the physical realm but in the spiritual world as well. When we add to our wisdom and understanding, it grows stronger and stronger. The writer of Hebrews said, "But strong meat belongeth to them that are of full age, even those who by reason of use have their senses exercised to discern both good and evil" (Hebrews 5:14). We should be working to strengthen our spiritual senses and increase in wisdom day by day.

Today's Word to the Wise: Always seek to increase your wisdom; it has a powerful impact as it grows in your life.

The Memory of the Just

The memory of the just is blessed: but the name of the wicked shall rot.—**Proverbs 10:7**

The great evangelist D.L. Moody was challenged by a British preacher named Henry Varley who said, "Moody, the world has yet to see what God will do with a man fully consecrated to him." Moody resolved, "By God's help, I aim to be that man." It is estimated that one hundred million people heard Moody preach as he traveled across America and England with the gospel. Thousands came to faith in Christ through Moody's meetings. As he approached the end of his life, he viewed Heaven as something to anticipate. Moody wrote:

> "Some day you will read in the papers that D.L. Moody of East Northfield, is dead. Don't you believe a word of it! At that moment I shall be more alive than I am now; I shall have gone up higher, that is all, out of this old clay tenement into a house that is immortal—a body that death cannot touch, that sin cannot taint; a body fashioned like unto His glorious body. I was born of the flesh in 1837. I was born of the Spirit in 1856. That which is born of the flesh may die. That which is born of the Spirit will live forever."

More than one hundred years after his death Moody is remembered as a powerful servant of God because he lived in obedience to God and His Word. Each day we are building a legacy that will live on after we are gone. With every decision we make and action we choose, we strengthen or weaken our character and our testimony, and we influence people for good or for evil. There are no neutral days—each one matters. We should commit ourselves as Moody did to being fully consecrated to God and following Him every day so that we will leave behind a godly legacy.

Today's Word to the Wise: Live today in such a way that you will be remembered with respect and joy after you are gone.

Guided by Integrity

The integrity of the upright shall guide them: but the perverseness of transgressors shall destroy them.—**Proverbs 11:3**

A Christian businessman named Joe Lee recounted an early work experience that helped shape the future course of his life. As a teenager he got a job on one of the largest cattle ranches in California. One day, he was instructed to drive a truck into the mountains to move cattle from one pasture to another. On the way, he saw that a fence had fallen down and the cattle had gotten out. Rather than continuing on, he stopped, rounded up those cattle and spent the rest of the day repairing the fence.

He was afraid that he would get in trouble for not carrying out his assignment, but he knew he needed to report in. When he told the foreman what he had done, instead of being scolded he was praised for taking initiative. "Act like you would if you owned the place," his boss told him. That principle of integrity—taking diligent care of everything placed in his hand—made Joe Lee a great success in the business world and more importantly as a Christian.

Solomon wrote: "Whatsoever thy hand findeth to do, do it with thy might" (Ecclesiastes 9:10). Integrity does not cut corners or look for ways to avoid responsibility. Instead it steps up to the plate and gives the best possible effort to do what is expected—and maybe a little more. This kind of attitude toward work and responsibility is certain to set you apart in any field, and it will be rewarded. Even more important than men noticing, God will see your diligence and bless it. Someone said, "Even if the task is not worthy of you, diligence is." Although everyone else may be taking shortcuts, you can do what is right.

Today's Word to the Wise: Treat every responsibility and opportunity as vitally important, and your integrity will keep you on the right path.

Avoiding Trouble Is Better than Surviving It

A prudent man concealeth knowledge: but the heart of fools proclaimeth foolishness.—**Proverbs 12:23**

A number of years ago a car company aired an eye-catching commercial. They showed a car made by one of their competitors heading toward a wall. In slow motion, they played out the crash. The car was well made, and it kept the passengers from being hurt. Then they showed one of their own cars heading toward the same wall, but instead of crashing into the wall, it was able to stop short. The announcer came in to drive home the message: is it better to live through a wreck or to avoid getting in one in the first place?

Prudence helps us avoid danger because it recognizes what is going on around us. Our English word *prudence* comes from the Latin word for "seeing ahead." One of the most important ways in which prudence is displayed is in the matter of our speech. Prudent people do not feel the need to tell everything they know to everyone they meet. Someone once said, "If I don't tell you what I know, how will you know that I know so much?" The temptation to be recognized as one of those "in the know" often leads us to speak when we should be silent.

While there is a time to speak out and confront evil, most of us speak too much rather than too little. We would avoid a great deal of trouble if we prudently kept our mouths closed instead of proclaiming the latest gossip. If we continue to open our mouths about everyone and everything, we will certainly create trouble for ourselves and others. If you have a problem with a person, you should talk to them and God about it—and no one else.

Today's Word to the Wise: Rather than looking for ways to get out of trouble, it would be better to prudently avoid it in the first place.

Get Up and Work

The soul of the sluggard desireth, and hath nothing: but the soul of the diligent shall be made fat.—**Proverbs 13:4**

A city dweller traveled far into the country to visit a distant relative. He found his second cousin sitting on the stump of a tree. "How have things been?" he wanted to know. "Not bad at all," the country dweller replied. "I was going to have to cut down all these trees, but a cyclone blew through and saved me the trouble." "That's amazing," the city man said. "But there's more," the countryman continued. "There was a huge pile of brush I needed to clear, and lightning set fire to it and burned it all up." "That's remarkable," the visitor exclaimed. "What are you doing now?" "Waiting for an earthquake to come along and shake the potatoes out of the ground!"

Hard work as a virtue has fallen out of favor in our society. The trend is toward people working fewer and fewer hours, and not working as hard in those hours as they once did. Many are looking for loopholes to avoid work altogether. In recent years, more people have been added to the Social Security disability payment system than have gotten jobs. Certainly there are some people who cannot work because of injury or illness, but a great number of these cases are people whose disability is very hard to define.

It may not be in fashion, but God still expects His people to work. "Six days shalt thou labour, and do all thy work" (Exodus 20:9). When we do not work, we lose the provision that labor provides. Many people wish they had more—a nicer home, a newer car, or better clothes. Yet most people stay stuck in the wishing stage instead of finding a way to work harder to provide for what they need.

Today's Word to the Wise: Rather than wishing for things and not having them, we should be working to provide for our needs and our families.

Don't Learn from Fools

A scorner seeketh wisdom, and findeth it not: but knowledge is easy unto him that understandeth. Go from the presence of a foolish man, when thou perceivest not in him the lips of knowledge.—**Proverbs 14:6–7**

In his parable written in the 1920s about wise money management, George Samuel Clason tells the story of a young man named Arkad who desired to learn the secrets of wealth. He arranged a bargain with a rich man in Babylon, who agreed to teach him the principles he needed to succeed. Once Arkad began following those principles, he began to accumulate wealth.

Looking to expand his resources, Arkad gave the money he had been saving to a bricklayer who was supposed to use it to buy jewels to resell at a profit. Unfortunately, the bricklayer was swindled by dishonest merchants who sold him worthless pieces of glass. When he told this story to his mentor, Arkad was rebuked for trusting someone without knowledge. "About brickmaking he gives good advice," Arkad later ruefully concluded.

When we try to learn from those who do not have knowledge and wisdom, we end up in worse shape than we were when we started. Those who learn from fools will simply become more foolish. There are people in our world who are highly credentialed with many degrees and honors, who despite their learning are still utterly foolish in the eyes of God. As Bob Jones, Sr. said, "Education without God makes men clever devils." There is no source of true wisdom apart from God.

Psalm 1:1 says, "Blessed is the man that walketh not in the counsel of the ungodly, nor standeth in the way of sinners, nor sitteth in the seat of the scornful." In both spiritual matters and issues of daily life, we should only listen to those with godly wisdom.

Today's Word to the Wise: Be sure that you are only listening to those who are instructing you in godly wisdom.

The Revenues of the Wicked

In the house of the righteous is much treasure: but in the revenues of the wicked is trouble.—**Proverbs 15:6**

People think if they just had more money, everything would be different. Many who acquire this longed-for wealth suddenly find that things are different—they get worse. Jack Whittaker won the Powerball lottery jackpot of over $314 million on Christmas day 2002. At the time, it was the largest prize won by a single winner in United States history. Whittaker was already a successful businessman, but the sudden windfall proved to be anything but a blessing for his family.

Over the next decade, both his granddaughter and her boyfriend died from apparent drug overdoses, his daughter passed away, he was robbed on more than one occasion, he was arrested for driving under the influence, and was sued by a number of people and businesses, including Caesar's Atlantic Casino for $1.5 million in bounced checks to cover gambling losses.

The devil knows we are often susceptible to the temptation of taking shortcuts in an attempt to get rich, but that path always leads to ruin. The more successful a person is at attaining wealth through illegitimate means, the worse off they are—no matter how much their bank account grows. Great temptations lie in the path of those who desire riches. Paul reminded Timothy, "But they that will be rich fall into temptation and a snare, and into many foolish and hurtful lusts, which drown men in destruction and perdition" (1 Timothy 6:9).

Although God does not promise that every one of His children will be wealthy, He does promise to meet and supply our needs. We do not have to look for quick or dishonest ways to accumulate wealth because we can trust His provision. Cultivate contentment instead, and you will be spared many sorrows.

Today's Word to the Wise: If you acquire your resources through hard work, you will escape the trouble that comes with ill-gotten gains.

Make Your Choice

*A man's heart deviseth his way: but the L*ORD *directeth his steps.*
—Proverbs 16:9

President Ronald Reagan's family was often poor while he was growing up because his father was an alcoholic. He told the story later in his life that an aunt had offered to purchase a pair of shoes for him. When she took him to the cobbler, young Reagan was asked, "Do you want square toes or round toes?" Unable to decide, Reagan didn't answer, so the cobbler gave him a few days to choose.

Several days later the cobbler saw Reagan on the street and asked him again what kind of toes he wanted on his shoes. Reagan still couldn't decide, so the shoemaker replied, "Well, come by in a couple of days. Your shoes will be ready." When the future president did so, he found a pair of shoes—one square-toed and one round-toed. "This will teach you to never let people make decisions for you," the cobbler said to his indecisive customer. "I learned right then and there," Reagan said later, "if you don't make your own decisions, someone else will."

Often when faced with a difficult decision, we give in to the temptation to put it off. We hope that it will get easier in the future, but that is rarely the case. Instead the wavering between choices paralyzes us and leaves us unable to take action and do what is right. Elijah asked the people on Mt. Carmel, "How long halt ye between two opinions?" (1 Kings 18:21). This is not "halt" in the sense of stopping, but rather to be lame or to limp. When we are indecisive, we cripple ourselves and make it difficult to accomplish great things for God. It is impossible to know everything before making a decision; so learn what you can, seek wise counsel, pray, and then choose your course and follow through.

Today's Word to the Wise: Once you have the relevant information in hand to resolve a question, prayerfully make your decision and trust God to direct your steps.

Listening to Reproof

A reproof entereth more into a wise man than an hundred stripes into a fool.—**Proverbs 17:10**

The evangelist Gipsy Smith would often counsel with people after the end of a service that he preached. He once told of meeting with a man who told him he was not getting anything out of his Bible reading. The man said he received no inspiration although he had "gone through it several times." "Let it go through you once," replied Smith, "then you will tell a different story."

One of the easiest ways to distinguish between someone who is wise and someone who is foolish is to see how he responds to reproof. Because we all make mistakes, we all need correction. The problem arises when we respond to that correction with pride rather than heeding it. This not only robs us of improvements needed in our character and conduct, but it demonstrates that we are not walking in wisdom.

In addition to the reproofs we receive from friends and authorities, we need to carefully approach the Word of God looking for things that need to change. "All scripture is given by inspiration of God, and is profitable for doctrine, for reproof, for correction, for instruction in righteousness: That the man of God may be perfect, throughly furnished unto all good works" (2 Timothy 3:16–17).

Often we are tempted to go to the Bible to point out the mistakes of others rather than reading it to find things that are worthy of reproof in our own lives. If we do not listen to the reproofs of Scripture, we will not be equipped to do the work to which God has called us. It may be painful to receive reproof, but it is far better than continuing on the path of folly. As we respond properly to reproof, we demonstrate skill and wisdom in living.

Today's Word to the Wise: When you are reproved, accept it gladly and willingly, realizing the help that you are being offered.

The Fruit of Kind Words

A man's belly shall be satisfied with the fruit of his mouth; and with the increase of his lips shall he be filled.—**Proverbs 18:20**

During the latter part of his life, President James Madison, who lived to be eighty-five years old, suffered from a variety of physical problems. As a result, he was constantly trying different medicines and potential cures. It is said that an old friend who lived nearby sent Madison a box of vegetable pills which he had made himself, and asked Madison to let him know how they worked. After some days went by, he received one of Madison's famous carefully worded letters. It went something like this: "My dear friend, I thank you very much for the box of pills. I have taken them all; and while I cannot say I am better since taking them, it is quite possible that I might have been worse if I had not taken them."

Often our words are used to wound people rather than to build them up and encourage them. (This can even be true of the words we direct toward ourselves.) People who are constantly critical find that their words divide relationships and discourage others. The Bible tells us that we will receive the fruit from the kind of words we speak. Someone once said, "Lord, remind me to make my words sweet because I may have to eat them." In truth, we all "eat" from the words we use.

While we should always tell the truth, that is not an excuse to be cruel or to unleash whatever we are thinking on others. Ephesians 4:15 tells us we should be "speaking the truth in love." If it is necessary to correct someone, you can still be kind and encouraging. There is no excuse for being harsh or unkind.

Today's Word to the Wise: Be a blessing to both yourself and others with kind and gracious words, and you will find your life better as a result.

Deferring Anger

The discretion of a man deferreth his anger; and it is his glory to pass over a transgression.—**Proverbs 19:11**

When John D. Rockefeller was running the Standard Oil Company, he was well known for his disdain for losing money. One day an executive made a bad decision that cost the company $2 million. His senior staff spent the day trying to avoid his presence to make sure they were not caught up in his wrath. One partner, Edward Bedford had an afternoon appointment with Rockefeller that he could not avoid. When he entered the office, he found Rockefeller making notes on a piece of paper.

They briefly discussed the loss, and then Rockefeller showed Bedford what he had written. According to Bedford's account: "Across the top of the page was written, 'Points in favor of Mr. _____.' There followed a long list of the man's virtues, including a brief description of how he had helped the company make the right decision on three separate occasions that had earned many times the cost of his recent error." Bedford said, "In later years, whenever I was tempted to rip into anyone, I forced myself first to sit down and thoughtfully compile as long a list of good points as I possibly could. Invariably, by the time I finished my inventory, I would see the matter in its true perspective and keep my temper under control."

The difference between those who control their anger and those who do not has nothing to do with the severity of the events that befall them. It has everything to do with their care to control their actions. It brings glory to God when we refuse to allow anger to control our actions and responses. We have both the ability and the responsibility to control our emotions and our anger.

Today's Word to the Wise: Those who quickly fly off the handle damage their personal and business relationships, as well as their testimonies.

You Can Trust God

Say not thou, I will recompense evil; but wait on the LORD, and he shall save thee.—**Proverbs 20:22**

Charles Spurgeon told this story of his grandfather James and his faith in God. "He had a large family and a very small income, but he loved his Lord, and he would not have given up his preaching of the gospel for anything." One day the cow on which the family relied for milk for the children suddenly died. James Spurgeon's wife was greatly concerned, but he said, "God said He would provide, and I believe He could send us fifty cows if He pleased."

On that same day, a group met in London—a group James Spurgeon did not know—that wanted to help meet the needs of poor pastors. They raised a large sum of money, and began sending it to different pastors in need to help their families. When they reached the end of the list, there were still five pounds left. One man suggested sending it to James Spurgeon. Another said, "No, let's not send just five pounds. Let me add five more to go with it." Others joined in, and the day after his cow died, James Spurgeon received twenty pounds in the mail.

You can trust God to keep His promises and provide for your needs. This is true for our physical needs as well as the needs that arise when others do wrong toward us. There is always the temptation to "get even" and lash out at those who are unkind or unfair, but God's Word commands: "Dearly beloved, avenge not yourselves, but rather give place unto wrath: for it is written, Vengeance is mine; I will repay, saith the Lord" (Romans 12:19). We demonstrate faith in God, not just in our prayers for His provision, but also in our patient belief in His justice.

Today's Word to the Wise: When you are wronged, trust God to take care of you and deal with it rather than taking vengeance yourself.

Ears of Compassion

Whoso stoppeth his ears at the cry of the poor, he also shall cry himself, but shall not be heard.—**Proverbs 21:13**

William Booth was greatly stirred by the needs of the poor of London, and he realized that most churches were doing nothing to reach the "undesirables"—drunkards, morphine addicts, prostitutes, and the poor. He set out to reach them with what he called the 3 S's: Soup, Soap and Salvation. Thousands were saved among those who most churches had no interest in reaching. Booth gave his life for the cause of reaching others.

In his 80s, Booth's work began to be hindered by blindness. He briefly lost his sight and then recovered it, but later he lost his vision permanently. His son Bramwell came to bring him the bad news that he would never see again. Booth replied, "God must know best, Bramwell. I have done what I could for God and the people with my eyes. Now I shall do what I can for God and the people without my eyes."

A heart of love for those in need was always a key part of the life and ministry of Jesus Christ. "But when he saw the multitudes, he was moved with compassion on them, because they fainted, and were scattered abroad, as sheep having no shepherd" (Matthew 9:36). It is easy for us to be caught up in the busyness of life in our modern world and forget to stop and care about those in need. It is not just in far off lands that people are lost, poor, and hungry—they are in our own neighborhoods and towns as well.

There is no way for us to do what God wants us to do as Christians without caring for and reaching out to those in need. The followers of Jesus should live as He lived. Peter said that Jesus "went about doing good" (Acts 10:38). This statement should describe our lives as well.

Today's Word to the Wise: Loving those in need and reaching them with the gospel is truly living as Jesus did.

The Blessing of Generosity

He that hath a bountiful eye shall be blessed; for he giveth of his bread to the poor.—**Proverbs 22:9**

When 67-year-old carpenter Russell Herman died in 1994, his will included a staggering set of bequests. Included in his plan for distribution was more than $2 billion for the City of East St. Louis, another $1.5 billion for the State of Illinois, $2.5 billion for the national forest system, and, to top off the list, Herman left $6 trillion to the government to help pay off the national debt. That sounds amazingly generous, but there was a small problem—Herman's only asset when he died was a 1983 Oldsmobile. He made grand pronouncements, but there was no real generosity involved. His promises were meaningless because there was nothing to back them up.

True generosity is not determined by the amount that we give but by our hearts. When Jesus saw the widow give two mites in the temple, He responded, "Verily I say unto you, That this poor widow hath cast more in, than all they which have cast into the treasury" (Mark 12:43). The sacrificial gift that she gave demonstrated how much she loved God and His work. The best way to determine what we love most is not by our words but by how we use our time and our money.

There is no shortage of need in our world. Some, like the scribe and the Pharisee in the parable of the Good Samaritan, pass by without caring enough to get involved and help. No doubt such people would profess their love for God and others, but it is not visible from their actions. Those who obey the command to love God and their neighbor find ways to help. Even if giving requires a sacrifice they are willing to make it because of the depth of their love.

Today's Word to the Wise: What you do to meet the needs of others and support the work of God reveals what you truly love most.

True Security

Wilt thou set thine eyes upon that which is not? for riches certainly make themselves wings; they fly away as an eagle toward heaven.
—**Proverbs 23:5**

James Marshall left his family's home in New Jersey as a young man and, like so many others, began a migration west. After contracting malaria while living in Missouri he was advised to go further west, and in 1845 he arrived in California. He worked a number of different jobs and served in the army during the Mexican-American War in 1846. After a short period of service, he returned to his ranch and entered a partnership with his friend, John Sutter, to build a sawmill.

When the two men discovered that the spillway they had constructed was too narrow to handle the amount of water needed to operate the mill, they began the process of enlarging it. On the morning of January 24, 1848, as Marshall examined the channel, he found large flakes of pure gold, sparking one of the greatest gold rushes in history. But Marshall did not profit from his discovery. The mill project failed. A vineyard he bought went bankrupt. His mines did not produce. In his old age, reduced to abject poverty, Marshall died alone in a small shack.

Wealth is easy for us to trust. If God blesses us and we begin to accumulate financial resources, we must be careful not to place our trust in those resources. Paul instructed his protégé Timothy to issue a warning to the rich members in his church: "Charge them that are rich in this world, that they be not highminded, nor trust in uncertain riches, but in the living God, who giveth us richly all things to enjoy" (1 Timothy 6:17). Riches do not provide true security because they can quickly vanish away. Instead our confidence should be in the presence and promises of God which never fail. Only then can we find true security.

Today's Word to the Wise: Place your confidence in that which is eternal and certain rather than in riches which soon fade away.

Preparation

*Prepare thy work without, and make it fit for thyself in the field; and afterwards build thine house.—***Proverbs 24:27**

In the early 1900s the world watched with excitement and intense interest as the race to be the first to reach the South Pole unfolded. The two frontrunners were Norwegian explorer Roald Amundsen and British naval officer Robert Falcon Scott. Scott's expedition set out hoping to arrive first. After weeks of strenuous and dangerous travel, Scott and four other men reached the South Pole—only to find that Amundsen and his party had beaten them by five weeks. Disappointed in their failure, they set out on the eight hundred mile journey back to safety.

That return journey proved fatal. Scott and his group failed to connect with the dog teams that were meant to meet them on the way and speed their trip to safety. The party was trapped by a massive blizzard, their supplies ran out, and all of them perished. Scott was lauded as a hero and received posthumous honors from the British Empire. But as historians began to study his surviving notes and the accounts of others, they came to realize that the fate of Scott and his party was largely due to his failures as a leader, specifically his failure to plan for the adversity and hardships he and his men would face in the hostile Antarctic.

Wisdom places great value on planning and preparation because of the important connection between how we start and how we finish. Jesus pointed out the importance of planning when He asked, "For which of you, intending to build a tower, sitteth not down first, and counteth the cost, whether he have sufficient to finish it?" (Luke 14:28). Many of the problems we have come because we simply did not prepare to avoid them before beginning our work. Seek wise counsel, pray, search the Scriptures, and determine your direction before you begin—it brings great protection.

Today's Word to the Wise: Before launching into a significant new project, make sure you have properly prepared for what lies ahead.

Slow Down

Go not forth hastily to strive, lest thou know not what to do in the end thereof, when thy neighbour hath put thee to shame.—**Proverbs 25:8**

The first person to be arrested for speeding in the United Sates was apparently a taxi driver named Jacob German. He worked for the Electric Vehicle Company operating an electric powered cab in New York City. On May 20, 1899, he was pulled over for driving twelve miles per hour in an eight mile per hour zone. A policeman on a bicycle gave chase and took him to jail. According to most accounts German did not actually receive a ticket. The first speeding ticket wouldn't be issued until 1904 when a man named Harry Myers was caught breaking the speed limit in Dayton, Ohio.

In his famous sermon *Payday Someday* Dr. R.G. Lee referenced Jehu who the Bible says "drove furiously," and he remarked that Jehu had many relatives on the roads of America. The truth is that our passion for haste is hardly confined to the roadway. In fact, we live in a world that is obsessed with getting things done faster, reaching goals sooner, and making better time—often without stopping to consider whether we are even going in the right direction.

This haste can spill into our personal relationships with destructive results. A small matter can quickly trigger a large dispute without regard to if this is a fight worth having—or even considering the potential consequences that winning the fight might bring. Many relationships are destroyed because someone is simply too quick to fight. Someone once described a man as "Willing to fight at the drop of a hat...and willing to drop the hat if the other guy didn't." That's not a good approach for a believer. Instead we should be "swift to hear, slow to speak, slow to wrath" (James 1:19).

Today's Word to the Wise: If you are tempted to quarrel or fight, step back and carefully consider whether that is the right approach to take.

The Lazy Man's Way

The slothful man saith, There is a lion in the way; a lion is in the streets.
As the door turneth upon his hinges, so doth the slothful upon his bed.
The slothful hideth his hand in his bosom; it grieveth him to bring it
again to his mouth.—**Proverbs 26:13–15**

I read about a hobo who back in the day was riding a train to make his
way west. He stopped in the town of Denver, hoping that people would
have pity on him and give him something to eat, but everywhere he went,
he seemed to get the same response. Finally in disgust he made his way
back to the train station. Under his breath he muttered, "This has got to
be the laziest town I've ever been to. Every person I met wanted me to do
work for him!"

A lazy person can always find some excuse not to work—no matter
how ridiculous it is. That's because he has surrendered everything for the
sake of avoiding labor. Taking the path of least resistance is a guarantee
to never accomplish anything good for this world or the next. Every work
of lasting importance requires labor, effort, and sacrifice. Whether or not
the world values work, we as believers have a responsibility to be diligent
in our efforts and overcome laziness.

It is important that we understand the role God intends for work to
play in building and strengthening our character. Adam had assignments
and responsibilities even before the fall. After the fall, work became
harder as part of the curse of sin. God told Adam, "cursed is the ground
for thy sake" (Genesis 3:17). The necessity to labor and struggle is good for
us. Avoiding work is like not taking medicine because it tastes bad. It may
avoid temporary unpleasantness, but in the end we are harming ourselves.

Today's Word to the Wise: Rather than making excuses and seeking ways
to get out of work, diligently do the tasks that are set before you.

Stay in Your Place

As a bird that wandereth from her nest, so is a man that wandereth from his place.—**Proverbs 27:8**

John Frederick Parker was one of the original officers when the Metropolitan Police Department for Washington, D.C. was established in 1861. He had an undistinguished record, having been reprimanded on more than one occasion for sleeping or being drunk while on duty. Despite his checkered past, Parker was assigned to guard the booth of President Abraham Lincoln during the performance of "Our American Cousin" at Ford's Theater on April 14, 1865.

During the intermission of the play, Parker and several other men left the theater and went to a nearby tavern for drinks. As a result when John Wilkes Booth arrived at the presidential box, there was no security guard to stop him from entering and killing President Lincoln. Confronted later by Mary Todd Lincoln who blamed him for her husband's murder, Parker said, "I did wrong, I admit, and have bitterly repented." John Parker failed to stay in the place where he should have been, and tragedy followed.

It is easy for us to find excuses for not being where we should be and doing what we should do, but there is great value in diligence and reliability. Instead of being distracted, bored, or tempted by something else, we must be faithful in our responsibilities. This is true in our families, on our jobs, in the church, and everywhere we belong. A man or woman who is where they should be, doing what they should do, is far safer than one who is not. Think of David staying behind in Jerusalem and seeing Bathsheba on the rooftop. While he should have resisted the temptation, if he had been where he was supposed to be, the temptation would never have happened. Don't wander away from the place where God has put you in search of greener pastures.

Today's Word to the Wise: Be diligent about fulfilling whatever assignments God has placed in your life—it can literally be a matter of life and death.

Prayers God Hates

He that turneth away his ear from hearing the law, even his prayer shall be abomination.—**Proverbs 28:9**

One of the wonderful attributes of God is His willingness to hear and answer prayer. The Bible is filled with promises about prayer, and we should certainly claim those promises. Yet there are prayers that God will not hear and answer. As shocking as it may be to contemplate, there are prayers that God actually hates. These are prayers that are offered by those who refuse to submit in obedience to the Word of God yet expect to be heard anyway.

The prophet Amos declared to the people that God was not interested in hearing from them because of the sin that they harbored in their hearts. "I hate, I despise your feast days, and I will not smell in your solemn assemblies. Though ye offer me burnt offerings and your meat offerings, I will not accept them: neither will I regard the peace offerings of your fat beasts" (Amos 5:21–22).

In his book *Prayer: Asking and Receiving,* Dr. John Rice told the story of Charles Blanchard who followed his father as the second president of Wheaton College. Blanchard's wife had fallen ill, and doctors were unable to do anything to help. As a last resort they decided to try an operation. As he prayed about his wife's condition, Dr. Blanchard was convicted of a certain matter in his heart which he had not addressed. He confessed that sin, prayed again, and his wife immediately began to recover and the operation was cancelled.

Many times we wonder why God does not answer our prayers. We bombard Heaven fruitlessly, forgetting the warning of Scripture: "If I regard iniquity in my heart, the Lord will not hear me" (Psalm 66:18). Sin that we tolerate in our hearts not only breaks our fellowship with God but it keeps our prayers from being answered.

Today's Word to the Wise: Before you ask God for things in prayer, make sure that your heart is tuned to following and obeying His Word.

The Fear of Man

*The fear of man bringeth a snare: but whoso putteth his trust in the
Lord shall be safe.*—**Proverbs 29:25**

One of the most gifted speakers in church history was John
Chrysostom—the name comes from the Greek word meaning
"golden tongued." John was sent from Antioch to what was then
Constantinople where he preached fearlessly in the capital of the Eastern
Roman Empire. His denunciation of the lavish extravagance of the
rich and ruling class and his condemnation of excess infuriated many,
including Empress Eudoxia who arranged for him to be exiled. When he
was told of his fate, Chrysostom responded: "What can I fear? Will it be
death? But you know that Christ is my life, and that I shall gain by death.
Will it be exile? But the earth and all its fullness are the Lord's. Poverty I
do not fear; riches I do not sigh for; and from death I do not shrink."

Far too many today are more worried about what people think than
about what God thinks. The desire not to offend others (which is not a
bad thing in itself) is often elevated to be the most important thing. As a
result, many shrink from speaking the truth. In America we have enjoyed
a great measure of freedom from persecution, but the proclamation of
clear Bible principles is rapidly falling out of favor. There may come a day
when we face persecution and even death for speaking the truth.

The decision we make in that hour will be determined by who we
fear more—God or man. As we commit ourselves to following Christ
and being faithful to Him regardless of the consequences, we may
be persecuted, but we will please the One who matters most. When
Stephen was stoned for his fearless preaching he said, "Behold, I see the
heavens opened, and the Son of man standing on the right hand of God."
(Acts 7:56).

Today's Word to the Wise: A believer who is obeying and fearing God
has nothing to fear from any man.

1 Kings 6–7 » Luke 20:27–47 » Proverbs 29

A Deceived Generation

There is a generation that are pure in their own eyes, and yet is not washed from their filthiness.—**Proverbs 30:12**

The Scottish poet Robert Burns' best known poem is entitled *To a Louse, On Seeing One on a Lady's Bonnet at Church.* In the poem Burns describes the audacity of the little creature crawling around with impunity on the fine bonnet worn by a high society matron to the service. The poem concludes with these lines (put in modern English from Burns' original):

> And would some Power the small gift give us
> To see ourselves as others see us!
> It would from many a blunder free us,
> And foolish notion:
> What airs in dress and gait would leave us,
> And even devotion!

All of us are capable of thinking ourselves as being far better than we actually are. Studies show that people routinely over-estimate their skills, intelligence, and abilities in comparison to others. One study famously found that half of all men rated themselves in the top ten percent nationally in athletic ability.

Often we do not see problems in our own lives, though we can be quite skilled at detecting the problems of others. As Jeremiah 17:9 reminds us, "The heart is deceitful above all things, and desperately wicked: who can know it?" If we are depending on our ability to evaluate ourselves, we are heading for trouble. We need an absolute standard of truth against which we can measure ourselves. That standard is the Word of God. It is "a discerner of the thoughts and intents of the heart" (Hebrews 4:12). To properly judge ourselves, we must be diligent students of the Bible and apply what we read to our lives.

Today's Word to the Wise: We need to make our evaluations and measurements by the unchanging Word of God rather than our thoughts or feelings.

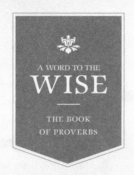

A WORD TO THE

WISE

THE BOOK
OF PROVERBS

MAY

The Curse of Prosperity

For the turning away of the simple shall slay them, and the prosperity of fools shall destroy them.—**Proverbs 1:32**

I read about a young man just starting out in business who told his pastor that he would be faithful to tithe and asked for God's blessing on his work. The man was faithful to give as he had promised, and his income continued to increase. He became one of the highest givers in the church. But as his income continued to grow, it got harder and harder for him to feel good about writing a check to give so much money to God.

Finally he called the pastor and said, "I made $6 million last year. I can't afford to give God $600,000. What can I do?" The pastor responded, "I can pray that God reduces your income back down to where you can afford to tithe." It didn't take long for the businessman to decide that tithing was a better deal. That story illustrates one of the dangers that comes with God's blessing. As we get more, it can become an idol that will ultimately lead to our destruction.

Paul warned Timothy about false teachers who would come in and equate prosperity with God's blessing, "supposing that gain is godliness" (1 Timothy 6:5). We should not fall into the trap of thinking that because someone has more they must be receiving God's favor. The popular message that God wants all of His children to be rich and financially well off is not grounded in Scripture. In fact, the Bible teaches that while God does bless people with prosperity in some cases, in other cases material gain is actually part of His judgment. The destructive power of the love of money leads those who have some wealth to want still more. They are never satisfied or content, thus missing the blessing of God's peace.

Today's Word to the Wise: Examine your heart carefully to be sure that money has not taken God's rightful place.

Rejoicing in Evil

Who rejoice to do evil, and delight in the frowardness of the wicked;
—**Proverbs 2:14**

"I need to quit texting, because I could die in a car accident," twenty-one-year-old college student Chance Bothe wrote to a friend. Moments later, still texting, he missed a curve on the road and plunged thirty feet into a ravine. Miraculously he did not die, but he suffered a serious brain injury and numerous broken bones. It was six months before he was able to leave the hospital, and he had to relearn how to walk, talk, and take care of himself. While he knew what he was doing was dangerous, he continued to do it.

The story is shocking, yet each day millions of people do things that they know are wrong, dangerous, and sinful without believing that they will suffer the consequences. Our culture has adopted a casual attitude toward sin—even worse, sinful behavior is often seen as comical and a source of fun and delight. While the world may have forgotten how awful sin is and how much God hates it, believers cannot afford to take that attitude.

A casual approach to sin or finding humor and pleasure in sin exposes us to the dangers of temptation. A fear of God and an understanding of His holiness protects us from sin and its consequences. This fear caused Joseph to flee when he was tempted by Potiphar's wife. Rather than finding sin attractive, he viewed it as destructive. When Potiphar's wife approached Joseph with her immoral offer he replied, "How then can I do this great wickedness, and sin against God?" (Genesis 39:9)

This attitude is especially important in our entertainment choices. If we are laughing about sin night after night on television or enjoying reading about it in books or online, we will be far more vulnerable when temptation comes. Wisdom keeps the right attitude toward sin—hating it just as God does.

Today's Word to the Wise: Do not adopt the attitude that sin is a laughing matter. Regard it as God does—as great wickedness.

A Sign of God's Love

My son, despise not the chastening of the LORD; neither be weary of his correction: For whom the LORD loveth he correcteth; even as a father the son in whom he delighteth.—**Proverbs 3:11–12**

When Christians endure suffering and affliction they often find it hard to maintain a proper perspective toward the goodness of God and His kindness in bringing correction into our lives. Of course not every trial is a result of sin in our lives. We live in a fallen world where the ravages of sin impact both the saved and the lost alike. Yet it is always wise to stop and examine our lives and see if there is correction from our Heavenly Father involved.

Charles Spurgeon said, "It is not every affliction that benefits the Christian; it is only a sanctified affliction. Take heed if God is trying you, that you search and find out the reason. Have you lost that joy you once felt? There is some cause for it. Many a man would not have half so much suffered if he would but look to the cause of it. I have sometimes walked a mile or two, almost limping along because there was a stone in my shoe, and I did not stop to look for it. And many a Christian goes limping for years because of the stones in his shoe, but if he would only stop to look for them, he would be relieved. What is the sin that is causing you pain? Get it out."

The author of Hebrews quoted this admonition from Solomon because it is a truth that is worth repeating. "My son, despise not thou the chastening of the Lord, nor faint when thou art rebuked of him" (Hebrews 12:5). Instead of allowing ourselves to be discouraged or getting angry with God and giving up, we should view His chastisement as evidence that we are His children and that He loves enough to correct us.

Today's Word to the Wise: If you view chastisement as a sign of God's love, it will be easier for you to respond correctly in repentance.

Staying on Course

I have taught thee in the way of wisdom; I have led thee in right paths.
When thou goest, thy steps shall not be straitened; and when thou
runnest, thou shalt not stumble.—**Proverbs 4:11–12**

The use of the term "red herring" to describe something that distracts
someone from their main goal dates back to at least the 1500s. The
writer Thomas Nashe penned, "Next, to draw on hounds to a scent, to
a red herring skin there is nothing comparable." Despite this literary
depiction, there appears to be little evidence that hunters actually used
herring to train their dogs to stay after their prey, but the phrase stuck. It
came to be used as a general figure of speech to describe a false trail that
leads nowhere but instead draws attention away from the main thing.

The devil is a master at using distractions to draw us away from what
God intends for us to do. He is perfectly willing to use good things to
keep us away from the best things. I once heard a sermon titled "Rabbit
Chasers." The preacher was a man with rural roots who described how
in his childhood they would take their dogs into the woods to hunt
opossum, but they found that the dogs would stop hunting opossums
to chase rabbits instead. He talked about how anything that distracts us
from God's best is a waste.

When it comes to avoiding destructive distractions, wisdom offers
a great defense. Wisdom chooses the important and long-lasting over
the fleeting and temporary. Wisdom rejects the quick fix in favor of the
permanent solution. Wisdom shuns the approach of the world for the
path of God—even when that path is narrow and not chosen by many
others. In short, the more we are in touch with God's Word and God's
wisdom, the more closely we will follow God's path.

Today's Word to the Wise: Stay focused on God's plan and purpose for
your life, and do not allow anything to take you off course.

The Eyes of the Lord

For the ways of man are before the eyes of the Lord, and he pondereth all his goings.—**Proverbs 5:21**

In August of 2010 a group of thirty-three miners were trapped in a Chilean gold and copper mine by a cave-in. Amazingly they managed to survive for more than two months before they were finally rescued. Upon reaching the surface, one of the miners, Yonni Rojas, discovered that both his wife and his mistress had arrived to hold vigil and watch for his safe return! He thought that he had covered his tracks and that no one knew of his five year affair, but an unexpected mine disaster revealed his sin, not just to his family, but to the entire world.

Charles Spurgeon said, "You say that you can handle your secret sins, that there is no one hurt by them. But you may as well ask the lion to let you put your head into his mouth. You cannot regulate his jaws: neither can you regulate sin. Once done, you cannot tell when you will be destroyed. You may put your head in and out a great many times; but one of these days it will be a costly venture."

As Christians we must never lose sight of the fact that God sees and knows everything that we do and think. No matter how carefully we may hide from others, nothing is hidden from His sight. Hebrews 4:13 says, "Neither is there any creature that is not manifest in his sight: but all things are naked and opened unto the eyes of him with whom we have to do." God knows what we are doing and what we desire to do, and He has not changed His mind regarding sin. God hates sin too much and loves us too much to allow us to get away with secret sin.

Today's Word to the Wise: It is far better to confess and forsake your sin immediately than to wait until it results in public shame.

Sudden Destruction

Therefore shall his calamity come suddenly; suddenly shall he be broken without remedy.—**Proverbs 6:15**

Despite its location on a low island on the Texas Gulf Coast and the destruction brought by a hurricane on the neighboring city of Indianola, the residents of Galveston did not see a need to build a sea wall to protect their city from a major storm. Though the United States Weather Bureau was aware that a tropical storm was passing through the Caribbean, they did not have the means to track it. The warnings that were issued were far too little and too late.

On September 8, 1900, a massive hurricane, which caused the deadliest natural disaster in United States history, struck the thriving Texas town. Modern estimates place it as a category four hurricane. Wind speeds reached over one hundred miles per hour before the measuring equipment was destroyed. A storm surge of more than fifteen feet swept over the low island and destroyed thousands of homes and buildings. Estimates of the total loss of life were as high as twelve thousand people. Burial plots could not be found for the massive number of bodies, and after attempts to dispose of them at sea were thwarted by the tides, massive funeral pyres were built to burn the remains.

The residents of Galveston thought they were living in perfect safety when in fact they were in enormous danger. This is also true of those who are casual about their relationship with sin. The fact that God's mercy may sometimes delay immediate judgment does not mean that sin is hidden from His eyes or is acceptable to Him. As Moses warned the children of Israel, "be sure your sin will find you out" (Numbers 32:23). Rather than being lulled into complacency, we should run to God in repentance and seek His forgiveness before we fall under His judgment.

Today's Word to the Wise: Rather than waiting for judgment and destruction, repent of any sin in your life and return to a right relationship with God.

A Matter of the Heart

Hearken unto me now therefore, O ye children, and attend to the words of my mouth. Let not thine heart decline to her ways, go not astray in her paths.—**Proverbs 7:24–25**

One of the things that the Centers for Disease Control in Atlanta, Georgia, does is track the different things that end life. According to their statistics, more Americans die of heart disease every year than any other single cause. No one keeps similar statistics on spiritual tragedies, but if there were a way to measure the cause of them, certainly problems of the heart would be at the top of the list. If we allow our hearts to be turned away from God, disaster will certainly follow.

We see this truth illustrated in the life of Solomon. Though God gave him great wisdom, wealth, and power, Solomon did not remain constant in his devotion. In his youth he worshiped and valued God, building the magnificent Temple in Jerusalem. But he disobeyed the Word of God by taking many wives from foreign nations. Over time they destroyed his allegiance to the God of Israel. "For it came to pass, when Solomon was old, that his wives turned away his heart after other gods: and his heart was not perfect with the LORD his God, as was the heart of David his father" (1 Kings 11:4).

What goes on in the heart cannot be concealed forever. Sooner or later it will be apparent in our actions. Jesus said, "For out of the heart proceed evil thoughts, murders, adulteries, fornications, thefts, false witness, blasphemies" (Matthew 15:19). If we love God as we should, there will be no room for the things of the world to take root. The warning John issued to the church at Ephesus shows the vital importance of the heart: "Nevertheless I have somewhat against thee, because thou hast left thy first love" (Revelation 2:4).

Today's Word to the Wise: Above all else, guard your heart and make sure your love for God stays fervent and tender.

Leadership and Wisdom

Counsel is mine, and sound wisdom: I am understanding; I have strength.
By me kings reign, and princes decree justice. By me princes rule, and
nobles, even all the judges of the earth.—**Proverbs 8:14–16**

Because Solomon asked for a wise and understanding heart when
God offered him anything he desired, he was granted a measure
of wisdom that no one before or since has possessed. Early in his reign
that wisdom was displayed when he had to decide which of two women
was the mother of a child; both claimed the baby. Apparently, the "lower
courts" had been unable to discern which woman was telling the truth,
so they brought them both to Solomon for him to judge between them.
What happened next cemented Solomon's reputation as a man with great
insight and wisdom.

"And the king said, Bring me a sword. And they brought a sword
before the king. And the king said, Divide the living child in two, and
give half to the one, and half to the other" (1 Kings 3:24–25). The woman
who was the mother wanted the child to live, even if she couldn't be the
one to raise him. The woman who was the false claimant was willing to
let the child be killed. Thus Solomon revealed who the mother was. The
people of the kingdom were astonished for "they saw that the wisdom of
God was in him, to do judgment" (1 Kings 3:28).

Every person in leadership (and most of us are leaders in some aspect
of our lives) needs the wisdom of God. In our human wisdom, we do not
have the ability to make good decisions in the problems and decisions
we face. Many people, through trusting their own wisdom, have made
tragically destructive choices that have impacted their lives and the lives
of those they lead. We should seek to apply the principles of Scripture
and follow the leading of the Holy Spirit so that we lead wisely.

Today's Word to the Wise: Seek God's wisdom for every area of your life
so you can glorify Him in your actions.

What You Do for Yourself

If thou be wise, thou shalt be wise for thyself: but if thou scornest, thou alone shalt bear it.—**Proverbs 9:12**

When he was just twenty years old, Benjamin Franklin set out to improve his character. He created a list of thirteen virtues that he wanted to cultivate in his life. They were: temperance, silence, order, resolution, frugality, industry, sincerity, justice, moderation, cleanliness, tranquility, chastity, and humility. His plan was to work on one each week and then go on to the next. When he reached the end of the list, he would start over again.

The problem with this approach is that in our own strength we do not have the ability to develop the behavior that God expects from us. Though Franklin's parents were devout churchgoers and he was a good friend with noted evangelist George Whitefield, Franklin was not a believer. His lack of reliance on God meant that no matter how diligently he tried, he could never truly improve himself in a lasting way.

The key to success in life and living in a manner that is pleasing to God is found only in the power of God. Paul wrote, "This I say then, Walk in the Spirit, and ye shall not fulfil the lust of the flesh" (Galatians 5:16). It is not our willpower and strength that overcomes temptation and displays godly character. It is a life surrendered to the Holy Spirit and operating under His power and influence.

Wisdom teaches us to obey God and His Word with profound and lasting results. In his will Ben Franklin left 1,000 pounds (about $4,400 in that day) to the city of Philadelphia with the stipulation that it be allowed to accumulate interest for two hundred years before being spent. By the time it was used, his bequest was worth some $5 million. Wisdom also accumulates, and the benefits last a lifetime and beyond.

Today's Word to the Wise: When we acquire and follow wisdom, we greatly enrich our own lives as well as the lives of others.

Blessing without Sorrow

The blessing of the Lord, *it maketh rich, and he addeth no sorrow with it.*—**Proverbs 10:22**

Fleeing religious persecution in England and seeking a place where they could worship God freely, the Pilgrims made the treacherous journey across the Atlantic Ocean to the shores of America in 1620. After a difficult trip, they finally reached the New World. Before going ashore to establish a new colony, they wrote and signed a document known as the Mayflower Compact. In it they stated that their purpose in founding the colony was "for the Glory of God, and advancements of the Christian faith."

William Bradford, who eventually served as the governor of Plymouth Colony, wrote in his diary that the Pilgrims "came to anchor in the Bay, which was a good harbor...and they blessed the God of Heaven, who brought them over the fast and furious ocean...and a sea of trouble." Though the Pilgrims endured hardship as they worked to carve a new home out of the rocky shores of New England, the hand of God continued to bless them and meet their needs.

The blessings of God are often misunderstood. Some people teach that if God is blessing you, nothing will ever go wrong and you will have everything that you want. But that is not the teaching of Scripture. The blessing of God is not primarily about material things, although it certainly may include those. Instead it is about the things that are eternal and can never be taken away.

To properly appreciate the blessings of God, we must first trust that He knows what is best for us and that He is powerful enough to be sure we receive what He wants us to have. This kind of faith allows us to be content regardless of our circumstances. With this attitude, we will be grateful for all the good things God gives.

Today's Word to the Wise: When we receive the blessings of God with gratitude and thanksgiving, we find true and lasting joy.

Justice in Practice

A false balance is abomination to the LORD: but a just weight is his delight.—**Proverbs 11:1**

A Michigan judge, Raymond Voet, has a long-standing policy forbidding the use of cellular phones in the courtroom. Any phone that rings aloud is confiscated, and the owner receives a fine. Over the years, attorneys, police officers, witnesses, and spectators have broken the rule and received the punishment.

During closing arguments at one trial, a smartphone started talking. "I can't understand you. Say something like Mom," the phone requested. It was the judge's new phone. "I'm guessing I bumped it. It started talking really loud. That's an excuse, but I don't take those excuses from anyone else. I set the bar high, because cell phones are a distraction and there is very serious business going on," he said. "The courtroom is a special place in the community, and it needs more respect than that." During the next break in the trial, Judge Voet held himself in contempt, and paid the standard twenty-five dollar fine that he issues anyone who disturbs a trial. "Judges are human," Voet said. "They're not above the rules. I broke the rule, and I have to live by it."

To live a life that is pleasing to God, we need to deal justly both with ourselves and others. The priority God places on justice is very high indeed. The prophet Micah wrote, "He hath shewed thee, O man, what is good; and what doth the LORD require of thee, but to do justly, and to love mercy, and to walk humbly with thy God?" (Micah 6:8). There will always be temptations to cut corners in our dealings with others or to excuse something in ourselves that we condemn in others. We should reject these temptations and act justly.

Today's Word to the Wise: Hold yourself to the same standards to which you hold others, and be just in all your interactions.

The Tongue of the Wise

There is that speaketh like the piercings of a sword: but the tongue of the wise is health.—**Proverbs 12:18**

When future president Abraham Lincoln was just nine years old, his mother Nancy died after drinking milk from a cow that had eaten a poisonous plant. Though she had only nine years in which to impact his life, she used them well. Later Lincoln would say, "All that I am, or hope to be, I owe to my angel mother." But it was not just in her teaching that she touched his life. Lincoln also said, "I remember my mother's prayers and they have always followed me. They have clung to me all my life."

In contrast to the good example set by Nancy Lincoln, consider another mother. She was angry and abusive toward her youngest son. When classmates teased him, calling him "Ozzie Rabbit" because he was small and had big ears, she told her son that they were right. The boy's older brother later said, "We learned very early that we were a burden… she wanted to be free of responsibility." That boy, Lee Harvey Oswald became a household name when he assassinated President John Kennedy.

Our words have enormous power. They can deeply wound or they can heal. Knowing this truth, we should be very careful how we speak to others. Colossians 4:6 instructs, "Let your speech be alway with grace, seasoned with salt, that ye may know how ye ought to answer every man." Words that we excuse as teasing may cut much deeper than we realize. Words that praise character and effort encourage others to persevere in godliness.

Today's Word to the Wise: Use your words today to pray for others and to encourage and strengthen others.

Loving the Truth

A righteous man hateth lying: but a wicked man is loathsome, and cometh to shame.—**Proverbs 13:5**

Before he became president of the United States, Abraham Lincoln was a successful attorney in Illinois. His specialty was railroad law—a new field at the time. When the son of a friend was charged with murder and put on trial in 1858, Lincoln agreed to defend him at no cost. During the trial a witness named Charles Allen testified that he had seen the accused, Duff Armstrong, hit and kill James Metzker on the night of August 29, 1857. Allen's testimony was that though he was 150 feet away, the light of the full moon allowed him to clearly see that Armstrong was the killer.

Once he had Allen committed and on the record with his sworn testimony, Lincoln sprang his trap. He pulled out an almanac for the previous year and showed that the moon on that date was not full but only one quarter—and that at the time of the crime it had barely risen. There was no way that Allen could have seen Armstrong commit the crime as he had testified. The jury acquitted William Armstrong on their first ballot. The truth overcame the lie, and justice was done.

When we are honest and truthful, we demonstrate our commitment to following God and obeying His commands. The temptation to shade the truth, to tell "white lies," or to try to get off the hook by lying always leads to disaster. Much of our society has abandoned honesty as a virtue, but that does not make it any less important for us to continue to love the truth. Jesus said, "And ye shall know the truth, and the truth shall make you free" (John 8:32). Though it may seem that lying will work out better in the short run, the truth is always the best course in the end.

Today's Word to the Wise: If you are committed to the truth, it will protect you and bring you God's blessings.

The Way that Seemeth Right

There is a way which seemeth right unto a man, but the end thereof are the ways of death.—**Proverbs 14:12**

For skiing enthusiasts there are few places that top the rugged Cascade Mountains in Washington state. For "extreme skiers" who look for the most remote and steep locations, one of the best places to ski is the Stevens Pass on Cowboy Mountain. Just outside that ski park is a place known as Tunnel Creek. Though it is not maintained by the ski resort, it is known for deep snow that is perfect for skiing—and for avalanches.

In February of 2012 more than a dozen world class skiers gathered for an excursion down Tunnel Creek. The trip ended in disaster as nearly three feet of newly fallen snow combined with temperature changes created a deadly avalanche. Three of the skiers—professionals who had spent much of their lives on the slopes—perished in the massive snow slide. The wife of one of the victims asked him that morning if the excursion was safe. She later said, "He looked me right in the eye and said: 'Of course. I wouldn't be going if it weren't.'" They thought that what they were doing was safe, but they were tragically and fatally wrong.

Human wisdom and understanding is fallible. Studies have shown that people routinely underestimate dangers and overestimate their abilities to cope with them. This is true in all aspects of life, but it is especially true in the spiritual realm. The prophet Jeremiah put it this way: "O Lord, I know that the way of man is not in himself: it is not in man that walketh to direct his steps" (Jeremiah 10:23). God has given us a perfect and inerrant guide—His Word. Rather than relying on how things look and feel to us, we should trust and follow His precepts.

Today's Word to the Wise: Trust God's Word and His wisdom above your own, and you will be greatly protected from danger.

Sharing Knowledge

The lips of the wise disperse knowledge: but the heart of the foolish doeth not so.—**Proverbs 15:7**

One of the iconic characters of early America was John Chapman, better known as Johnny Appleseed. Chapman was born in Massachusetts just before the start of the American Revolution. When he was about eighteen years of age, he left home and headed west. For more than fifty years he crisscrossed the states of Pennsylvania, Ohio, Indiana, and Illinois. Chapman took apple seeds and planted nurseries across the region. He built fences to protect the new trees, and he contracted with local farmers or merchants to sell the trees as they grew.

John Chapman was also a missionary. He loved to tell children stories from the Bible. One of his hearers described his voice this way in an article about Johnny Appleseed published in *Harper's New Monthly Magazine*: "strong and loud as the roar of wind and waves, then soft and soothing as the balmy airs that quivered the morning-glory leaves about his gray beard." Along with his supply of apple seeds he also carried tracts and Bible portions to share with those he met.

The life of Johnny Appleseed is a powerful reminder to us of one of the purposes God has for us here on Earth—to share the gospel and the truths of Scripture with those we meet. Rather than being isolated from the world, we are to be "the sons of God, without rebuke, in the midst of a crooked and perverse nation, among whom ye shine as lights in the world" (Philippians 2:15).

Christians are not meant to be hoarders of the Good News or the blessings we have received from God. Peter said we are to "minister the same one to another, as good stewards of the manifold grace of God" (1 Peter 4:10). As we share what we have, God multiplies it to do even more.

Today's Word to the Wise: The purpose of wisdom is not just for us to store it up for ourselves but to share it with others as well.

Righteous Leadership

It is an abomination to kings to commit wickedness: for the throne is established by righteousness.—**Proverbs 16:12**

It seemed like a fairly simple burglary when a group of five men were arrested the night of June 17, 1972, while breaking into the Democratic National Committee headquarters in the Watergate complex in Washington, D.C. The arrest and subsequent trial were largely ignored during the election that year, and President Nixon was overwhelmingly reelected to a second term in a landslide. The story, however, was more involved than first appeared, and the Nixon presidency began to unravel.

The revelation that the burglary was connected to the Committee to Reelect the President and that Nixon and his staff had impeded the investigation eventually led to the door of the Oval Office. Tape recordings secretly made in the White House gave investigators evidence of high level involvement. By the time the dust had settled, more than three dozen people, including many top administration officials, had been convicted and sent to prison for their roles in the break-in and the subsequent cover-up. President Nixon resigned in disgrace rather than waiting for an almost certain impeachment, and only a pardon from President Ford kept him from facing trial as well.

Often those in leadership (and all of us are leaders and influencers in at least one area) are tempted to think that they can afford to cut corners or do things that they would condemn others for doing. They may think that their position entitles them leeway from honesty and integrity—but it does not. Every time a leader approves of or tolerates sin, he is weakening the very framework that supports his position. Because all authority comes from God—" there is no power but of God" (Romans 13:1)—any sinful act is an attack not just on His authority, but on the leader's authority as well.

Today's Word to the Wise: Any sin tolerated in the life of a leader not only damages him but brings hurtful consequences to his followers as well.

Dangerous Fools

Let a bear robbed of her whelps meet a man, rather than a fool in his folly.—**Proverbs 17:12**

In July of 2011, a hiker was attacked by a female grizzly bear near the Wapiti Lake trail in Yellowstone National Park. The man and his wife were visiting the park as hundreds of thousands do each year. Apparently they surprised the mother grizzly and her cubs. The National Park Service issued a statement saying, "In an attempt to defend a perceived threat to her cubs, the bear attacked and fatally wounded the man." Though the man did not intend to harm the bear or her cubs, she did not know that and responded according to her nature—with fatal results.

As dangerous as it is to cross paths with a mother bear and her cubs, the Bible tells us that it is even more dangerous to cross paths with a fool. The folly in the heart of a fool is not limited to his own life. Instead it tends to infect others and bring devastation into their lives. Think of Achan taking loot from the city of Jericho when God had forbidden it. He undoubtedly thought he had pulled off the perfect crime. Once they had captured another city or two, he could bring out the things he had hidden in his tent and no one would ever know.

What he forgot was that God knew what had happened. That was the height of folly, and it brought destruction not only to Achan and his family but also to dozens of others. "Did not Achan the son of Zerah commit a trespass in the accursed thing, and wrath fell on all the congregation of Israel? and that man perished not alone in his iniquity" (Joshua 22:20). Although you cannot control everyone who is part of your life, you can guard against the influence of fools.

Today's Word to the Wise: Beware of the company or influence of a fool. His folly will bring destruction to your life.

Take Time to Listen

He that answereth a matter before he heareth it, it is folly and shame unto him.—**Proverbs 18:13**

"Mice in Council" is one of Aesop's better known fables. A group of mice, tired of constantly living in fear of being attacked and eaten by a cat, hold a meeting to decide on a course of action. A number of possibilities were debated and rejected before one mouse stood with a proposal that proved to be very popular. "I think I have hit upon a plan which will ensure our safety in the future, provided you approve and carry it out. It is that we should fasten a bell round the neck of our enemy the cat, which will by its tinkling warn us of her approach."

The mice were prepared to vote to approve the plan when an elderly mouse stood and said, "I agree with you all that the plan before us is an admirable one. But may I ask who is going to bell the cat?" Often people say things that sound good in the moment, but when they are fully considered, the flaws begin to appear. Other times, only one side of a situation is presented for consideration. The problem comes in when we take action based on the early information without taking all sides into account. That approach leads to foolish decisions and can result in calamity.

We should take time to carefully weigh all aspects of a matter, making sure that we have the full story before proceeding to make a decision. Choices based on partial and incomplete information rarely turn out well. Do not allow impatience or haste to push you toward moving forward unless you are sure you have understood both the current situation and the possible outcomes of any decision you make. Only then are you ready to make a wise and safe decision.

Today's Word to the Wise: Take the time to make sure you have listened to and understood all aspects of a matter before you decide on a solution.

The Protection of Obedience

He that keepeth the commandment keepeth his own soul; but he that despiseth his ways shall die.—**Proverbs 19:16**

When the massive Hurricane Charley slammed into Florida in 2004 with 145 mile per hour winds, it destroyed more than twelve thousand homes. A later study by a group of insurance companies found that almost all of those homes had something in common—they were built prior to 2001. In that year, a new building code was adopted which required homes to be strengthened to withstand hurricane force winds.

Jeff Burton, building code manager for the Institute for Business and Home Safety said, "There is very, very strong evidence that buildings built under the 2001 code that were built properly and inspected...fared much, much better than buildings that were built prior. The building code, as it exists today did its job." There is a reason for the building code, and those who follow it find that it works. The same is true for the Word of God.

When we view the Bible as a list of things we must do or cannot do, we are tempted to resent the commandments of God. Many people completely abandon any pretense of holiness or godly living because they don't want to be tied down by rules. When the storm winds blow, those who have not built their lives according to God's code find themselves facing destruction and ruin.

It is important that we understand the purpose of God's commandments. First John 5:3 tells us, "...and his commandments are not grievous." They are given for our protection. God does not arbitrarily declare some things off limits to make sure we aren't having fun. The commands of God are given for our own good. When we follow them carefully, we receive both protection from evil and blessings from above.

Today's Word to the Wise: View God's commandments as a protection, and you will find them a blessing rather than a burden.

A Faithful Man

Most men will proclaim every one his own goodness: but a faithful man who can find?—**Proverbs 20:6**

Late in 1944 with the war going very badly for the Japanese, a young lieutenant name Hiroo Onoda was sent to Lubang Island in the Philippines. His orders were simple. He was to do everything possible to slow the American advance by conducting guerilla attacks. Under no circumstances was he to surrender or to kill himself. Onoda took his orders seriously. Even when the American forces captured the island early in 1945 and most of the other men in his unit surrendered, Onoda continued to fight.

He and three others took to the hills where they continued the struggle. Their continuing attacks alerted authorities to their presence, and leaflets were dropped telling them the war was over. Onoda believed it was a trick and continued the fight. Eventually, the other members of his party surrendered or were killed, but he continued to launch guerilla attacks. Finally in 1974, his former commanding officer was flown to Lubang Island to meet with Lieutenant Onoda. He formally relieved the tenacious soldier of his duty so Onoda could leave the war behind without disobeying his orders and being dishonored.

The war had been over for nearly thirty years, but Lieutenant Onoda was still faithful to obey the command he had been given decades before. In a day when we see many fall away from following God, we are sometimes tempted as Elijah was to wonder if there are any faithful people left. There most definitely are. And we have the opportunity to add to that number by being faithful ourselves. Jesus asked this question, "Nevertheless when the Son of man cometh, shall he find faith on the earth?" (Luke 18:8). Each of us should resolve to live in such a way that we will be found faithful when we see Jesus.

Today's Word to the Wise: God is looking for faithful men and women to serve Him. Will you be one today?

Wandering from the Truth

The man that wandereth out of the way of understanding shall remain in the congregation of the dead.—**Proverbs 21:16**

In September of 2012, an Alzheimer's support group highlighted a news story that would point out the seriousness of Alzheimer's and the difficulties facing those caring for Alzheimer's patients. A sixty-seven-year-old man who was living in a nursing home with what was described as "severe dementia" wandered away from the facility. He had to use a walker to get around, and even though it was raining, he was wearing house slippers instead of shoes.

The police and staff focused their search in the immediate vicinity of the nursing home, believing that he would be found nearby. To their shock and amazement, he had somehow made his way to a bus station, purchased a ticket, and made the trip back to his former hometown—124 miles away. Statistics indicate that nearly two-thirds of Alzheimer's patients wander from time to time. In that respect the disease is much like the spiritual danger that all of us face—that of wandering away from the Lord without understanding the dangers we face.

The old hymn "Come Thou Fount of Every Blessing" contains the line: "Prone to wander Lord I feel it, prone to leave the God I love." The prophet Isaiah wrote, "All we like sheep have gone astray; we have turned every one to his own way; and the LORD hath laid on him the iniquity of us all" (Isaiah 53:6). The truth is that no one remains in a close relationship with God by accident; it requires conscious and repeated effort. If we allow ourselves to just drift along, we will begin to wander away from God. Like a ship that has not set an anchor, we will be carried along with the currents, often without even realizing it. Then one day we find ourselves far adrift. Cling to the truth and to God, and you will avoid wandering.

Today's Word to the Wise: Guard your heart carefully against the tendency we all have to wander away from God.

Planning for the Future

A prudent man foreseeth the evil, and hideth himself: but the simple pass on, and are punished.—**Proverbs 22:3**

Anthropologist Gregory Bateson told an amazing story about the New College at Oxford in England. The college is "new" only by Oxford standards, having been founded in 1379. During the 1400s a great dining hall was built for the students to use. One of the stunning architectural features of the hall is the presence of a number of massive exposed oak beams which are two feet thick and forty-five feet long.

According to Bateman's story, in the late 1900s the beams were found to be infested with beetles which were destroying their structural integrity. Knowing they needed to be replaced, but unsure where to find such massive trees, the college leaders were stymied. It was the college forester who came forward with the solution. Hundreds of years before, oak trees had been planted on college lands for the specific purpose of providing replacements in the future. While generations of foresters had harvested other trees, they had left the oaks to grow strong and tall. Because the need had been foreseen, a provision had been made to meet it.

God's children should be characterized by wisdom regarding the future. Someone once said, "Failing to plan is planning to fail." While none of us know exactly what will happen tomorrow and we should never be presumptuous about the future, we should plan for things that can be foreseen. Trusting God does not imply that we fail to make provision for the future for ourselves and our families. When making plans for the material things, we must also remember to plan for spiritual things. This means we should prepare to avoid temptation and sin. It is far easier to keep from sinning if you avoid being tempted. Jesus taught His disciples to pray, "Lead us not into temptation" (Matthew 6:13).

Today's Word to the Wise: Carefully evaluate future dangers and do what you can to avoid them so you will not suffer the consequences of failing to plan.

Be an Example

My son, give me thine heart, and let thine eyes observe my ways.
—**Proverbs 23:26**

The first Naval officer killed in the Iraq war in 2003 was twenty-seven-year-old Lieutenant Thomas Adams. He was one of seven who died when his Sea King helicopter collided with another aircraft over the Persian Gulf. Lieutenant Adams was serving as a liaison officer with the British Royal Navy at the time. In serving his country Adams was following a long family tradition. He was a descendant of President John Adams, and many other members of his family had served the nation from the Revolutionary War to the Civil War to modern times.

Adams' legacy is a wonderful example of the legacy we can leave for future generations by the way we live in the present. President John Adams believed in the United States and devoted his life to helping form and build the new nation. His children and grandchildren followed in his footsteps because of the example that he set for them. By observing his ways the course of their lives was set—a pattern that has lasted for generations.

Part of God's plan for His people is that each generation sets an example for the next to follow. Paul wrote to the church at Corinth, "Be ye followers of me, even as I also am of Christ" (1 Corinthians 11:1). Each day we should be aware that there are others watching us, especially in our family and in our church family. They see how we respond to success and victory, and how we respond to difficulty and defeat. They watch our lives to see if our actions match our words. They observe our behavior at home to see if it matches our conduct in public. While none of us are perfect, we should strive to continually set a godly example for those who come after us to follow.

Today's Word to the Wise: Live in such a way that as your children and grandchildren follow your example, their lives will bring honor and glory to God.

The End of Sloth

Yet a little sleep, a little slumber, a little folding of the hands to sleep: So shall thy poverty come as one that travelleth; and thy want as an armed man.—**Proverbs 24:33–34**

Some people refer to Paul Railton of Consett, England, as the laziest man in the world. That would be difficult to prove, but his legal troubles certainly provide evidence that he is in the running for the title. In December of 2009, a cyclist saw Railton "walking" his dog by driving his car slowly and holding the leash out the car window. The cyclist reported him to authorities. Railton pled guilty to a charge of "not being in proper control of a vehicle" and was fined sixty-six pounds and ordered not to drive for six months.

As our society moves further and further away from understanding the value of hard work, we are seeing a rise in laziness. This disease is undermining not just the foundations of our nation, but it is striking the church as well. It is always easy to justify rest and relaxation. While there is a place for rest—following the pattern God established in the beginning of Creation by resting on the seventh day—fewer people are being overworked than would like to think they are. Instead too many continually "hit the snooze button" and waste their lives through laziness.

However much we would like to think otherwise, there always comes a day of reckoning for laziness. No good intention can overcome the law of work which God has placed in the universe. When we do not labor, eventually the consequences arrive. Taking the easy way out in the present always damages the future—and it will never produce the desired result. Charles Spurgeon said, "There is no fatigue so wearisome as that which comes from lack of work." Take the tasks which are before you and give them your full effort.

Today's Word to the Wise: Laziness may bring temporary perceived benefits, but in the end it always results in disaster.

The Protection of Self-Control

He that hath no rule over his own spirit is like a city that is broken down, and without walls.—**Proverbs 25:28**

Alexander the Great was a conquering, military genius like few others in history. But although he commanded great armies, he frequently struggled with the control of his anger. At a banquet held to celebrate a victory, flattering courtiers heaped praise on the young leader. In the process someone made remarks which downplayed the courage and achievements of the Macedonian Hetairoi—the Companion Cavalry that was the elite of Alexander's army. Their general Clitus was enraged and spoke out to remind Alexander they had saved his life in a recent battle.

Clitus told Alexander that he was being flattered by those who told him only what he wanted to hear and that they were trying to drive a wedge between the conqueror and his most loyal supporters. Alexander did not receive that rebuke well. While he looked for a sword to strike his loyal general, friends ushered Clitus from the room. But Clitus soon returned through another door to continue his rebuke. Alexander snatched a spear from a guard and hurled it into Clitus' body, killing him. Afterward Alexander repented, but it was too late to undo his rash act. It is said that for several days he refused to eat or drink, mourning the death of his friend. Alexander conquered many great cities and empires, but he could not conquer his anger.

Paul wrote, "But the fruit of the Spirit is love, joy, peace, longsuffering, gentleness, goodness, faith, Meekness, temperance: against such there is no law" (Galatians 5:22–23). Temperance is what we often refer to as self-control. It is the ability to submit to the Holy Spirit and respond properly, resist temptation, defer anger, and control frustration. A person who has no self-control is demonstrating that he or she is not in submission to the Holy Spirit.

Today's Word to the Wise: As you yield to the Holy Spirit and walk in His leading, you will exhibit the fruit of temperance.

Repeating Folly

As a dog returneth to his vomit, so a fool returneth to his folly.
—Proverbs 26:11

A number of years ago, retired NASA engineer Edgar C. Whisenant wrote a book called *88 Reasons Why the Rapture Will Be in 1988*. The book, which he self-published, placed the expected date of the Rapture between September 11 and September 13 of 1988 and became a massive bestseller. By the end of the year in which it was published, more than 4.5 million copies had been sold. Whisenant was certain he had the date right. He said, "Only if the Bible is in error am I wrong; and I say that to every preacher in town. I would stake my life on Rosh Hashanah 1988."

Whisenant's later books predicting the Rapture in 1989, 1993, and 1994 did not sell nearly so well as the first one, but he kept right on making those predictions despite the clear teaching of Scripture that we are not meant to know the date and time of Christ's return.

Because we are only human, all of us are going to make mistakes. One of the things that sets fools apart, however, is that they continue to make the same mistakes over and over again. They never learn from their errors, no matter how painful their experiences may be. That is because they are committed to their folly.

We should be teachable and learn from our mistakes. As Psalm 32:9 puts it, "Be ye not as the horse, or as the mule, which have no understanding: whose mouth must be held in with bit and bridle, lest they come near unto thee." The path of wisdom is to consider the lessons we are being taught when things go wrong. Rather than blaming others or talking about "bad luck," we should look to see if we have violated a principle of Scripture and bring our lives into compliance with God's Word.

Today's Word to the Wise: Commit yourself to being teachable so you do not foolishly continue to repeat mistakes.

A Debt to Be Paid by each Generation

Be thou diligent to know the state of thy flocks, and look well to thy herds. For riches are not for ever: and doth the crown endure to every generation?—**Proverbs 27:23–24**

In his farewell speech at West Point, General Douglas MacArthur praised the courage and willingness to sacrifice of the American soldier: "His name and fame are the birthright of every American citizen. He needs no eulogy from me, or from any other man. He belongs to history as furnishing one of the greatest examples of successful patriotism. He belongs to posterity as the instructor of future generations in the principles of liberty and freedom. He belongs to the present, to us, by his virtues and by his achievements.

"In twenty campaigns, on a hundred battlefields, around a thousand campfires, I have witnessed that enduring fortitude, that patriotic self-abnegation, and that invincible determination which have carved his statue in the hearts of his people. From one end of the world to the other, he has drained deep the chalice of courage. I do not know the dignity of their birth, but I do know the glory of their death. They died unquestioning, uncomplaining, with faith in their hearts, and on their lips the hope that we would go on to victory. Always for them: Duty, Honor, Country."

The freedom we enjoy as Americans was purchased at great cost. But it is not a once-for-all purchase. The price must continue to be paid if the freedom is to continue. The same is true in the spiritual realm. Jude said we must "earnestly contend for the faith which was once delivered unto the saints" (Jude 3). The faith has been delivered, but we must still be willing to stand and fight for it. Let it never be said that we allowed the flame of faith to go out.

Today's Word to the Wise: Commit to stand for freedom and truth in your generation.

Confession and Mercy

He that covereth his sins shall not prosper: but whoso confesseth and forsaketh them shall have mercy.—**Proverbs 28:13**

In May of 1948 three men robbed a bank in Hoyt, Kansas, getting away with $1,000. Shortly thereafter two men were killed in a car wreck. Police believed that the men killed were the robbers, and the case was closed. Four years later, however, something unusual happened. On a Sunday morning at the Seward Avenue Baptist Church, a young man named Al Johnson stepped to the pulpit and revealed to the congregation that the day before he had gone to the district attorney and confessed his role in the crime.

"I thought about the bank robbery many times," Johnson, who was a teenager when the crime occurred, said. "I prayed about it and asked the Lord to give me an answer. It seemed that He would give me only one answer and that was to give myself up." Johnson also revealed that he had borrowed the money to repay the bank his share of the stolen funds. The statute of limitations had expired, but Johnson said that even if it meant going to prison, he could not keep the secret any longer. Johnson agreed to help the authorities locate the other two men who were involved in the robbery.

Sometimes we think the best approach is to hide our sin, either to avoid embarrassment and exposure, or to avoid the potential consequences. That approach never works in the long run. There is a God who sees everything—nothing is ever hidden from His view. His hatred of sin is so intense that He will never allow us to prosper by covering our sin. The toll of hidden sin on the physical, emotional, and spiritual health of the sinner is vast. It is far better for us to confess and seek the mercy and forgiveness of God.

Today's Word to the Wise: Hidden sin destroys the one who hides it from the inside out—confess immediately and find God's mercy.

2 Chronicles 4–6 » John 10:24–42 » Proverbs 28

Pride Brings Us Low

A man's pride shall bring him low: but honour shall uphold the humble in spirit.—**Proverbs 29:23**

Evangelist J. Wilbur Chapman told of a father and son in Scotland who were taking a walk in the wintertime. It was cold, and the boy had his hands in the pockets of his overcoat. As they came to some slippery rocks, the father said, "You had better let me now hold your hand." But the little boy didn't want to take his hands out, so he refused. In just a few moments, his feet slipped and he took a hard fall.

The boy reconsidered his former position, but not all the way. Now he said, "I will take your hand." He reached up and clung to his father's hand as strongly as he could. When they came to the next slippery place, his grip was not strong enough to hold him up, and he fell once again. This time his pain overcame his pride. "You may take it now," he said to his father. The older man took the boy's hand tightly in his. Every time they came to a slick place, he kept the boy from falling.

That is a wonderful illustration of the pain and heartbreak that pride brings into our lives. When we insist on going our own way and fighting our battles in our strength, we will always fail. Only when God's hand holds us and lifts us up can we possibly succeed. James said, "But he giveth more grace. Wherefore he saith, God resisteth the proud, but giveth grace unto the humble" (James 4:6). Nebuchadnezzar learned this truth in great sorrow when he refused to give up his pride. God turned the mighty ruler into little more than an animal for seven years until he was willing to recognize that it was not him but God who truly ruled. At the end of this time, he humbly reflected, "And those that walk in pride he is able to abase" (Daniel 4:37).

God still gives grace to the humble. When you in humility ask Him for his help, He will always honor your request.

Today's Word to the Wise: When you humble yourself, you break down the barrier that hinders God's work in your life.

The Strength of Preparation

The ants are a people not strong, yet they prepare their meat in the summer;—**Proverbs 30:25**

In the London Olympic Games, skeet shooter Kim Rhode did something no one else had ever done before—won her fifth gold medal in five consecutive Olympics. She was just a teenager when she won her first gold medal in the Atlanta Games in 1996, making her the youngest shooting gold medalist in history. She successfully defended her title again and again. In fact, in London she set a new Olympic record by hitting 99 out of 100 targets.

Her secret? According to an interview in The New York Times, Rhode fires between 500 and 1000 shells every single day all year long. Her estimate is that she has fired at more than 3,000,000 targets. The truth is that Kim Rhode did not really win the gold medal in London— she won it by going to the range every day and preparing herself so thoroughly that she was able to perform at the highest level when the decisive moment came.

All of us who wish to serve God must be willing to pay the price to prepare for that service. Paul wrote to Timothy, "If a man therefore purge himself from these, he shall be a vessel unto honour, sanctified, and meet for the master's use, and prepared unto every good work" (2 Timothy 2:21). Sometimes we put the cart before the horse by trying to be of service without first making sure that our lives are ready for use.

This of course does not mean that we cannot do anything for God until some far off day in the future when everything is perfected. If we take that approach we will never do anything. Instead it means that we are to be daily preparing in such a way that when the moments of challenge and opportunity arise, we are ready to glorify Him.

Today's Word to the Wise: You will never accomplish all that you can and should for God unless you first prepare yourself for His use.

Kind Words

She openeth her mouth with wisdom; and in her tongue is the law of kindness.—**Proverbs 31:26**

It is impossible to overstate the power that our words have on others. A great illustration of this truth is found in the life of Winston Churchill. Churchill's father was so focused on his career that he had little time for his son. In the biography *Winston Churchill: The Era and the Man,* Virginia Cowles described the incredible impact that never receiving his father's approval had on young Churchill. He was shocked and pained to find that his father approved of his desire to join the army, not because he thought it was a good idea but because he thought the boy was too dumb to do anything else.

Churchill's father never invested in building their relationship. Cowles writes: "Winston was eagerly awaiting the day when his father would accept him as an equal. During the boy's two years at Sandhurst, Lord Randolph had occasionally taken him to dinners and weekend parties and he was confident that they were moving toward a closer understanding. But Lord Randolph never really dropped his mask. 'If ever I began to show the slightest idea of comradeship, he was immediately offended,' Winston wrote many years later, 'and when once I suggested that I might help his private secretary to write some letters, he froze me into stone.'"

Churchill's father died when he was still a very young man, and he never received the approval he so desperately sought. When we express praise or condemnation, we are shaping the view others have of themselves in powerful ways. While there are times when correction is needed, even then we should address the other person with kindness. Reproof is usually far better received when it is kindly delivered rather than harshly spoken. Since our words have so much power, it is important that we choose them with wisdom.

Today's Word to the Wise: Choose your words with care so that they are kind and edifying to those who hear them.

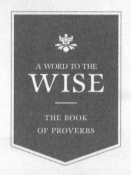

A WORD TO THE

WISE

—

THE BOOK
OF PROVERBS

JUNE

Choosing to Fear God

For that they hated knowledge, and did not choose the fear of the LORD:
—Proverbs 1:29

A reporter saw Jim Taylor, star running back on the Green Bay Packers football team standing in the team's hotel lobby more than forty-five minutes before the bus was scheduled to take the team to the stadium for a playoff game. "Why are you here so early, Jim?" he asked. "I don't want to get left at the hotel," the Hall of Fame running back answered. The Packers were coached by Vince Lombardi, and soon after his arrival in Green Bay, he instituted a schedule that came to be known as "Lombardi Time." He would announce the start of a practice or the departure time for an event, only to begin early—either leaving those who showed up "on time" behind or critiquing them for being late.

The essence of Lombardi Time is that if you were not fifteen minutes "early" you were late. In honor of the famed coach, the clock at Lambeau Field that faces Lombardi Avenue is still set fifteen minutes ahead. Lombardi was known as a fierce disciplinarian, and his players were expected to comply with his rules without question or argument. Despite his great talent, Jim Taylor was more afraid of disappointing his coach than of almost anything else.

Many people in our society today view God casually. This is not just true in the world, but sadly this attitude has also infected the church. Despite this tide of neglect for the character and nature of God, we must make the choice to swim against the current and maintain our fear of the Lord in recognition of His holiness. When Isaiah saw a glimpse of God's throne in Heaven he said, "Woe is me! for I am undone...for mine eyes have seen the King" (Isaiah 6:5). Make it your choice to maintain a holy fear of God.

Today's Word to the Wise: Choose to fear God and you will be protected from many dangers.

The Paths of the Righteous

That thou mayest walk in the way of good men, and keep the paths of the righteous.—**Proverbs 2:20**

In a remote mountainous region in central China, there lies what many hikers believe is one of the most dangerous hiking trails in the world. Along the south peak of Mt. Huashan, a trail winds its way to a summit approximately a mile and half high. The views are breathtaking, but you literally take your life in your hands to get there. One particularly notable section of "trail" close to the peak is known as *Changkong Zhandao* or "Floating in Air Road." For some two hundred feet there is no trail but a narrow wooden walkway fastened to the side of the sheer cliff with an iron chain attached above to cling to as you make your way along. Because of the elevation, snowstorms can arise with little warning, leaving the steep trail and steps covered with ice. Without extreme care, hikers can find that mountain trail dangerous and even deadly.

As we make our way through life, God has given us a path to follow and instructions to obey. The prophet Isaiah said, "And thine ears shall hear a word behind thee, saying, This is the way, walk ye in it, when ye turn to the right hand, and when ye turn to the left" (Isaiah 30:21). In the pages of Scripture we find the guidelines which allow us to walk safely through the world. The enemy attempts to get us off course, luring us into danger.

While some of his bypaths may seem alluring, there is only one safe path for us to take—the path of the righteous. Every sin is a step off that path and leads to destruction. Instead of taking risks to see how far we can go without disaster, we should stay safely on God's course.

Today's Word to the Wise: While there are many temptations to lead us away from the paths of righteousness, we must remember that they all lead to disaster.

Incomparable Riches

Happy is the man that findeth wisdom, and the man that getteth understanding. For the merchandise of it is better than the merchandise of silver, and the gain thereof than fine gold. She is more precious than rubies: and all the things thou canst desire are not to be compared unto her.—**Proverbs 3:13–15**

Though his grandfather and uncle were well-known preachers, Robert Rundle initially planned a career in the business world. But God burdened his heart for missions while he was in school, and Rundle determined to go to western Canada and work among the Cree Indians. He arrived in Fort Edmonton, Saskatchewan in 1840. For the next eight years he traveled and ministered in the wild country, taking the gospel to remote areas. Badly injured in a horseback accident, he was forced to return to England. His health never allowed him to return to the mission field, and he pastored for much of the rest of his life.

Near the resort town of Banff, Alberta, Mount Rundle, which is named in Robert Rundle's honor, towers in the Canadian Rockies. Though Rundle did not see massive numeric results, his sacrifice and ministry left a lasting impact. The Cree Indians said of Rundle, "He came among us poor, and poor he went away, leaving us rich." The world would hardly judge Rundle a success, but God measures with a different standard.

The way we spend our time, our talents, and our resources reveals a great deal about what matters the most to us. There are some who gain great worldly wealth and yet have very little in the eyes of God. A man with much gold is highly esteemed here on Earth, yet in Heaven God uses gold to pave the street. Instead of focusing on the temporal, we should devote our lives to that which is eternal—that which is worth far more than any form of wealth.

Today's Word to the Wise: If you devote your life to that which matters for eternity, you will accumulate true riches which can never be lost.

Holding on for Dear Life

Take fast hold of instruction; let her not go: keep her; for she is thy life.—**Proverbs 4:13**

In April of 2011, a line of deadly tornadoes ripped across the state of Alabama, leaving 250 people dead in its wake. Near Wellington, Alabama, the Hardy family realized the storm was coming too late to find a permanent shelter. They considered trying to take shelter in a metal clubhouse, but it had already been turned on its side by the strong winds. In desperation, they took shelter in a small stand of trees. They tied a rope around the children and huddled around them in the trees as the storm passed. A family member said that while they had been scratched by flying dirt and debris, no one suffered serious injuries.

Imagine how tightly you would cling to the trees and rope in such a situation. The fact that your life or the life of your child might depend on your grip would give you all the motivation you needed to hang on with every ounce of power you could muster.

Although there are no warning sirens or news alerts, each of us is living in the path of destructive storms. There are temptations and destructive philosophies abounding around us. If we do not have a secure place of protection, we will be destroyed.

Because the Word of God is so readily available to us, we often take it for granted rather than treasuring it as the precious resource it is. When you view the Bible as a lifeline designed to keep you safe through the storms of life, you begin to take it more seriously. If you knew the truth you were hearing in church on Sunday was the difference between life and death, you wouldn't have trouble listening to the message. If you remembered that your daily time in God's Word was your lifeline to spiritual strength, you would be less likely to neglect it. Truth is that important, and it deserves our careful attention.

Today's Word to the Wise: When we understand how important God's principles for wise living are, we will cling tightly to them.

The Deceitfulness of Sin

Her feet go down to death; her steps take hold on hell. Lest thou shouldest ponder the path of life, her ways are moveable, that thou canst not know them.—**Proverbs 5:5–6**

One of the largest freshwater turtles is the alligator snapping turtle. Found primarily in the southeastern United States, these massive turtles have been known to weigh as much as 250 pounds. They are carnivorous, and while their diet is primarily fish, they have been known to eat almost anything else they can find in the water—even small alligators. Though they are very large, the force of their jaws is not greater than that of other turtles. Instead of force, the alligator snapping turtle relies on a uniquely deceitful method of foraging for fish.

The turtle will lie completely still on the floor of a lake or river with its mouth wide open. At the end of the turtle's tongue is a small, pink, worm-shaped appendage. The turtle wiggles the end of its tongue so that it looks like a worm moving through the water. When a fish comes to eat the worm, the turtle's jaws rapidly close, trapping the fish so that it cannot escape.

Similarly to the snapping turtle's lure, temptation comes in the guise of something desirable, but it always ends in destruction. If we could see the ruin rather than the temptation, it would be far easier to resist. Satan knows this, so he cleverly disguises what is deadly in the guise of something pleasurable. If the devil came to us in a red suit with a pitchfork and forked tail, we would not be tempted. Instead as Paul wrote, "Satan himself is transformed into an angel of light" (2 Corinthians 11:14). Recognizing that our enemy is a master of disguise, both for himself and in his temptations, we need to always be on guard to protect our purity.

Today's Word to the Wise: When sin seems most alluring, remember the certainty of destruction at the end of the path of sin.

Get Out!

Do this now, my son, and deliver thyself, when thou art come into the hand of thy friend; go, humble thyself, and make sure thy friend. Give not sleep to thine eyes, nor slumber to thine eyelids. Deliver thyself as a roe from the hand of the hunter, and as a bird from the hand of the fowler.—**Proverbs 6:3–5**

The final eruption of Mount St. Helens in May of 1980 was not a sudden event. For two months prior to the massive blast—the most deadly and destructive in American history—earthquakes and volcanic activity signaled a major event was underway. Authorities had plenty of time to sound the alarm and warn those living nearby of the looming danger. Despite the seriousness of the threat, some people chose to disregard the warnings.

Of those who refused to evacuate, probably the best known is Harry Randall Truman. The eighty-three-year-old man was the owner and caretaker at the Mount St. Helens Lodge at Spirit Lake. He had survived the sinking of his troop ship by a German submarine off the coast of Ireland during World War I, and he was not about to leave just because scientists thought there was danger. Truman told reporters, "I don't have any idea whether it will blow. But I don't believe it to the point that I'm going to pack up." On May 18, 1980, Truman and his lodge were buried beneath 150 feet of mud and debris from the volcanic eruption. His body was never found.

It is foolish to recognize the danger or temptation and think that we will somehow be exempt from the consequences if we linger. If we believe Scriptures' warnings concerning temptation, we will surely flee. The only real protection that we have is the approach taken by Joseph when he was tempted by Potiphar's wife. "…and he left his garment in her hand, and fled, and got him out" (Genesis 39:12).

Today's Word to the Wise: Every place of temptation is a place of deadly peril—heed God's warning and flee.

Until the Morning

Come, let us take our fill of love until the morning: let us solace ourselves with loves.—**Proverbs 7:18**

Just five days after accepting the position as head coach of the Notre Dame Fighting Irish football team, George O'Leary resigned in disgrace. An investigation revealed that more than twenty years before he had included false claims on his résumé, including saying that he had lettered in football when he was not even on the team and that he had a master's degree which he had not earned. The lies had not been discovered at any of his previous coaching jobs, but the high profile of the position at Notre Dame led to his exposure.

In a statement O'Leary said: "Due to a selfish and thoughtless act many years ago, I have personally embarrassed Notre Dame, its alumni, and fans. With that in mind, I will resign my position as head football coach." Though a considerable amount of time had passed between O'Leary's deception and its discovery, it did come to light with devastating results. He had seemingly reached the heights of his profession, only to wake up and find it all taken away.

When we are tempted with the allure of sin, we must remember that no matter how enjoyable the sin may be in the moment, there will certainly come a day of reckoning. This is the decision that Moses faced, and the Bible says he responded: "Choosing rather to suffer affliction with the people of God, than to enjoy the pleasures of sin for a season" (Hebrews 11:25).

No one has ever successfully sinned without consequence. Though sin may be hidden for days, weeks, or even years, "God is not mocked: for whatsoever a man soweth, that shall he also reap" (Galatians 6:7). Contemplating the coming of morning and the day when we must account for what we have done will help us resist temptation.

Today's Word to the Wise: Do not fall for the lie of Satan that you can sin without consequence—morning always comes.

Our Faithful God

When he gave to the sea his decree, that the waters should not pass his commandment: when he appointed the foundations of the earth:
—Proverbs 8:29

John Newton was a wicked and immoral man before his conversion. Active in the slave trade which he would later work hard to outlaw, Newton was on his way home to England from Africa when a storm nearly sank his ship and he cried out to God for mercy. Newton eventually became a faithful pastor in Olney, England, where he wrote the poem we know as the wonderful hymn "Amazing Grace." Late in his life Newton was almost completely blind and deaf, but he insisted on continuing to do what he could for the Lord.

In his diary Newton wrote: "Oh, for grace to meet the approach of death with a humble, thankful, resigned spirit becoming my profession. That I may not stain my character by impatience, jealousy, or any hateful temper but may be prepared and permitted to depart in peace and hope and be enabled, if I can speak, to bear my testimony to thy faithfulness and goodness with my last breath. Amen." A friend who visited Newton just before his death recorded some of his final words. Newton told his friend, "My memory is nearly gone, but I remember two things: That I am a great sinner and that Christ is a great Saviour."

No matter what else happens in our lives, we can always rely on the faithfulness of God. From the very creation of the world all of His decrees and promises have been kept. His Word never fails, and we can trust Him to keep His promises. Trials and difficulties do not shake our faith when we focus on the God who never changes. The author of Hebrews wrote, "Jesus Christ the same yesterday, and to day, and for ever" (Hebrews 13:8).

Today's Word to the Wise: No matter how difficult things may seem, you can always count on God to be faithful and to keep His promises.

The Invitation of Wisdom

She hath sent forth her maidens: she crieth upon the highest places of the city, Whoso is simple, let him turn in hither: as for him that wanteth understanding, she saith to him, Come, eat of my bread, and drink of the wine which I have mingled.—**Proverbs 9:3–5**

In his short story *The Masque of the Red Death* first published in 1842, Edgar Allen Poe describes a terrible plague sweeping across the land. Prince Prospero invites a number of noblemen to come to his palace to escape the plague. They lay in great stores of provisions, then weld the doors shut behind them to keep out the danger. Though the invitation appears to offer safety, in the end it only brings death as the plague is revealed at a great masked ball to already be within the palace.

In contrast, God offers an invitation to come and claim the wisdom that provides safety, security, and protection from danger. His invitation is genuine, and we should eagerly respond to it.

When we answer the invitation of wisdom—God promises to give it to us freely. James said, "If any of you lack wisdom, let him ask of God, that giveth to all men liberally, and upbraideth not; and it shall be given him" (James 1:5). Because our need of wisdom is so great, God graciously provides it when we ask.

Why then do God's people not always have the wisdom they need? Part of the answer is found in the invitation of wisdom: it is extended to those who are willing to acknowledge their need. The invitation is extended to the "simple"—those who need instruction. When God appeared to Solomon and offered him whatever he desired, the young king responded, "I am but a little child: I know not how to go out or come in" (1 Kings 3:7). Solomon was wise enough to see his need for wisdom, and he was humble enough to ask for it. God will give us wisdom if we will but acknowledge our need and ask Him for it.

Today's Word to the Wise: If you answer the invitation of wisdom, every part of your life and service for God will be improved.

Missed Opportunities

He that gathereth in summer is a wise son: but he that sleepeth in harvest is a son that causeth shame.—**Proverbs 10:5**

The three days of fighting at Gettysburg, Pennsylvania, in early July, 1863, were a major turning point of the Civil War—but they could have been even more decisive. The final day of the battle saw a major defeat for the Confederate army under General Robert E. Lee, and he was forced to retreat from the battlefield. When his army reached the Potomac River, Lee found it in flood stage and was unable to cross. It was ten days before Lee was able to get his men across the river and back to safety in Virginia.

During those ten days, General George Meade of the Union Army did not attack. Lee's forces were trapped against the river and badly outnumbered. They were low on supplies and ammunition following the great battle and probably could have been crushed with a decisive attack. Instead Meade dithered, and as a result, the war lasted almost two more years. Meade's failure to seize that opportunity caused great hardship and suffering. Eventually it would be the more decisive General U. S. Grant who would defeat Lee and end the war.

Someone wisely said, "The opportunity of a lifetime must be seized in the lifetime of the opportunity." There is a season for harvest, and if we do not take advantage of it, that opportunity may well be gone forever. Though there are sometimes second chances, some opportunities once lost can never be regained. We should wisely take advantage of the things God places in our paths. An opportunity to witness to a lost person, to comfort one who is grieving, or to meet a need of someone who is suffering may never come again. Do what you can today, realizing that none of us are given the promise of tomorrow.

Today's Word to the Wise: Be alert to the opportunities you have—if they are not seized immediately they may be lost forever.

Keep What Is Precious

A gracious woman retaineth honour: and strong men retain riches.
—Proverbs 11:16

Things bought at garage sales don't usually end up on the evening news, but a Chinese bowl bought by a New York family in 2007 became famous in April of 2013. The new owners paid just three dollars for what turned out to be a bowl from the Northern Song Dynasty that was more than one thousand years old. Until someone told them what they really had, the family had the bowl stuck on the mantle over their fireplace. When they placed the bowl with Sotheby's Auction House for sale, it was estimated to go for approximately $200,000. Instead a dealer from London purchased it for more than $2,000,000.

Why would the first owners sell something so valuable for just three dollars? The answer is that they didn't appreciate what it was worth. We may shake our heads at that, but the truth is that every day men and women give up things far more valuable than money could buy for something that is ultimately worthless.

When a woman sacrifices her integrity and steals from her employer to be able to buy something she wants or a man sacrifices his purity to commit immorality to satisfy his lust, something of great worth is being given up for something very cheap. This is a clear indication of misplaced values. When parents ignore their children's need to further a career (or even a ministry), they are giving up something that cannot be regained for the sake of something that will not last.

We need to live by God's values—caring most about those things that matter most to Him. This commitment must be demonstrated not just in our words but in the way we invest our time and our resources. When we value things that matter, we will not give them away cheaply.

Today's Word to the Wise: Don't make the mistake of giving away what is truly valuable and precious for that which is fleeting.

The Triumph of Truth

The lip of truth shall be established for ever: but a lying tongue is but for a moment.—**Proverbs 12:19**

In one of his addresses to ministerial students, Charles Spurgeon related the following story. "On one occasion, when Mr. Wesley was preaching, he said, 'I have been falsely charged with every crime of which a human being is capable, except that of drunkenness.' He had scarcely uttered these words before a wretched woman started up and screamed out at the top of her voice, 'You old villain, and will you deny it? Did you not pledge your bands last night for a noggin of whisky, and did not the woman sell them to our parson's wife?' Having delivered herself of this abominable calumny the virago sat down amid a thunder-struck assembly, whereupon Mr. Wesley lifted his hands to Heaven, and thanked God that his cup was now full, for they had said *all* manner of evil against him falsely for Christ's name-sake."

Doing right is certainly no guarantee that people will speak well of you. In fact, in some cases it seems to motivate them to criticize and condemn, even when they cannot do so honestly. That does not mean, however, that you have to descend to their level and answer falsehood with falsehood. Honesty and integrity establish a foundation that cannot be destroyed from the outside in, only from the inside out.

There may be a temporary benefit derived from lying. People often lie to get out of trouble or to prevent something they have done from being discovered, but any such benefits will always be short lived. The truth will eventually be revealed, and those who commit to it in the beginning find themselves vindicated in the end. In the final analysis, what others say of us doesn't matter compared to what God says. God weighs us in the balance of truth.

Today's Word to the Wise: Do not let false accusations derail you from doing right. God guarantees that truth will prevail in the end.

The Company You Keep

He that walketh with wise men shall be wise: but a companion of fools shall be destroyed.—**Proverbs 13:20**

The courtroom was hushed as Saleem Williams testified that his friend, nineteen-year-old Monique Robinson, had handed him the gun and told him to pull the trigger. Williams had already pled guilty to his role in the September 2011 murder of a twenty-two year old man in Phoenixville, Pennsylvania, named Selvin Lopez-Mauricio. Now he was testifying against Robinson, his girlfriend, as part of his agreement with prosecutors. Williams claimed that he would not have been involved in the murder at all except for her influence.

The people we choose as our close friends and companions truly have a dramatic and powerful influence on our lives. Someone said, "You will be the same in five years as you are now except for the books you read and the people you meet." Those with whom we choose to spend our time have a powerful influence on us, either for good or evil.

There are no neutral parties when it comes to influence. We either spend our time with those who are wise and are better for it, or we spend our time with those who are foolish and suffer the consequences.

There is an old saying, "A man is known by the company he keeps." While that statement is true, it is only part of the picture. Not only does the character and nature of those with whom we fellowship say something about us, but it shapes and molds who we are as well. While we should strive to be a positive influence and role model for others, it is foolish to spend all of our time with people of bad influences and not expect them to impact our lives and character. Healthy people don't make contagious people well by being around them—they just get sick themselves.

Today's Word to the Wise: Select your friends carefully—you are making a choice not just of companions but of your very future.

Don't Buy that Bridge

The simple believeth every word: but the prudent man looketh well to his going.—**Proverbs 14:15**

In the long history of con artists, George C. Parker holds a special place of dishonor. He is remembered as one of the most successful and daring swindlers in American history. He set up an office in New York City and "sold" some of the city's most famous attractions to tourists. His favorite was the Brooklyn Bridge, but he also sold the Statue of Liberty, Madison Square Garden, and Grant's Tomb. He produced elaborately forged documents and deeds to convince his targets that he was the rightful owner of the landmarks he was selling.

Parker was so persuasive that on more than one occasion, police had to come and explain why the new "owners" of the Brooklyn Bridge couldn't put up tollbooths to collect money from those who tried to cross. After his third conviction for fraud, Parker was sentenced to life at Sing Sing Prison in New York, where he spent the last eight years of his life. He dishonestly made a fortune preying on people who foolishly believed his empty words. He was not only an expert salesman, but he realized that many people were gullible and he used that to his advantage.

God expects us to be careful and prudent with the resources that He entrusts to us. Of course, this applies to far more than financial matters. Prudence and wisdom also keep us from falling for the lies of temptation and protect us from great suffering and heartbreak. We should not be easily fooled, but rather we should investigate what we are told and be certain that it is true before making a decision. Paul wrote, "See then that ye walk circumspectly, not as fools, but as wise" (Ephesians 5:15). Develop godly discernment through reading and meditating on God's truths and remaining responsive to the Holy Spirit. Walking with prudence will save you from a world of sorrow.

Today's Word to the Wise: Though we should not go through life as cynics, we also should not gullibly believe everything we are told.

When Less Is More

Better is little with the fear of the LORD than great treasure and trouble therewith. Better is a dinner of herbs where love is, than a stalled ox and hatred therewith.—**Proverbs 15:16–17**

In his narrative poem "The Faultless Painter" about the Italian artist Andrea del Sarto, Robert Browning used the expression "less is more." Because of his careful attention to detail, del Sarto was known as a painter *senza errori*—without errors. However, his perfectionism also seems to have reduced his output. It was this tendency that Browning highlighted with the phrase that has entered into our language. Though the expression "less is more" is often true, it seems many struggle with understanding the spiritual truth behind the words.

There is a driving spirit of discontent in our day that makes it hard for people to be satisfied with what they have. In truth, if our focus is on our "stuff" we will never be content because there is always one more thing that we don't have or one more person who has more. Ecclesiastes 5:10 says it this way: "He that loveth silver shall not be satisfied with silver; nor he that loveth abundance with increase: this is also vanity." No matter how much we get, it will never be enough.

There are some things far more important than possessions. If we have those things we will be content even if there are no great material blessings. It is in that contentment that we will find something that cannot be purchased for any amount of money.

It is said that on her deathbed Queen Elizabeth I said, "All my possessions for one moment of time." Though she was fabulously wealthy, in the end even her resources could not purchase what she wanted most. Let our hearts be set on that which is eternal, and we can be truly happy.

Today's Word to the Wise: If you love and fear God as you should, the number and value of your possessions will not be your primary focus.

A Balanced Father

By mercy and truth iniquity is purged: and by the fear of the LORD men depart from evil.—**Proverbs 16:6**

Charles Spurgeon told of a godly Christian man who became a magistrate in the Scottish village of Wishaw. One day a man was brought into his courtroom who had been the judge's childhood friend. Their paths had diverged, and while the judge did right, his friend had lived a life of sin and crime. Those in the courtroom who knew the relationship between the two thought that the judge might go easy on his old friend. Instead he sentenced him to the maximum fine for his offense.

Once the sentence had been pronounced, the judge left the bench, went to the officer of the court, and paid the fine from his own pocket. He both did his duty as a judge in upholding the law and showed mercy toward his old friend by paying the fine. This balance of truth and mercy is vitally important for fathers as they work to rear their children "in the nurture and admonition of the Lord" (Ephesians 6:4). Too much focus on rules provokes rebellion. Too much focus on mercy promotes riotous living.

In this daunting task—bringing up children to love and fear God in a world that is radically opposed to Him and His law—fathers need to maintain this healthy balance between mercy and truth. By doing so, we are giving them a powerful illustration of how God deals with us.

It was a sobering realization to me as a dad that much of our children's view of God would be shaped by how I treated them as their father. Truly this is a task beyond human strength. "Except the LORD build the house, they labour in vain that build it" (Psalm 127:1). But He will help as we ask for His power and wisdom for this vital task.

Today's Word to the Wise: By setting a godly example of the balance of mercy and truth, fathers prepare their children to walk with God.

Stop Before You Start

The beginning of strife is as when one letteth out water: therefore leave off contention, before it be meddled with.—**Proverbs 17:14**

In June of 2012, a large wildfire threatened the town of Elbert, Colorado. Many people were forced to evacuate their homes, and it took more than one hundred firefighters to finally control the blaze which consumed more than six hundred acres. Alex Averette, a member of the volunteer fire department, was the first to spot and report the blaze. Months later he admitted to investigators that he had started a small fire with a cigarette lighter "for the experience." But the fire quickly grew out of control and threatened thousands of lives. Averette was arrested and charged with arson.

Many times we think we will be able to control the consequences of a word or action, only to find that things rapidly spin out of control. It is impossible to gather water back up after it is poured on the ground. Likewise, it is very difficult to restore broken relationships once careless words and deeds have damaged them. Before the fight has started, there is no problem keeping things in check. Once it has begun, however, things often spiral far beyond what was intended in the beginning and the problems become much more difficult to resolve.

Just as the difficulty of overcoming a habit like smoking can be avoided by never starting it, the problem of restoring a battered relationship can be avoided by not allowing the conflict to begin. While there are some things that are worth fighting for—such as the truth of the gospel—in many cases it is simply a matter of pride that causes a battle to begin. Like water that is poured out, the words once spoken cannot be recalled. God expects us to control our tongues through the power of His Spirit, and when we do, we will avoid damaging our relationships.

Today's Word to the Wise: Avoiding arguments and broken relationships is much easier than picking up the pieces after a pointless conflict.

The Mouth of the Fool

A fool's lips enter into contention, and his mouth calleth for strokes. A fool's mouth is his destruction, and his lips are the snare of his soul.
—**Proverbs 18:6–7**

When the Cornerstone Bank in Waco, Nebraska, was robbed of $6,000 in November of 2012, the bank employees were able to give the police a fairly good description of the teenage girl who pulled off the crime and the car in which she escaped. As it turned out, the investigators didn't really need those descriptions, because the thief recorded a YouTube video boasting of her criminal prowess.

Fanning out the cash in front of the camera, nineteen-year-old Hannah Sabata held up a sign that read, "I just stole a car and robbed a bank. Now I'm rich, I can pay off my college financial aid, and tomorrow I'm going for a shopping spree." Later she held up another sign which said, "I told my mom today was the best day of my life…she just thinks I met a new boy." Hannah's brief criminal career ended later that week when police took her into custody.

The number of people who have gotten into trouble because of something they said goes far beyond boasting criminals. Lies, gossip, criticism, and slander will damage, not just those about whom they are spoken, but the speaker as well. The words that come from our mouths reveal the condition of our hearts and minds. Jesus said, "O generation of vipers, how can ye, being evil, speak good things? for out of the abundance of the heart the mouth speaketh" (Matthew 12:34).

We should exercise great care in our speech, knowing the power of our words. Though there is a time when we should speak, more often the problem comes from speaking too much instead of speaking too little. Let wisdom guide every conversation.

Today's Word to the Wise: The words that we speak reveal the condition of our hearts and can bring blessing or calamity upon us. We should be careful to choose them wisely.

The Value of Correction

Smite a scorner, and the simple will beware: and reprove one that hath understanding, and he will understand knowledge.—**Proverbs 19:25**

As the 1963 college football season drew to a close, Alabama coach Bear Bryant faced a dilemma. He was known as a strict disciplinarian, but his star player, quarterback Joe Namath, had broken a team rule. Normally he would be suspended, but with the Sugar Bowl against highly ranked Mississippi coming up, that meant the team would be forced to use a lesser player and might not win the game. Most of Bryant's staff opposed a suspension, but in the end, Bryant enforced the rule. Namath sat and watched as his teammates pulled out a 12–7 win without his help.

The message was received loud and clear, not just by Namath but also by every other member of the team—no one is above the rules. The following season, Namath returned to the team and led a highly focused group to an undefeated regular season and the national championship. His public correction benefitted him, but its biggest impact was probably on his teammates. They received the benefit of the principle Paul relayed to Timothy: "Them that sin rebuke before all, that others also may fear" (1 Timothy 5:20).

When we correct those who do wrong, we provide a vital example to all who see it. If they see people sinning and getting by, they are tempted to follow their example. Solomon wrote, "Because sentence against an evil work is not executed speedily, therefore the heart of the sons of men is fully set in them to do evil" (Ecclesiastes 8:11).

For those whose hearts are devoted to wisdom, correction is not a grievous insult, but rather an opportunity to increase their understanding and avoid mistakes in the future. If we respond in pride and anger when we are reproved rather than with gratitude and humility, we are missing one of God's great tools to impart wisdom to us.

Today's Word to the Wise: One of the important reasons for enforcing discipline is the impact that seeing correction has on others.

Known by Our Actions

Even a child is known by his doings, whether his work be pure, and whether it be right.—**Proverbs 20:11**

In his story "The Goat and the Goatherd," Aesop tells of a young man who was charged with tending a flock of goats. One of the goats wandered off and refused to return. The boy called him, whistled to him, and shouted at him, but the goat would not budge. Finally the exasperated youth threw a rock at the goat. It hit the goat and broke his horn. Afraid that he would get in trouble for harming the animal, the goatherd begged the goat not to say anything to the owner. The goat replied, "You silly fellow, the horn will speak though I be silent."

Though it may be possible for a time to deceive people by our words, eventually our actions will reveal what is really in our hearts. In the final analysis, what we do holds far more weight than what we say in shaping how others view us. If we say all the right things but do not match those words with our deeds, our message will be lost in the fog of hypocrisy. The world is looking for believers whose lives match what they profess to believe. There is enormous power in a witness that is supported by a life.

James wrote, "But whoso looketh into the perfect law of liberty, and continueth therein, he being not a forgetful hearer, but a doer of the work, this man shall be blessed in his deed" (James 1:25). God blesses those who do what they read in His Word. The prayers for blessing some people offer are not answered because their deeds do not place them in a position to receive God's blessing. Recognizing the importance of our testimony, it is vital that our deeds, both in public and in private, are in keeping with what we proclaim as the truth.

Today's Word to the Wise: Your actions carry far more weight in establishing your testimony than do your words.

Esther 1–2 » Acts 5:1–21 » Proverbs 20

The Poverty of Pursuing Pleasure

He that loveth pleasure shall be a poor man: he that loveth wine and oil shall not be rich.—**Proverbs 21:17**

We live in a society that is obsessed with the pursuit of pleasure. While this is not a new thing, the lengths to which it is being taken today are beyond what has been known throughout most of history. The airwaves are filled with ads which promise happiness and success for those who have more stuff than they know what to do with. These ads are used for everything from cars to toothpaste. But they—and the mindset they promote—are based on a lie.

A study published in *US News and World Report* some years ago did some digging into what people's expectation of life really was. Rather than just asking general questions, those who conducted the study were specific about what people thought they would need to have in order to feel like they had achieved the "American Dream." Interestingly enough, the responses were quite similar regardless of the current income the respondents had. For the average person in the study to feel like they had made it, based on their specific answers for what kinds of things they wanted, their income would need to basically double. This was true for those making $25,000 and those making $100,000. When you added up all the possessions and purchases that they felt would make them content, it was roughly twice as much money as they currently had—and that clearly isn't attainable for most people.

As those around us focus on increasing their income, to increase their ability to spend, to increase their appetite for more, they do not realize that they are chasing a circular dream that can never make them happy. No amount of money and no group of belongings can bring contentment to a heart that does not already hold it.

Today's Word to the Wise: Because happiness can never be found in accumulating possessions, we should abandon the fruitless quest and seek God instead.

The Friendship of Angry Men

Make no friendship with an angry man; and with a furious man thou shalt not go: Lest thou learn his ways, and get a snare to thy soul.
—Proverbs 22:24–25

In March of 1991, a twenty-four-year-old man named Carl Kerr went to a friend's house along with several other people. He and his friend, twenty-one-year-old John Sheppard, were drinking and watching television when an argument broke out. Witnesses later told police that while Sheppard was normally even-tempered, he "got very angry when things didn't go his way." He left the room and returned with an ax and struck Kerr with it nine times, killing him. After just ninety minutes of deliberation, the jury found Sheppard guilty, and he was sentenced to life in prison without the possibility of parole.

While that is an extreme example of the principle Solomon lays out for us in Proverbs on the danger of friendship with an angry man, the damage done by such relationships is a real danger. Even if we never suffer direct physical harm, we are learning a destructive pattern of behavior when we keep company with those who cannot keep control of their emotions and anger.

The friends with whom we choose to develop relationships and spend time have an enormous impact on our lives. They help shape our attitudes and our responses when things go right and when things go wrong. While a good friend helps us do what is right (think of Jonathan and David as an example of the power of such a relationship), a bad friend helps us do what is wrong (think of Jonadab and Amnon).

The reality is that we do not choose the impact our friends have on us. That happens automatically as a result of the relationship. The choice we have is in the friends we select. Choose your friends carefully because they will play a major role in determining your future.

Today's Word to the Wise: If you observe someone who is not exhibiting self-control, do not establish a friendship with them.

Hope and the Fear of the Lord

Let not thine heart envy sinners: but be thou in the fear of the LORD *all the day long. For surely there is an end; and thine expectation shall not be cut off.*—**Proverbs 23:17–18**

Many people lose their faith in God when they do not immediately see good rewarded and evil punished. Instead of continuing to believe and fear Him, their hearts turn away from following God and seek satisfaction elsewhere. Even if we do not quickly see what God has promised come to pass, it is still certain. Abraham waited twenty-five years for the birth of his promised son, Isaac. Though there was a moment when his faith wavered with Hagar, he continued to believe until the promise was fulfilled.

After Isaac was born, God instructed Abraham to offer him as a sacrifice. Rather than struggling against God's direction, Abraham obeyed. The level of his belief and fear of God commanded his obedience. Though no one had ever been raised from the dead at that point, Abraham believed that if he did what God said, Isaac would not remain dead. The Bible tells us that Abraham acted in faith, "Accounting that God was able to raise him up, even from the dead; from whence also he received him in a figure" (Hebrews 11:19). We should demonstrate that same level of hope and fear in our obedience as believers.

Though hope and fear may seem like opposite traits, our belief that God will do what He promises is reinforced by our fear of His holiness and righteousness. We can depend on His unchanging nature and unfailing love no matter what the circumstances may seem to be. We should never allow those who are doing evil and seem to be doing well to make us doubt the goodness of God—or His judgment of sin.

Today's Word to the Wise: Knowing that you can completely rely on God for everything gives you the hope to continue fearing Him no matter what happens.

Standing in Adversity

If thou faint in the day of adversity, thy strength is small.
—**Proverbs 24:10**

In April of 2007, Seung-Hui Cho, a senior at Virginia Tech University, went on a rampage. By the time his murderous spree ended in suicide, Cho had killed thirty-two people and wounded seventeen more. Most of those killed were shot as they sat in classes in the engineering school. Cho chained the doors shut to ensure it would be hard for his intended victims to escape. Panic broke out as students began to realize what was happening. When Cho came to one classroom, he found the door barred by the professor, seventy-six year old Liviu Librescu.

Librescu, a Romanian Jew who survived the Nazi Holocaust, told the students to open the windows and escape outside. He saved the lives of a number of his students before falling victim to the gunman's bullets. His son later told of the emails he received from young people who had been in the classroom when their professor saved their lives by literally placing himself in the line of fire. In the moment of adversity, his courage rose to the occasion and he proved himself a hero.

Most of us don't face tests that are quite that severe, but each of us faces moments when our faith and courage is put to the test. The opportunity to share the gospel with a friend or co-worker or stay silent, the temptation to take something that doesn't belong to us or leave it—these are moments of adversity. These moments do not *determine* whether or not we have strength of character—they *reveal* it. The crucible of adversity is the moment when what is in our hearts is shown to the world. Our responsibility to God is to live every day in His strength so that we do not fail the test.

Today's Word to the Wise: When the moment arises and you are put to the test, resolve to stand firm no matter what.

Apples of Gold

A word fitly spoken is like apples of gold in pictures of silver.
—**Proverbs 25:11**

John Bunyan is known for his famous allegory *Piligrim's Progress*. He wrote this book while imprisoned for preaching without a license from the Church of England. Before he became a preacher, however, Bunyan was a tinker in Bedford, England. He was a wicked man with no care or thought for the things of God. In his book *Grace Abounding*, Bunyan recounts the crucial events that placed him on the path to salvation. Bunyan wrote that he was sitting outside a neighbor's shop "cursing, swearing, and playing the madman, after my wonted manner."

A woman inside, though she was not a Christian herself, was shocked by the depth of Bunyan's profane declarations and told him that his words made her tremble. The unexpected reproof sobered Bunyan and took root in his heart. It even led him to consider the path on which he was headed. Not long after that experience, he was saved. Simple words of correction from an unsaved woman radically altered Bunyan's life.

Our words have great power. They can build up and encourage someone who is struggling, or they can tear down and discourage someone who is seeking help. When we choose our words, we should always be aware of the impact that they can have on others. David wrote, "I said, I will take heed to my ways, that I sin not with my tongue: I will keep my mouth with a bridle, while the wicked is before me" (Psalm 39:1).

There is a time for strong words in confrontation of sin. There is a time for comforting words when someone has a broken heart. There is a time for instructing words when someone needs guidance. Wisdom rightly assesses the situation and then uses words which are appropriate to meet the need of the moment.

Today's Word to the Wise: Since your words can have such a powerful impact on others, choose them carefully and be sure they are filled with grace.

Don't Grab the Dog's Ears

He that passeth by, and meddleth with strife belonging not to him, is like one that taketh a dog by the ears.—**Proverbs 26:17**

A Christian worker noticed that his young son was prone to getting involved in fights between two brothers who lived across the street. One day he took the boy on a walk. As they passed one house, a large German shepherd bounded into the yard and ran along the fence beside the sidewalk. The father waited for a moment and then asked, "Would you like to reach over the fence and grab his ears?" Of course the boy had no interest in that. Then the father quoted this verse and pointed out that by intervening in fights between the two other boys, he was doing something very much like that foolish act.

There are few people who face so little trouble in their own lives that they need to go borrowing it by getting involved in the strife of others. Yet for a variety of reasons, we often give in to the temptation to take part in a conflict that does not involve us. While these actions and interventions may be well-motivated, they are not the path to peace and serenity.

To put it bluntly, we should be minding our own business. If there is a role for us to play in a conflict, it will probably find us fairly quickly. There is no need to jump into other people's battles. If we feel the need to get involved, we should first spend time in careful evaluation to determine whether it is an area where we can contribute to an actual solution. Only if the answer to that is yes should we take part.

Today's Word to the Wise: You will have plenty of difficulty in your life without taking on struggles and conflicts that rightly belong to others.

Faithful Wounds

Faithful are the wounds of a friend; but the kisses of an enemy are deceitful.—**Proverbs 27:6**

Charles Spurgeon said, "Give me for a friend a man who will speak honestly of me before my face; who will not tell first one neighbor, and then another, but who will come straight to my house and say: 'I feel there is wrong in you, my brother, that I must tell you of.' That man is a true friend. He has proved himself to be so, for we never get any praise for telling people of their faults; we rather hazard their dislike."

Many people suffer because they lack a friend who is deep and committed enough to offer correction when it is needed. Often the reason no one points out a flaw in time for us to correct it without serious damage is found in our response to those who attempt to offer correction. A man or woman who responds with anger or frustration to such an attempt will soon stop receiving them—but that is a very dangerous position to be in.

Ecclesiastes 4:13 says, "Better is a poor and a wise child than an old and foolish king, who will no more be admonished." None of us are wise and godly enough not to need friends to help us improve. None of us are able to identify all of our blind spots and see where we may be vulnerable. Corporations pay huge sums of money to people who attempt to break through their security systems in order to identify weaknesses before they can be exploited. Our friends—true friends—provide such a warning system for us if we have the humility and wisdom to listen to them. The fact that correction comes from a friend does not make it painless. But we should view it as a needed wound—and appreciate it.

Today's Word to the Wise: Respond to your friends in such a way that they are willing to speak up when you need correction.

The Hunger of Vain Companions

He that tilleth his land shall have plenty of bread: but he that followeth after vain persons shall have poverty enough.—**Proverbs 28:19**

In the parable of the prodigal son, Jesus told of a young man who gravely insulted his father, took all of the money from his inheritance, and left home. In a land far away, his wealth made him the center of attention, but once his money was gone and a famine came, the boy found that all of his so-called friends had vanished. Knowing how Jewish people regard pigs, and knowing what pigs eat, think of the depths of desperation expressed in this statement: "And he would fain have filled his belly with the husks that the swine did eat: and no man gave unto him" (Luke 15:16).

The people who are our closest friends have an enormous influence on our lives. They are either setting good examples and encouraging us to do better, or they are setting bad examples and encouraging us to do things that are of no lasting value. The Hebrew word translated "vain" in Proverbs 28:19 is the same word used in Genesis 41:27 when Joseph interpreted Pharaoh's dream that warned of the coming famine. The seven years of famine were represented by "seven empty ears" of corn. They were ears of corn, but they had no value in them.

Those people who have no vision from God for their lives, who are not willing to labor to reach their vision and provide for their needs, are not productive people. While we should love, pray for, and encourage them, we should not make them our examples. A person who is surrounded by such people may start out working hard to do better, but over time they will be influenced by such vain companions. Instead look for people whose lives and attitudes challenge you to do more for God, and you will benefit greatly.

Today's Word to the Wise: If you surround yourself with empty people who have no drive and ambition, you will suffer poverty along with them.

The Rejoicing of the Righteous

In the transgression of an evil man there is a snare: but the righteous doth sing and rejoice.—**Proverbs 29:6**

In the early part of the 1600s, Germany suffered two huge tragedies. The Thirty Years' War, one of the longest periods of continual war in modern history, swept across Europe. In addition, the Bubonic Plague rampaged through the population. Millions perished from war and disease. The German town of Eilenburg had four pastors at the beginning of 1637, but by the end of the year, only one—Martin Rinkart—was left alive.

During that awful year, more than 4,400 people died. Rinkart conducted all of the funerals, sometimes as many as forty or fifty in a single day. In May, his beloved wife died. Yet through all of that heartbreak, Rinkart retained his faith. He later penned a hymn of rejoicing that is still sung today.

> Now thank we all our God
> With hearts and hands and voices;
> Who wondrous things hath done,
> In whom this world rejoices.
> Who, from our mother's arms,
> Hath led us on our way,
> With countless gifts of love,
> And still is ours today.

If you observe people very long you will see that while some go through difficult times and fall apart, others go through the same difficulties and maintain a strong and vibrant faith. The difference is not in the hardship, but in the faith that chooses how to respond. When we are resting in the love and goodness of God, we can sing and rejoice even in the midst of our trials.

Today's Word to the Wise: No matter what our circumstances, the righteousness given to us through Christ gives us reason to rejoice.

Hiding in the Rocks

The conies are but a feeble folk, yet make they their houses in the rocks;
—**Proverbs 30:26**

When the Jewish revolt against the Romans was squelched and Jerusalem was captured in 70 AD, a small band of Jewish fighters broke away and fled to the mountain fortress of Masada to continue their struggle for freedom. Herod had built a great palace and fortifications there years before. The narrow winding passes that led to the top of the mountain helped the Jews hold off the Romans for nearly three years before the siege was finally able to breach the defenses. Nearly a thousand Jews committed suicide rather than being captured by the Romans. According to historical accounts only two women and three small children survived.

There was no comparison between the military might of the Roman legions and the band of Jewish revolutionaries. What equalized them for so long was that the Jews had a fortified place of safety from which to fight. We are involved every single day in a spiritual struggle. It is not a casual battle, but a matter of life and death. Peter reminds us, "Be sober, be vigilant; because your adversary the devil, as a roaring lion, walketh about, seeking whom he may devour" (1 Peter 5:8).

Knowing the seriousness of the threat that we face, wisdom encourages us to find safety in a place that offers a defense from danger. Like the defenseless conies, we must seek shelter from a relentless enemy. God offers us a sure place of protection in His Word. David cried out, "From the end of the earth will I cry unto thee, when my heart is overwhelmed: lead me to the rock that is higher than I" (Psalm 61:2). Before trouble comes, find your place of refuge by filling your heart and mind with Scripture. When trouble comes, use the sword of the Spirit as your weapon.

Today's Word to the Wise: Take refuge in the eternal truths of Scripture, and you will find safety from the attacks of Satan.

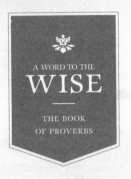

A WORD TO THE

WISE

THE BOOK
OF PROVERBS

JULY

A Path to Avoid

My son, walk not thou in the way with them; refrain thy foot from their path: For their feet run to evil, and make haste to shed blood.
—**Proverbs 1:15–16**

In August of 2012, vacationers at the beach in Terracina, Italy were shocked when a car pulled up next to a man who had just left the water and shot him seven times. The man was Gaetano Marino, leader of the Camorra crime family. He was known as "Stumpy" because his hands had been blown off nearly twenty years earlier when a bomb he was attempting to set for someone else went off prematurely. Police said they believed the killing was part of a struggle for control of the cocaine business between rival mob factions. Marino was part of a "family business" that placed him on a path that led to his death.

The law of sowing and reaping has not been repealed. When we set out on a course of action, there are consequences that we can and should anticipate (both good and bad). These consequences ought to play a large role in our choices. Many people get into trouble when they decide to associate with those who put them on the wrong path. Though they never intend to end up in great danger, they begin walking an evil road, which always results in destruction.

The only guarantee of safety is to avoid such paths. Continuing down the wrong road and hoping to get off at the last moment is a recipe for disaster. The assumption that we know enough to evaluate where the danger will strike and that we can afford to continue on a sinful path up until that moment is both arrogant and false. Instead we should quickly turn away from an evil path and from evil companions. Only in repentance can we be safe from the consequences of sin.

Today's Word to the Wise: If you follow the path of those who enjoy sin, you will meet the same bitter end that they do.

A Godly Government

For the upright shall dwell in the land, and the perfect shall remain in it. But the wicked shall be cut off from the earth, and the transgressors shall be rooted out of it.—**Proverbs 2:21–22**

After decades of service to his country in both war and peace, George Washington completed his second term as president. In his Farewell Address to the nation he wrote: "Of all the dispositions and habits which lead to political prosperity, religion and morality are indispensable supports. In vain would that man claim the tribute of patriotism who should labour to subvert these great pillars of human happiness, these firmest props of the duties of men and citizens."

America was never a Christian nation in the sense that everyone was a believer, but there is no question that strong Christian principles guided the foundations of our government. As we see that changing before our eyes—as the government begins to punish good and promote evil—it is more important than ever that we do what we can to influence the shape of our society. While we have the right and the duty to be involved in the government as citizens, the ultimate solution to these problems can only be found in the spiritual arena.

Paul, who understood what it was like to live under a government that was in direct opposition to God, urged Timothy to pray and make supplication, "For kings, and for all that are in authority; that we may lead a quiet and peaceable life in all godliness and honesty" (1 Timothy 2:2). We must be faithful in praying for our leaders at all levels of government. In addition, we must be diligent about sharing the gospel with others. The actions of men are never ultimately the result of the law but of the heart. As Christ rules in the hearts of His children, their actions and our nation will change for the better.

Today's Word to the Wise: Be faithful to pray for our leaders and our nation so we can live in righteousness and safety.

A God Blessed Nation

The curse of the LORD is in the house of the wicked: but he blesseth the habitation of the just.—**Proverbs 3:33**

In 1938, as the Nazis continued to build their military might and the clouds of war loomed darker over Europe, Irving Berlin brought out a song he had first written in 1918 but then set aside. Sung by Kate Smith on an Armistice Day radio broadcast, "God Bless America" quickly became a national favorite. The introduction to the lyrics refers to the song as "a solemn prayer." But it is important for us to remember that this prayer can only be answered in context of our national behavior.

We cannot expect God to bless our nation unless we are willing to be a righteous nation. When the government is working in obedience to God's design to reward good and punish evil (see Romans 13:3), there is a positive impact on the entire society and a basis for seeking God's blessing. The Psalmist wrote: "Blessed is the nation whose God is the LORD; and the people whom he hath chosen for his own inheritance" (Psalm 33:12).

Those of us who love God and believe His Word have a special responsibility as citizens. Though this world is not our home and our ultimate loyalty must always be to the eternal, we have also been commanded to "shine as lights in the world" (Philippians 2:15). Paul wrote these words to a church born from persecution by an unrighteous government. One of the first members of that church was the jailer who was converted when Paul and Silas were freed from his prison by an earthquake. These people realized that the evil of their government and their society did not excuse them from doing right; it made it even more important that they follow God's commands.

Today's Word to the Wise: As we see our nation turning its back on God, it is more important than ever that we take a stand for right and truth.

A Shining Light

But the path of the just is as the shining light, that shineth more and more unto the perfect day.—**Proverbs 4:18**

Today as we celebrate the anniversary of America's Declaration of Independence, it is worth looking back to remember that the foundations of this nation were laid in faith. President Ronald Reagan acknowledged that heritage in his Farewell Address to the nation just before leaving office. He said: "The past few days when I've been at that window upstairs, I've thought a bit of the 'shining city upon a hill.' The phrase comes from John Winthrop, who wrote it to describe the America he imagined. What he imagined was important because he was an early Pilgrim.

"He journeyed here on what today we'd call a little wooden boat; and like the other Pilgrims, he was looking for a home that would be free. I've spoken of the shining city all my political life, but I don't know if I ever quite communicated what I saw when I said it. But in my mind it was a tall, proud city built on rocks stronger than oceans, windswept, God-blessed, and teeming with people of all kinds living in harmony and peace; a city with free ports that hummed with commerce and creativity."

No nation can be truly great apart from the blessing of God, and no nation can be blessed by God without godly people praying and living according to His Word. The biggest problem facing our nation is not evil in high places, although that does exist. The biggest problem is that God's people have stopped being shining lights, choosing instead to hide their lights and silence their voices. As society becomes darker, it is more vital than ever that we speak out—sharing the gospel and declaring the truth of Scripture, shining more brightly in contrast to a world that has turned its back on God.

Today's Word to the Wise: Regardless of the spiritual health of our nation, each believer has an obligation to God to shine as a light in the darkness.

Rejected Reproof

And say, How have I hated instruction, and my heart despised reproof;
And have not obeyed the voice of my teachers, nor inclined mine ear to
them that instructed me!—**Proverbs 5:12–13**

Mount Everest, the highest peak on Earth, has long been the goal of climbers around the globe. In the decades since it was first scaled, individuals and groups have come to the remote Himalayas in an effort to reach the top. During the 1990s Everest "tourism" reached a new high as guides began selling services to take larger and larger groups up the mountain. In 1996 writer Jon Krakauer was part of one such expedition—a trip that ended in tragedy. His book *Into Thin Air* recounts the series of decisions and poor choices that left eight climbers and guides dead on the mountain when a massive storm caught them on the trail and they were unable to return to safety.

There were plenty of warnings for those who chose to heed them. Many people abandoned their efforts to reach the summit of Everest and remained safe below. Others thought that their skill or their guides would enable them to make it despite the storm. Some of those who refused to listen to the warnings perished on the mountain.

When we decide that we know better than those who are sounding the alarm and giving warnings of danger, we are taking a grave risk. It may be that they are wrong and there is no danger, but that is seldom the case. Usually when we are being warned, it is for a reason. God graciously gives us teachers and spiritual leaders to provide words of caution to save us from destruction. Pride does not want to admit that it might need correction, and as a result, often ends in tragedy. Humility listens to these words and heeds them, taking advantage of the protection and safety available.

Today's Word to the Wise: Do not let arrogance keep you from benefitting from the protection offered by the reproof of others.

Lasting Reproach

A wound and dishonour shall he get; and his reproach shall not be wiped away.—**Proverbs 6:33**

He was considered by the British to be America's best Revolutionary War general—the most skilled at both battle tactics and the command of men. His reputation as a fearsome warrior was so great that on at least one occasion he won a battle without fighting at all. When the British hired a group of their Indian allies to lay siege to an American fort, this general sent a single messenger to tell them that the "Black Eagle" (his Indian name) was coming. They immediately gave up the siege, and the fort was spared.

His abilities, however, were marred by pride and a quick temper, and he often clashed with commanders and subordinates alike. He was accused of claiming credit he did not deserve and was charged with misappropriating funds. Perhaps because of the feeling that he had been wronged, when the opportunity arose, Benedict Arnold attempted to hand West Point and George Washington over to the British. When the plot was discovered, he was forced to flee to England, where he spent the rest of his life. Despite his great courage and skill in battle and his many contributions to the American cause, the name Benedict Arnold remains synonymous with traitor more than two hundred years later.

While there is mercy and forgiveness with God, and He promises to pardon us when we repent and confess, there are also consequences of sin that can never be undone. The shame and stigma of sin remain long after whatever fleeting pleasure has vanished from memory. There is no undoing the harm caused by sin to a reputation. The only defense is to be on guard and refuse the temptation to sin in the first place. Once we have yielded to temptation, we have also surrendered control of our future reputation.

Today's Word to the Wise: Keep your guard up at all times so that the sin of a moment does not become the shame of a lifetime.

Job 32–33 » Acts 14 » Proverbs 6

The Deceit of the Devil

(She is loud and stubborn; her feet abide not in her house: Now is she without, now in the streets, and lieth in wait at every corner.) So she caught him, and kissed him, and with an impudent face said unto him, I have peace offerings with me; this day have I payed my vows.
—**Proverbs 7:11–14**

In addition to his long career as a political leader, including several years spent as Secretary of State and candidate for President, William Jennings Bryan often filled pulpits as a preacher. His powerful rhetoric opened the Word of God and challenged men and women to repent. In one memorable illustration, he told of a man from his hometown of Salem, Illinois, who once had been a drunkard. The man was convicted of the error of his ways and signed a temperance pledge to stop drinking. But, as Bryan told the story, each time he went into town, he continued to tie his horse up at the hitching post in front of the tavern where he used to drink. It wasn't long before he was back inside with his old friends, drinking once again.

The devil for centuries has been convincing people that they are different—that they can get close to the edge of temptation without going over. He delights when Christians believe that they are strong enough to resist continual exposure to temptation without giving in. He knows he is close to triumph when we forget Paul's admonition, "Wherefore let him that thinketh he standeth take heed lest he fall" (1 Corinthians 10:12).

The devil doesn't play fair. He doesn't care what he has to use to lure us to sin. Anything—even good things—can become tools in his hands. We need to walk through the world with our guard up and our eyes fixed on Jesus. Only then can we triumph over temptation and win the victory.

Today's Word to the Wise: Satan is a master of deceit. Only by clinging to the truth can we hope to overcome his deception.

The Mouth of Wisdom

Hear; for I will speak of excellent things; and the opening of my lips shall be right things. For my mouth shall speak truth; and wickedness is an abomination to my lips. All the words of my mouth are in righteousness; there is nothing froward or perverse in them.—**Proverbs 8:6–8**

One of the oldest delegates to the United States Constitutional Convention in Philadelphia was Roger Sherman of Connecticut. In addition to his long and successful career as a lawyer and politician, he was for many years a professor of religion at Yale, training many of the early leaders of the United States. Sherman was widely respected by his colleagues, and as a result had great influence among them. Thomas Jefferson said of him: "That is Mr. Sherman, of Connecticut, a man who never said a foolish thing in his life."

For a period of time the convention appeared to be hopelessly deadlocked as the representatives of the different states could not agree on representation for the new nation. Sherman was one of the main designers of the plan known as the Great Compromise that set up the Senate where every state had the same number of representatives and the House where the larger states would have more representatives based on their population. Because of his reputation for integrity and wisdom, Sherman was able to get his plan passed, and the new government was formed.

Those who spend time with us quickly develop an assessment of the honesty and wisdom of our words (or the lack thereof). It is, as the old saying goes, impossible to fool all of the people all of the time. Our words reveal what we truly value and the condition of our heart. A heart filled with wisdom will not result in a mouth filled with harmful or foolish words.

Today's Word to the Wise: Our words have great power, and we should take care to ensure that what we say is filled with wisdom and truth.

True Knowledge

The fear of the LORD is the beginning of wisdom: and the knowledge of the holy is understanding.—**Proverbs 9:10**

In Roman times, a general who had won a great victory was given a triumph—a great parade through the streets of Rome to celebrate his accomplishments and give him honor and glory. In his book *Apologetics*, Tertullian (one of the leading pastors of the early church) said that each time a general made this trip, he was accompanied by a slave who had a single assignment. Periodically along the route as the crowds cheered the conquering hero, the slave would whisper in the general's ear, "*Respice post te! Hominem te esse memento! Memento mori!*": "Look behind you! Remember that you are but a man! Remember that you will die!"

The humanistic philosophy that surrounds us has its focus on man rather than on God. Our society glories in our achievements and accomplishments. We revel in breaking records and establishing new goals. We believe in conceit that we can solve all of our problems with better education and social structures apart from God. While that approach is alluring to our fallen natures, it is based on a lie. There is no truth or knowledge apart from God. He is the source of all good things, and there is nothing meaningful or lasting that we can achieve apart from Him.

Describing the Roman society of his day, Paul wrote, "And even as they did not like to retain God in their knowledge, God gave them over to a reprobate mind, to do those things which are not convenient" (Romans 1:28). Truly that could be said of our age as well. When people leave God out of their thoughts, true wisdom vanishes. They may have advanced degrees and great education, but they lack true knowledge. Only when we turn to God and fear Him can we say we have understanding.

Today's Word to the Wise: God is to be the center of our hearts and our thoughts—only then do we possess true knowledge.

Staying on the Right Path

He is in the way of life that keepeth instruction: but he that refuseth reproof erreth.—**Proverbs 10:17**

There were 128 runners in the field for the cross country race at the 1993 NCAA Division II Track and Field Championships. As they set out on the 6.2 mile run, they were following a course that had been marked for them by the race officials. Toward the end of the course, one of the runners in the middle of the group realized something was wrong. Mike Delcavo of Western State College in Colorado saw that the main pack had missed the turn. "I was waving for them to follow me and yelling 'This is the right way,'" he told an interviewer after the race.

Delcavo was right—but only four other runners followed him. The rest continued on the shortcut, which allowed them to run a shorter distance and finish the race sooner. In a widely-criticized decision, race officials allowed the abbreviated route to stand as the "official course" and Delcavo officially finished 123rd.

The world does not always reward staying on track—literally or figuratively, but the path we follow is important to God. One day, those of us who have already trusted Christ for our salvation will appear before the Lord for an evaluation of our service. Our entrance into Heaven is sure—that was settled when we received Christ. But rewards for how we spent our lives are not so sure. When we stand before the Lord, no shortcuts will be recognized, and only those who have run the race by His guidebook will be honored.

Second Timothy 2:5 says, "And if a man also strive for masteries, yet is he not crowned, except he strive lawfully." There may be times when most of the people around you are going in a direction that Scripture forbids. Don't allow your convictions to be swayed by the actions of others. Be willing to stand firm for truth, even if it means you stand alone.

Today's Word to the Wise: No matter which way the majority goes, if you stick to the Word of God you will always be on the right path.

Unbribable Justice

Though hand join in hand, the wicked shall not be unpunished: but the seed of the righteous shall be delivered.—**Proverbs 11:21**

When Diana Valencia was arrested in Texas on drug charges in September of 2008, there was little doubt regarding her guilt. Anyone caught with two kilos of cocaine is going to have difficulty explaining it was an innocent mistake. Valencia, however, came up with a novel attempt at getting off—she and her sister decided to bribe the judge who would be hearing her case. The plan might have worked, since the judge was willing to take the money—except the FBI got involved.

Agents had been suspicious of Judge Manuel Barraza, and they cut a deal with Valencia's sister to record her meetings with the judge. She taped a total of five conversations with the judge in which they agreed on the price for getting her sister off. Barraza was arrested and convicted and lost his judicial position because of his attempts to circumvent justice for profit.

Many people think that they can enjoy sin and then find some means of avoiding the consequences. As one old preacher said, they sow wild oats and then pray for crop failure. But no matter what devices we come up with, God is a sure and certain judge. We cannot bargain with or bribe Him. His hatred of sin parallels His perfect holiness. He does not turn away from sin.

The only hope that we have when we have sinned is to repent and seek forgiveness through the blood of Christ. John wrote, "If we confess our sins, he is faithful and just to forgive us our sins, and to cleanse us from all unrighteousness" (1 John 1:9). Sin that we attempt to hide or cover will always result in condemnation; sin that we confess will be forgiven.

Today's Word to the Wise: God's justice may be delayed for a time, but it will be carried out no matter what attempts are made to avoid it.

The Way of a Fool

The way of a fool is right in his own eyes: but he that hearkeneth unto counsel is wise.—**Proverbs 12:15**

Though it doesn't rain often in the Arizona desert, when it does rain, it tends to rain heavily, and flash floods are a common occurrence. In many places the natural washes and arroyos take the water across roadways. Often people attempt to drive through the water and find themselves trapped as the force of the current takes them off the road. Sometimes people even die trying to drive through the floodwaters. Many times they require rescue by local authorities.

In an effort to combat this, Arizona passed what is officially called Section 28–910 of the Arizona Revised Statues, but more commonly known as the "Stupid Motorist Law." This law makes it illegal for people to drive around barriers in an attempt to cross flooded streets—and provides for a $2,000 fine for anyone who does so and has to be rescued. Despite the warnings, the potential fine, and the example of those who have been injured or killed in the attempt, people still try to make their way through floodwaters with deadly results.

We all have the tendency to convince ourselves that the warnings only apply to others. Yet the end result of such folly is damaging. Our own wisdom and understanding is a poor guide to making decisions.

We see an illustration of this in the Old Testament at the death of Joshua. As long as Joshua and the leaders who had known Joshua lived, the children of Israel served the Lord. Once they were gone, however, the people went their own ways. Several times in the book of Judges we find the expression: "In those days there was no king in Israel, but every man did that which was right in his own eyes" (Judges 17:6). Rather than doing that which is right in our own eyes, we should obey what God declares.

Today's Word to the Wise: Instead of doing what makes sense to you, judge everything by what the Bible says.

Learning from Mistakes

Poverty and shame shall be to him that refuseth instruction: but he that regardeth reproof shall be honoured.—**Proverbs 13:18**

Much of the foundation for the modern computing world was laid by Thomas Watson, Sr. who founded the International Business Machine Company and made it a leader in the world of data processing. He was the one who popularized the company motto "Think" which still appears throughout buildings owned by IBM. One of the things that distinguished Watson from many of his less successful peers was his belief in the value of mistakes. He correctly felt that the difference between success and failure was not in avoiding mistakes but in learning from them.

In the 1940s, an employee reportedly made a catastrophic mistake— an error that would cost IBM $1 million. That is a lot of money today, but in those days it was an enormous sum. Certain that he was about to be fired, the erring employee typed up a letter of resignation and took it to Watson's office. To his shock, Watson refused to accept his letter or fire him and said, "Fire you? I've just invested one million dollars in your education, and you think I'm going to fire you?"

Because we are only human, it is certain that we will make mistakes. One of the primary things that distinguishes between the wise man and the fool is whether he learns from those mistakes. When we fail, when we are corrected, when we are reproved, we should realize that we have been presented with a wonderful learning opportunity. One business consultant told a potential client, "When you hire us, you are getting to avoid over one hundred years of other people's mistakes." Rather than responding in pride and refusing to learn, we should humbly submit to correction when we make mistakes—and then not repeat them.

Today's Word to the Wise: Learn from your mistakes (and those of others) and you will be prepared for promotion and honor.

Slow to Wrath

He that is slow to wrath is of great understanding: but he that is hasty of spirit exalteth folly.—**Proverbs 14:29**

"The Bear and the Bees," like most of Aesop's fables, focuses on behavior in an animal world that contains lessons for people to apply to their lives. In this story, a hungry bear found a hollow tree in the woods in which bees had built a hive that was filled with honey. The bear approached cautiously, not wanting to alert the bees to his presence. Before the bear could reach the honey he craved, one lone bee returning from the clover field saw him and stung him.

Enraged, the bear attacked the tree, trying to get at the honey—but in doing so he roused all of the bees in the hive. They flew out to defend their sweet treasure. The bees stung the bear over and over until he fled for his life. Finally he found a pool of water and dove under the surface until the bees went away. Aesop's point was that it is far better to suffer a small injury than to allow our fury to put us in great danger.

The difference between those whose anger controls them and those who control their anger is not found in whether things happen to provoke anger. All of us are going to experience disappointments, hurts, and insults from time to time. The question is how we will respond. We have the choice of keeping our anger in check no matter what has transpired. While there is a time and a place for righteous anger, far more often we "fly off the handle" and respond in the heat of the moment. Thomas Jefferson said, "When angry, count to ten before you speak. If very angry, count to one hundred." Knowing that an immediate reaction is likely to be wrong, we should carefully consider our response when we are provoked.

Today's Word to the Wise: If you quickly grow angry and lose your temper, your wrath will place you in great danger.

Seeking Knowledge

The heart of him that hath understanding seeketh knowledge: but the mouth of fools feedeth on foolishness.—**Proverbs 15:14**

During the War of 1812, British soldiers captured Washington, D.C. and set fire to a number of government buildings. Among those destroyed was the Library of Congress. In 1815 former President Thomas Jefferson agreed to sell his personal library to the nation to start the replacement process. Congress purchased nearly 6,500 books from Jefferson. In 1851 an accidental fire destroyed many of the books Jefferson had donated. Recently the Library of Congress has been working on recreating Jefferson's personal collection, trying to acquire a copy of every book in the original set.

Back in his day, some criticized Jefferson's collection as being too broad. But Jefferson defended the wide array of topics: "There is in fact no subject to which a member of Congress may not have occasion to refer." Jefferson had an appreciation for knowledge and understood how important it is, both to individuals and to nations, to be careful students.

This is true in the spiritual realm as well. The word "disciple" comes from the Greek word for a student or pupil. Though in our society formal education ends at a relatively young age, learning should never stop. The Apostle Paul knew more than most about the things of God. He had a personal encounter with Jesus on the road to Damascus and then spent years in the desert being taught the truths of God. Yet when he wrote to the Romans he declared, "O the depth of the riches both of the wisdom and knowledge of God! how unsearchable are his judgments, and his ways past finding out!" (Romans 11:33). No matter how much we know, there is always more to study and learn. We should heed the instruction of 2 Peter 3:18 and "grow in...the knowledge of our Lord and Saviour Jesus Christ."

Today's Word to the Wise: Never be content with how much you know about God and His Word. Always be learning.

Finishing Well

The hoary head is a crown of glory, if it be found in the way of righteousness.—**Proverbs 16:31**

In the midst of a youth-obsessed culture where people go to great lengths to hang on to youth chemically, surgically, and psychologically, it is easy to forget how much God values wise and godly men and women in their later years. These elders in the faith, those who have walked with God for many years, have great wisdom to impart both to their own families and to those who are younger in the faith. Rather than dreading growing old, we should rejoice in the opportunities it presents.

In his book *The Best Is Yet To Be* Henry Durbanville wrote, "I feel so sorry for folks who don't like to grow old…I revel in my years. They enrich me…I would not exchange…the abiding rest of soul, the measure of wisdom I have gained from the sweet and bitter and perplexing experiences of life; nor the confirmed faith I now have in the…love of God, for all the bright and uncertain hopes and tumultuous joys of youth. Indeed, I would not! These are the best years of my life…The way grows brighter; the birds sing sweeter; the winds blow softer; the sun shines more radiantly than ever before. I suppose 'my outward man' is perishing, but 'my inward man' is being joyously renewed day by day."

For our later years to be godly ones, we must walk in the way of righteousness during our young and middle years. Many of the people in the Bible who suffered serious moral failures—Noah, Judah, David, and others—were in the latter part of their lives when they sinned greatly. They abandoned the glory of old age and the consistency of their testimony for momentary pleasure. We should heed these examples as a caution of the need to finish well in our Christian walk.

Today's Word to the Wise: Resolve today to follow God carefully so your final years will be found in the way of righteousness.

The Best Medicine

A merry heart doeth good like a medicine: but a broken spirit drieth the bones.—**Proverbs 17:22**

Norman Cousins was a well-known author and teacher when he was diagnosed with several serious illnesses, including heart disease. Doctors gave him little hope of recovery. Rather than giving up, Cousins decided to try something unusual—he laughed. In his best-selling book *Anatomy of an Illness,* Cousins described the effect of finding ways to make himself laugh, including watching old comedies. He wrote, "I made the joyous discovery that ten minutes of genuine belly laughter had an anesthetic effect and would give me at least two hours of pain-free sleep. When the pain-killing effect of the laughter wore off, we would switch on the motion picture projector again and not infrequently, it would lead to another pain-free interval." Cousins lived 36 years after his first diagnosis.

He had discovered a powerful spiritual principle—our attitude has a major influence on our physical health and well-being. God does not intend for His children to live in misery and despair. If our spirits are broken we are not as effective in witnessing or serving God. Instead we should find our joy in the Lord regardless of what is happening around us. Circumstances may change, but He never does.

When Ezra and Nehemiah led the people of Israel in celebrating the Feast of the Tabernacles after the wall of Jerusalem was rebuilt, the people mourned when they realized how they had violated the law of God. Nehemiah encouraged them, reminding them that God was merciful and forgiving. "Then he said unto them, Go your way, eat the fat, and drink the sweet, and send portions unto them for whom nothing is prepared: for this day is holy unto our Lord: neither be ye sorry; for the joy of the LORD is your strength" (Nehemiah 8:10). Keep your heart happy and enjoy the presence of God in your life every day.

Today's Word to the Wise: Do not let any circumstance or difficulty take the joy of the Lord away from you.

The Waste of Laziness

He also that is slothful in his work is brother to him that is a great waster.—**Proverbs 18:9**

Frank Gilbreth may be best remembered today for the book about his family written by two of his children, *Cheaper by the Dozen* (Frank and his wife Lillian had twelve children), but in his day he was best known as a major innovator in the world of work. First in the bricklaying trade where he got his first job and then later in the Army during World War I, Gilbreth was an expert in studying work and finding ways to do things faster and more efficiently. Not surprisingly, many workers objected to being studied, analyzed, and told they were expected to do more work in the same amount of time.

Laziness is not just shown when people avoid work; it also appears when they are present on the job but not producing. Many people have perfected the art of looking busy while doing as little as possible. This is unfair both to their employer and to themselves. But it is even more of a disgrace for a child of God to behave this way. Paul wrote, "Servants, obey in all things your masters according to the flesh; not with eyeservice, as menpleasers; but in singleness of heart, fearing God: And whatsoever ye do, do it heartily, as to the Lord, and not unto men" (Colossians 3:22–23).

Our work should be the same whether we are working in isolation or with the boss standing directly behind us. God expects us to be diligent in our effort rather than giving in to the temptation to coast by on less than our best. Recognizing the value of our time and effort, and more importantly the value of our testimony, we should give the full measure of effort to every task, whether great or small.

Today's Word to the Wise: Knowing that your work is a reflection of your testimony as a child of God, diligently do your best in every part of your work.

Before It's Too Late

Chasten thy son while there is hope, and let not thy soul spare for his crying.—**Proverbs 19:18**

Parents have many things they need to teach their children. There are physical, social, emotional, moral, and most of all spiritual lessons they need to learn in order to be prepared for life. The earlier those lessons are taught, the better off children are. If we fail to instruct them, they will pay the consequences. Sometimes parents fall into the trap of thinking that it is mean or unkind to discipline children, so they let them get away with things that deserve loving, firm correction. This inevitably leads to tragedy.

Children are born with a sin nature that leaves them prone to doing wrong. God's grace combined with loving discipline and teaching from parents leads children to make wise choices. Neglecting to train children is unkind in the long run.

There is a powerful illustration of this truth in the life of Eli. Though he was a godly priest, his sons were wicked, and Eli did not stop them or correct their behavior. God spoke to Samuel when he was just a boy and delivered this condemnation of Eli: "For I have told him that I will judge his house for ever for the iniquity which he knoweth; because his sons made themselves vile, and he restrained them not" (1 Samuel 3:13).

Unrestrained behavior soon becomes the habit of a lifetime. There is a time when wise chastening has the hope of changing behavior, but that time will pass. If the investment in training and disciplining is not made when children are young, it becomes very difficult to change later. There is a unique window of opportunity to shape morals and character in youth that is never repeated. We need to be careful to take advantage of it. In the end, the temporary relief of avoiding discipline will produce a bitter harvest.

Today's Word to the Wise: Teach, instruct, and discipline your children while they are young—before it is too late.

Cutting Corners

Divers weights, and divers measures, both of them are alike abomination to the Lord.—**Proverbs 20:10**

There are always people looking to take advantage of others and make money dishonestly. Many times we hear their stories and think, "If they just worked that hard at something honest, they would have true benefit for their labor!" But there is a far more important reason to be honest—the fear of angering God through our dishonesty. Simply put, God hates it when we cut corners and cheat people in an effort to get rich.

Back in 1993, four executives from a Florida rental car company were convicted and jailed for defrauding their customers. Using what con artists have long referred to as a "salami technique" (you slice off tiny pieces in hopes that no one will notice and that those little pieces will build up to a large amount of money over time), they cheated at least 47,000 customers over a four year period. They had modified the computer billing software to overstate the size of the gas tanks on the cars. Whenever a customer returned the car without filling it up, the gas charge would be increased to cover those "extra" gallons of gas purchased. It took a long time to uncover the scam because most of the customers were only charged small amounts—sometimes as little as $2.00—and very few people noticed.

God demands that we be honest and aboveboard in all of our dealings. With His blessing and favor, what we are able to acquire through honest effort will be enough. Whether we are selling a product or selling our time to an employer, we need to be diligent to ensure we are giving full value for what we receive. Even if you are convinced that no one will ever discover your scheme, God will know. It is far better to live with transparency and honesty.

Today's Word to the Wise: Take great care to be honest with everyone in your life and never cut corners to gain an advantage.

Don't Spend it All

There is treasure to be desired and oil in the dwelling of the wise; but a foolish man spendeth it up.—**Proverbs 21:20**

According to the Organization for Economic Cooperation and Development (OECD), the United States has one of the lowest savings rates in the developed world. Over the past ten years, our savings rate—the amount the average household keeps rather than spending from what they earn—has declined. In fact, OECD figures for 2012 show the rate overall at just 4 percent. By contrast, many other developed countries have a rate of over 10 percent. The fact that most people in America save almost nothing is a testimony to the spirit of foolishness that has gripped our nation.

The person who spends everything he makes (and often more) is not living according to wisdom. While hoarding all of our money is not God's plan for us, neither is using it all up as soon as we get it. In addition to tithing, giving offerings, and providing for the needs of our family, we should be saving some money to provide for needs in the future. It is presumptuous for us to assume that the car will never break down, the washing machine will never need to be replaced, and the roof will never leak. Knowing that such unexpected events will occur, we should do what we can to make provision for the future by saving in the present.

At the same time as we make our plans and preparations for the future, we should remember that our preparation is not our true source of security. James reminds us, "Ye know not what shall be on the morrow. For what is your life? It is even a vapour, that appeareth for a little time, and then vanisheth away" (James 4:14). Rather than trusting in our strength and resources, we should be relying on God as our provider. Only then are we ready to face the future.

Today's Word to the Wise: Make sure that the way you spend and save your money reflects the principles of wisdom found in Scripture.

Skipping the Thorns

Thorns and snares are in the way of the froward: he that doth keep his soul shall be far from them.—**Proverbs 22:5**

If you have ever picked blackberries, especially wild blackberries, you know two things. First, when they are plump, ripe, and juicy, blackberries are delicious. Second, picking them can be painful. Blackberry bushes are scientifically known as brambles—they are thick and thorny, and the berries are difficult to get to without getting cut up. This is why in the 1920s scientists began work on creating a truly wonderful invention—the thornless blackberry bush. These varieties now offer the sweet and succulent blackberries without the thorns that made picking blackberries so painful.

The obvious question is: Why would anyone deal with the thorns if there was an alternative? The obvious answer is: They wouldn't unless they either didn't know there was an alternative or unless they were foolish. The same is true in life. The Bible tells us that the way of the froward—those who are stubbornly determined to go their own way rather than God's way—is filled with thorns. Yet it is possible to avoid those thorns by walking in God's way instead.

Of course we realize that as the old saying goes, "Bad things happen to good people." That is a result of living in a world that has been cursed by sin. But there are specific painful consequences that naturally occur when we decide that we know better than God how we should live. People sometimes say that they are being judged by God for doing wrong, but in most cases they are simply experiencing the pain that God's Word warned would come when they go their own way. Though these thorns and snares are real and present, they can be avoided if we turn far away from the wisdom and pleasures of the world and follow Christ.

Today's Word to the Wise: Rather than foolishly insisting on going our way and suffering the consequences, we should gratefully yield to God's plan.

Take it Seriously

Apply thine heart unto instruction, and thine ears to the words of knowledge.—**Proverbs 23:12**

In May 2013, thirteen-year-old Arvind Mahankali correctly spelled the word "knaidel" (a German-Yiddish word for a dumpling) to win the 86th Scripps National Spelling Bee. Mahankali had finished third each of the two previous years. In both of those years he was eliminated when he failed to correctly spell a German-derived word. In preparation for his third attempt, Mahankali diligently worked to strengthen his area of weakness. "This year I prepared German words and I studied them, so when I got German words this year, I wasn't worried," he said after his victory.

No one has yet invented a way to magically acquire knowledge—or anything else worthwhile—without effort. If we are going to learn what we need to know to succeed in life, whether in our ministry, our career, our family, or even our hobbies, we are going to have to devote the time and effort required to gain the skills and knowledge we need…and then continue to devote the time and effort required to maintain what we have learned. Renowned concert pianist Vladimir Horowitz said in an interview that if he skipped one day of practice he could tell a difference in his performance. If he skipped two or three days, other top-notch pianists could tell. If he skipped a week, members of the audience would notice.

We need to take learning seriously. A person who is dedicated to acquiring skills and information on the job will quickly stand out from his peers. A parent who is serious about gathering the tools to more effectively meet his children's needs will reap great benefits in his children. And a Christian dedicated to studying and applying God's Word will gain wisdom. We must obey the admonition of 2 Timothy 2:15: "Study to shew thyself approved unto God, a workman that needeth not to be ashamed, rightly dividing the word of truth."

Today's Word to the Wise: Take the business of acquiring and applying truth seriously, and you will be on the path to success.

Missed Opportunities

If thou forbear to deliver them that are drawn unto death, and those that are ready to be slain; If thou sayest, Behold, we knew it not; doth not he that pondereth the heart consider it? and he that keepeth thy soul, doth not he know it? and shall not he render to every man according to his works?—**Proverbs 24:11–12**

A total of 636 people were murdered in New York City during 1963, but one of those victims is still remembered because of the circumstances of her death. Early in the morning of March 13, Kitty Genovese was returning home from work when she was attacked by a knife-wielding assailant named Winston Moseley. Though she screamed for help, no one came to her aid. Finally one man raised his window and yelled at the attacker and he fled. But no one helped Genovese. Severely injured, she staggered toward the doorway to her apartment and then collapsed. A few minutes later, Moseley returned and finished his evil work. At least six different people saw or heard the attack and did not respond.

Many times we are not certain about what God wants us to do in a particular case. But there should be no doubting or questioning how we should act when we are presented with an opportunity to help someone in urgent need. This is one of the lessons of the parable of the Good Samaritan—when we see someone in distress, we should do whatever we can to help. A very simple action can be the difference between hope and despair, between success and failure, and in some cases even between life and death. We must not miss these opportunities. James warns us, "Therefore to him that knoweth to do good, and doeth it not, to him it is sin" (James 4:17). There are no accidents with God. When we come across a situation where someone needs help, He has placed us there to provide help.

Today's Word to the Wise: God wants you to do what you can to help the people in need with whom you cross paths today.

A Soft Tongue

By long forbearing is a prince persuaded, and a soft tongue breaketh the bone.—**Proverbs 25:15**

The value of kindness over harshness is clearly illustrated in Aesop's fable of "The Wind and the Sun." The two were arguing over which was stronger. They saw a man walking down the road toward them, and the Sun proposed a contest to resolve the dispute. He said, "Whichever of us can cause that traveler to take off his cloak shall be regarded as the stronger." They agree on the terms of the challenge, and the Wind took the first turn while the Sun went behind a cloud.

The Wind blew hard upon the traveler. Harder and harder he blew to make the man cold, but that only succeeded in making the traveler clutch his cloak more tightly around him. At last the Wind gave up in despair. Then the Sun came back out from behind the cloud and began to shine upon the man. The brighter his face became, the hotter the man grew. Soon he found it too hot to continue and took off his cloak. Through kindness, the Sun accomplished what the Wind could not by force, and he won the contest.

While it may be satisfying to give someone a "piece of our mind" or tell them exactly what we think, that approach is unlikely to produce a positive result. If we want to have influence with others, our words need to be kind and soft rather than harsh and grating. Paul put it this way: "Let your speech be alway with grace, seasoned with salt, that ye may know how ye ought to answer every man" (Colossians 4:6). By patiently continuing to use kind words and a soft tone, we improve the prospects for a positive response. Remember, the goal is not to win an argument or a fight; it is to influence behavior for the better.

Today's Word to the Wise: When you are trying to influence someone, make sure that your words are kind and you will find greater success.

Self-Inflicted Wounds

He that sendeth a message by the hand of a fool cutteth off the feet, and drinketh damage.—**Proverbs 26:6**

Mark McCormack was one of the first professional sports agents. Among his early clients were three of the best golfers in the world at the time: Arnold Palmer, Jack Nicklaus, and Gary Player. McCormack's company, the International Management Group, later branched out to many areas beyond sports. In his best-selling book *What They Don't Teach You at Harvard Business School*, McCormack describes a vivid illustration he used to impress on his employees the importance of hiring only the best people available.

He had received a set of Russian dolls—the kind where each doll has a smaller doll inside it. Each one is painted to look alike, so that the only difference is that they get smaller as they go. He told his managers, "If you hire people who are less talented and intelligent, our company will continue to shrink." The point was clear: they needed to be looking for good people to hire if their company was to prosper and grow.

That is true in the secular business world, and there is a lesson in that story for our lives in any field. If we are depending on people who are fools, we are headed for trouble. There are clear indications that we can see in the words and actions of others that let us know whether they are living according to wisdom or according to folly. In any situation where it is necessary to rely on someone who is a fool, you must recognize the danger of unintended consequences that can arise from their actions. Try to find ways to minimize this risk by surrounding yourself with wise people and relying on them as much as possible.

Today's Word to the Wise: Do everything you can to avoid a position where you have to rely on fools to get things done.

Avoiding Pitfalls

*A prudent man foreseeth the evil, and hideth himself; but the simple
pass on, and are punished.*—**Proverbs 27:12**

In March 2013, the southbound side of Interstate 77 near the North
Carolina-Virginia border was closed for hours following a massive
chain of accidents. Police later reported that seventeen different collisions
involved ninety-five cars and trucks. The wrecks left three people dead
and more than two dozen injured, many of them seriously. The cause
of the accidents was people driving into a thick fog that descended over
the interstate that Sunday afternoon. A police spokesman said, "Visibility
at the time this accident occurred was down to about one hundred feet
or less."

As people continued to drive blindly forward, they could not see the
danger that was just ahead until it was too late. Prudence reminds us to
be on guard for danger—not just in the present but in the future as well.
Because of the way our minds work, we often tend to discount what may
happen in the future simply because it hasn't happened yet. It's like the
old joke about the optimist who fell from the top of a large building. As
he passed the 10th floor on his way down he said, "I'm okay so far!" That
approach places us in a precarious position because if we fail to foresee
the danger, we are almost certain to find it.

When the Bible talks about someone who is "simple" it means
someone who has not received instruction. One of the purposes of
Proverbs (and indeed all of Scripture) is to give us an education that
equips us to live wisely. Paul told Timothy, "All scripture is given by
inspiration of God, and is profitable for doctrine, for reproof, for
correction, for instruction in righteousness" (2 Timothy 3:16). The Bible
offers us a guidebook that warns of dangers in the road ahead and tells us
how to avoid them. We should carefully heed these warnings.

Today's Word to the Wise: Do not suffer pain in the future because you
failed to look ahead today.

Hardened Hearts

Happy is the man that feareth alway: but he that hardeneth his heart shall fall into mischief.—**Proverbs 28:14**

There is probably no greater illustration of the danger and destructiveness of a hardened heart in Scripture than the story of Pharaoh. When God sent Moses to bring the children of Israel out of Egypt and lead them to the Promised Land, He told Moses that Pharaoh's heart would be hardened—and that is exactly what happened. When the plagues began to fall upon Egypt, Pharaoh realized that the God of Israel was real and powerful, yet he did not yield to the commands of God given through Moses. As one plague after another ended, Pharaoh continued to refuse to obey: "But when Pharaoh saw that there was respite, he hardened his heart, and hearkened not unto them; as the LORD had said" (Exodus 8:15).

Each time we choose in stubbornness and rebellion to go against what God has said, it has an effect on our heart. Over time, if we continue to sin in this way, it becomes easier to do wrong and more difficult to do right. Our hearts become like hard and stony ground where there is no room for the seed of the Word to take root and grow. The end of this process is always tragedy because it results in continued disobedience—and eventually in disastrous consequences.

When we feel our hearts becoming cold and hard we need to repent and seek God's face. In His mercy He offers us hope for renewal. Through the prophet Ezekiel God promised, "And I will give them one heart, and I will put a new spirit within you; and I will take the stony heart out of their flesh, and will give them an heart of flesh" (Ezekiel 11:19). When we properly fear God, we will be careful not to allow our hearts to become hardened against His Word.

Today's Word to the Wise: Guard your heart carefully and make sure that it stays soft and receptive toward the things of God and His Word.

The Danger of Pride

A man's pride shall bring him low: but honour shall uphold the humble in spirit.—**Proverbs 29:23**

Hank Gathers of Loyola Marymount University was one of the best college basketball players in the nation. During the 1988–1989 season he became the second player in NCAA history to lead all players in both scoring and rebounding in the same year. Gathers' next season, his senior year, the Lions basketball team was even better and won the regular season conference championship. Before a conference tournament game at the end of the season Gathers told a reporter who was interviewing him, "God couldn't guard me tonight."

Just minutes into the game, Gathers scored on a fast break dunk and then collapsed on the floor. Paramedics were unable to revive him, and the twenty-three year old was pronounced dead on arrival at the hospital. Gathers had been suffering from an irregular heartbeat, but because he felt like the medication that was prescribed interfered with his ability to play basketball, he had apparently stopped taking it which led to his early death.

When we have success in any area—career, family, or ministry—the temptation is for us to take the credit and allow pride to fill our hearts. That is a dangerous place. Through the prophet Isaiah, God declared, "I will not give my glory unto another" (Isaiah 48:11). The reason pride is such a danger is because it seems so reasonable to us in the moment. Like the great king Nebuchadnezzar walking the walls of Babylon, we are tempted to look at the work and accomplishments of our lives and proclaim, "Is not this great Babylon, that I have built for the house of the kingdom by the might of my power, and for the honour of my majesty?" (Daniel 4:30). If we give in to that temptation we are dishonoring God and heading for destruction.

Today's Word to the Wise: If you detect traces of pride in your heart, repent immediately and humble yourself before God judges your pride.

The Majesty of God

Who hath ascended up into heaven, or descended? who hath gathered the wind in his fists? who hath bound the waters in a garment? who hath established all the ends of the earth? what is his name, and what is his son's name, if thou canst tell?—**Proverbs 30:4**

When Satan received permission from God to launch a devastating attack on Job, he succeeded in taking away Job's belongings and even most of his family, but he did not succeed in taking away his faith. The Bible records, "In all this Job sinned not, nor charged God foolishly" (Job 1:22). But Job was suffering greatly, and throughout the book he expressed his desire to be able to confront God and find out why all of these things were happening to him.

When God did appear, rather than explaining Himself, He begins describing the enormous power He possessed—enough power to create and control everything in the world. After listening to God's voice, Job no longer wished to present his case. He said, "Behold, I am vile; what shall I answer thee? I will lay mine hand upon my mouth. Once have I spoken; but I will not answer: yea, twice; but I will proceed no further" (Job 40:4–5).

As far as the record given to us in Scripture goes, Job never did receive an explanation for the tragic events he experienced. God replaced all that he had lost and more, but He did not declare the purpose behind what had happened. God does not need to give explanations or reasons—He is the mighty Creator and all things belong to Him. Since they are His, He has the perfect right to dispose of them however He pleases. We should not demand a God who conforms to our sense of justice but rather bow to the God who defines justice by His actions.

Today's Word to the Wise: If we have a proper picture of the power and majesty of God, it changes both the way we see Him and the way we see ourselves.

You Can't Buy Love

The heart of her husband doth safely trust in her, so that he shall have no need of spoil.—**Proverbs 31:11**

In William Shakespeare's famous play *The Merchant of Venice*, a character named Bassanio hoped to win the hand of a wise and beautiful woman named Portia. Her father's death had left her a wealthy woman, and many men wanted to marry her to get rich. In her father's will, he had stated that her hand would be given in marriage to the suitor who would choose correctly when presented with three caskets—one of gold, one of silver, and one of lead. The rich princes who came to court Portia chose gold or silver and failed the test. Finally Bassanio arrived and wisely chose the lead casket with the inscription "Who chooseth me must give and hazard all he hath." He passed the test and married Portia.

True love is generous, but you cannot buy love by giving. The husband of the wise woman in Proverbs 31 does not need "spoil"—the gain of battle or business—with which to secure her affection. He knows where her heart is, and as a result he has confidence. Love that is based on anything outward—wealth, possessions, or beauty—never produces security because it is based on something that can be lost.

Only when love springs from within can it be a lasting foundation on which to build. God does not intend for us to buy our way into each other's hearts. Instead He commands us to love the other as we would love ourselves—not because loving feels good to us, but from a desire to give to the other. All of the possessions in the world will not create love. Neither will lack of all possessions destroy love. Build your relationships on this firm foundation.

Today's Word to the Wise: True love cannot be bought or bartered for with gifts and possessions—it can only come from within.

A WORD TO THE

WISE

THE BOOK
OF PROVERBS

AUGUST

Why People Sin

She crieth in the chief place of concourse, in the openings of the gates: in the city she uttereth her words, saying, How long, ye simple ones, will ye love simplicity? and the scorners delight in their scorning, and fools hate knowledge?—**Proverbs 1:21–22**

It is possible to clean a pig, but unless you intend to never let it go outside, it is pretty much impossible to keep a pig clean. Anyone who has visited a hog farm has seen them rolling around in the mud and muck. Now for most of us that isn't our idea of a good time—but the pigs like it. Because pigs have almost no sweat glands, they are prone to overheating. Coating themselves with mud gives them relief from the heat. In addition, the mud acts as a kind of sunscreen, protecting the pig from getting sunburned. Finally, mud gives the pig relief from biting insects that they have no other means of avoiding. The short answer to why pigs roll in the mud is that to pigs it feels good—they like it.

When we see people sinning, covering their lives in the filth and muck of the world, we sometimes wonder why they choose that. The simple answer is that because of our fallen nature, sin is attractive. Even though it may stink, it feels good to the sin nature to be covered in sin. Though we have been given a new nature as Christians, we still have the flesh and old patterns and desires. Left unchecked, our flesh will draw us back to the mire of sin just as pigs are drawn to mud. To counter this effect we have the indwelling presence of the Holy Spirit. Paul wrote, "This I say then, Walk in the Spirit, and ye shall not fulfil the lust of the flesh" (Galatians 5:16).

Today's Word to the Wise: Our love for God and the presence of His Holy Spirit work together to make sin revolting to us.

Forgotten Covenants

Which forsaketh the guide of her youth, and forgetteth the covenant of her God.—**Proverbs 2:17**

On December 29, 2006, the United States Treasury received a payment from the government of England for $83 million. It was the final payment on a loan negotiated in 1946 to help England recover from the devastating effects of World War II. The original loan of $3.5 billion (about $55 billion in today's money) was made at 2 percent interest, and the funds were used to prop up the staggering British Empire. Over the years, the payments continued to be made until the loan was finally marked paid in full. Even though six decades had passed from the original loan, the terms of the agreement were not forgotten.

Such dedication and commitment should not be rare, but in our day, all too often people make covenants they are not willing to keep. We see evidence of this in the spiraling divorce rate, people walking away from their homes and mortgages and people breaking employment contracts. Whether they never intended to keep the commitments they made or whether they feel they are justified in breaking them because "things have changed," people are abandoning their covenants at an alarming rate.

As God's children we should never lose sight of the fact that He is a party to every agreement that we make. Every promise, every commitment, and every covenant we enter should be carried out to completion. God is quite blunt in evaluating those who break their commitments: "When thou vowest a vow unto God, defer not to pay it; for he hath no pleasure in fools: pay that which thou hast vowed" (Ecclesiastes 5:4). Keeping our promises is important for Christians because it is so much a part of God's character. In his prayer at the dedication of the Temple, Solomon said, "There hath not failed one word of all his good promise" (1 Kings 8:56).

Today's Word to the Wise: Do not forget or neglect to keep the covenants and promises you have made to God and others.

Confidence

Be not afraid of sudden fear, neither of the desolation of the wicked, when it cometh. For the LORD shall be thy confidence, and shall keep thy foot from being taken.—**Proverbs 3:25–26**

Many Christians risked and gave their lives opposing the evils of Hitler's Holocaust. One of the best known of these was Corrie ten Boom. She and her family saved some eight hundred Jews from the death camps in the "hiding place" behind the wall in Corrie's bedroom before they were betrayed to the Gestapo. Corrie's father and sister both died in prison, but Corrie survived and traveled around the world telling a story of faith and courage that has challenged many. She once said, "When a train goes through a tunnel and it gets dark, you don't throw away the ticket and jump off. You sit still and trust the engineer."

Despite what some prominent preachers like to say, God does not promise us that everything is going to go well and things will always turn out the way we think they should. There will be dark times when you cannot see the way forward and don't know where to go. The truth is that whether or not I can see the way clearly, God can. He revealed this facet of His nature to the prophet Isaiah describing Himself as, "Declaring the end from the beginning, and from ancient times the things that are not yet done, saying, My counsel shall stand, and I will do all my pleasure" (Isaiah 46:10).

Years ago, a son went to his father, disturbed about how the book he was reading would turn out. His favorite character was in jeopardy and he was afraid. "Don't worry," his father advised, "I've read the whole book, and it turns out fine." God is in control of your life, and it will work out according to His plan—He hasn't just read the Book, He wrote it!

Today's Word to the Wise: No matter how dark your surroundings and circumstances may be, you can still have complete faith in God.

Words of Life

My son, attend to my words; incline thine ear unto my sayings. Let them not depart from thine eyes; keep them in the midst of thine heart. For they are life unto those that find them, and health to all their flesh.
—**Proverbs 4:20–22**

Hymn writer Philip P. Bliss was killed in a train wreck along with his wife in 1876 when he was just thirty-eight years old. In his short life he penned many songs of faith and inspiration that we still sing today. One of the best known is "Wonderful Words of Life." Bliss wrote the song two years before his death. A new publication was being planned called *Words of Life* that was meant to encourage believers to read and study the Scriptures. The name was taken from John 6:68 which reads: "Then Simon Peter answered him, Lord, to whom shall we go? thou hast the words of eternal life." Bliss was asked to write a new song for their use, and he penned these words:

> Sing them over again to me,
> Wonderful words of life,
> Let me more of their beauty see,
> Wonderful words of life;
> Words of life and beauty
> Teach me faith and duty.

God has given us the Bible to teach us how to live. This is what wisdom is all about. Yet often people are looking for new ideas and new directions rather than going by what God says. While man has learned much about science and the natural world over the years, the principles God established in Scripture do not need to be updated or revised. They simply need to be followed. When the Word of God is in our hearts and our minds, it will guide our steps, build our faith, and keep us from sin.

Today's Word to the Wise: Knowing how precious and powerful the Word of God is, study and meditate on it every day.

Be Careful Where You Drink

Drink waters out of thine own cistern, and running waters out of thine own well.—**Proverbs 5:15**

If you have ever traveled in other countries, you have probably received the advice, "Don't drink the water." But it is not just third world countries where water poses a danger. In 1999 hundreds of people who attended the Washington County Fair in New York became seriously ill after drinking water that had been contaminated by *E. coli* bacteria. Two people—a young child and an elderly man—died. Authorities believe that runoff from the stock barn may have contaminated the water supply, making it dangerous.

In detailing for his son the importance of purity and faithfulness to his wife, Solomon placed great emphasis on being satisfied with what God has given you. Though he foolishly did not heed his own counsel and God's commandments in this area, Solomon nevertheless highlighted a key point we must remember: the pursuit of satisfaction outside the means God has provided always leads to tragedy.

The first temptation in the Garden of Eden offered knowledge and the opportunity to "be as gods, knowing good and evil" (Genesis 3:5). The devil used the same tactics in the temptation of Christ—inviting Him to avoid the cross and take authority over the world by worshipping Satan. But where Adam failed the test, Christ passed, refusing to use any means except those ordained and provided by God.

This principle is true in every area of life, but it is particularly applicable to the area of marriage. There is a loud drumbeat in our society encouraging people to look outside the marriage relationship for satisfaction. That is a tragic mistake. If you are not content with who God has given you, you will certainly not be content with someone else. Give thanks for who He has given you, and keep the vows you have made.

Today's Word to the Wise: Trust God to provide for you the means to meet your needs, and you will save yourself from great heartache.

You Are Not an Exception

Can a man take fire in his bosom, and his clothes not be burned? Can one go upon hot coals, and his feet not be burned? So he that goeth in to his neighbour's wife; whosoever toucheth her shall not be innocent.
—**Proverbs 6:27–29**

In 2010 Adam Galinsky, Professor of Ethics and Decision in Management at the Kellogg School of Management, conducted a series of experiments to measure the effect of power on people and their moral judgments. His findings will not surprise any student of Scripture or human nature. When people in the experiment were placed in positions of authority, or even told that they were in a higher position than others, their judgment of both themselves and others changed radically.

Galinsky summarized his findings by saying, "In all cases, those assigned to high-power roles showed significant moral hypocrisy by more strictly judging others for speeding, dodging taxes, and keeping a stolen bike, while finding it more acceptable to engage in these behaviors themselves. The powerful impose rules and restraints on others while disregarding these restraints for themselves, whereas the powerless collaborate in reproducing social inequality because they don't feel the same entitlement."

Right and wrong do not change, regardless of position or power. There are no exceptions to God's rules, and no one is above His law. His moral standards are absolute, and He accepts no excuses from those who violate them. Though we may convince ourselves otherwise because of our special circumstances, we are wrong. The world has done everything it can to destroy the concept of absolute truth, but God's Word is not subject to revision or alteration. It is settled, and it is true. God has not changed His mind about anything that He has spoken, and He holds each one of us accountable for obedience to His commands.

Today's Word to the Wise: No matter how you rationalize sin, God will not overlook or excuse it, and you will suffer the consequences.

The Sweet Smell of Temptation

I have decked my bed with coverings of tapestry, with carved works, with fine linen of Egypt. I have perfumed my bed with myrrh, aloes, and cinnamon.—**Proverbs 7:16–17**

In September of 2006 the United Nations General Assembly was the scene of a geopolitical confrontation. President George W. Bush addressed the body on Tuesday. The next day, one of his most ardent foes, Venezuelan dictator Hugo Chavez, took the microphone to decry the United States leader. "The devil came here yesterday," Chavez said, referring to Bush, "and it smells of sulfur still today." Of course neither the American president nor the Venezuelan leader is actually the devil— but the devil is very real nonetheless.

The idea that the devil would appear smelling of sulfur is ancient folklore, apparently because of Scripture's description of brimstone being part of the punishment of Hell. But in truth, when Satan and his minions come to tempt us, they bring a very different smell. If they actually showed up stinking of evil, we would be on guard and more likely to resist temptation. Instead they come to us with the sweet smells of perfume designed to lull us into complacency so that we will be more likely to yield to the enticements placed before us.

Paul warned the church at Corinth that Satan was able to appear as "an angel of light" (2 Corinthians 11:14). Like a skilled fisherman, he knows exactly what bait to use to get us to pay attention to the lure rather than the hook. The stench of sin comes to us well disguised in hopes that we will lose sight of the end result. Every temptation is based on the immediate moment—making the pleasure that is offered all we consider. Yet when we see beauty and sweetness on display, we should remember to look behind the curtain. We may not be able to smell the sulfur, but it is there.

Today's Word to the Wise: Do not allow the sweet smell of temptation to lure you into doing wrong.

What Delights God

Then I was by him, as one brought up with him: and I was daily his delight, rejoicing always before him; Rejoicing in the habitable part of his earth; and my delights were with the sons of men.—**Proverbs 8:30–31**

Joshua Bell is widely regarded as one of the best violinists in the world. When he was a little boy, Bell pulled out the drawers of his dresser, strung rubber bands across them, and "played" music on the bands, changing the position of the drawers to get different notes. When his parents saw that, they started him with violin lessons. Bell's concerts routinely sell out, but in January of 2007 he took part in a unique experiment. Dressed in jeans, a t-shirt, and a baseball cap, Joshua Bell stood in the L'Enfant Plaza Subway Station in Washington and played his violin.

A reporter watched to see what people would do. Bell played six classical pieces on his Stradivarius for nearly an hour. More than a thousand people passed by. Only seven stopped to listen for as much as a minute. A world class violinist playing some of the most beautiful music ever written on a violin made by the greatest master of the craft did not attract attention from the crowd—they had no delight in what he was doing.

When we think about the things that bring delight to God, we often immediately focus our attention on external things—what we can see or feel. Yet the Bible tells us that God delights in wisdom, and that same delight is available to us. The things in which we delight tell us clearly what things we love. When we find it difficult to focus on reading the Word or hearing it preached and taught, we are revealing that our delight is not in the things of God. He has made so much available to us, and it is a tragedy if we miss out on what delights God.

Today's Word to the Wise: Make sure that the things that delight God are a delight to you as well.

Loud Ignorance

A foolish woman is clamorous: she is simple, and knoweth nothing.
—Proverbs 9:13

We live in an age when volume of speech too often substitutes for careful thought. People confidently declare their opinion whether or not it is based on substance. Someone said, "The problem today is that those who know the least know it the loudest." The fact that someone is speaking loudly or even eloquently does not guarantee that they are saying something that is worth hearing. One of the characteristics of a foolish man or woman is that they speak frequently and loudly. Ecclesiastes 5:3 says, "A fool's voice is known by multitude of words."

Because words of folly are so prevalent, it often leads to a casual attitude toward our speech. But what characterizes the world should not characterize us as children of God. Our words are powerful and important, and we should carefully guard what we say. Jesus said, "But I say unto you, That every idle word that men shall speak, they shall give account thereof in the day of judgment" (Matthew 12:36).

When we consider the importance God places on every word, it should lead us to speak wisely—and often, not at all. There is no shame or disgrace in keeping silent when we have nothing constructive to add to a conversation—in fact, it may be the course of greatest wisdom. There is no shame in not knowing the answer to a question. The shame comes when we babble on with nothing of value to say. The Lord has given us His inspired Word and His Holy Spirit to teach us wisdom. The more that our hearts and minds are filled with God's Word and the more we are yielded to the Holy Spirit, the more wisely we will be able to speak. When we speak God's truth, we will never speak foolishly.

Today's Word to the Wise: Knowing that we will give account for our words, we should choose them with care and fill them with wisdom.

Consider the End

He that walketh uprightly walketh surely: but he that perverteth his ways shall be known.—**Proverbs 10:9**

Chilon of Sparta was considered one of the wisest men of the ancient world. Acclaimed as one of the Seven Sages of Greece, he was instrumental in bringing about the Peloponnesian League which greatly strengthened the city of Sparta. Chilon is probably best remembered for his motto which was rendered into Latin as *finem respice*—"consider the end." That was good advice six centuries before Christ was born, and it is good advice today.

Every path we choose leads to a destination. The path of upright and godly living leads to one destination. The path of perverted and ungodly living leads to another destination. It is not always possible to immediately discern where a person is headed, but if you watch them long enough, it will become clear. Even before a person reaches the conclusion of his path, it becomes plain where he is going.

There is no way for us to conceal our direction and escape the consequences of our choices forever. Eventually the day of reckoning comes, but that day is not the product of random chance or circumstance. It is the culmination of a series of choices. Some will reach the end and hear, "Well done, thou good and faithful servant" (Matthew 25:21). Others who have never placed their trust in Christ will hear, "I never knew you: depart from me, ye that work iniquity" (Matthew 7:23).

Over the years as I have counseled with people who are dealing with sin, I've seen that they rarely considered the consequences of what they were about to do. If they had considered the end at the beginning, they might have made a different decision. Instead of falling for the lie of the present, we should always consider the future when we are tempted and do what is right.

Today's Word to the Wise: The way you decide to walk today determines the destination you will reach tomorrow.

Reaping What You Sow

The righteousness of the perfect shall direct his way: but the wicked shall fall by his own wickedness. The righteousness of the upright shall deliver them: but transgressors shall be taken in their own naughtiness.
—**Proverbs 11:5–6**

In his short story *How Much Land Does a Man Require?* Leo Tolstoy tells of a peasant named Pakhom who is not content with his lot in life. He believes that if he had more land, he would be content. So Pakhom sets out to buy more land, working hard to get the money to acquire more and more, but contentment continues to elude him. His possessive nature leads to arguments with his neighbors, and he finds himself unable to trust anyone.

Finally he hears of a simple group of people known as the Bashkirs who own huge plots of land. Pakhom goes to them and makes an arrangement. For the sum of one thousands rubles, they will give him as much land as he can walk around in a single day. The catch to the deal is that if he fails to return to the starting point before the sun sets, he will forfeit all his money and receive no land. Starting early in the morning, Pakhom begins to walk, going far to ensure he will receive as much land as possible. Late in the day he realizes he has gone too far and begins running back. He reaches the line just as the sun sets—and falls dead. Pakhom is buried in a grave six feet long, answering the question in the title of the story.

When we allow any sinful desire to linger in our hearts, it will not stay small. Instead it will continue to grow until it takes control of our lives. When we tolerate wickedness inwardly, it will eventually be expressed outwardly, and it will lead to death, as sin always does.

Today's Word to the Wise: If we do not control our lusts and desires, they will quickly capture us and lead us to destruction.

Confident of Victory

The wicked are overthrown, and are not: but the house of the righteous shall stand.—**Proverbs 12:7**

One of the best-known poems of Percy Bysshe Shelley is *Ozymandias*. In it, Shelley tells of a report brought by a traveler from a distant land of the remnants of a statue erected to a great ruler. The ravages of time have left only the legs still standing. The head of the ruler is mostly buried nearby in the sand, but the inscription boasting of his prowess was still there on the pedestal. The poem concludes with these lines:

> "My name is Ozymandias, king of kings:
> Look on my works, ye Mighty, and despair!"
> Nothing beside remains. Round the decay
> Of that colossal wreck, boundless and bare
> The lone and level sands stretch far away.

There are times when it appears the wicked are prospering. Perhaps you know someone who is dishonest or immoral but seems to be doing very well. This can be confusing and discouraging when we are trying to do right. The prophet Jeremiah knew this feeling. He asked God, "Wherefore doth the way of the wicked prosper? wherefore are all they happy that deal very treacherously?" (Jeremiah 12:1). When we are in this position, it is important for us to remember that God is keeping record of all that is done, and there will come a day of reckoning.

Rather than allowing the seeming prosperity of the wicked to discourage us, we should remember that at best it is only fleeting. One day all of the possessions and power they accumulate will disappear along with them, and in that day it will not profit them at all. When the judgment comes, those who have turned away from obeying God will see too late the folly of their evil ways. On that day we will know the value of the decisions we have made to follow and obey God.

Today's Word to the Wise: Because we are God's children and He keeps His promises, we can be confident of final victory.

A Fountain of Life

The law of the wise is a fountain of life, to depart from the snares of death.—**Proverbs 13:14**

Jesus was always talking to people about their need for salvation. One of my favorite stories is found in John 4 where Jesus witnessed to the Samaritan woman at Jacob's Well by the city of Sychar. By the time their conversation was done, she was not just a believer in Jesus as her Messiah and Saviour, but she was bringing others to hear Him.

The well where this conversation took place had been dug by Jacob and his men centuries before. It was still giving water in Jesus' time, and it is still there today. A British visitor during the 1800s described the well this way: "…a narrow opening, just wide enough to allow the body of a man to pass through with arms uplifted, and this narrow neck, which is about four feet long, opens into the well itself, which is cylindrically shaped, and opens about seven feet, six inches in diameter. The well appears to have been sunk through a mixture of alluvial soil and limestone fragments, till a compact bed of mountain limestone was reached, having horizontal strata which could be easily worked; and the interior of the well presents the appearance of having been lined throughout with rough masonry." The well, which was dug by hand, is nearly 150 feet deep.

While we usually take water for granted today, in Bible times finding a source of good water could literally be the difference between life and death. It was worth a great deal of time and effort to obtain and defend.

In the spiritual realm the Bible is compared to a constant source of life-giving water. Ephesians 5:26 refers to "the washing of water by the word." Just as Jacob treasured his well and took care to ensure it would last for generations, we should treasure the Bible and labor to learn, study and obey it.

Today's Word to the Wise: Treat the Scriptures as a precious source of life and you will be delivered from temptation and death.

The Folly of Overconfidence

A wise man feareth, and departeth from evil: but the fool rageth, and is confident.—**Proverbs 14:16**

In September of 1923 the *USS Delphy*, under the command of Lieutenant Commander Donald Hunter, led a flotilla along the California coast on a training exercise. Partway through the trip a dense fog settled over the small fleet. Rather than stopping until they could tell for certain where they were and what direction they were headed, Hunter led the other ships full speed ahead, confident he knew what to do.

The resulting shipwreck came to be known as the Honda Point Disaster. It was the largest peacetime loss of ships in United States history. Seven of the destroyers ran aground and were sunk. Twenty-three sailors died, and dozens more were injured. If they had simply waited until the fog cleared, the disaster would have been avoided. Instead, overconfidence led to a great disaster and loss of life.

We all face the temptation to overestimate our abilities and knowledge, but that leads us down a dangerous road. Paul reminds us, "For I say, through the grace given unto me, to every man that is among you, not to think of himself more highly than he ought to think; but to think soberly, according as God hath dealt to every man the measure of faith" (Romans 12:3). Pride leads us into overconfidence—and into danger.

The path of wisdom requires that we properly evaluate potential dangers. It is foolish to think we are immune to dangers. When we take that approach, we fail to take precautions that would prevent tragedy. The fences placed around the wild animals in the zoo are there for a reason. They are not decorative; they are protective. Similarly, the dangers of this world are real. The devil is seeking to destroy us. Rather than taking a lax attitude toward our security, we need to keep our guard high.

Today's Word to the Wise: Beware of overconfidence in yourself. Rely on God's Word and wise counsel as you make your decisions.

A Delightful Voice

The sacrifice of the wicked is an abomination to the LORD: but the prayer of the upright is his delight.—**Proverbs 15:8**

In June of 2013 news broadcasts across the country featured a little boy named Grayson Clamp doing something he had never done before. The three-year-old was born without the auditory nerves that carry sound to the brain. Attempts to restore his hearing with a cochlear implant were unsuccessful, so doctors at the University of North Carolina tried an experimental procedure to implant an auditory nerve directly into Grayson's brain. This procedure proved successful, and millions of people enjoyed seeing the look of wonder and joy on the little boy's face when he heard his father's voice for the first time.

Hearing the voice of someone we love is always a pleasure. I think of the missionaries who served in the past when it took weeks for letters to travel back and forth from home to the field. With the technology available today, communication is instant. Even then, it is a delight to hear from a friend or family member who is far away. Just as we respond to those familiar voices with pleasure, God delights in hearing from His children.

Why do we pray? Certainly it is not to inform God of what we need. He already knows everything about our situation, and, far better than we could devise, He knows the answer that will be best for us. Prayer is meant in part to remind us of how dependent on God we truly are.

But prayer is not just for our benefit. God enjoys hearing us pray! When we come to Him in faith and make our petitions before His throne of grace, His heart rejoices. He likes hearing our voices. Let us never go long without going to Him in prayer.

Today's Word to the Wise: We should never think that our prayers annoy or burden God. He delights to hear from His children.

Where You Learn Best

Understanding is a wellspring of life unto him that hath it: but the instruction of fools is folly.—**Proverbs 16:22**

In 2008 and 2009 public schools in Atlanta, Georgia, saw an impressive increase in student test scores. Schools where a majority of the students had been struggling were suddenly producing students scoring well above grade level. Accolades followed, and many teachers and principals received raises and bonuses. Atlanta School Superintendent Beverly Hall was named national superintendent of the year. Teachers and leaders from other parts of the country wanted to know the secret to Atlanta's amazing success.

Then the house of cards came crashing down. Following rumors of widespread cheating, special investigators appointed by the governor of Georgia determined that the improvement of test scores had nothing to do with student performance and everything to do with educators' manipulation. In 2013 nearly three dozen educators were indicted on charges of racketeering, theft, conspiracy and lying. The investigation revealed that they would gather in "grading parties" where teachers would sit around and change the students' wrong answers to correct ones. Many of the teachers claimed they had not wanted to go along with the scheme but felt "forced" to do so.

Unfortunately, not everyone who is in a position of leadership is going to give you wise teaching and counsel. Some will look for shortcuts and encourage you to do the same. They will tell you how to get around the rules—both man's rules and God's rules—and show you the "benefits" they have gained by doing so. If you listen to these teachers of folly, your life will suffer. Look instead for those who live and teach God's wisdom and accept their input and direction. The instruction of fools may seem wise for a short time, but it leads to disaster.

Today's Word to the Wise: Be vigilant in who you allow to influence your life. Seek out those with understanding and wisdom.

Blind Hearts

He that hath a froward heart findeth no good: and he that hath a perverse tongue falleth into mischief.—**Proverbs 17:20**

Almost 8 percent of men of Northern European ancestry suffer from some degree of color blindness. The problem is not actually blindness but the inability to see shades of certain colors, most often in the red and green color families. Deficiencies in the cone receptors of the eye lead to the problem, which is sixteen times more common in men than in women. Even less common is a condition known as total color blindness, in which the person sees everything in black and white and cannot identify any colors at all.

But far worse than not being able to see color is not being able to see good. Yet that is the end result of a heart that is turned away from following God. The modern teaching that man is basically good and there is good in everyone is clearly contradicted by Scripture. Romans 3:12 says, "They are all gone out of the way, they are together become unprofitable; there is none that doeth good, no, not one."

And yet, there *are* many good things all around us. God has created a wonderful world full of beauty and pleasure, meant for our enjoyment. He has given us Christian friends with whom we can fellowship. He has given us His Holy Spirit to live within our hearts and guide us in our way. He has given us His perfect Word to provide comfort, direction and blessing. Yet many look around and find themselves unable to identify anything good in their lives. When the discouraged prophet Elijah complained that only he was faithful, God told him there were seven thousand more doing right. Rather than constantly looking for what is wrong, we should focus on the good things God has given us.

Today's Word to the Wise: Guard your heart and do not let it become calloused so that you can continue to see the good things around you.

Sustaining Spirit

The spirit of a man will sustain his infirmity; but a wounded spirit who can bear?—**Proverbs 18:14**

Viktor Frankl was a prominent Jewish psychologist in Vienna during the 1930s. During the Holocaust, he and virtually all of his family members were rounded up and placed in concentration camps. One by one, his family perished at the hands of the Nazis. By the time the American army liberated the camp Frankl was in, the only other surviving member of his family was a sister who had fled to Australia before the war started.

After the war, Frankl wrote a book about his experiences called *Man's Search for Meaning*. He detailed the suffering he endured, but he also noted the vital importance of attitude and outlook to whether a person survived that awful experience. Though Frankl was not a Christian, he hit upon an important truth found in Scripture. The spirit of man—our inward thoughts and emotions—plays a vital role in our success or failure.

Certainly Daniel had a great deal about which he could have complained. His nation had been conquered, and he had been carried far from home and placed in a training program designed to destroy his allegiance to God. Yet rather than allow his circumstances to dictate his outlook, he kept his spirit right. On the night the handwriting appeared on the wall in Belshazzar's palace, the queen described Daniel this way: "an excellent spirit, and knowledge, and understanding…were found in the same Daniel" (Daniel 5:12).

We do not have to let what is going on around us dictate our inward thoughts and attitude. Paul wrote, "For which cause we faint not; but though our outward man perish, yet the inward man is renewed day by day" (2 Corinthians 4:16). As believers we have access to a source of strength and power that will allow our spirit to overcome injury and trouble.

Today's Word to the Wise: Guard your spirit well. Keep it in submission to the Holy Spirit, and life will not overcome you.

The Truth Comes Out

A false witness shall not be unpunished, and he that speaketh lies shall not escape.—**Proverbs 19:5**

A pastor who grew up on a farm in a small town in Missouri recounted a painful lesson from his childhood. His father tasked him with clearing the thistles from a field where their cows would be grazing later in the year. The day was hot, and he had no appetite for the work, so rather than digging out the thistles as he was told, he simply cut them down. The job was finished, and he went on to other things. Because the field was over the hill from the farmhouse, his shortcut could not be seen. But a few weeks later when his father moved the cows to that field, there was a sea of purple thistle flowers that revealed the deception.

Though people lie for many reasons, one of the most common motives is an attempt to get out of trouble—to escape the consequences for what they have done. They hope that in covering up the truth they can avoid the pain of facing what they did. This pattern was set early in human history. After Cain killed his brother Abel, God confronted him regarding what he had done. "And the LORD said unto Cain, Where is Abel thy brother? And he said, I know not: Am I my brother's keeper?" (Genesis 4:9).

The reality is that lies are not just wrong, but they are self-perpetuating. One lie leads to another and then another, and eventually the entire edifice of dishonesty comes crashing down—leaving the person in far worse shape than he would have been in had he simply confessed when initially confronted. Telling the truth is always the best course, even if the immediate results are unpleasant. In the end, the lies and cover-ups always fall apart, leaving heartbreak and pain behind.

Today's Word to the Wise: No matter how tempting it may be to try to lie our way out of trouble, we must remember that the truth will come out.

The Importance of Honesty

Divers weights are an abomination unto the Lord; and a false balance is not good.—**Proverbs 20:23**

The American quarter is something of a throwback in its design. It has grooves around the outside, known as "reeded" edges in the coin business. The reason for this unique design dates back far into the past. When governments began minting coins from precious metals, usually gold or silver, dishonest people quickly saw an opportunity. They would file the edges away, taking a little from each coin, which over time would add up to a significant sum of money.

Isaac Newton, who in addition to being a brilliant scientist and devout Christian, was in charge of the Royal Mint in England and devoted much of his time to prosecuting counterfeiters and "coin clippers." To combat this kind of theft, a new coin design was introduced. Having grooves along the edge of the coin made it impossible to file away part of the metal without it immediately being spotted. Though United States coins haven't been made with silver for decades, the design remains.

When people decide to get ahead by dishonest means, they will do almost anything. Clever thieves exert diligent effort to find creative ways to take advantage of others, yet this approach is doubly wrong. First, it is wrong to lie and cheat to try to get ahead. Second, it is wrong because it misses the value that God places on work. Jesus said, "My Father worketh hitherto, and I work" (John 5:17).

Work is honorable and part of God's plan for His creation. Adam was given assignments prior to the fall. God's plan is for us to work to provide for our needs and for our families. Rather than looking for shortcuts, accept your work assignments as being from God and pursue them diligently.

Today's Word to the Wise: Rather than looking for ways to get ahead by taking advantage of others, treat them fairly and honestly.

An Accurate Evaluation

The soul of the wicked desireth evil: his neighbour findeth no favour in his eyes.—**Proverbs 21:10**

David was a "man after God's own heart," but he committed adultery and murder. Noah was a "preacher of righteousness," but he planted a vineyard and became drunk on the wine. Peter was a strong leader of men, but he denied the Lord in the moment of crisis. We have sin natures that do not go away when we are saved, and because of that sin nature, there lurks in our hearts a desire for evil.

The Bible is filled with stark reminders of the depths of depravity to which people can sink if they allow their evil desires to linger and grow. Evil creates an appetite for more evil. It is not satisfied with a little evil; it keeps wanting more and more. The more we give in to temptation, the stronger the appetite for sin grows. This is not just true for the lost. Both the Bible and history are filled with examples of believers who committed horrible sins. Thankfully we do not fight the battle against sin alone. In the hymn "A Mighty Fortress Is Our God," Martin Luther said it well: "Were not the right Man on our side, our striving would be losing."

Jeremiah wrote, "The heart is deceitful above all things, and desperately wicked: who can know it? I the LORD search the heart, I try the reins, even to give every man according to his ways, and according to the fruit of his doings" (Jeremiah 17:9–10). We need to recognize that God's evaluation of our heart is the only one that is reliable, and He judges our thoughts and desires not by what seems right to us but rather by the unchanging truths of His Word.

Today's Word to the Wise: If you leave evil desires unchecked, they will grow until they destroy both your life and the lives of others.

When God Settles Accounts

The eyes of the LORD preserve knowledge, and he overthroweth the words of the transgressor.—**Proverbs 22:12**

David's sin with Bathsheba was perhaps the lowest point of his life. Yet rather than immediately repenting and seeking God's forgiveness, he began devising plans to cover his sin. He went to great lengths to try to make it look like Uriah was the father of Bathsheba's baby, and when that didn't work he arranged Uriah's murder. David devoted great effort and used his office for his cover-up. Humanly speaking, he did a pretty good job covering his tracks, yet the Bible says, "But the thing that David had done displeased the LORD" (2 Samuel 11:27).

No sin is ever hidden from the eyes of God. We may hide sin from the eyes of men for days, weeks, months, or even years, but no sin stays hidden forever. God has set an unchangeable law into the foundation of the world—the law of sowing and reaping—that guarantees that sin will be discovered. Moses warned the tribes of Rueben, Gad, and Manasseh to be faithful to fulfill their responsibility to fight with the other tribes to win the Promised Land for Israel. "But if ye will not do so, behold, ye have sinned against the LORD: and be sure your sin will find you out" (Numbers 32:23).

We have two basic choices. We can attempt to hide our sins and continue on the wrong path, or we can repent of doing wrong and seek God's forgiveness and mercy. Only one of those choices is a good one. The prophet Isaiah wrote, "Let the wicked forsake his way, and the unrighteous man his thoughts: and let him return unto the LORD, and he will have mercy upon him; and to our God, for he will abundantly pardon" (Isaiah 55:7).

Today's Word to the Wise: The sins that we commit cannot be hidden. Unless confessed and forsaken, they will bring judgment in our lives.

Worth Paying For

Buy the truth, and sell it not; also wisdom, and instruction, and understanding.—**Proverbs 23:23**

In 1867 United States Secretary of State William Seward made one of the best deals in the history of the country. After several years of negotiations with Russia, he completed an agreement to purchase what is now the state of Alaska. The price of $7 million was a significant sum of money in those days, and many people derided the decision. The Alaska purchase was referred to as "Seward's folly" and "Seward's ice box." One critic even referred to Alaska as a "polar bear garden."

In the end, the purchase proved to be an amazing investment. Seward paid about two cents per acre for a land area equal to one fifth of the rest of the United States. The discovery of gold, oil, and other natural resources in later years made the purchase an even better payoff. Though it is doubtful that Seward had any idea of all that would follow from his purchase, he was wise enough to recognize an opportunity and take advantage of it while it was available.

Each day we are presented with a variety of options for how we will use our time, our talents, and our money. While the options may be nearly limitless, our resources are not. That means we must make choices—selecting some things and rejecting others. The path of wisdom is to choose what is important and eternal and make our investments in those areas. Solomon counseled his son to "buy the truth" because it is something that lasts. There will always be things that we must leave behind, sometimes even good things, if we want to spend our lives on what is best. By filling our hearts and minds with the Word of God, we will be able to identify what matters most and choose wisely.

Today's Word to the Wise: Keep your focus on the things that really matter and make sure you are investing in what is eternal.

Standing for Blessings

He that saith unto the wicked, Thou art righteous; him shall the people curse, nations shall abhor him: But to them that rebuke him shall be delight, and a good blessing shall come upon them.—**Proverbs 24:24–25**

In September of 1919 the governor of Massachusetts faced a difficult decision. The policemen of Boston, long underpaid and overworked had formed a union to demand better pay and working conditions. When their demands were not met, more than two thirds of the policemen went on strike, leaving the city unprotected. Crime quickly became an overwhelming problem. The governor faced a dilemma. He sympathized with the policemen and recognized their genuine complaints, but he was unwilling to allow them to hold the city and state hostage.

Though his political aides were sure it would end his career, the governor called out the state National Guard and sent them to restore order. Told that he would lose the next election, he replied, "It does not matter whether I am elected or not." Instead of angering the people, his action gathered widespread praise. He easily won re-election, then was nominated to be Vice President of the United States. Calvin Coolidge—the former Massachusetts governor—became president when Warren Harding died in office. His courageous refusal to further his career by going along with those who wanted him to encourage wrongdoing was in the end the key to his rise to higher office.

Often we are tempted to lower our standards and allow bad behavior to continue unchecked for the sake of keeping peace and getting along with others. Those who would counsel us to not take a stand are not giving us words of wisdom. While we should not be unkind or carry a poor disposition, we should also be clearly known and identified with those who stand for what is true and right. When we do this, we will find unexpected blessings are the result.

Today's Word to the Wise: Stand for what is right, even if it does not appear to be the best or easiest course in the short run.

Love Your Enemies

If thine enemy be hungry, give him bread to eat; and if he be thirsty, give him water to drink: For thou shalt heap coals of fire upon his head, and the LORD shall reward thee.—**Proverbs 25:21–22**

Though she is part of one of the most famous pictures of the last fifty years, very few people recognize the name Kim Phuc. She was nine years old when her village in Vietnam was hit by napalm bombs. The Pulitzer Prize winning photo that seared her image into the minds of people all over the world showed her running down the road screaming after having been horribly burned in the attack. Though doctors expected her to die, she survived, but she spent more than a year in the hospital and endured seventeen surgeries.

Though she lived, more than just her body was scarred. The wounds left deep marks on her spirit. Telling the story she said, "The anger inside me was like a hatred high as a mountain, and my bitterness was black as old coffee. I hated my life. I hated all people who were normal, because I was not normal. I wanted to die many times. Doctors helped heal my wounds, but they couldn't heal my heart." A friend of her family invited her to church for a Christmas service, and that night everything changed. "I could not wait to trust the Lord," Kim said. "[Jesus] helped me learn to forgive my enemies, and I finally had some peace in my heart."

All of us have injuries we have suffered in life. In most cases they are not as severe as Kim Phuc's physical injuries, but the emotional injuries we suffer bring pain and sorrow. Rather than hating those who have hurt us and trying to get even, we should show them love and kindness. This is the model Christ set on the cross when He prayed, "Father, forgive them; for they know not what they do" (Luke 23:34).

Today's Word to the Wise: Through the power of God's Spirit you can show kindness and forgiveness to those who have hurt you.

Everything You Hear

He that hateth dissembleth with his lips, and layeth up deceit within him; When he speaketh fair, believe him not: for there are seven abominations in his heart.—**Proverbs 26:24–25**

There is an old saying that you shouldn't believe everything you hear. There is great wisdom in that because many people are skilled at using words to manipulate and encourage others to do evil. People often forget that one of the most evil leaders in history, Adolf Hitler, was elected to office, in part because of his oratorical skills. One journalist who covered his campaign speeches wrote: "There were no qualifications in what he said; everything was absolute, uncompromising, irrevocable, undeviating, unalterable, final. He seemed…to speak straight from the heart, and to express their own deepest fear and desires…Such uncompromising radicalism lent Hitler's public meetings a revivalist fervour."

Millions were swept along by the powerful current of Hitler's words, and millions perished as a result. Not everyone who speaks eloquently and fervently has your best interests at heart. Rather than judging their speech by the power and force of their words, you should judge it by whether or not it is in line with the principles of Scripture. There are plenty who are intentionally striving to deceive others. We often focus on Satan as the source of deception, but in truth he has many willing accomplices in his evil schemes to mislead and destroy people.

In warning of false teachers who would come, Jesus said, "Wherefore by their fruits ye shall know them" (Matthew 7:20). Rather than allowing ourselves to be swept along by rhetoric, we should be carefully watching to see if the life of the speaker matches his words. Those who sound good but do not live rightly should be discarded as influences, lest we come under their sway and be led astray. Be a careful and thoughtful hearer and you will be guarded from evil.

Today's Word to the Wise: Take great care in choosing to whom you will listen and do not blindly follow just because their words sound good.

A Happy Answer

My son, be wise, and make my heart glad, that I may answer him that reproacheth me.—**Proverbs 27:11**

A lthough he came from a powerful and wealthy family, William Penn was greatly persecuted in England because he was a Quaker. After being acquitted in a criminal trial that hinged on his refusal to be part of the Church of England, Penn received permission to go to America and found a new colony—Pennsylvania. Unlike most of the other colonies, Pennsylvania offered a great deal of religious freedom. Penn not only helped shape the new nation of America, but he left behind a great deal of wise advice as well.

His work *Some Fruits of Solitude in Reflections and Maxims* was popular in colonial America. In it Penn wrote this about the importance of spending the time to train young people to do right rather than relying on money to make up for parental shortcomings. "Men are generally more careful of the Breed of their Horses and Dogs than of their Children. Those must be of the best Sort, for Shape, Strength, Courage and good Conditions: But as for these, their own Posterity, Money shall answer all Things. With such, it makes the Crooked Straight, sets Squint-Eyes Right, cures Madness, covers Folly, changes ill Conditions, mends the Skin, gives a sweet Breath, repairs Honor, makes Young, works Wonders."

It is a double tragedy when parents fail to teach and train their children. It is a tragedy for the children because they miss "the nurture and admonition of the Lord" (Ephesians 6:4) that every child needs to be equipped for life. But such careless parents also rob themselves of the joy of seeing children develop into men or women of God. Many parents mourn missed opportunities in their later years when it is too late to go back and shape the child's life.

Today's Word to the Wise: The time you spend investing in teaching your children wisdom will pay dividends throughout their lives.

Humility in Prosperity

The rich man is wise in his own conceit; but the poor that hath understanding searcheth him out.—**Proverbs 28:11**

During the 1960s an entrepreneur named Johnny Ling put together one of the first massive conglomerate companies with interests in many different fields. For a time LTV, as his new company was known, was one of the fastest growing businesses in the country. In fact they grew so quickly that they attracted the attention of a Congressional committee looking into anti-trust violations. Called before Congress regarding his recent purchase of US Steel, Ling testified that there was no one in his company who "knew a thing about steel." This was his way of assuring Congress that the deal did not pose a threat.

When the economy slowed in the late 1960s, LTV and the companies they had purchased came crashing down in financial ruin. One economic writer later observed, "Maybe Ling would have been better off if someone had known something about steel." There is a temptation when someone has been successful in one area of life—particularly if that success has been financial—to regard them as experts in many other areas as well, but this is folly. Success and riches can easily leave a person conceited and self-focused.

Paul instructed Timothy, "Charge them that are rich in this world, that they be not highminded, nor trust in uncertain riches, but in the living God, who giveth us richly all things to enjoy" (1 Timothy 6:17). Financial success is no reason to think highly of ourselves. These riches are often fleeting and are not a stable foundation on which to build either security or our opinion of ourselves. The only true source of wisdom and stability is found in God. Anything else is subject to change—and because of His hatred of pride, God harshly judges those who are lifted up in their own conceit.

Today's Word to the Wise: Rather than allowing success to make us proud, we should maintain a humble spirit even when things are going well.

A No Win Situation

If a wise man contendeth with a foolish man, whether he rage or laugh, there is no rest.—**Proverbs 29:9**

Some three hundred years before the birth of Christ, a Greek king named Pyrrhus of Eiprus was trying to resist the invading Roman armies. Pyrrhus was a gifted tactician, and he was able to defeat the Romans twice during what came to be known as the Pyrrhic War. Though he was victorious, his armies suffered heavy casualties. According to Plutarch, when he congratulated Pyrrhus on his victory after the second battle, he said without joy that one more such victory would utterly undo him. Some battles are simply not worth winning.

Anyone who has interacted with a fool understands this truth. No matter what you do—how carefully you plan your words, how logically you craft your arguments, or how rightly you position yourself—the fool simply will not listen. You cannot reason with such a person because they are not willing to listen to wisdom and truth. No communication strategy is effective. As Proverbs 29:9 points out, neither humor nor anger will make your point.

There is a saying among businesses that deal with outside inspection and licensing: "Arguing with an inspector is like wrestling a pig in the mud. Sooner or later you figure out that the pig enjoys it." The same is true when we find ourselves forced to deal with fools.

None of us have complete control of our lives. We cannot completely avoid having to deal with foolish people. But when you recognize that you are dealing with a fool, remember that you are facing a no win situation. The best course of action is to end the conversation as quickly as possible and spend your time with those who are willing to heed wisdom.

Today's Word to the Wise: Surround yourself with wise men and women, and spend as little time arguing with fools as possible.

Believing the Word

Surely the churning of milk bringeth forth butter, and the wringing of the nose bringeth forth blood: so the forcing of wrath bringeth forth strife.—**Proverbs 30:33**

In addition to being a skilled medical doctor, Walter Wilson of Kansas City was a fervent personal soul winner. He often used his extensive knowledge of medicine and the natural world to make a spiritual point to those with whom he spoke. He told the story of how he once encountered a young skeptic who had been taught to believe that the Bible simply wasn't true. The young man challenged Dr. Wilson, claiming that the Christian faith rested on ancient fairy tales. "Nothing in the Bible is true," the young man said. Dr. Wilson replied, "If I show you a verse in Scripture that is true, will you listen to what I have to say?" The young man agreed. Dr. Wilson opened his Bible to Proverbs 30:33—and the skeptic agreed to listen to the gospel without insisting the truth of that Scripture be demonstrated on him.

There is great power in the Word of God because it came to us from God Himself. Peter wrote, "According as his divine power hath given unto us all things that pertain unto life and godliness, through the knowledge of him that hath called us to glory and virtue" (2 Peter 1:3). Throughout history, men have laughed at what the Bible says, only to be proven wrong in their doubting. And though our faith does not rest on archaeology, history, or science, there are no contradictions between what God says and what has been proven true in these fields.

The problem with the Bible is not that it is outdated or errant, but that it is not believed and obeyed. Jesus answered Satan's temptation by saying, "It is written, Man shall not live by bread alone, but by every word that proceedeth out of the mouth of God" (Matthew 4:4).

Today's Word to the Wise: Since all Scripture is the reliable and infallible Word of God, you can always trust it to guide your life.

A Willing Worker

She seeketh wool, and flax, and worketh willingly with her hands.
—Proverbs 31:13

The story is told of a man who wrote to the great missionary David Livingstone to tell him that there were men willing to come and join him in the work if he would let them know of a good road to take to get there. Livingstone replied, "If you have men who will only come if they know there is a good road, I don't want them. I want men who will come if there is no road at all." While talents and training can play a role in success, the attitude with which we approach our work is vital. A right attitude can determine if we will achieve what we can and should in both ministry and career.

As we look at the virtuous woman described in Proverbs 31 often our focus is on her work. While there is certainly a great deal of work being accomplished, God also calls attention to the manner in which she works. She does not view her tasks as painful drudgery, but instead takes them on with a willing heart and spirit. This is the way God expects His children to work.

A great deal of the success Nehemiah enjoyed while rebuilding the wall around Jerusalem was found in the way the people approached the massive project. They could have viewed it as an overwhelming and impossible job, but instead they followed his lead and succeeded. Nehemiah records: "So built we the wall; and all the wall was joined together unto the half thereof: for the people had a mind to work" (Nehemiah 4:6). When we take on our assigned responsibilities with a willing heart, we are more likely to do them well and to stay on task until the work is complete. Do not allow the world's contempt of work to infect your attitude.

Today's Word to the Wise: Make sure that you approach your work with a willing attitude and you will find greater success.

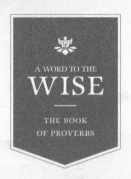

A WORD TO THE

WISE

THE BOOK
OF PROVERBS

SEPTEMBER

Before It Is Too Late

Then shall they call upon me, but I will not answer; they shall seek me early, but they shall not find me:—**Proverbs 1:28**

The patience and longsuffering of God is so beautifully illustrated in the story of Noah and the ark. When God determined to judge the world with a great flood because of the wickedness of man, He would have been fully justified to do so immediately. Instead, He allowed more than one hundred years to pass, during which time Noah proclaimed the coming judgment to those around him. The Bible says, "By faith Noah, being warned of God of things not seen as yet, moved with fear, prepared an ark to the saving of his house; by the which he condemned the world, and became heir of the righteousness which is by faith" (Hebrews 11:7).

Although God kept the opportunity open for decades, one day time ran out. Many people make the mistake of thinking that they have plenty of time to make things right with God. Someone said, "The problem is that people who rely on a midnight conversion may die at 10:30." None of us knows when we will reach the point when God will say "Enough," and the door of repentance will be closed forever. But we do know that if we continue to reject His call, one day a deadline will be reached. Paul wrote, "Behold, now is the accepted time; behold, now is the day of salvation" (2 Corinthians 6:2).

What is true of the lost is true of Christians as well. Because we are not immediately judged when we sin, we may fall into Satan's snare of thinking that God does not see or care. Just as with the lost, there comes a day when a Christian who refuses to confess and walk in the light finds that the opportunity to repent is gone.

Today's Word to the Wise: Do not make the mistake of thinking that you have plenty of time to repent—do it immediately.

How We View Work

*To deliver thee from the way of the evil man, from the man that speaketh
froward things; Who leave the paths of uprightness, to walk in the ways
of darkness;*—**Proverbs 2:12–13**

In the early days of America, the Puritans who came here from England
seeking religious freedom played a vital role in shaping the culture and
thought of life. One area in which they had a special impact was on the
view of work—what is sometimes referred to as the "Protestant work
ethic." To them, work was not a curse but a necessary and important part
of life and service to God.

Cotton Mather described the belief that Christians have two
important callings: one to salvation and one to work. Comparing these
two to the oars on a boat he wrote, "If [the Christian] mind but one of his
callings, be it which it will, he pulls but on one side of the boat, and will
make a poor dispatch to the shore of eternal blessedness."

As we plan our work for the day, it is worth taking time to reflect on
the importance of work in God's plan for us. Work did not start with
the fall and the curse. Work started on the day God created Adam. "And
the LORD God took the man, and put him into the garden of Eden to
dress it and to keep it" (Genesis 2:15). While work became harder after
sin entered into the world, productivity was part of God's original design
for us.

Instead of viewing work as a necessary evil, we should view our
job—whatever it is—as a calling from God. Paul wrote that we are to
work "Not with eyeservice, as menpleasers; but as the servants of Christ,
doing the will of God from the heart" (Ephesians 6:6). As a Christian you
should strive to be the best worker in your place of employment.

Today's Word to the Wise: When we view our work rightly as part of
our service to God, we become both better workers and better Christians.

Surprise Side Effects

Be not wise in thine own eyes: fear the LORD, and depart from evil. It shall be health to thy navel, and marrow to thy bones.—**Proverbs 3:7–8**

If you have ever seen an advertisement for a prescription medication, you've undoubtedly heard a long list of side effects—things that are not the intended purpose of the medication, but may be a result of taking it. People should probably pay more attention to those lists. A recent study by the Indiana University School of Medicine analyzed more than five thousand common medications. They found that the two hundred most commonly prescribed drugs—antidepressants, antivirals, and Parkinson's medications—have an average of one hundred side effects.

In that context we usually think of side effects as being negative, but sometimes these can be beneficial. For example, a popular hair-restoring prescription was originally intended as a blood pressure medication, but many of those taking the drug noticed that their hair was growing. What is true of positive side effects in the world of medication has a parallel in the spiritual realm as well.

God expects us to do what He says because He says it. We do not need reasons and explanations—God said it and that settles it. Yet in many cases there are positive benefits that come from obedience to the commands of Scripture. For example, Paul wrote, "Children, obey your parents in the Lord: for this is right. Honour thy father and mother; which is the first commandment with promise; That it may be well with thee, and thou mayest live long on the earth" (Ephesians 6:1–3).

Doing what God says is good for us spiritually, but it also produces a positive impact on our lives physically, emotionally, and mentally. When we find principles and commandments in the Word of God, we should not view them as restrictive and onerous, but instead as opportunities to reap the benefit of living as God intends.

Today's Word to the Wise: When you walk according to wisdom, it produces benefits in every part of your life.

Follow the Signs

Enter not into the path of the wicked, and go not in the way of evil men. Avoid it, pass not by it, turn from it, and pass away.—**Proverbs 4:14–15**

A bus of high school students on their senior trip had been enjoying their visit to America's great historical sites along the East Coast. They had visited Washington, Philadelphia, and New York City and seen the heritage of freedom left behind for them. As they made their way into Boston on the chartered bus, the driver suddenly stopped. Over the highway into the town was a low bridge—too low for the bus to get under. Traffic quickly began to back up behind the bus.

Unable to go either forward or back, the group sat there until policemen finally came. After the police blocked off traffic, the bus driver was able to back up to the closest exit so he could take another route. Before sending him on his way, the police gave him a ticket for failing to heed the warning sign that instructed all trucks and high profile vehicles to take the exit and avoid the bridge.

The Bible is filled with warning signs—instructions from God that caution us against taking paths that will lead to trouble. Often we see these signs and continue on our way, not stopping to realize that those signs are there for a reason and that if we keep going despite their warning there will be consequences.

Some people rationalize their conduct, choosing to believe that those "old fashioned" warnings were given for another age and time and do not apply to us today. Others think that they are exempt from God's cautions and warnings. Even though Scripture and experience teach otherwise, they decide that they can get away with living as they please. The wise man or woman observes and obeys the warning signs and avoids much pain and suffering.

Today's Word to the Wise: Pay attention to the warnings given in Scripture, and you will avoid a great deal of trouble.

Wisdom Listens

He shall die without instruction; and in the greatness of his folly he shall go astray.—**Proverbs 5:23**

It is tragic when someone suffers injury or dies because of an accident, but it is even more tragic when the event could easily have been prevented. Many of the things that cause pain and suffering in our world are well known in advance. For example, few people who have smoked for decades are legitimately surprised when they get lung cancer. The warning labels on the package detail the likely result of the use of the product. Yet many do not receive the instruction that is provided for them.

We must guard against the tendency to reject instruction because we do not wish to be corrected or because we do not like or appreciate the person delivering the warning. It is bad not to be warned, but it is far worse to be warned and not heed that warning. All of the instruction in the world—the faithful preaching and teaching of the Word, wise counsel, godly input—does no good if we do not listen and apply those truths to our lives. It is a characteristic of a fool to not be willing to receive instruction, and sadly it often produces a tragic end.

When David decided to number the people of Israel, he was warned by Joab against that course of action, but he refused to listen. "Notwithstanding the king's word prevailed against Joab, and against the captains of the host. And Joab and the captains of the host went out from the presence of the king, to number the people of Israel" (2 Samuel 24:4). Joab was in charge of David's army, but he was also David's nephew, and they often clashed. David refused to heed the warning he was given, and a great plague came on Israel as a result.

Today's Word to the Wise: Demonstrate that wisdom is at work in your life today by heeding the instruction of God's Word and God's people.

Victory over Temptation

Lust not after her beauty in thine heart; neither let her take thee with her eyelids.—**Proverbs 6:25**

Reuben Robinson, better known as "Uncle Bud," was an unlikely candidate to be a greatly used preacher and evangelist. He had no formal education, and a severe speech impediment rendered him difficult to understand. Yet on the night he was saved as a twenty-year-old man, he felt God's call to preach, and he obeyed. For sixty years he served as an evangelist, seeing more than one hundred thousand saved in his meetings as he crisscrossed the country preaching the Word. Once he had the opportunity to visit New York City. Upon his return he remarked, "Lord, I thank You for letting me see the sights of New York. And, Lord, I thank You that I didn't see anything I wanted!"

We cannot stop the devil from placing temptation in our path, but we can certainly stop it from taking root in our heart. We do not generally sin from casual temptation but rather when we allow it to linger in our hearts and our thoughts. As we dwell on it, our desire for it draws us away from the Lord.

We sometimes speak of someone "falling" into sin, but in truth the normal process of sin is not a sudden fall but a long, slow walk. When Lot left Abraham he had no idea that one day his family would be destroyed by his move to Sodom. He simply placed his tent so that he could watch that godless city out his front door. Little by little he left behind what he knew to be right until one day he was fully enmeshed in the wickedest place of his day. When you are faced with temptation today, remember that one of the surest ways to victory is to ignore the earliest nudges of temptation.

Today's Word to the Wise: One of the most important parts of avoiding sin is halting temptation before it takes root in our hearts.

The Diligence to Avoid

Therefore came I forth to meet thee, diligently to seek thy face, and I have found thee.—**Proverbs 7:15**

We usually think of diligence as a positive character trait. In most cases, persistence until you reach your goal without allowing anything to derail you is a good thing. There is, however, a kind of diligence that is a danger, and that is the diligence of temptation. We see this principle in action in the story of Joseph and Potiphar's wife. Often we focus on the critical moment when Joseph fled out of the house to avoid her, but this was not a one-time event. The Bible says: "And it came to pass, as she spake to Joseph day by day, that he hearkened not unto her, to lie by her, or to be with her" (Genesis 39:10).

As Satan attempts to get us to sin, he is persistent. He is willing to exert great effort day after day to wear down our defenses and lull us into a false sense of security. Even after Jesus completely overcame Satan's temptation the Bible says, "And when the devil had ended all the temptation, he departed from him for a season" (Luke 4:13). If the complete and total victory of Jesus over temptation only provided relief "for a season" we should not expect our experience to be any different.

The devil knows that we are prone to overconfidence. When we have successfully overcome a particular challenge, the natural tendency is to relax. We must not forget that a temptation defeated today is not vanquished, and we can never afford to let down our guard. Knowing the persistence of temptation, we must be just as diligent to fill our hearts and minds with the Word of God and allow our lives to be filled and directed by the Holy Spirit. Only then can we know lasting victory.

Today's Word to the Wise: Victory over temptation and sin today does not guarantee victory tomorrow. Keep your guard up and be alert.

Leaving an Inheritance

*I lead in the way of righteousness, in the midst of the paths of judgment:
That I may cause those that love me to inherit substance; and I will fill
their treasures.*—**Proverbs 8:20–21**

To say that I am thoroughly enjoying having grandbabies in our life
is an understatement. They are a delight beyond measure to both
my wife and me. Someone once said, "If I'd known how much fun
grandchildren were, I would have had them first!" The joy these little ones
bring is certainly amazing, but each time I see their faces, I remember
that I have a responsibility to leave them an inheritance—not so much of
money or possessions, but of my faith.

Our faith is not just for ourselves or our children, but for our
grandchildren as well. It is meant to span from generation to generation,
being passed down as part of a godly inheritance from parents to their
children and then to their children. Moses told the people of Israel, "That
thou mightest fear the LORD thy God, to keep all his statutes and his
commandments, which I command thee, thou, and thy son, and thy
son's son, all the days of thy life; and that thy days may be prolonged"
(Deuteronomy 6:2).

God's plan for the family is that it be a far-reaching instrument
for building, strengthening, and nurturing faith in Him. We should be
establishing memorials that we can point back to in coming years to
show our children and grandchildren how God has worked in our lives.
When God parted the Jordan River so that the Israelites could cross into
the Promised Land, He instructed Joshua to build a memorial altar. This
was so the future generations would have a visible reminder of God's
power and protection over His people. In the same way, we should be
intentionally planning ways in which we can leave these reminders for
our family for years to come.

Today's Word to the Wise: Conduct your life in such a way that an active,
living faith is part of the inheritance you leave for your family.

Counterfeits

For she sitteth at the door of her house, on a seat in the high places of the
city, To call passengers who go right on their ways: Whoso is simple, let
him turn in hither: and as for him that wanteth understanding, she saith
to him,—**Proverbs 9:14–16**

Wolfgang Beltracchi, who often described himself as "a German hippie," never received any formal art instruction. The self-taught painter, however, had a great gift—he could mimic the styles of some of the most famous Surrealist and Expressionist painters perfectly. Although he had some success selling his work, Beltracchi went into the art forging business in the 1980s, because it paid much better. His wife sold the "newly discovered" masterpieces that he was churning out, and they became multi-millionaires.

Beltracchi's work fooled numerous experts. His paintings hung in well-known museums and were purchased by celebrities around the world. He even sold one forgery to the widow of the artist whose work he was copying! Beltracchi continued producing high quality forgeries until 2008 when a suspicious appraiser tested the pigments in one of his paintings and found paint from forty years after the painting was supposedly done. When the German authorities arrested him, they seized many more "masterpieces" waiting to be sold.

The devil is not original. His plan is to imitate what God does but change it just enough so that rather than bringing life and joy, it brings death and pain. Notice how the beginning of the invitation of folly to those who are simple is the same as the invitation of wisdom recorded earlier in the chapter: "Whoso is simple, let him turn in hither: as for him that wanteth understanding, she saith to him," (Proverbs 9:4). Of course the advice given is very different, but there is a lesson here in how Satan approaches us. He wants to deceive us, and we must be on guard so he does not achieve his goal.

Today's Word to the Wise: Be alert to the counterfeits offered by Satan and reject them.

A Source of Strength

The way of the LORD is strength to the upright: but destruction shall be to the workers of iniquity.—**Proverbs 10:29**

In his great allegory *Pilgrim's Progress,* John Bunyan paints many wonderful pictures of the Christian's journey to Heaven. One of these is found in a story called "The Fire in the Wall." Pilgrim sees a strange sight—there is a fire burning at the edge of a wall. He sees a man standing there throwing buckets of water on the fire, trying to put it out. "Yet did the fire burn higher and higher," Pilgrim says. "Why is this?" He does not understand until Interpreter shows him the other side of the wall. On the other side, a man is pouring oil on the fire, keeping it burning brightly. "This is Christ," Interpreter explains, "Who continually, with the oil of His grace, maintains the work already begun in the heart."

When we do God's work and walk in God's way, we have the promise of God's grace to strengthen us for our lives. Paul wrote, "I can do all things through Christ which strengtheneth me" (Philippians 4:13). Sometimes we rely on our own resources and try to do the work ourselves, but such an effort is doomed to failure. We cannot do what God intends for us to do without the strength that He provides. When we have that supernatural source of strength, however, great things become possible.

When Elijah was fleeing from Jezebel, an angel came to him and said, "Arise and eat; because the journey is too great for thee" (1 Kings 19:7). In the strength provided by the food the angel prepared, Elijah was able to run for forty days and nights. God's power enables us to accomplish that which He has planned for us. Knowing how helpless we are without His power, we should be constantly seeking His grace and favor for His work.

Today's Word to the Wise: Do not attempt to face your battles in your own strength—instead rely on the strength that God provides.

Pleasing God

They that are of a froward heart are abomination to the Lord: but such as are upright in their way are his delight.—**Proverbs 11:20**

It should be the desire of every Christian to glorify God and please Him with our lives. In this, as in all things, Jesus sets a perfect example for us to follow. We see an expression of this after Jesus was baptized by John. "And lo a voice from heaven, saying, This is my beloved Son, in whom I am well pleased" (Matthew 3:17). We see it again on the Mount of Transfiguration when Peter suggested they stay with Jesus, Moses, and Elijah on the mount. "While he [Peter] yet spake, behold, a bright cloud overshadowed them: and behold a voice out of the cloud, which said, This is my beloved Son, in whom I am well pleased; hear ye him" (Matthew 17:5).

We do not gain favor or merit with God based on our performance— His grace has already "made us accepted in the beloved" (Ephesians 1:6) because of the sacrifice of Jesus Christ. Our standing with Him has been secured by the precious blood of Jesus. Still, it pleases God to see us walking in His ways, just as He was pleased with Jesus who said, "And he that sent me is with me: the Father hath not left me alone; for I do always those things that please him" (John 8:29). It should be the desire of every child of God to live in such a way that we bring delight to Him through our actions.

Because we have God's Word, we can order our lives according to the wisdom of God. As we read it, study it, memorize it and meditate on it, our thoughts and actions are brought into line with God's thinking. When the Bible is the governing force in our lives, we can be certain that we are pleasing Him.

Today's Word to the Wise: Live each day in such a way that your actions are a delight to God.

The Satisfaction of Work

He that tilleth his land shall be satisfied with bread: but he that followeth vain persons is void of understanding.—**Proverbs 12:11**

Although it may have originated in Russia, the origins of the children's story *The Little Red Hen* are uncertain. This little parable describes a hen who found some wheat seeds and invited the other barnyard animals to help her grow and harvest the wheat. Despite her repeated asking for assistance, none of them are interested in planting, weeding, watering, harvesting, milling, or baking. Yet when the delicious bread is finished, they are more than happy to help eat it. Instead the Little Red Hen says, "I'll eat it myself." She had done all of the work, and she deserved the satisfaction of reaping the fruit of her efforts.

Our society does not value work as it once did. There are many government programs providing funding for those who are unwilling to labor. (This is different than providing help for those who cannot help themselves.) These programs produce a negative incentive. When there is no connection between work and reward, it is not hard to understand why people regard work as something to be avoided if at all possible. Those who are able to work but refuse to do so cheat themselves of the satisfaction and accomplishment that comes from diligent labor.

Instead of drifting along with the culture, God's people should be shining examples of diligent workers. Whether or not the task is enjoyable or pays as much as we think it should, work is part of God's plan for our lives. We must remember that ultimately our labor is for the Lord, not our human boss. Colossians 3:23–24 admonishes, "And whatsoever ye do, do it heartily, as to the Lord, and not unto men; Knowing that of the Lord ye shall receive the reward of the inheritance: for ye serve the Lord Christ."

Today's Word to the Wise: Do all of your work diligently, realizing that you rob yourself as well as others when you do less than your best.

Bringing Joy to Others

Hope deferred maketh the heart sick: but when the desire cometh, it is a tree of life.—**Proverbs 13:12**

One of the most vividly drawn and memorable characters in all of Charles Dickens' work is Miss Havisham from *Great Expectations*. Though she is a wealthy woman, she lives as a recluse, dressed in a yellowed wedding gown. Every clock in her house is stopped at twenty minutes before nine, and remnants of a banquet are rotting on the dining room table. She even wears only one shoe. The story explains that she was jilted on her wedding day and never got over her heartbreak. In fact, she takes in and raises a girl, training her for the specific purpose of breaking a man's heart so that she could have her revenge.

While this is an exaggerated and fictional character, it is also a powerful illustration of the damage that can be done by broken dreams. Of course not all dreams and expectations can or should be met. But when we have made a commitment to someone, we should diligently strive to fulfill it. Once we have created a hope in someone's heart, there will be repercussions if that hope is delayed or dashed.

This word of caution is especially important for parents (and grandparents). A promise or offer made in casual conversation to a child may be quickly forgotten by the adult, but the child takes it deep into his heart and places great hope in seeing it fulfilled. When it is not, a rift in the relationship can easily develop. We need to exercise caution not to make careless promises, and we need to do everything possible to keep the commitments we make. The same is true in our marriages. When promises are repeatedly made and broken, a level of distrust and wounded spirit often result. How much better it is to make those dreams come true and to see joy and life spring up in those we love.

Today's Word to the Wise: Take care that you are not heedlessly dashing someone's legitimate dreams and expectations.

No Laughing Matter

Fools make a mock at sin: but among the righteous there is favour.
—**Proverbs 14:9**

Edwin Cooper was famous across America, yet almost no one knew his real name. Coming from a family of circus clowns, Cooper began performing before audiences when he was just nine years old. In the 1950s, after a stint with the Barnum and Bailey Circus, he became a fixture on television as Bozo the Clown. In addition to entertaining both young and old, Cooper had a message for his "buddies and partners" every week: get checked for cancer. Cooper was so busy working, however, that he neglected to follow his own advice. By the time his cancer was discovered, it was too late for it to be treated. Edwin Cooper died at just forty-one years of age from a disease he had warned many others to watch out for.

Sin is far more deadly than the most aggressive and fast growing cancer. It kills and destroys everything it touches. From the fall of Adam in the Garden of Eden until now, sin takes no prisoners. This is the purpose behind everything Satan does. Jesus said, "The thief cometh not, but for to steal, and to kill, and to destroy" (John 10:10). Because of his evil nature and his hatred of everything good, the devil brings destruction to everything within his reach.

When we regard sin as God does, we find nothing amusing or humorous about it. We will not make it the subject of the jokes we tell or listen to. We will not allow ourselves to be tempted to get a little closer to the line to see if we are still safe. God hates sin with a holy and righteous fury, and so should we. When we find ourselves amused by sin, it is time for us to focus on the cross. Seeing the price paid for our sin reminds us that it is no laughing matter.

Today's Word to the Wise: Avoid those who find sin funny or entertaining, and you will be protected from deadly evil.

A Smooth Course

The way of the slothful man is as an hedge of thorns: but the way of the righteous is made plain.—**Proverbs 15:19**

For decades, people who like to drive at inordinate speeds have descended on the Bonneville Salt Flats in Utah. Many of the world land speed records were set here. The miles of this smooth and densely packed salt pan in northwestern Utah offer drivers of cars, trucks, and motorcycles the opportunity to achieve their maximum speed in relative safety. Because the course is flat and straight, the only consideration is how fast a top speed can be achieved.

There is nothing like a smooth road to make travel easier. The Hebrew word used for *plain* in today's verse is the idea of a road that was elevated—a highway. Though we use the term for any major road these days, the original meaning described a road that had been built up so that it would be flat and level, without the dips and valleys that would make travel difficult in the days before motorized transportation. This word *plain* is the word God chose to describe the lives of those who are following His principles of wisdom.

It is important to note that this verse is not teaching the careless prosperity theology so popular in our day. It does not say that the way of the righteous is easy and without trouble. Instead it teaches that as we walk in God's way, we find an easier path through life than we would have otherwise found. There will still be suffering and persecution, but we will not be dealing with the painful consequences of sinful behavior and bad decisions. Like a driver searching for the fastest route to his destination, let us look for God's way through our lives.

Today's Word to the Wise: Dedicate yourself to living by God's commandments, and you will find a plain path to follow God.

Where Success Comes From

Pride goeth before destruction, and an haughty spirit before a fall.
—Proverbs 16:18

In the days leading up to Super Bowl XLII in February of 2008, the New England Patriots were riding an impressive winning streak. They hadn't lost a game all season, and one more win would make them only the second undefeated team in NFL history. They were heavily favored to defeat the New York Giants in the Super Bowl, and team officials made plans to capitalize on the expected victory. Steps were taken to trademark the phrase 19-0, and hats and shirts with that commemoration of a perfect season were printed up ahead of time. Unfortunately for the Patriots, the Giants were not interested in rolling over and playing dead. They fought for every yard and point, and when the game was over the Giants had pulled off a shocking 17–14 upset.

The natural sinful tendency is for us to feel overconfident for our accomplishment and achievements. Yet, in truth, though we should work hard, all that we accomplish is the result of what God has given us. Paul reminded the church at Corinth that all of their success was due to God's grace and not their own ability. "For who maketh thee to differ from another? and what hast thou that thou didst not receive? now if thou didst receive it, why dost thou glory, as if thou hadst not received it?" (1 Corinthians 4:7).

There is no place for pride in God's plan for our lives. In fact when we are proud, we position ourselves for judgment. The only true and lasting form of glory is that which God gives to those who banish pride. Peter wrote, "Humble yourselves therefore under the mighty hand of God, that he may exalt you in due time" (1 Peter 5:6). Exalting ourselves for our accomplishments sets us up for a great fall.

Today's Word to the Wise: Banish pride from your heart and mind so that you can receive God's promotion and honor.

The Acid Test

The fining pot is for silver, and the furnace for gold: but the LORD *trieth the hearts.*—**Proverbs 17:3**

On the surface, there are several metals that look similar to gold. Centuries ago, people discovered that unscrupulous operators would take advantage of this to trick people into paying for worthless metal. In order to determine whether gold was genuine or not, scientists devised an "acid test." The item that is supposed to be gold is rubbed on a black stone, leaving a mark behind. Gold is what is called a noble metal, meaning that it is resistant to the corrosive effects of acid. If the mark is washed away by the acid, then the metal is not real gold. If it remains unchanged, the genuine nature of the gold is proven.

It is not always immediately apparent from the outside whether or not someone is a genuine believer doing the work of God from a good heart. Some are tares among the wheat while others are doing the right things but for selfish motives. It is only when faith and works are put to the test that it will become clear. Not all of these tests will yield the results that people expect. Jesus said, "Many will say to me in that day, Lord, Lord, have we not prophesied in thy name? and in thy name have cast out devils? and in thy name done many wonderful works? And then will I profess unto them, I never knew you: depart from me, ye that work iniquity" (Matthew 7:22–23).

Those who are believers will stand at the Judgment Seat of Christ where their works will be tested. Those who have put their trust in Christ can never lose the eternal life Christ promised, but their work for the Lord will be inspected. Paul wrote, "Every man's work shall be made manifest: for the day shall declare it, because it shall be revealed by fire; and the fire shall try every man's work of what sort it is" (1 Corinthians 3:13). Only that which has been done with pure motives and for the glory of God will survive that judgment.

Today's Word to the Wise: Make sure that your faith and your works will stand up to the acid test.

Get the Whole Story

He that is first in his own cause seemeth just; but his neighbour cometh and searcheth him.—**Proverbs 18:17**

In the children's story *Alice in Wonderland*, Alice observes the trial being held for the Knave of Hearts who is accused of stealing some tarts baked for the Queen. Like everything else in the story, the trial is an exercise in the absurd. The silliness reaches its pinnacle when the King and Queen tire of the process and are ready to move forward.

"It's a pun!" the King added in an offended tone, and everybody laughed, "Let the jury consider their verdict," the King said, for about the twentieth time that day.

"No, no!" said the Queen. "Sentence first—verdict afterwards."

"Stuff and nonsense!" said Alice loudly. "The idea of having the sentence first!"

Of course we recognize immediately that it is folly to render judgment prior to hearing the entire story—we have no basis for making a decision. Yet often we fall into the trap of basing our decisions on partial information. The first version of the story that we hear is not always complete and accurate. While that version may sound convincing wisdom takes the time to get the whole story before making a decision.

We live in a hurry up world. Some people act like instant coffee takes too long. But when it comes to making important decisions wisdom counsels us to slow down and make sure the details are right. There was almost a civil war in Israel after the death of Joshua. The people were ready to fight based on a rumor—a rumor that turned out to be inaccurate. "And the children of Israel *heard say*, Behold, the children of Reuben and the children of Gad and the half tribe of Manasseh have built an altar" (Joshua 22:11). Make sure you know the whole story before taking action.

Today's Word to the Wise: Do not be hasty in reaching conclusions—make sure you have the whole story before making up your mind.

Not Just for Kids

Hear counsel, and receive instruction, that thou mayest be wise in thy latter end.—**Proverbs 19:20**

O ften we think counsel is only for young people. They face major issues and decisions—where to go to school, who to marry, what kind of work they should do—that certainly will be made better with godly advice and input. The need for counsel, however, does not end in youth or even middle age. Throughout our lives, we need to continue getting input from others. Wisdom is not just meant to get us headed in the right direction—it is meant to guide us throughout our lives.

Solomon himself serves as a tragic example of what failing to adhere to this principle produces. Though he was granted great wisdom by God, Solomon did not walk in wisdom all the days of his life. He indulged his sinful appetites, and his heart turned away from following God. The nation of Israel suffered greatly as a result, and after Solomon died a civil war divided the nation. The decisions that Solomon made reflected foolishness in action.

Although Solomon was wiser than anyone else, he was not the only wise person in Israel. There were men who had served his father David who could have given him godly counsel and encouraged him to avoid the marriages that pulled him into idolatry. There is no record, however, that Solomon had any interest in hearing their advice. Thinking he had it all figured out, he went his own way—towards disaster.

In light of what we know of Solomon's reign, there is an ironic statement found in his later writings which says, "Better is a poor and a wise child than an old and foolish king, who will no more be admonished" (Ecclesiastes 4:13). When Solomon was inspired to write those words, one must wonder if he recognized himself and shook his head at his own folly.

Today's Word to the Wise: Continue to seek counsel from wise and godly people throughout your life.

Success at Making Excuses

The sluggard will not plow by reason of the cold; therefore shall he beg in harvest, and have nothing.—**Proverbs 20:4**

William Sydney Porter, better known by his pen name O. Henry, became one of the most popular authors in America at the turn of the last century. He wrote for years, but his literary career really took off from a most unlikely place—prison. Porter had been convicted of embezzling from the bank where he worked in Texas. (There is some evidence that it was not theft but carelessness that led to the loss of funds in the bank.) While serving his five-year prison sentence, Porter wrote and published some of his best-known stories, establishing himself as a premiere author.

In his interactions with others, O. Henry displayed the same wit that filled his stories. Once he attempted to get a royalty check from a New York publisher without success. He went to the office to try to collect in person, only to be told that the person who signed checks was not available because of a sprained ankle. "My dear sir," O. Henry said, "does he sign them with his feet?"

When we are trying to avoid doing something we don't want to do, almost any excuse will suffice. It's much easier to plow a field on a cool day than a hot one, yet Solomon points out that a lazy man will even use the cold as his excuse not to work. Rather than looking for reasons to avoid the tasks that are set before us, we should be faithful and diligent about our work. Success at making excuses may avoid temporary effort, but it leads to more pain in the end. When a sluggard goes hungry, he has time to regret that he did not work when he had the opportunity. God has established rewards for work that can never be obtained by making excuses.

Today's Word to the Wise: Rather than making excuses, work diligently and you will reap the rewards of your labor.

Guard Your Tongue

Whoso keepeth his mouth and his tongue keepeth his soul from troubles.—**Proverbs 21:23**

James said that one of the clearest measures of growth and maturity in a believer is the ability to control the tongue. "For in many things we offend all. If any man offend not in word, the same is a perfect man, and able also to bridle the whole body" (James 3:2). Despite the fact that it is difficult to tame the tongue, it is critically important that we do so. Our words have great power. They can strengthen and encourage others—or tear them down.

Dr. Bob Jones, Sr. said, "There is nothing today that is doing more to deaden the spiritual testimony of Christianity than the long, backbiting, mean tongues of some supposedly orthodox Christians. There are Christians that talk much about a separated life and boast about what they do and do not do and speak with great pride about their loyalty to orthodoxy, who spend their time dipping their tongues in the slime of slander and speaking the death warrant to the reputation of others. The Bible is filled with condemnation of people that slander other people. It condemns with great severity people who even take up a reproach about other people. It is just as bad to carry a rumor around after it starts as it is to start it."

Our words have a great impact on our own lives as well. When we violate God's law by gossiping or speaking falsely against others, we create pain, suffering, and divisions in the body of Christ which is meant to be united. Do not allow your words to tear apart what God has brought together. Paul wrote, "Let no corrupt communication proceed out of your mouth, but that which is good to the use of edifying, that it may minister grace unto the hearers" (Ephesians 4:29).

Today's Word to the Wise: Recognize the power of your words, and guard them carefully to ensure they build up rather than tear down.

Part of Our Nature

Foolishness is bound in the heart of a child; but the rod of correction shall drive it far from him.—**Proverbs 22:15**

There is an old story that dates centuries back of a scorpion who set out to see the world. His progress was halted when he reached a river that was too wide for him to cross because he could not swim. A frog passed by, and the scorpion asked for a ride across the river. The skeptical frog asked, "How do I know you won't sting me?" The scorpion answered with unassailable logic, "Because if I sting you, I'll die too." That convinced the frog and they set out across the river. Halfway across the scorpion stung the frog despite his promise. Feeling the paralysis spreading through his body and realizing he was about to die, the frog asked, "Why did you do that? Now we will both die." The scorpion replied, "Because it's my nature."

Despite the pronouncements of educators, sociologists, and politicians man is not basically good. While it may appeal to our pride to say that we are good, the plain (and obvious) truth is that man's innate nature is evil. David wrote, "The LORD looked down from heaven upon the children of men, to see if there were any that did understand, and seek God. They are all gone aside, they are all together become filthy: there is none that doeth good, no, not one" (Psalm 14:2–3).

We do not become sinners—we are sinners from birth. The sin nature is bound in our hearts and only the grace of God can replace it with a new nature and conform us to His image. Even after our conversion, the old tendencies to sin remain. Unless the Spirit of God is filling our lives and guiding our steps, we will revert to walk in our old ways.

Today's Word to the Wise: Recognize the presence of your old sinful nature and daily yield to the Holy Spirit so He has control.

In the End

Hear thou, my son, and be wise, and guide thine heart in the way. Be not among winebibbers; among riotous eaters of flesh: For the drunkard and the glutton shall come to poverty: and drowsiness shall clothe a man with rags.—**Proverbs 23:19–21**

A lot of people think they are having a good time as they go along with their friends doing things that are wrong. They may drink, gamble, eat, and party to find temporary pleasure. But in the end, going against God's law always brings negative consequences. Tragically, many people never stop this downward spiral, while others wait until they have reached the bottom of the barrel before turning to God for help.

Sam Jones was a greatly used evangelist who saw thousands saved in his meetings. But before he became a Christian, he was a hopeless alcoholic. Jones was so brilliant that he passed the bar exam to become a lawyer after only one year of study, yet he drank himself out of job after job until he hit rock bottom. Jones remembered that day well: "I went to the bar and begged for a glass of liquor. I got the glass and started to drink and looked into the mirror. I saw my hair matted, the filth and vomit on my clothes, one of my eyes totally closed, and my lips swollen. And I said, 'Is that all that is left of the proud and brilliant lawyer, Sam Jones?' I smashed the glass on the floor and fell to my knees and cried, 'Oh, God! Oh, God, have mercy!'"

The grace of God transformed him into a powerful preacher, but how much better would it have been for Sam Jones to turn to God before he reached such a low point—or before he started down the path of sin at all. Any pleasure sin offers is fleeting and temporary, but the consequences are painful and lasting.

Today's Word to the Wise: Instead of following sin to its bitter end, confess and repent—turn to God for mercy and forgiveness.

Getting Even

Say not, I will do so to him as he hath done to me: I will render to the man according to his work.—**Proverbs 24:29**

An elephant and a giraffe walked together to a watering hole on the African plain. It was a cool and pleasant evening, and they were talking about life. When they reached the water hole, they saw a large turtle sunning himself on a log. Without saying a word, the elephant walked over and kicked the turtle, sending him spinning out over the water until he landed with a huge splash. "Why did you do that?" the giraffe asked his friend. "Thirty years ago I came to this same water hole and that turtle snapped at my trunk," the elephant replied. "You have an amazing memory," the giraffe said. "Yes," said the elephant. "I have turtle recall!"

Even those of us who struggle to remember what we were supposed to get at the grocery store or why we walked into the room find it easy to remember those who have treated us wrongly. We tend to nurse our injuries, rehearsing the details and thinking about ways in which we could get even. Holding on to the pains of the past harms us in two ways. First, the more time we spend focused on them, the more painful they become. Rather than allowing the wound to heal, we keep picking at the scab and making it worse.

Second, the longer we think about injuries done to us, the more likely we are to attempt revenge for what happened. This leads to all sorts of evils. Paul wrote, "Dearly beloved, avenge not yourselves, but rather give place unto wrath: for it is written, Vengeance is mine; I will repay, saith the Lord" (Romans 12:19). The pain that we suffer is real, but faith in God allows us to trust Him to bring true justice to those who have done us wrong.

Today's Word to the Wise: Trust God to bring justice rather than trying to get even yourself.

Know When to Quit

Hast thou found honey? eat so much as is sufficient for thee, lest thou be filled therewith, and vomit it. Withdraw thy foot from thy neighbour's house; lest he be weary of thee, and so hate thee.—**Proverbs 25:16–17**

Each year on the fourth of July the Nathan's Famous Hot Dog Company sponsors a hot dog eating contest. In 2013 Joey Chestnut won the competition for the seventh year in a row, setting a new record by eating sixty-nine hot dogs and buns in just ten minutes. The second runner up "only" managed to eat fifty-one. According to a nutritionist, Chestnut consumed almost twenty-seven thousand calories in that ten minute eating spree. Chestnut received a prize of $20,000 for his eating performance.

Few of us are in danger of eating seventy hot dogs in one day, let alone nearly seven a minute for ten minutes straight. Still, we live in a world where "enough" is never enough. Many people devote their lives to acquiring wealth and possessions, living with a focus only on the temporal. As a result, they live in a perpetual state of dissatisfaction. They struggle to get the latest and biggest and newest toys and never enjoy a moment of peace.

God's plan for us is contentment. This contentment is not based on having "enough" but having faith to believe that the presence of God makes up for whatever we lack. Hebrews 13:5 says it this way: "Let your conversation be without covetousness; and be content with such things as ye have: for he hath said, I will never leave thee, nor forsake thee." Knowing that God is with us should give us the peace of mind to be content with His provisions. Being satisfied with what He has chosen to provide is a vital step to wisdom.

Today's Word to the Wise: Despite being surrounded by a world focused on possessions and wealth, we should live contentedly with what God provides.

Sticks and Stones

The words of a talebearer are as wounds, and they go down into the innermost parts of the belly.—**Proverbs 26:22**

Most of us learned the saying when we were little: "Sticks and stones may break my bones, but words will never hurt me." In reality, words are amazingly powerful—they can either build up and encourage, or tear down and cause deep wounds. Whether the words spoken against someone are true or false, they are able to deeply injure.

When David was fleeing from King Saul, he briefly took shelter with Ahimelech the priest. A man from Edom named Doeg saw David there and reported him to Saul. In his jealous rage, Saul had all the priests and their families killed. When he heard this news, David wrote a powerful condemnation of Doeg. "Thy tongue deviseth mischiefs; like a sharp razor, working deceitfully. Thou lovest evil more than good; and lying rather than to speak righteousness. Selah. Thou lovest all devouring words, O thou deceitful tongue. God shall likewise destroy thee for ever, he shall take thee away, and pluck thee out of thy dwelling place, and root thee out of the land of the living. Selah" (Psalm 52:2–5).

While we should always tell the truth, sometimes telling the truth becomes an excuse for repeating stories that do not need to be told. There are stories that are completely true but benefit no one by being repeated. Character assassination in the name of truth is not godly speech. We should guard our tongues and not delight in having the latest gossip to share. Paul wrote to the church at Ephesus: "But speaking the truth in love, may grow up into him in all things, which is the head, even Christ" (Ephesians 4:15). Speaking in love prevents us from carelessly wounding others and falling under the judgment of God.

Today's Word to the Wise: Make a dedicated and conscious effort to avoid wounding others with your words.

The Necessity of Friendship

Iron sharpeneth iron; so a man sharpeneth the countenance of his friend.—**Proverbs 27:17**

A number of years ago, a man named James Hewett compiled a book of sermon illustrations. In it he included some stories from his own life. He said that one of his neighbors was trying to install a television antenna on his roof and was really struggling to get it done by himself. Hewett walked over and offered to help. He had a collection of nice tools and had everything needed for the task. When they finished the job, his neighbor looked at his rather impressive tool kit and asked what he made with such tools. "Friends mostly," Hewett answered.

All of us need friends. God did not intend for us to go through life flying solo. In fact while everything God created was good, there was something that He said needed to change. "And the LORD God said, It is not good that the man should be alone; I will make him an help meet for him" (Genesis 2:18). This principle applies to more than just a marriage relationship—it demonstrates the need for friendship as well.

Ecclesiastes 4:9–10 puts it this way: "Two are better than one; because they have a good reward for their labour. For if they fall, the one will lift up his fellow: but woe to him that is alone when he falleth; for he hath not another to help him up." We need friends to strengthen and encourage us as we strive to do right. We need friends to rejoice with us in the good times and weep with us in the bad times. The necessity of friendship requires that we be willing to make investments to build and maintain these important relationships. Jesus sent the disciples out two by two. Likewise, rather than trying to do it alone, we should rely on our friends.

Today's Word to the Wise: Put forth the work and effort to build solid friendships, and every part of your life will benefit.

The Blessings of Faithfulness

A faithful man shall abound with blessings: but he that maketh haste to be rich shall not be innocent.—**Proverbs 28:20**

Richard Cecil was a greatly used pastor in England in the late 1700s. He was closely connected with John Newton and Wilber Wilberforce in their efforts to end the slave trade. The spirit that kept him faithful to God through a long life of service was demonstrated when he was just a boy. One day, Richard's father, who worked for the British East India Company, took the boy into the city with him. He told Richard to wait at a certain gate until he returned. In the busyness of his day, he forgot the boy and returned home alone. He said, "Dear me! I left him in the morning standing under such and such a gateway, and I told him to stay there till I came for him. I should not wonder but that he is there now." He did, in fact, find Richard Cecil at the very spot where he was told to wait.

We live in an impatient world, yet God expects us to be faithful even if results are not immediately apparent. Faithfulness is not a nice accessory to the Christian life—it is an absolute essential. Paul wrote, "Moreover it is required in stewards, that a man be found faithful" (1 Corinthians 4:2). The reason faithfulness is so important is because God did not promise us an easy life where everything goes the way we want it to go. God expects us to trust and follow Him just as much in the dark as we do in the light.

It's easy to say that God has been good to us when things go well, but the truth is God is good all the time. Determining to be faithful is the only reasonable response to His everlasting love, and that faithfulness will allow us to remain consistent through the ups and downs of life.

Today's Word to the Wise: When we faithfully serve God and patiently trust Him, our lives will be filled with His blessings.

A Leader's Example

If a ruler hearken to lies, all his servants are wicked.—**Proverbs 29:12**

In their best-selling business book *In Search of Excellence,* Tom Peters and Bob Waterman tried to discover what made some companies perform so much better than others. One of the companies they visited was Hewlett-Packard. The founders of this company, William Hewlett and Dave Packard, wanted their company to be filled with people who approached their jobs with interest and excitement. To that end they took the unusual step of establishing an "open lab stock" policy where employees were allowed and encouraged to take tools and parts home to use on their own projects and inventions. The consultants wrote: "Legend has it that Bill Hewlett visited a plant on a Saturday and found the lab stock area locked. He immediately went down to maintenance, grabbed a bolt cutter, and proceeded to cut the padlock off the lab stock door. He left a note that was found on Monday morning: 'Don't ever lock this door again. Thanks, Bill.'"

They then described a conversation with a young engineer who had only been with the company for a year. "Commenting on some problems with a new personnel procedure, he said: 'I'm not sure Bill and Dave would have done it that way.' It's truly remarkable to find the value set stamped in so quickly, and with such clarity." Peters and Waterman reported the same attitudes across the company. Why did the employees have that spirit? Because the leaders did.

Each of us is a leader in some part of our lives. From pastors and bosses to parents and teachers, we serve as examples to others—and they will follow those examples. If we conduct our lives with honesty and integrity, it will make a positive impact on them. Of course, the reverse is also true. Never forget those who are watching you.

Today's Word to the Wise: You are a leader in at least some aspect of your life, and your followers will copy your behavior—good or bad.

Taking Initiative

The locusts have no king, yet go they forth all of them by bands;
—**Proverbs 30:27**

Every day we are presented with opportunities to help people in need—spiritually, physically, or emotionally. Yet often these opportunities are missed because we do not seize the initiative and take action. When Peter and John went to the Temple to pray and saw the lame man there begging, they did not receive a special revelation or direction from God to help him. They simply saw his need and realized they should do something about it. "Then Peter said, Silver and gold have I none; but such as I have give I thee: In the name of Jesus Christ of Nazareth rise up and walk" (Acts 3:6).

An English pastor of the 1800s, Sydney Smith, wrote these words about those who fail to take action when they should: "A great deal of talent is lost in the world for want of a little courage. The fact is, that to do anything in the world worth doing, we must not stand back shivering and thinking of the cold danger, but we must jump in and scramble through as well as we can. A man waits, and doubts, and consults his brother, and his particular friends, till one day he finds that he is sixty years old, and that he has lost so much time in consulting that he has no time to follow their advice."

Most of the great things done for God are not the result of grand plans. They usually grow from the initiative taken by Christians to do something about a problem or need that they see. It does not take a revelation from God or a directive from a leader to respond to a challenge or crisis. God wants His people to be active rather than passive, responding in whatever way they can to the needs of those they meet.

Today's Word to the Wise: Do whatever you can to meet the needs in front of you rather than waiting for a perfect time to act.

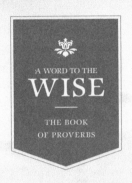

A WORD TO THE

WISE

THE BOOK
OF PROVERBS

OCTOBER

Crown Jewels

My son, hear the instruction of thy father, and forsake not the law of thy mother: For they shall be an ornament of grace unto thy head, and chains about thy neck.—**Proverbs 1:8–9**

One of the biggest tourist attractions in England is found at the Tower of London—the Crown Jewels. The crowns and regalia there have graced the heads of monarchs for centuries. Some of the pieces date back more than eight hundred years. The best-known piece of the collection is the Imperial State Crown. It contains more than three thousand gemstones, including the Second Star of Africa, the Black Prince's Ruby, the Stuart Sapphire, St. Edward's Sapphire, and Queen Elizabeth's Pearls. This is the crown that Queen Elizabeth wears for the Opening of Parliament and other state occasions. These beautiful pieces are a token of honor and tradition that has lasted for centuries.

When we walk in God's paths, keeping the instructions and principles taught to us by our earthly and spiritual parents, there are many benefits. We are spared the judgment for wrongdoing that comes when we violate these precepts, and we are able to receive the blessings that God promises for obedience. But one of the most important things in God's plan for our lives is that we pass on what we have received. The monarchs of England do not retain the Crown Jewels for themselves—they add to them to make them more beautiful and valuable and then pass them on to future generations.

God wants us to live in obedience so that we set an example for those who come behind us. Some have the privilege of coming from generations of believers while others are the first Christians in their family. In either case, we should live so that those who come after us have a legacy of grace to follow.

Today's Word to the Wise: When you walk in the way of godliness and wisdom, it decorates your life in a way that brings glory to God.

A Heart of Wisdom

When wisdom entereth into thine heart, and knowledge is pleasant unto thy soul; Discretion shall preserve thee, understanding shall keep thee:
—**Proverbs 2:10–11**

Wisdom works from the inside out. It must be in our heart before it can be in our actions. Doing right on the outside is important, but if things are not right on the inside, it will be revealed in time. We see a prime example of this in the life of Solomon. He was young when he became king of Israel, and Solomon recognized his need of help and asked God for wisdom. God was pleased and made Solomon extremely wise. His reputation spread around the world and leaders from far away, such as the Queen of Sheba, came to see his beautiful palace and hear him answer difficult questions.

Unfortunately, Solomon did not maintain wisdom in his heart. He allowed it to be replaced with idolatry. First Kings 11:1, 3–4 says, "But king Solomon loved many strange women together with the daughter of Pharaoh, women of the Moabites, Ammonites, Edomites, Zidonians, and Hittites; And he had seven hundred wives, princesses, and three hundred concubines: and his wives turned away his heart. For it came to pass, when Solomon was old, that his wives turned away his heart after other gods: and his heart was not perfect with the LORD his God."

We do not receive a lifetime supply of wisdom all at once. We must continually seek it through the pages of God's Word and from godly counselors. The direction of our lives will be shaped by our heart attitude toward wisdom. The benefits that come from having it are great and well worth the effort. As long as we are seeking and valuing wisdom, both our lives and those with whom we come in contact will be blessed.

Today's Word to the Wise: Keep God's principles in your heart and mind and they will guard and keep you from danger.

Both Hands Full

Length of days is in her right hand; and in her left hand riches and honour. Her ways are ways of pleasantness, and all her paths are peace. She is a tree of life to them that lay hold upon her: and happy is every one that retaineth her.—**Proverbs 3:16–18**

A young boy accompanied his mother on her trip to the general store. He was quite well behaved, and the man behind the counter was impressed as he watched the little fellow. When they were ready to check out, the man told the boy to reach into the jar of candy that was by the register and help himself. But the boy kept his hands down in his pockets and wouldn't respond. Finally, the man reached into the jar, got some candy, and handed it to the boy. When they left the store his mother asked, "Why didn't you get the candy when he told you to?" The boy replied, "Because his hands are way bigger than mine!"

God loves us and wants us to have good things for our lives, and His hands are far bigger than ours. One of the great blessings He offers to us is the instruction of wisdom. Wisdom comes to us with both hands full of blessings. When we walk in God's ways we reap enormous benefits. This is not to say that we can expect God to give us all the goodies we can think of. It is a prescription for living in a way that creates positive results and avoids negative ones.

A person who walks in folly may do things which shorten life, bring shame, and create financial hardship. These are not so much signs of the judgment of God as the natural consequences of walking outside of His commandments. The learning and living of wisdom is vital if we want to experience a happy and blessed life.

Today's Word to the Wise: Resolve to walk according to God's principles of wisdom, and every part of your life will be improved.

It All Flows from the Heart

Keep thy heart with all diligence; for out of it are the issues of life.
—**Proverbs 4:23**

High in northwest Minnesota, the Itasca State Park holds the origin of one the largest and most powerful natural features of our world—the Mississippi River. More than 2,500 miles long, the great river carries millions of gallons of water down the middle of the country. The Mississippi is vital to commerce, farming, transportation, and navigation for our nation, but it begins with a very small stream. The headwaters of the Mississippi River are the place where it all begins.

The Bible tells us that our heart is the source for the decisions and choices of life. We set the course for our future by the direction of our heart—everything else flows from that. Great wickedness comes when we allow our heart free reign to exercise evil. This was the reason God sent the Flood to destroy the world. "And GOD saw that the wickedness of man was great in the earth, and that every imagination of the thoughts of his heart was only evil continually" (Genesis 6:5).

This principle works both directions. When our heart is aligned with the things of God, blessings follow. Additionally, when our heart is right with God and the hearts of those with whom we fellowship are also right with God, our hearts will be knit to one another. During the good part of Saul's reign, Israel's first king was strengthened by a select group of his followers. First Samuel 10:26 records, "And Saul also went home to Gibeah; and there went with him a band of men, whose hearts God had touched."

If your heart is right, your actions and choices will reflect a desire for the things of God rather than the things of the world—and you will be blessed.

Today's Word to the Wise: Knowing the vital impact your heart will have on your future, guard it with great care.

A Source of Joy

Let thy fountain be blessed: and rejoice with the wife of thy youth.
—Proverbs 5:18

Marriage is under attack in our society. On one hand, the push for same-sex marriage is seeking to change the very definition of the institution which God created. On the other hand, there is a lack of respect and commitment for marriage, even among those who still understand what marriage is. Often we hear jokes about marriage that reveal contempt rather than holy reverence for the institution that is part of God's original plan for mankind. Marriage did not come after the fall but before it—and God takes the covenant commitment made by a man and wife very seriously.

God intends for marriage to be a source of joy and help in our lives. While it is not God's plan for every individual to marry, marriage is God's gift to many. For marriage to be what God intends it to be, effort on the part of both spouses is required. It cannot be done properly unless it is done unselfishly. There aren't any secrets or shortcuts—it is simply a matter of living day after day with the best interests of the other person in mind.

The pattern of humility and service that is required for a joyful marriage is set for us in the life of Christ. Picture Him on His knees in the Upper Room washing the feet of His disciples—including Judas who would betray Him that very night. The disciples had been discussing their comparative ranks in the coming kingdom and asking which of them would be the greatest. Yet Jesus, the Lord of Heaven and Earth, was humble before them, performing the task of a slave to meet their needs. When we approach marriage with care for the other person rather than insisting on getting everything we want, marriage becomes a source of joy and strength as God intends.

Today's Word to the Wise: God intends for marriage to be a source of joy, and those who are married are responsible to help create that joy.

Twice as Bad

These six things doth the LORD hate: yea, seven are an abomination unto him: A proud look, a lying tongue, and hands that shed innocent blood, An heart that deviseth wicked imaginations, feet that be swift in running to mischief, A false witness that speaketh lies, and he that soweth discord among brethren.—**Proverbs 6:16–19**

Despite the flippant portrayal of God that our modern society has created, we know from the pages of Scripture that the High and Holy God of Heaven and Earth hates sin. This is not a casual dislike—it is an intense hatred. A person need only look at the cross and see the price sin required to understand God's wrath toward sin. Even though God hates all sin, there are some sins that call down His special condemnation and judgment. On the list of seven abominable sins found here in Proverbs, one makes the list twice—lying.

This is not filler. God did not run out of things to include on the list of seven and repeat one to complete a number. Lying is a sin that God holds in special judgment and hatred. Why? Because lying was at the very heart of Satan's rebellion against God. Jesus told the Pharisees, "Ye are of your father the devil, and the lusts of your father ye will do. He was a murderer from the beginning, and abode not in the truth, because there is no truth in him. When he speaketh a lie, he speaketh of his own: for he is a liar, and the father of it" (John 8:44).

Too often Christians give themselves permission to tell "white lies" or stretch the truth, thinking that it is not that big of a deal. But it is a big deal to God. Complete honesty and integrity in our lives is the standard. Anything less means we are siding with Satan and doing his evil work. Those of us who know Christ should walk in and speak His truth.

Today's Word to the Wise: God expects and demands honesty from you in both word and action.

Don't Believe It

With her much fair speech she caused him to yield, with the flattering of her lips she forced him.—**Proverbs 7:21**

The 2004 presidential election was expected to be close, and it was. Early in the afternoon of election day the first round of exit polls showed Senator John Kerry with a significant lead over incumbent President George Bush in several key states. A long-time Democratic strategist with the Kerry campaign, Bob Shrum walked up to the Senator and said, "Can I be the first to call you Mr. President?" Of course when the actual votes were counted, Mr. Bush defeated Mr. Kerry, and Shrum's premature statement was proven incorrect. It was later revealed that he had said something very similar to then Vice President Al Gore during the 2000 election four years earlier.

There are many tools that people use to try to influence others, but one of the most effective is flattery. The old saying, "Flattery will get you nowhere" is belied by centuries of human experience. Flattery often works quite effectively at shaping the opinions and actions of another. For example when Daniel's enemies wanted King Darius to sign the decree forbidding anyone from praying to any god except the king himself, they did not reveal their true purpose. They painted a picture of bringing honor and respect to Darius, and he foolishly went along with their plot. Only the intervention of an angel prevented Daniel from being devoured by the lions.

That story points out the danger of flattery. It is a safe conclusion that the person trying to get you to do something by flattery is thinking far more about themselves than about what is good for you. While valid compliments are both appropriate and powerful, flattery focuses on unearned praise and tries to build up pride in the heart of the hearer.

Today's Word to the Wise: Be on guard when someone comes to you with flattering words; you can be sure they do not have your best interest at heart.

Seeking Wisdom Early

I love them that love me; and those that seek me early shall find me.
—Proverbs 8:17

The expression "the early bird gets the worm" entered the English language more than five hundred years ago, possibly from an even older German variation of the proverb. The idea that people can improve their chances of success by starting early is not new. Despite its demonstrated truth, too often we find excuses to put things off rather than beginning promptly. This principle applies in many areas, and it is especially applicable to the topic of wisdom in our lives.

There is a clear promise given to us here—when we seek wisdom early, we will find it. Solomon's own life illustrates this principle. He was a young man, around twenty years of age, when he became king over Israel. At the beginning of his reign when God offered him whatever he wanted, he asked for wisdom. David had taught him the vital importance of wisdom, and, when presented an opportunity to ask for great things from God, Solomon correctly selected wisdom.

Not only should we seek God's wisdom early in our lives, but it is important to seek wisdom early in the day as well. Though we live in a culture that values self-reliance, it is important for God's children not to approach life with the arrogant assumption that they need no help. In truth we must have God's help every day. Jeremiah wrote, "It is of the LORD's mercies that we are not consumed, because his compassions fail not" (Lamentations 3:22). We cannot live as God intends unless we walk in wisdom. Each morning we should set aside time to read God's Word and ask for His guidance and direction through the day. Since we have His promise that this request will be answered, we are foolish indeed if we fail to ask.

Today's Word to the Wise: The sooner we seek and begin to follow God's wisdom, the better our lives will be.

Behind the Door

But he knoweth not that the dead are there; and that her guests are in the depths of hell.—**Proverbs 9:18**

Frank Stockton's short story *The Lady or the Tiger?* first published in 1882, was for many years a favorite of high school English and literature classes. The story tells of a barbaric king who administered justice in his kingdom in a unique way. When a man was accused, he was placed in an arena with two doors before him. Behind one was a bloodthirsty tiger that would kill him in an instant. Behind the other was a beautiful maiden who would immediately become his wife.

In Stockton's tale, a commoner fell in love with the king's daughter. When the king discovered this, he was furious and sentenced the young man to his fate. Before the appointed day, the princess discovered which door concealed the tiger and which concealed the woman who would marry the man she loved—a woman she knew and hated. Just before the man chose his door and his destiny, she signaled toward the door on the right. The story does not answer the question of which fate she selected for the young man, leaving it up to the reader to determine what her choice would be. Would she rather see him alive with someone else or would she rather see him dead?

Like the man in that fictional story, we face a choice when temptation comes—a choice that is literally life and death. The difference is that we can *know* what is behind the door. While sin presents a beautiful face, it conceals death. The path of sin always leads to the same end. James wrote, "Then when lust hath conceived, it bringeth forth sin: and sin, when it is finished, bringeth forth death" (James 1:15). The only hope we have is to yield to God's Spirit and take the way to escape that He provides when temptation comes.

Today's Word to the Wise: When you are tempted to sin, remember what lies behind that door and do what is right.

The Hand of the Diligent

He becometh poor that dealeth with a slack hand: but the hand of the diligent maketh rich.—**Proverbs 10:4**

B iographical accounts of his early life vary, but it is generally believed that when Andrew Carnegie came to America from Scotland as a thirteen-year-old boy, he had less than a dollar. Like a large number of young people in his day, Carnegie went to work in a factory instead of going to school. Looking to better his life, he found a job first as a telegraph messenger and then later as a telegraph operator. In this position, his prodigious memory and diligent work brought him to the attention of some of Pennsylvania's leading industrialists. At eighteen he went to work for Thomas Scott at the Pennsylvania railroad, and by twenty he was made superintendent of the operation. Carnegie went on to become one of the wealthiest men in the world. While he was apparently not a born-again Christian, his life gives ample evidence to the importance and value of diligence.

As the old saying goes, "I'm a great believer in luck. The harder I work the luckier I get." A diligent worker stands out. The so-called Protestant work ethic has largely vanished from our world today. As a result, anyone who shows up on time, works hard, and gives an employer full value for wages paid will quickly get noticed. The Word of God tells us that the alternative to such work is poverty.

God's plan is not for people who are able to work to sit around and expect others to care for their needs. Paul wrote, "For even when we were with you, this we commanded you, that if any would not work, neither should he eat" (2 Thessalonians 3:10). When we view work as an opportunity to excel rather than a drudgery to complete, we can accomplish great things.

Today's Word to the Wise: If you treat every task you have as important and do it diligently, your work will be blessed.

A Need for Counsel

Where no counsel is, the people fall: but in the multitude of counsellors there is safety.—**Proverbs 11:14**

The news of the *Challenger* space shuttle explosion in January of 1986 was a major shock to almost everyone. Millions of school children watched the coverage of the launch because a teacher from New Hampshire, Christa McAuliffe, was part of the crew. To some, however, the tragedy was not unexpected. A year prior, engineers for Morton Thiokol (the company that made some of the key components of the shuttle) had discovered a serious problem. Under very cold conditions, the seals called o-rings that were part of the solid rocket boosters would fail, with potentially devastating results.

In July of 1985 an engineer named Roger Boisjoly wrote a memo to his superiors in which he said: "It is my honest and very real fear that if we do not take immediate action to dedicate a team to solve the problem… then we stand in jeopardy of losing a [space shuttle] flight…." Those concerns went unheeded on a cold morning in January of the following year. Morton Thiokol executives made what was later described as a "management decision" that the launch could proceed safely. Tragically, they were wrong, and seven people perished in an accident that could have been avoided.

There is a tendency—a dangerous and potentially deadly tendency—to think that we have things figured out and don't need help and input from others. The Bible stresses the importance of receiving and heeding wise counsel, but sometimes we only apply that principle to the young. It is for everyone; even those of us who have been saved for many years still benefit from the safety of godly counselors. Humble yourself enough to receive and follow good counsel, and you will be protected as a result.

Today's Word to the Wise: None of us are smart enough to resolve all of life's problems and questions—we need wise and godly counsel.

It Starts with your Thoughts

The thoughts of the righteous are right: but the counsels of the wicked are deceit.—**Proverbs 12:5**

In his book *Influence*, Dr. Robert Cialdini of Arizona State University relates the story of a shop owner who was preparing to go on vacation and left tasks for her staff to perform. She had a line of jewelry that hadn't been selling well, and she wanted it cleared out. In her haste, however, she left a note that was unclear. When she returned, she was delighted to find that every piece of the jewelry was gone. "I guess marking those pieces half price was the right call," she told her assistant. "Half price? I thought you wanted the price doubled!" the shocked girl replied. The pieces that hadn't been selling went out the door immediately once the price was raised because it changed the way people thought about them.

Our thoughts determine our actions. What seems to us to be shocking and out of character behavior would be explained if we could see the thought processes that had been going on internally. Jesus said, "A good man out of the good treasure of his heart bringeth forth that which is good; and an evil man out of the evil treasure of his heart bringeth forth that which is evil: for of the abundance of the heart his mouth speaketh" (Luke 6:45).

It is impossible to do rightly while thinking wrongly for an extended period of time. What is inside will come out. If you want your life to be marked by righteous actions, you must think righteous thoughts. That is why Paul wrote, "Finally, brethren, whatsoever things are true, whatsoever things are honest, whatsoever things are just, whatsoever things are pure, whatsoever things are lovely, whatsoever things are of good report; if there be any virtue, and if there be any praise, think on these things" (Philippians 4:8).

Today's Word to the Wise: If you fix your thoughts on the things of God, your actions will be pleasing to Him.

The Value of Work

Wealth gotten by vanity shall be diminished: but he that gathereth by labour shall increase.—**Proverbs 13:11**

Before James Garfield went into politics and became president, he taught at what is now Hiram College in Ohio. The ambidextrous Garfield would amuse his students by writing on a chalkboard with both hands—one in Greek and the other in Latin—at the same time! It is said that on one occasion a father came to Garfield and complained that the academic course at the school was too long and arduous and asked if it could be shortened. "Certainly," Garfield replied. "But it all depends on what you want to make of your boy. When God wants to make an oak tree, He takes a hundred years. When He wants to make a squash He requires only two months."

In a world filled with people looking for shortcuts to success and ways to avoid work, we are called by God to work—patiently, diligently, and consistently. The commandment to observe the Sabbath day includes this instruction: "Six days shalt thou labour, and do all thy work" (Exodus 20:9). Regardless of what those around us do, we have the responsibility to labor and work hard. This is the only path to true and lasting success. There are no shortcuts in God's economy.

Rather than looking for the easy way to get ahead, we should recognize the value and importance of work. The old Puritan preacher Cotton Mather described the balance between working for God and doing earthly work as being like the two oars on a boat. If you only pull on one oar you will not make progress toward your goal. Only when both oars are pulling together are you moving forward. While it may take time—perhaps even a great deal of time—work eventually produces rewards that are lasting.

Today's Word to the Wise: Be willing to put in the time and effort to achieve your goals, and you will be amazed at the results.

Work or Talk

In all labour there is profit: but the talk of the lips tendeth only to penury.—**Proverbs 14:23**

According to a recent study published in *Forbes* magazine on behavior in the workplace, 90 percent of employees said that they wasted at least some time each day at work. On average those employees were wasting about forty-five minutes per day. By far, the biggest time waster reported was talking to co-workers, with 43 percent of people saying they wasted time in this way. Economists estimate the value of wasted time each year to be in the billions of dollars.

When we view work properly, we recognize the value and importance of it. God has designed work not only to build and strengthen our character, but also to produce positive results. In God's plan, there is a connection between labor and reward. That is why in the Old Testament those who owned fields were commanded to leave some behind so that the poor could come and find food. "And when ye reap the harvest of your land, thou shalt not wholly reap the corners of thy field, neither shalt thou gather the gleanings of thy harvest" (Leviticus 19:9). The New Testament echoes this command in 2 Thessalonians 3:10: "For even when we were with you, this we commanded you, that if any would not work, neither should he eat."

Of course work has little appeal to our fallen nature. Instead, people look for ways to acquire wealth without effort. This explains the popularity of the lottery, which, as someone noted, is a tax on people who are bad at math. All of the dollars paid out in prize money are taken from those who buy tickets in hopes of getting rich quick. Many people who do win end up in much worse shape financially after the passage of time. God's plan is that we would work willingly and trust Him to reward us.

Today's Word to the Wise: When it is time to work, work hard and diligently, and your efforts will be rewarded.

The God Who Hears Our Prayers

The LORD is far from the wicked: but he heareth the prayer of the righteous.—**Proverbs 15:29**

When God appeared to Moses at the burning bush and commanded him to return to Egypt to free the Jewish people from their slavery, He was responding to their pleas for deliverance. The Bible says, "And the LORD said, I have surely seen the affliction of my people which are in Egypt, and have heard their cry by reason of their taskmasters; for I know their sorrows" (Exodus 3:7). When we pray we are not simply engaging in a religious ritual—we are talking to a God who hears us.

This knowledge is a critical part of the process to receiving answers to our prayers. John wrote, "And if we know that he hear us, whatsoever we ask, we know that we have the petitions that we desired of him" (1 John 5:15). Sometimes we receive what we ask for immediately, but other times prayer becomes a lengthy process. George Müller famously prayed for more than fifty years for the conversion of two of his friends. One was saved just before he died and the other not long after Müller passed away. In time, his prayers of many decades were answered.

The temptation when we do not quickly receive the answer is to begin to lose faith—to doubt that God is hearing us. This was the downfall of Abraham and Sarah. When God's promise of a son was not fulfilled they took matters into their own hands. Their plan created conflict and was fraught with disaster. Rather than losing heart and getting discouraged, we should continue to trust God even when we must wait for an answer. He does still hear and answer prayers, and we can count on Him to give us what is best in His timing.

Today's Word to the Wise: Rejoice in the knowledge that God hears your prayers today and allow that fact to strengthen your faith.

Effective Instruction

The wise in heart shall be called prudent: and the sweetness of the lips increaseth learning.—**Proverbs 16:21**

In the play *A Man for All Seasons*, about the life of Sir Thomas More of England, the following exchange occurs between More and a young man seeking advice for his future:

Sir Thomas More: Why not be a teacher? You'd be a fine teacher; perhaps a great one.

Richard Rich: If I was, who would know it?

Sir Thomas More: You; your pupils; your friends; God. Not a bad public, that.

Even those who are not professional teachers are involved in instruction. God's plan for His church is not just that the pastor will teach but that members will instruct and encourage each other. Paul told Titus to encourage the older women in the church, "That they may teach the young women to be sober, to love their husbands, to love their children" (Titus 2:4). He told Timothy, "And the things that thou hast heard of me among many witnesses, the same commit thou to faithful men, who shall be able to teach others also" (2 Timothy 2:2). All of us are teachers in at least one area of our lives.

If we want to be effective in our teaching, it is crucial that we carefully guard the words that come from our lips. When we speak with harshness or condescension, we put up barriers to learning. If we speak with kindness and encouragement, we are much more likely to get a positive response. One of the things about Jesus that amazed those who heard Him was the way in which He spoke. Luke records: "And all bare him witness, and wondered at the gracious words which proceeded out of his mouth. And they said, Is not this Joseph's son?" (Luke 4:22). May that truly be said of our speech as well.

Today's Word to the Wise: Be sure that your words are kind so you can influence others for good.

The Things We Value

Wherefore is there a price in the hand of a fool to get wisdom, seeing he hath no heart to it?—**Proverbs 17:16**

In 2004, a painting by Anna Mary Robertson, better known as Grandma Moses, was brought to the *Antiques Roadshow* for appraisal. Born before the Civil War, Robertson did not take up painting until late in her life. Her primitive style eventually became extremely popular, and her work commanded a high price. The man who brought the painting to be evaluated had lived nearby and his mother was a friend of Grandma Moses. He said, "She was just a wonderful friend of the family. And she would let my mother buy these paintings, which she thought had relatively little value. I guess my mother did, too. She probably bought eight or ten paintings in all, and my guess would be for perhaps under ten dollars each."

The painting that was bought for around $10 was appraised as being worth $60,000! In her early days of painting, Grandma Moses did not think of her works as being very valuable, so she parted with them for next to nothing. How often do we give up that which is priceless for a little temporary pleasure or advantage? How often do we abandon that which matters most for that which matters least?

The best way to determine what matters the most to someone is not to hear what they say but to see what they do. The things we pursue and give our lives to are the things that we truly value the most. Fools do not seek wisdom because they do not place any value on it. Wise people will seek wisdom even at great expenses because they understand how important it is to successful living. When we value what God values we are on the path to wisdom.

Today's Word to the Wise: The things that we value are revealed in the choices we make and to what we give our time, money, and effort.

A Friend Who Sticks

A man that hath friends must shew himself friendly: and there is a friend that sticketh closer than a brother.—**Proverbs 18:24**

Jonathan Edwards was one of the greatly used men of God in the early days of America. He is probably best remembered for the powerful sermon "Sinners in the Hands of an Angry God." That sermon broke through the proud self-reliance of many and helped spark the revival known as the Great Awakening in the churches of New England. Later, Edwards' own church turned against him when he insisted that only those who had been saved should be eligible for church membership. Voted out of his church, Edwards became the president of what is now Princeton University. Just a month after taking office, he received a smallpox vaccine, but contracted the disease and died. On his death bed, just before lapsing into unconsciousness, he said, "Now, where is Jesus of Nazareth, my true and never-failing Friend?" Indeed, Jesus is our true and never-failing Friend as well.

Friendship is one of the greatest blessings God has given to us. A true friend is a source of encouragement, counsel, wisdom, correction, and strength. In our moments of greatest trial, if we have such a friend we can find hope despite the darkness around us. Of course that is not always the case. Think of Job who in his suffering was visited by three men who were supposed to be his friends. Rather than bringing hope and encouragement, they condemned and criticized Job. Finally Job had enough: "Then Job answered and said, I have heard many such things: miserable comforters are ye all" (Job 16:1–2). Even if we are utterly forsaken and alone, there is still hope. David wrote, "When my father and my mother forsake me, then the LORD will take me up" (Psalm 27:10). There is never a burden or problem you will face that God will not be there for you.

Today's Word to the Wise: No matter what trials you endure or how many forsake you, Jesus will always be a faithful friend.

Don't Listen

Cease, my son, to hear the instruction that causeth to err from the words of knowledge.—**Proverbs 19:27**

One of the most important influences on the direction of your life is the people to whom you choose to listen. If you listen to those who encourage, motivate, uplift, and instruct in righteousness, you are likely to do right. If you listen to those who discourage and criticize, you are likely to stray from following God. The fact that we become like those to whom we listen makes it essential for us to choose wisely who we allow to influence us.

In his poem "It Couldn't Be Done," Edgar A. Guest wrote:

> There are thousands to tell you it cannot be done,
> There are thousands to prophesy failure,
> There are thousands to point out to you one by one,
> The dangers that wait to assail you.
> But just buckle in with a bit of a grin,
> Just take off your coat and go to it;
> Just start in to sing as you tackle the thing
> That "cannot be done," and you'll do it.

Don't listen to voices that are filled with discouragement and doubt. Instead, find those who encourage you to do right and well. Find those who uplift your spirit and keep you going when you want to quit. Find those whose speech is like that instructed in Ephesians 4:29, "Let no corrupt communication proceed out of your mouth, but that which is good to the use of edifying, that it may minister grace unto the hearers." We do not have to allow our minds and spirits to fall under the influence of those who would lead us astray. By measuring the input we receive from others against the Bible, we can determine if it is worth hearing.

Today's Word to the Wise: You cannot listen to those who constantly promote foolishness without it having an effect on your life.

Dig Until You Reach Water

Counsel in the heart of man is like deep water; but a man of understanding will draw it out.—**Proverbs 20:5**

If you travel to Greensburg, Kansas, you can pay a visit to what is billed as the "World's Largest Hand-Dug Well." Construction on the well began in the 1880s. As the railroads made their way across Kansas, a reliable source of water for the steam engines was essential. The work was done by teams of men using hand tools—shovels, picks, half barrels, pulleys, and rope. As they made their way downward, they lined the well shaft with limestone rock. The finished well is more than one hundred feet deep and more than thirty feet in diameter. It took enormous effort to reach the water, but it produced lasting results.

The Bible likens wise counsel to water in a deep well. Good advice is not just lying around on the surface—it takes work to find. There are plenty of people who have no idea what they are talking about but will be more than happy to give you a "piece of their mind." And sadly there will be plenty of people to give you advice that goes directly against the authority and commandments of Scripture. Anyone who wishes to be truly wise and reap the benefits of godly counsel is going to have to reject the simple approach and put forth effort—but the effort is worth it.

The Bible says, "Blessed is the man that walketh not in the counsel of the ungodly" (Psalm 1:1). If we reject the counsel of the world and seek the counsel of wise men, it will bring God's blessings on our lives and keep us on the right path. Do not let the effort required to find good counsel keep you from this important task.

Today's Word to the Wise: If you put forth the effort to find and receive wise counsel, you will be rewarded.

What Matters Most to God

*To do justice and judgment is more acceptable to the L*ord *than sacrifice.*
—**Proverbs 21:3**

Some people believe that God is pleased with whatever we happen to bring before Him—that all worship is equally acceptable to God. But a quick review of Scripture clearly shows that this is not the case. Cain brought an offering, but it was not accepted because it was not given in obedience. Nadab and Abihu offered "strange fire" before the Lord in the tabernacle and were struck dead as a result. King Uzziah went into the temple to offer the sacrifices of the priests, and God struck him with leprosy. Ananias and Sapphira brought an offering to Peter, but because they lied about it, they fell down dead in front of the congregation.

Our sacrifices do not buy us favor with God. The sacrifice of Jesus on the cross has forever settled the question of position with God for all who believe. The prophet Isaiah wrote, "He shall see of the travail of his soul, and shall be satisfied: by his knowledge shall my righteous servant justify many; for he shall bear their iniquities" (Isaiah 53:11). Our gifts to God are given in gratitude for His grace to us, not to improve our standing with Him.

Hebrews 13:15–16 says, "By him therefore let us offer the sacrifice of praise to God continually, that is, the fruit of our lips giving thanks to his name. But to do good and to communicate forget not: for with such sacrifices God is well pleased." God does not need anything that we have. Everything already belongs to Him. When we live with praise in our hearts toward Him and love in our actions toward others, He is pleased. Rather than trying to buy God's favor and forgiveness, we should give freely because we have already received them through His grace.

Today's Word to the Wise: God is far more interested in the condition of our heart than He is in the size of our offerings.

The Pathway to Peace

Cast out the scorner, and contention shall go out; yea, strife and reproach shall cease.—**Proverbs 22:10**

Paul "Red" Adair was one of the most famous firefighters in the world. Adair was not the kind of firefighter who rushed into burning homes or office buildings. Instead his highly specialized team travelled around the world to put out fires at oil wells and gas fields. Adair served in the Army during World War II as a bomb disposal expert, and he used his knowledge of high explosives to good effect in his dangerous line of work. One of his most famous firefighting efforts was in the Gassi Touil field in Algeria. The fire burned out of control for more than five months—the pillar of flame reaching some 450 feet in the air—before Adair was called in to put out the blaze.

The secret to Adair's technique lay in the recognition that fire requires oxygen to burn. The blast from the high explosives would temporarily stop the fire by removing the oxygen until a cap could be put in place to stop the flow of oil or gas that was feeding the fire.

In the same way that oxygen is a component of fire, critical people are a component of strife and trouble. The harsh and unkind words of a continual critic create a combustible atmosphere that inevitably leads to conflict.

If you want to enjoy a calm and peaceful life then you must, as Romans 14:19 says, "follow after the things which make for peace." One of those things is limiting your exposure to critical people. While it is not possible for us to avoid these types of people completely, we do need to take whatever steps we can to reduce their impact on our lives. Like a raging oil fire that is capped after an explosion to take away oxygen, peace follows when critical people are removed.

Today's Word to the Wise: When you spend time around highly critical people, you can expect to have a life filled with strife.

Consider Carefully

Eat thou not the bread of him that hath an evil eye, neither desire thou his dainty meats: For as he thinketh in his heart, so is he: Eat and drink, saith he to thee; but his heart is not with thee. The morsel which thou hast eaten shalt thou vomit up, and lose thy sweet words.
—**Proverbs 23:6–8**

The Medici were one of the most famous and powerful families of Italy during the Middle Ages. Their involvement in politics, religion, art, and science left a major impact on the entire world. They were known as a ruthless family, willing to do virtually anything to get their way—even in their dealings with each other. In 2007, scientists from the University of Florence unearthed the grave of Francesco de Medici, the Grand Duke of Tuscany. Their finding of highly elevated levels of arsenic in his bones and hair fragments gives credence to the rumor that he had been poisoned. It is very likely that the poisoner was his own brother, Cardinal Ferdanando de Medici, who wanted the title for himself and poisoned Francesco at a family meal.

Not every banquet that is set before you is safe to eat. The devil knows how powerful an attractive "meal" is in tempting us to sin. This approach worked in the very first temptation in the Garden of Eden: "And when the woman saw that the tree was good for food, and that it was pleasant to the eyes, and a tree to be desired to make one wise, she took of the fruit thereof, and did eat, and gave also unto her husband with her; and he did eat" (Genesis 3:6). Like a sports team running the same play again and again because the opponent hasn't adjusted, Satan continues to make sin look attractive to lure men and women to sin and destruction.

Today's Word to the Wise: Before you take the first bite, consider carefully who has prepared the food that is put before you.

The Allure of Change

My son, fear thou the LORD and the king: and meddle not with them that are given to change: For their calamity shall rise suddenly; and who knoweth the ruin of them both?—**Proverbs 24:21–22**

It is a natural part of life for things to change. (For instance, anyone who has needed medical care understands that "the good old days" weren't a good time to have a serious illness.) The conveniences of modern technology, though sometimes used for ill, also offer wonderful opportunities to take the gospel to more people. Yet we live in a world that is *obsessed* with change, and that spirit has had a serious impact on churches as well. Change is sometimes needed, but those who are constantly seeking change for the sake of change are on a path to disaster.

In Luke's account of Paul's missionary journey to Athens he wrote, "(For all the Athenians and strangers which were there spent their time in nothing else, but either to tell, or to hear some new thing)" (Acts 17:21). In the process of seeking change, many people abandon things that should not be lost. The notion that change is a good thing in and of itself is a lie that the devil has used to great effect through the centuries. While there are good changes that should be made, they should be made with great care.

In logic there is something known as the Fallacy of Chesterton's Fence which says, "Don't ever take down a fence until you know why it was put up." That is sound advice for every part of life. While it may seem attractive to go around replacing the old with the new, this is something that should only be done with much thought and the seeking of wise counsel. Do not follow those who are constantly promoting change simply because they are unsettled and discontent. They are likely to lead you to a destructive end.

Today's Word to the Wise: Do not allow yourself to be infected with the spirit of constant change.

False Boasting

*Whoso boasteth himself of a false gift is like clouds and wind without rain.—***Proverbs 25:14**

In July of 2013, one of the oldest and most prestigious honorary intellectual societies in the nation, the American Academy of Arts and Sciences, was stunned by the resignation of its president and chief executive officer, Leslie Berlowitz. The Academy, founded during the Revolutionary War, has more than four thousand members dedicated to advancing knowledge and conducting research. Berlowitz was forced to resign after it was revealed that she falsely claimed to have received a doctorate from New York University. Ironically one of the books she had written was titled *Restoring Trust in American Business.*

The prevailing attitude in our society reflects the spirit of "tooting your own horn," even falsely when it seems advantageous to do so. In contrast, the prevailing attitude commanded in Scripture is one of humility. Jesus observed how the Pharisees competed to get the best and most prominent seats when they gathered. But He instructed His followers to not seek a place of prominence for themselves: "But when thou art bidden, go and sit down in the lowest room; that when he that bade thee cometh, he may say unto thee, Friend, go up higher: then shalt thou have worship in the presence of them that sit at meat with thee. For whosoever exalteth himself shall be abased; and he that humbleth himself shall be exalted" (Luke 14:10–11).

There is a great temptation to want others to see and notice what we are doing. We want them to think well of us. While we should certainly live in an honest and upright manner which is worthy of praise, that is not the reason we do it. Instead, we should allow God to determine our level of fame and attention. Faithfulness to Him will always be rewarded, whether or not it is ever seen or noticed by others.

Today's Word to the Wise: Trust God to give you whatever praise and promotion He sees fit rather than putting yourself forward.

Not a Fun Game

As a mad man who casteth firebrands, arrows, and death, So is the man that deceiveth his neighbour, and saith, Am not I in sport?
—Proverbs 26:18–19

Laughter is one of the kindest gifts God has given to humans. It lightens the heart and, as researchers continue to find, has positive health benefits.

As helpful as laughter may be, however, we need to be cautious about having fun at the expense of others. Some people delight in saying hurtful and critical things about their friends and then pass it off as "just teasing." Comments about physical attributes or intelligence can quickly become painful. The fact the person saying them may be laughing doesn't make them funny to the person about whom they are spoken. Such words can be discouraging and defeating to hear.

Many of us can still remember hurtful things that were said to us or about us on playgrounds and in classrooms decades ago. Those wounding words carry enormous power. Many are discouraged and defeated because they are subjected to a constant barrage of negativity and criticism.

When Job's friend Eliphaz came to comfort him after Job lost all of his children and his possessions, he said this about Job: "Behold, thou hast instructed many, and thou hast strengthened the weak hands. Thy words have upholden him that was falling, and thou hast strengthened the feeble knees" (Job 4:3–4). Part of what made Job such an upright man was the impact his words had on others. Rather than making jokes and having fun at the expense of others, we should ensure that our words are lifting them up and encouraging them to go forward and do right. Paul wrote, "Let your speech be alway with grace, seasoned with salt, that ye may know how ye ought to answer every man" (Colossians 4:6).

Today's Word to the Wise: Take great care in teasing and joking with others—it often creates grave problems.

The Influence of Friends

As in water face answereth to face, so the heart of man to man.
—**Proverbs 27:19**

In his short story *The Great Stone Face*, Nathaniel Hawthorne tells of a rock outcropping in the New England mountains that resembled a human face. The legend in the story is that someday a man will come whose face matches the stone and who will be the "greatest man of his time." A young boy named Ernest growing up nearby hopes that he will be able to find that great man. Over the course of his life, a number of prominent men come to the mountain, including a wealthy merchant, a victorious general, a rising politician, and a gifted writer. But each of them is flawed, and none of them resemble the stone face.

As an old man, Ernest, who has become a preacher, is asked to give a sermon at the base of the mountain. In the evening as the sun sets and the people listen, they make a discovery. Hawthorne wrote, "The face of Ernest assumed a grandeur of expression, so imbued with benevolence, that the poet, by an irresistible impulse, threw his arms aloft and shouted, 'Behold! Behold! Ernest is himself the likeness of the Great Stone Face!' Then all the people looked, and saw that what the deep-sighted poet said was true. The prophecy was fulfilled." Despite their acclaim, Ernest remained unconvinced. He went home hoping someday a great man would come.

This fictional story contains an important spiritual truth—we become like those who influence us. Just as we see a reflection of our face in a still pool of water, we see a reflection of our heart in those we have chosen as our friends. The basis of any friendship is shared beliefs and interests. Amos asked, "Can two walk together, except they be agreed?" (Amos 3:3). But our friends do not just reveal our hearts. They also help shape and mold them.

Today's Word to the Wise: Choose your friends with the greatest care because they will surely shape the future of your life.

Take a Stand

He that rebuketh a man afterwards shall find more favour than he that flattereth with the tongue.—**Proverbs 28:23**

In June of 1989, after weeks of protests for freedom and democracy in Tiananmen Square in Beijing, China, the authorities ordered a crackdown. The army was sent into the crowd to brutally break up the protests. While no exact count has ever been revealed, it is believed that at least hundreds (if not thousands) of protestors were murdered—many of them shot in the back. Perhaps the most enduring image of the protest was a single individual who came to be known simply as "Tank Man."

This one man holding two shopping bags saw a line of army tanks rolling toward the center of the city. He stepped into the street and stood in front of the lead tank. Even when they gunned their engines, he held his ground. When the tanks tried to maneuver around him, he moved to remain in front of them. Finally two men came out of the crowd and pulled him from the street. Though his fate is unknown, his courage has never been forgotten.

All of us face moments when we must choose to take a stand for right even if it means saying or doing something unpopular. Even if no one else stands with us, standing for right is always honored by God. Often we find that if we do take a stand, others will be inspired by our example and join with us. The influence that we have in those moments should not be missed. When Nebuchadnezzar commanded everyone to bow down before his golden idol, the three Hebrew children refused. Their courage was strengthened by being able to stand together. As a result, they presented a unified front to the heathen king. They were thrown into a burning furnace, but they emerged unharmed after walking with the Son of God through the fire.

Today's Word to the Wise: Even if you must stand alone, never be afraid to speak out boldly for what is right.

Righteous Leadership

When the righteous are in authority, the people rejoice: but when the wicked beareth rule, the people mourn.—**Proverbs 29:2**

A few years ago, the global consulting firm Ernst & Young did a survey of corporations in a number of different countries. Among the startling reports was that more than half reported suffering losses due to "significant fraud." Even more startling was the revelation that of those companies, an overwhelming majority of the losses were at the hands of managers—most often among those newly promoted to positions of leadership. A companion study showed that a large majority of workers believe they are more honest than their bosses.

All of us are responsible to God as leaders in at least some part of our lives. As such we have a serious responsibility to those who are following us. Whether that is one young child or hundreds of employees, the principle remains the same: we must set a righteous and godly example, or there will be serious consequences. Of course, a failure on the part of a leader does not justify wrongdoing on the part of a follower, but because of human nature, people frequently use the misconduct of those over them to excuse their own bad behavior.

Think of the life of Joseph. He was hated by his brothers because of the favoritism shown to him by Jacob. When the opportunity arose, they sold Joseph into slavery and took his coat of many colors home covered with blood so their father would think Joseph had been killed by a wild animal. Where did they learn to deceive their father? Years earlier, Jacob had conspired with his mother to deceive Isaac and claim the blessing from his brother Esau. The implications and influence of our example can stretch for generations, so it is vital we make sure it is a good one.

Today's Word to the Wise: Live your life with integrity so those who look up to you as an example will have a good one to follow.

Hang On and Keep Climbing

The spider taketh hold with her hands, and is in kings' palaces.
—**Proverbs 30:28**

In May of 2001, Erik Weihenmayer accomplished something that only about 150 people per year do—reaching the top of Mount Everest. The thing that made Erik's achievement unusual is that he is the first blind person to succeed in scaling the tallest mountain in the world. Erik was born with a disease called retinoschisis, and by the time he was thirteen he was completely blind. Rather than focus on what he could not do, he made the choice to focus on what he could do and went much further than almost anyone expected. Erik Weihenmayer's autobiography is titled *Touch the Top of the World: A Blind Man's Journey to Climb Farther Than the Eye Can See.*

Many times we face a choice—will we allow obstacles to stop us, or will we keep pressing on regardless of opposition and trouble? It would be nice if following God meant that things would always work out well and people would always like us. The reality is that many times doing what is right requires overcoming obstacles. We should not expect constant smooth sailing, nor should we allow troubles that arise to convince us to quit.

Consider the story of Jesus calming the storm for the disciples. "Now it came to pass on a certain day, that he went into a ship with his disciples: and he said unto them, Let us go over unto the other side of the lake. And they launched forth" (Luke 8:22). The disciples were acting in complete obedience to the command of Christ. They were in His physical presence—in close relationship to Him. Yet a great and terrifying storm arose, and they went to Jesus and begged for help. Jesus rebuked the storm, and they made their way safely to the other side. Do not let circumstances stop you from doing right.

Today's Word to the Wise: God does great things through people who refuse to be discouraged and quit His work.

Plan Ahead

She riseth also while it is yet night, and giveth meat to her household, and a portion to her maidens. She considereth a field, and buyeth it: with the fruit of her hands she planteth a vineyard.—**Proverbs 31:15–16**

Immediately following the fall of France to the invading German army in 1940, Winston Churchill and Franklin Roosevelt began discussing how to drive Hitler's forces back and liberate Europe. Planning this invasion began in earnest in 1942—a full two years before the Normandy invasion that came to be called Operation Overlord. The massive invasion that began the toppling of Hitler from power required so much manpower and machinery that it could not be quickly put together. Instead, long and careful planning was required to increase the likelihood of success.

While there are occasions when an opportunity suddenly arises, most significant accomplishments require diligent planning and preparation. For instance, over the years, our church family has built a number of buildings for the work of our ministry. We do not call for the bulldozers and steelworkers to show up first—instead we talk to architects and engineers. The construction of the building is what is visible, but that is the result of careful work that must begin long before the building starts to rise out of the ground.

The virtuous woman of Proverbs 31 planned meals for her family and their workers before the day started. That is careful short-term planning. Beyond that, the Bible tells us that she bought a field and planted a vineyard. This is careful long-term planning. It takes years before a vineyard becomes productive. But she was looking to the future, considering what she would need in the coming years, and making preparations for it.

Faith in God does not free us from the necessity of making wise plans. Instead of hoping things will work out somehow, we should do all we can to prepare for success. Then we must trust in the Lord for the outcomes.

Today's Word to the Wise: In all of your decisions, consider the long-term as well as the immediate outcomes.

A WORD TO THE

WISE

THE BOOK
OF PROVERBS

NOVEMBER

Consider Your Alliances

If they say, Come with us, let us lay wait for blood, let us lurk privily for the innocent without cause: Let us swallow them up alive as the grave; and whole, as those that go down into the pit: We shall find all precious substance, we shall fill our houses with spoil: Cast in thy lot among us; let us all have one purse:—**Proverbs 1:11–14**

Jehoshaphat was in many respects a good and godly king over Judah. But despite how much God blessed him, Jehoshaphat stopped following God with his whole heart. One of the biggest negative influences on his life was his friendship with the wicked king Ahab. "And Ahab king of Israel said unto Jehoshaphat king of Judah, Wilt thou go with me to Ramothgilead? And he answered him, I am as thou art, and my people as thy people; and we will be with thee in the war" (2 Chronicles 18:3).

In the following battle, Ahab was killed (just as Elijah had prophesied after the murder of Naboth), and Jehoshphat was nearly slain as well. But the consequences of Jehoshaphat's foolish alliance did not end in his lifetime. Following his death, his oldest son Jehoram took the throne. "And he walked in the way of the kings of Israel, like as did the house of Ahab: for he had the daughter of Ahab to wife: and he wrought that which was evil in the eyes of the LORD" (2 Chronicles 21:6).

While it is important for us to be kind and loving toward those who do not love and follow God, we should never make them our closest friends and companions. Jehu rebuked Jehoshaphat saying, "Shouldest thou help the ungodly, and love them that hate the LORD?" (2 Chronicles 19:2). Limit your close alliances to those who love and serve God.

Today's Word to the Wise: Close friendships with those who do not follow God and walk in His wisdom produce devastating results.

The Point of No Return

For her house inclineth unto death, and her paths unto the dead. None that go unto her return again, neither take they hold of the paths of life.—**Proverbs 2:18–19**

Located on the border between the United States and Canada, the three waterfalls of the Niagara River known as the Niagara Falls have the largest water flow rate of any falls in the world. Above the falls, Goat Island divides the river to flow over the Canadian Falls and the American Falls. The swift current of the river around the island forms amazing whitewater rapids that are often referred to as the "point of no return." Any boater who ventures past that point will be unable to escape being swept over the falls.

In every temptation we face, there comes a point of no return—a point where if we go any further, we will go over the edge into sin. At that point, our actions (or lack thereof) determine the outcome. Think of Joseph leaving his coat behind and fleeing from the house where Potiphar's wife was urging him to sin. In contrast, think of David lingering on the rooftop of the palace to look at Bathsheba. If David had done as Joseph did, the awful sin and suffering that followed would have been avoided. But by remaining in the place of temptation, David passed the point of no return.

Paul instructed Timothy, "Flee also youthful lusts: but follow righteousness, faith, charity, peace, with them that call on the Lord out of a pure heart" (2 Timothy 2:22). The longer we linger near temptation, the more likely we are to sin. Someone said that the reason people struggle with temptation is that they want to discourage it instead of defeat it. Recognizing the horrible consequences of sin, we should treat every temptation as a deadly danger to be avoided.

Today's Word to the Wise: The best way to overcome temptation is to take decisive action as soon as it appears.

Do What You Can

Withhold not good from them to whom it is due, when it is in the
power of thine hand to do it. Say not unto thy neighbour, Go, and
come again, and to morrow I will give; when thou hast it by thee.
—**Proverbs 3:27–28**

Edmund Burke, the great English politician and statesman of the eighteenth century, said, "No one ever made a greater mistake than he who did nothing because he could only do a little." We sometimes face the temptation to wait until we can do more before doing anything. Yet throughout Scripture and the history of the church, we see God doing great things with small gifts that came from willing hearts. The widow's mite, the little boy's lunch of loaves and fishes, the staff in the hand of Moses, the sling that David carried—none of these were mighty, yet they were used by God to accomplish great things.

Before He was crucified, Jesus was eating dinner when a woman came and anointed Him with spikenard. She was immediately criticized by those sitting around for wasting such a valuable commodity. The criticism was led by Judas who wanted the money to go into the treasury so he could embezzle it, but Jesus quickly corrected the critics. He pointed out that her gift was not a waste because it was an offering made from a loving heart. Jesus said, "She hath done what she could: she is come aforehand to anoint my body to the burying" (Mark 14:8).

We may not be able to do much, and there may never be buildings named in our honor because of our great donations. But God is much more concerned about the heart that motivates the gift than He is the size of the gift. He does not need our resources—it all belongs to Him already. What He desires is for us to do what we can.

Today's Word to the Wise: Rather than waiting until you have more, do all that you can with what you have today, and God will bless what you do.

Look Straight Ahead

Let thine eyes look right on, and let thine eyelids look straight before thee.—**Proverbs 4:25**

Marla Runyan gave her all to qualify for the Olympic Games in 1996, but her best time finished short of the mark to make the United States team. Undeterred by that failure, she returned in 2000 and made the team for the Sydney Olympics. Her eighth place finish in the 1,500 meter race was the best finish ever for a United States woman runner. The thing that makes Runyan's accomplishments even more remarkable is that she is legally blind. She is the first legally blind athlete to ever qualify for and compete in the Olympic Games. After her Olympic career was over she switched to running marathons and in 2002 posted the second fastest debut marathon time ever by an American woman.

Runyan can only see shapes and blurs, but she says that her lack of vision is actually an asset—she just focuses on the finish line in front of her rather than looking around to see what the other runners are doing. Not having visual distractions helps her compete and win her races. The same thing can be true in our lives. There will always be things that try to pull us away from what we should be focused on doing. Many times these will be good things, but we must be willing to set them aside and stay focused on what is most important.

The writer of Hebrews said, "Wherefore seeing we also are compassed about with so great a cloud of witnesses, let us lay aside every weight, and the sin which doth so easily beset us, and let us run with patience the race that is set before us, Looking unto Jesus the author and finisher of our faith" (Hebrews 12:1–2). No matter what is going on around us, Jesus never changes. As long as we focus on Him, we will stay on course.

Today's Word to the Wise: Keep your focus on Jesus, and the rest of life will fall into its proper place.

The Bondage of Sin

His own iniquities shall take the wicked himself, and he shall be holden with the cords of his sins.—**Proverbs 5:22**

Before Samson was even born, God had a special purpose for his life. The angel who told his mother that she would have a son said, "For, lo, thou shalt conceive, and bear a son; and no razor shall come on his head: for the child shall be a Nazarite unto God from the womb: and he shall begin to deliver Israel out of the hand of the Philistines" (Judges 13:5). God gave Samson a vast measure of strength which allowed him to win great victories over Israel's enemies. Despite the blessings he received from God, Samson took his responsibility to obey God's law lightly. He neglected to obey the God who gave him strength.

Samson frequently indulged immoral appetites, and he disregarded all but one aspect of his Nazarite vow—that of not cutting his hair. Eventually, however, through the influence of Delilah, Samson disclosed the secret to his strength (his obedience to his vow of not cutting his hair). His enemies cut off his hair while he slept, and when he awoke, his strength was gone, and he was captured. "But the Philistines took him, and put out his eyes, and brought him down to Gaza, and bound him with fetters of brass; and he did grind in the prison house" (Judges 16:21). Playing with sin became the downfall of Samson.

Sin promises pleasure and enjoyment, but it only delivers bondage. The illusion that we are in control is part of the allure of sin, but it is a lie. Like fetters wrapped around our souls again and again, the tentacles of sin take control and rob us of freedom. Like Samson, we usually do not recognize this is happening until it is too late. Knowing the deadly power of sin we must reject the false promises of temptation. This is the only way to maintain spiritual freedom.

Today's Word to the Wise: Sin is a master, not a servant. Though the bondage of sin may be invisible for a time, it is always there.

A Better Approach

My son, if thou be surety for thy friend, if thou hast stricken thy hand with a stranger, Thou art snared with the words of thy mouth, thou art taken with the words of thy mouth.—**Proverbs 6:1–2**

The Bible is filled with spiritual truths as well as advice for successful living in the "here and now." One of these is the warning against the co-signing of loans, what the Bible calls "surety." Many parents and grandparents have learned this lesson the hard way and are stuck with student loans that their children cannot or will not repay. In at least one high profile case, the loan company sued the parents of a student who had died before finishing his degree to try to get their money back.

Borrowing money is not necessarily a bad thing, but it is done much too freely in our society. It poses dangers that must be recognized, and if they are not, trouble is likely to follow. In many respects, borrowing resembles an old saying about government (sometimes attributed to George Washington): "Like fire, it is a dangerous servant and a fearful master. Never for a moment should it be left to irresponsible action."

If you choose to borrow or guarantee someone else's loan, you are placing yourself in a potentially dangerous position. The principles taught in Scripture teach that a far better approach is to save and to give rather than to co-sign. Many people stay in bondage for years because they have failed to heed this warning.

Today's Word to the Wise: Do not enter into foolish agreements that require you to make good for someone else's borrowing.

The Right Time to Repent

For the goodman is not at home, he is gone a long journey: He hath taken a bag of money with him, and will come home at the day appointed.
—Proverbs 7:19–20

Many times people—saved and unsaved alike—think that they will have plenty of time to repent and make things right with God. We think that we can sin up to a certain point, and then we will have time to settle our accounts with God. But the truth is that we do not know how long God's mercy will stay His hand of judgment. The fact that we are not immediately struck down the moment we sin is not a statement of God's indifference to our actions; it is a demonstration of His patience.

Consider, for instance, when David sinned with Bathsheba and then had her husband Uriah killed to cover up what he had done. He knew that it was wrong, but the plan he had devised to hide his sin appeared to be working so he stuck with it. It was not until he was confronted by Nathan that David repented.

We cannot count on knowing God's clock and getting in under the wire with a last minute repentance. The author of Hebrews wrote, "While it is said, To day if ye will hear his voice, harden not your hearts, as in the provocation" (Hebrews 3:15). The longer we put off making things right with God, the harder it becomes. Our hearts settle into a comfort zone with our sin, and our conscience becomes seared. In such a state, it usually requires severe chastisement from God for a true change to occur. It is far better to repent today than wait for tomorrow.

Today's Word to the Wise: If there is a matter in your life that needs repentance, do not wait—take care of it immediately.

The Assurance of Creation

When he prepared the heavens, I was there: when he set a compass upon the face of the depth: When he established the clouds above: when he strengthened the fountains of the deep: When he gave to the sea his decree, that the waters should not pass his commandment: when he appointed the foundations of the earth:—**Proverbs 8:27–29**

O ne of the purposes of creation is to show the power and majesty of God. In Psalm 19:1, David wrote, "The heavens declare the glory of God; and the firmament sheweth his handywork."

The Old Testament saint Job learned the value of seeing God's power displayed in creation. When God permitted Satan to take away everything he possessed, Job exhibited tremendous patience. But he also expressed a desire to understand—to have God explain why this was happening to him. When God did appear and speak, He did not provide the explanation Job was seeking. Instead He spoke at length (Job 38–41) about His power as demonstrated in the creation of the world. When God finished speaking, Job still did not have a reason for what he had gone through, but he did have a new appreciation for God. He said, "I know that thou canst do every thing, and that no thought can be withholden from thee" (Job 42:2).

When we are enduring difficult times, we too can look to creation to see the wisdom and majesty of God. We may not be able to understand the reasons for our present suffering (indeed, our finite minds may be unable to comprehend the purposes of God in allowing the suffering), but we can be renewed as we focus on the greatness of our God. Knowing the truth of creation and seeing the revelation of the power of God all around us, our faith will be strengthened and we will be encouraged to trust all of His precious promises.

Today's Word to the Wise: When you are tempted to doubt God, simply look around at His creation and be reminded of His power and faithfulness.

Recognizing Boundaries

Stolen waters are sweet, and bread eaten in secret is pleasant.
—Proverbs 9:17

Following the terrorist attacks on the United States on September 11, 2001, a new set of rules governing the air space over Washington, D.C. was put into place by the Federal Aviation Administration. In the first eighteen months after the new restricted zone was established, more than one thousand unauthorized flights flew into the off-limits area. Though none of these were attempted attacks, they all required a response from defense and security personnel. On several occasions, the White House and other government buildings were even evacuated. To curb the problem, the FAA established a special training course that all pilots who would be flying in the Washington, D.C. area were required to complete. The course would equip pilots to avoid straying into air space they are not allowed to enter.

Through His Word, God gives us the tools and guidance we need to avoid the things that are off limits. God knows that this training is necessary because the devil works hard to make sin as alluring as possible. He paints a beautiful picture of pleasure and enjoyment that will come when we yield to temptation and cross the boundaries God has established. The first temptation in the Garden of Eden succeeded because Adam was willing to join his wife in eating the forbidden fruit. It looked good, and I'm sure it tasted good, and Satan (falsely) promised that eating it would make them like God. So they ate. And death entered the world along with sin.

First John 2:16 describes the aspects of temptation this way: "For all that is in the world, the lust of the flesh, and the lust of the eyes, and the pride of life, is not of the Father, but is of the world." It is our job to learn to recognize what is forbidden and stay far away from it.

Today's Word to the Wise: Take the Bible as your training manual to equip and empower you to resist the allure of temptation.

There Is More to Learn

Wise men lay up knowledge: but the mouth of the foolish is near destruction.—**Proverbs 10:14**

General Douglas MacArthur grew up in a distinguished military family. His father won the Medal of Honor during the Civil War at the Battle of Missionary Ridge. Douglas went to West Point where he had the highest grade point average of any student in the previous twenty-five years. He would go on to be one of America's most courageous and creative military leaders. What most people don't realize is that MacArthur never stopped his military education. Despite his high academic standing at West Point, he did not consider his learning complete. He devoured military textbooks and visited battlefields in person to see how the terrain influenced the conflicts he had studied. He learned everything he could to prepare himself to be a better leader.

Wisdom encourages us to continue to learn—to "lay up knowledge"—just as a settler in pioneer days would spend the year cutting a large quantity of firewood and storing food in preparation for the winter months. The reality is that life is going to present us challenges and obstacles, and the more we can learn, the better prepared we will be to meet them. Education and learning are not just for children in school settings but for all of us throughout all of our lives.

Late in his life, not long before his execution, Paul wrote to Timothy from prison in Rome: "The cloke that I left at Troas with Carpus, when thou comest, bring with thee, and the books, but especially the parchments" (2 Timothy 4:13). Why did the aged apostle want Timothy to bring him books? Because he recognized the need for continued learning and study, particularly of the Word of God. We should never fall into the trap of thinking that we have learned all we need to know—there is always more to learn.

Today's Word to the Wise: Learn everything that you can so you will be better prepared to serve God and others.

Blessed in Freedom

By the blessing of the upright the city is exalted: but it is overthrown by the mouth of the wicked.—**Proverbs 11:11**

America has been blessed throughout our history to have men of great courage and faith stand in the gap and fight for our freedom. Veteran's Day is set aside to honor those who have served our country in this way. We have truly received a great gift through their sacrifice, and it is only right that we pause to remember and give thanks for the price they have paid for the freedom we too often take for granted.

One notable fighter in the Revolutionary War was Nathanael Greene. Known as the "Fighting Quaker," he laid aside the pacifism of his upbringing because of the importance of the cause of freedom. Greene rose through the ranks from private to general and became one of George Washington's most trusted officers. Largely self-taught, he studied scores of books on military history to equip himself for the tasks he was assigned.

In a letter to his wife, Nathanael Greene wrote: "It had been happy for me if I could have lived a private life in peace and plenty, enjoying all the happiness that results from a well-tempered society founded on mutual esteem. But the injury done my country, and the chains of slavery forging for all posterity, calls me forth to defend our common rights, and repel the bold invaders of the sons of freedom."

There is a long tradition of Christians placing their lives "between their loved homes and the war's desolation" as Francis Scott Key put it in "The Star Spangled Banner." We must not forget the price of freedom. If you have a loved one or friend who served in the military, take time to thank them today. We have been blessed by their sacrifice, and we should express our gratitude to them.

Today's Word to the Wise: Give thanks today to God and to those who have served in defense of our country for the freedom we are blessed to enjoy.

An Encouraging Word

Heaviness in the heart of man maketh it stoop: but a good word maketh it glad.—**Proverbs 12:25**

Edward Steichen was one of the first professional photographers to become well known to the general public. His gifted eye made him the highest paid photographer in the world for many years. He directed award-winning documentaries, and his work graced a number of museums around the world. But his remarkable photographic career almost didn't happen. As a teenager he bought a used camera and took his first fifty pictures. Only one was any good, and he almost gave up. His mother, however, insisted that one—a photo of his sister playing the piano—was so good he should continue.

There are many times when people are discouraged simply because of the nature of living in a fallen world. There are pains, disappointments, and defeats that each of us will face. The temptation in those trying times is to despair and give up. In those moments, a simple word of encouragement can be powerful. Solomon wrote, "Two are better than one; because they have a good reward for their labour. For if they fall, the one will lift up his fellow: but woe to him that is alone when he falleth; for he hath not another to help him up" (Ecclesiastes 4:9–10).

It is a blessing to have friends to offer that kind of help and encouragement when things are hard. But it also falls to us to be such a friend—to be ready to provide hope and comfort when others face difficulty. Sometimes we get wrapped up in looking for someone to come and encourage us when God wants us to be offering encouragement to others. There is never a bad time to provide genuine and hopeful words to a friend. Indeed by doing so you may help make the difference between success and failure.

Today's Word to the Wise: Find someone today who needs to hear an encouraging word and give it to them.

The Most Important Inheritance

A good man leaveth an inheritance to his children's children: and the wealth of the sinner is laid up for the just.—**Proverbs 13:22**

From time to time I stop and think about the legacy and inheritance that Terrie and I will leave to our children and grandchildren. There are many things that can be inherited, but the most important of all that we can leave behind is a heritage of faith in God and faithfulness to Him. God said this about Abraham: "For I know him, that he will command his children and his household after him, and they shall keep the way of the LORD, to do justice and judgment; that the LORD may bring upon Abraham that which he hath spoken of him" (Genesis 18:19).

A person who leaves millions of dollars, fine artwork and paintings, vacation houses, and other material possessions alone has failed their heirs. There is certainly no sin in leaving wealth to future generations, but that pales in importance next to assuring that the faith and confidence we have in God is passed on to future generations. This is not something that can be done intermittently—it requires a lifelong example.

The Bible records something interesting about the life of Enoch. "And Enoch lived sixty and five years, and begat Methuselah: And Enoch walked with God after he begat Methuselah three hundred years, and begat sons and daughters" (Genesis 5:21–22). It appears to have been the birth of his son that sparked Enoch's focus on his relationship with God. That relationship became so close that it was the defining testimony of Enoch's life. The writer of Hebrews said, "Before his translation he had this testimony, that he pleased God" (Hebrews 11:5). If that can be said by those who know us best, we have left the greatest inheritance of all.

Today's Word to the Wise: Live your life each day in such a way that there will be an unmistakable inheritance of faith your family can follow in the future.

The Fear of the Lord

In the fear of the LORD is strong confidence: and his children shall have a place of refuge. The fear of the LORD is a fountain of life, to depart from the snares of death.—**Proverbs 14:26–27**

In the closing days of World War II, the *USS Indianapolis* was tasked with a top secret mission—to deliver the atomic bomb that would be dropped on Japan to help end the war. On the return voyage home, the ship was attacked and sunk by a Japanese submarine. Because the mission was so secretive, the ship was not immediately missed. The men who survived the explosions and sinking of the ship floated in the water for five days. The group was repeatedly attacked by sharks. Many of them were seriously injured, and few had any food or water. By the time the survivors were spotted in the ocean and rescued, only 317 of the 1,196 sailors on board were still alive.

One of the survivors was Edgar Harrell. His son wrote a book about his father's experiences called *Out of the Depths*. In it Edgar Harrell recalled: "Clearly there were no atheists in the water that day. Gone was [the] attitude of pride that deceives men into thinking that there is no God, or if there is, they don't need Him. When a man is confronted with death, it is the face of Almighty God he sees, not his own. We were all acutely aware of our Creator during those days and nights."

When we recognize the reality that God is sovereign and everything in our lives depends on Him, it reminds us that He is not only to be loved but also to be feared. Though our culture may take a casual view of God, we must not. Instead we must recognize His power, share His hatred of sin, and live in the confidence and safety He offers.

Today's Word to the Wise: Recognizing the power and majesty of God leads us to properly fear Him and thus receive His protection.

Bringing Consolation

A merry heart maketh a cheerful countenance: but by sorrow of the heart the spirit is broken.—**Proverbs 15:13**

The fact that Nehemiah occupied the position of cupbearer to the king of Persia was unusual. The cupbearer was someone in whom the king had complete confidence. To protect the king from poison, the cupbearer would taste the prepared food and drink before it was served to the king. For Nehemiah, a member of a conquered people, to have a position like this means that he must have demonstrated a great deal of character and responsibility. When Nehemiah got the news of the sad state of Jerusalem, it had an impact on him that was noticeable. "Now I had not been beforetime sad in his presence. Wherefore the king said unto me, Why is thy countenance sad, seeing thou art not sick? this is nothing else but sorrow of heart" (Nehemiah 2:1–2). The words Nehemiah heard brought sorrow to his heart.

The emotional wounds that people receive as they go through life do not show up on x-rays or CAT scans, but they are still real. These hurts of the heart cannot be shrugged off or ignored because they have an impact on both our spiritual and physical well-being. Sometimes these wounds are overlooked or downplayed, but they do not go away or heal without help. The well-known pastor George Truett of Dallas, Texas, had a radio broadcast for many years. Each day he would end the program by saying, "Be good to everybody, because everybody is having a hard time."

The early church was blessed to have a man who provided great help and encouragement. His name was Joses, but he was such an encourager that the apostles called him Barnabas, which means "the son of consolation" (Acts 4:36). God wants us to offer consolation, help, and encouragement to those who are suffering from sadness and sorrow of heart.

Today's Word to the Wise: If you see someone with a sorrowful heart, do what you can to bring them comfort and encouragement.

Planting a Bitter Harvest

A froward man soweth strife: and a whisperer separateth chief friends.
—**Proverbs 16:28**

The court of Queen Elizabeth I was a swirling hotbed of intrigue. Her counselors and advisors constantly tried to undercut each other and gain her favor. Elizabeth skillfully played them against each other, promoting one then another to keep anyone from becoming too powerful. One of the most skillful players of the court game was Robert Devereux, the Second Earl of Essex. At Essex's direction, false accusations of treason or disloyalty were laid at the feet of some of the queen's most trusted servants—and such accusations were hard to prove false. Essex eventually reached too far and tried to depose Queen Elizabeth. He gathered a group of conspirators and marched into London. The group was arrested, and Essex was executed for treason. By his continual undermining of others, he planted the seeds for his rejection.

When we spend our time gossiping and telling stories about others—whether those stories are true or false—we are doing a great disservice to them and to ourselves. Much damage has been done to the body of Christ by those who gossip. Paul warned Timothy about the danger such people pose to the church. "And withal they learn to be idle, wandering about from house to house; and not only idle, but tattlers also and busybodies, speaking things which they ought not" (1 Timothy 5:13).

For some people, "prayer requests" are a spiritual cover given to the spreading of gossip. If someone needs prayer, talk to God and see if there is anything you can do to encourage them. Telling others about the latest news is not productive. Instead it destroys relationships and creates conflict. Purpose to never be one who spreads rumors and damages relationships.

Today's Word to the Wise: When you gossip and whisper about others, you are planting seeds for a bitter harvest.

Considered Speech

He that hath knowledge spareth his words: and a man of understanding is of an excellent spirit.—**Proverbs 17:27**

President Calvin Coolidge was famously known as a man of few words. His nickname was "Silent Cal." His wife, Grace Goodhue Coolidge, told the story of a young woman who sat next to her husband at a dinner party. She told Coolidge she had a bet with a friend that she could get at least three words of conversation from him. Without looking at her he quietly retorted, "You lose." Coolidge understood very well the value of using only carefully considered words—and those being few in number.

In a time when people reveal their most personal information in the most public ways without thought or hesitation, it is important for us to recapture this piece of wisdom. Truly wise believers do not feel the need to tell everything they know to everyone they meet—much less to total strangers. Instead they choose their words with care, recognizing the responsibility that comes with our speech. Jesus said, "But I say unto you, That every idle word that men shall speak, they shall give account thereof in the day of judgment. For by thy words thou shalt be justified, and by thy words thou shalt be condemned" (Matthew 12:36–37).

The reason our words are important to God is because they carry much power and can cause great damage. James wrote, "And the tongue is a fire, a world of iniquity: so is the tongue among our members, that it defileth the whole body, and setteth on fire the course of nature; and it is set on fire of hell" (James 3:6). Instead of allowing our words to spew forth and bring destruction, we need to tame our tongues and control them in the power of the Holy Spirit. Then our words will bring hope, healing, and blessing to others.

Today's Word to the Wise: Choose your words with great care; you will give an account for every single one.

Use Your Gifts

A man's gift maketh room for him, and bringeth him before great men.
—Proverbs 18:16

Bertoldo de Giovanni is hardly a household name, but without him we might never have known the name of Michelangelo. When the great sculptor was just a teenager, he became Bertoldo's student. Michelangelo's talent was already visible even at that young age, but he still needed to be taught to use his great gifts. It is said that one day Bertoldo entered the studio to find Michelangelo working on a sculpture far beneath his ability. The outraged teacher took a hammer and smashed the work to bits. Bertoldo said, "Michelangelo, talent is cheap; dedication is costly!" Michelangelo responded to the challenge and produced a lifetime of brilliant work.

God does not give us talents and abilities so that we can feel good about ourselves or receive praise from others. His purpose in gifting His children is so that we can use what He has given to us to build and strengthen the body of Christ. Paul told the church at Ephesus that God gave gifts to the church to be used: "Till we all come in the unity of the faith, and of the knowledge of the Son of God, unto a perfect man, unto the measure of the stature of the fulness of Christ" (Ephesians 4:13).

There is a danger when we do not use the talents God has given us. In addition to robbing His work of these talents, we place ourselves in danger of losing what we are neglecting. Jesus said, "For I say unto you, That unto every one which hath shall be given; and from him that hath not, even that he hath shall be taken away from him" (Luke 19:26). Identify the gifts that God has given to you, and put them to work for His Kingdom.

Today's Word to the Wise: Do not ever settle for less than doing the very best you can with the talents God has given you.

The Need for Knowledge

Also, that the soul be without knowledge, it is not good; and he that hasteth with his feet sinneth.—**Proverbs 19:2**

A few years ago an economist did a study to determine the impact of continued education on a worker's earning potential. Though the study focused on those in the engineering field, the basic principle applies in every field of work. The study concluded: "Without the added value from continually acquired knowledge, the lifetime earnings would be 67 percent less. This explains why it is necessary for individual information workers to start managing their own knowledge capital for maximum returns to themselves as well as to their employers."

God intends for His children to be learners. He does not regard ignorance as a virtue. The more that we know—the more skills we develop—the better we are able to serve Him. While this is true in the intellectual realm, it is even more true in the spiritual realm. For instance, Acts 8 records how Philip was being greatly used by God to bring revival to Samaria. From there, the Holy Spirit led him into the desert where he met an Ethiopian eunuch. This man had been to Jerusalem and was returning home without the answer to his spiritual need. The Bible account records that he was reading from the words of the prophet Isaiah a Messianic prophecy about Jesus. Philip immediately recognized the text and knew how to apply it. "Then Philip opened his mouth, and began at the same scripture, and preached unto him Jesus" (Acts 8:35).

Let us be careful students of Scripture, increasing our knowledge of the Word so we can be effectively used by God to witness and help others. Peter wrote, "But sanctify the Lord God in your hearts: and be ready always to give an answer to every man that asketh you a reason of the hope that is in you with meekness and fear" (1 Peter 3:15).

Today's Word to the Wise: The time you spend acquiring knowledge is never wasted.

The Glory of Youth

The glory of young men is their strength: and the beauty of old men is the gray head.—**Proverbs 20:29**

In December of 1874, in his paper *The Sword and Trowel*, Charles Spurgeon penned this challenge to young people: "You will not have another youth: soon it will not be in your power to offer to God your beauty and freshness. One occasionally sees in certain places announcements such as this, 'Smart young men wanted for the Guards.' Well, I am a recruiting sergeant. My colours are crimson, and I am eager to enlist both young men and women. I would be glad if I could do a bit of business and gather up recruits for Christ. Young men and women, step forward and fill the places of your fathers and mothers! We cannot have a better stock; none could be more welcome than your fathers' sons and daughters."

Service to God is a lifetime calling for Christians, and it should begin when we are young. It is said that after one meeting Moody reported "two and a half people" had been saved. When someone asked if he meant two adults and one child he said, "No. Two children and one adult. The children have a full life to serve God." We should be teaching and training our children and grandchildren the vital urgency of doing what they can in the strength of youth for the cause of Christ.

Hannah, who had been barren for many years, prayed for a son and promised him to God's service. When he was still very young, she took Samuel to Eli the priest where he began a life of fruitful service to God. The Bible says, "But Samuel ministered before the LORD, being a child, girded with a linen ephod" (1 Samuel 2:18). The church today needs a new generation of young people to rise up and dedicate their lives to serving God.

Today's Word to the Wise: Use the strength you have to serve God and encourage others, especially those who are young, to do the same.

Finding What You Follow

He that followeth after righteousness and mercy findeth life, righteousness, and honour.—**Proverbs 21:21**

When he finished his second term as president, Theodore Roosevelt took his son Kermit and set out on an expedition to Africa. An avid hunter, Roosevelt went with the aim of collecting specimens of African wild animals to be displayed at the Smithsonian Institution. The expedition was a major event, involving more than 250 porters and guides. Updates of the journey were sent to newspapers around the world so readers could follow the adventures of the former president. By the time the trip was over, Roosevelt and his son had shot more than five hundred big game animals, including seventeen lions, eleven elephants, and twenty rhinoceroses.

All of Roosevelt's skills as a hunter and the knowledge and training of his guides would have been for naught if he had gone on his hunt in Kansas. There are no wild lions, elephants, or rhinos there. Likewise, for you and me to get the results that we want, we must chart and follow a course that leads to the destination we desire. Many people today are following paths that lead to ruin and destruction, while at the same time hoping for good results. That approach is doomed to failure. Jesus said, "Enter ye in at the strait gate: for wide is the gate, and broad is the way, that leadeth to destruction, and many there be which go in thereat: Because strait is the gate, and narrow is the way, which leadeth unto life, and few there be that find it" (Matthew 7:13–14).

The success or failure of your life is not determined by the destination you want to reach, but rather by the destination toward which you set your course. You will find what you follow. The key to a life that is pleasing to God and successful in His sight is following those things which matter to Him.

Today's Word to the Wise: The destination that you reach in the future is determined by the paths you take today.

Humility and Wisdom

Bow down thine ear, and hear the words of the wise, and apply thine heart unto my knowledge. For it is a pleasant thing if thou keep them within thee; they shall withal be fitted in thy lips.—**Proverbs 22:17–18**

To truly hear the words of the wise, we must be willing to humble ourselves and listen. Solomon was gifted by God with great wisdom and was inspired to write much of Proverbs as an instruction to his son, but Rehoboam did not learn the importance of either wisdom or humility. Upon Solomon's death, the people came to Rehoboam and asked him to lighten the heavy load of taxes and service which Solomon had placed on them to finance all of his grand construction projects.

Rehoboam had two choices, and his decision revealed a great deal about his heart. He first went to his father's advisors (and it says something important that the wisest man in history had a group of counselors himself) and asked them what he should do. They correctly told him that granting the people's request would cement his place in their hearts. But then he went to his own friends—those his own age who did not have the wisdom and experience to give wise counsel—and they gave him very different advice.

Rehoboam foolishly listened to his peers. "And the king answered the people roughly, and forsook the old men's counsel that they gave him; And spake to them after the counsel of the young men, saying, My father made your yoke heavy, and I will add to your yoke: my father also chastised you with whips, but I will chastise you with scorpions" (1 Kings 12:13–14). As a result of his folly, the nation of Israel was permanently divided into two warring kingdoms. Receiving counsel requires that we humble ourselves to listen and follow the wisdom of others, even if it is not our preferred course.

Today's Word to the Wise: Never think that you are beyond the need for counsel and input from others.

A Source of Rejoicing

My son, if thine heart be wise, my heart shall rejoice, even mine. Yea, my reins shall rejoice, when thy lips speak right things.
—Proverbs 23:15–16

Professional baseball has been played in America since 1875, but on September 14, 1990, something happened that has never happened before or since. Late in his career, Ken Griffey, Sr., who had been a key member of the World Series champion Cincinnati Reds years before, was signed by the Seattle Mariners. His son Ken Griffey, Jr. was just starting his major league career. In the first inning of a game against the Angels, Griffey, Sr. hit a home run to left center field. His son followed him to the plate and hit another home run to almost exactly the same spot. It was the only time a father and son had hit back-to-back home runs in baseball history. Ken Griffey, Jr. said later that his father greeted him at the plate by saying, "That's how you do it, son!"

There are few joys that can compare to seeing our children and grandchildren succeed. Whether it's on a ball field, at a music recital, in an academic competition, or, most importantly, in a spiritual setting, seeing a child demonstrate character and competence is a true pleasure. But this victory is not something that just happens. Every right performance, every victory over temptation, every accomplishment is the result of a concerted effort to prepare for the moment of challenge.

Most of the kings over God's people after the nation of Israel was divided did not rule righteously. One of the few exceptions was Jehoshaphat. The reason for his success is spelled out for us: "And he walked in all the ways of Asa his father; he turned not aside from it, doing that which was right in the eyes of the LORD" (1 Kings 22:43). Set an example for those who follow you by living in wisdom.

Today's Word to the Wise: Teach your children and grandchildren to walk in God's ways so that you can rejoice in the way they live.

Count Your Blessings

Fret not thyself because of evil men, neither be thou envious at the wicked; For there shall be no reward to the evil man; the candle of the wicked shall be put out.—**Proverbs 24:19–20**

I read about a man who returned from a trip to Paris with a beautiful French doll for his young niece. When she opened the package the girl was so thrilled that she rushed inside to show her mother what she had received. "Did you thank your uncle for the present?" her Mother asked. "Yes, Mama," the girl replied, "But I didn't tell him so."

Sometimes we think that we are thankful people, but we neglect to express our gratitude. Often this is the result of failure to appreciate what we have. This ingratitude happens because we count the blessings of those around us instead of counting our own blessings. We fail to realize that even great blessings and prosperity may only be temporary. The fact that those who do not know God may have temporary success in "climbing the ladder" or accumulating the most toys does not change the fact that this is short-term success that produces no lasting or eternal result.

Instead of looking at others we should be focused on the amazing grace and blessings that God has given to us. David wrote, "Bless the LORD, O my soul, and forget not all his benefits" (Psalm 103:2). While we may not have everything we wish for, it is the promise of God that we will have everything we need. Those good things are not the result of our worth and merit, but of His grace. Since God is the source of all our blessings, He deserves the full measure of our praise.

Today's Word to the Wise: Rather than focusing on what others have, we should be expressing our gratitude to God for all that He has given us.

Sharing the Good News

As cold waters to a thirsty soul, so is good news from a far country.
—**Proverbs 25:25**

D r. R. A. Torrey told of a young Jewish woman who had been converted during his ministry in Chicago. When she went to work the next week, she began telling her co-workers what had happened. Many of them were upset and went to the manager to complain. The manager called her in and said, "We do not object to Christianity or to you being a Christian, but you must not talk about it in the office."

Though she was a single woman responsible for supporting her aging mother, she was unwilling to abandon her faith. "I cannot work somewhere that I cannot take my Master with me," she replied. She was told to return to her desk. She went back expecting to hear at any moment that she had been terminated, but nothing was said the rest of that day or the next. On Friday, she received a letter. Sure that it was her notice of dismissal, she opened it with trembling hands. It said, "We have a place of greater responsibility than the one you now occupy and with a larger salary than you are getting. We think you are just the person for this position."

Whether it results in promotion or termination, we should always be faithful to share the gospel with others. In the workplace this must be done in such a way that it does not steal time and effort from the boss, but there should be no doubt that we are believers from our speech and our conduct. In this season of the year when we think about gratitude in a special way, it is only fitting that we share with others the best gift we have ever received. We show gratitude for our salvation when we share the gospel with others.

Today's Word to the Wise: One of the best ways for us to show gratitude for the blessings we have received is to share the good news with those around us.

Resting in God's Faithfulness

The great God that formed all things both rewardeth the fool, and rewardeth transgressors.—**Proverbs 26:10**

A nne of Austria, mother of the famed Sun King Louis XIV, ruled the kingdom as regent while her son was a young boy. Through repeated tangles in the intrigues between competing factions at the court, she attempted to guide her young son to be a good ruler for France. One of her favorite sayings quoted often to him and others was: "God does not pay at the end of every week; nevertheless He pays."

We often think of God's faithfulness to keep His promises, but that faithfulness also extends to His rewards and punishments. Intertwined with God's faithfulness is God's sovereignty. We can trust Him to take care of matters—we do not have to take things into our own hands. Instead, we can rely on His perfect justice to work in His timing.

Life would be extremely difficult if it was up to us to determine and administer justice. There are times when we think someone has done wrong only to later discover that we didn't understand the reasons for what happened. Other times we think someone has failed only to later discover that they actually helped. God's perfect wisdom and knowledge always allow Him to know what should be done, and His power sees that justice will be served in the end.

Faith is based on the knowledge that we can count on God to do what He says. This gives us the confidence to trust Him and His unfailing goodness. James tells us that in God's character there "is no variableness, neither shadow of turning" (James 1:17). Give thanks today for the consistency and faithfulness of our Heavenly Father.

Today's Word to the Wise: Knowing that God will keep His promises to bless good and punish evil, we can leave matters in His hands.

How to Appreciate God's Blessings

The full soul loatheth an honeycomb; but to the hungry soul every bitter thing is sweet.—**Proverbs 27:7**

A rich British homeowner, coming downstairs one morning overheard the cook in the kitchen say, "Oh, if I only had five pounds, I would be content." She was a good worker, and he thought he would grant her wish. He walked into the kitchen and handed her a five pound note. She thanked him, and he left to go on about his day. But he paused outside the door to see if she would say anything else. Instead of expressing contentment, once she thought he was gone she said, "Why didn't I say ten pounds?"

The idea that if we just had a little more we would be content and happy is one of the most successful lies Satan has ever used against God's people. Contentment does not come from having more possessions, but from having more gratitude. There are some people with millions who are not content while there are others who don't even have hundreds who are. An active and working faith chooses to trust that God knows and cares about our situation. Jesus said, "your heavenly Father knoweth that ye have need of all these things" (Matthew 6:32).

Each time we complain about what we do not have, we are expressing our belief that we know what we need better than God. It is not wrong to ask Him for things—in fact He commands us to do so. The problem comes when we are not content with His answer. The tragedy of discontentment is that it renders us vulnerable to temptation and prevents us from realizing the abundance of blessings we have. If you are honest in evaluating what God has done for you, it won't take long for you to begin rejoicing that He "daily loadeth us with benefits" (Psalm 68:19).

Today's Word to the Wise: Faith trusts God to provide what we need and gives thanks for whatever He chooses to send our way.

The Cure for Covetousness

The prince that wanteth understanding is also a great oppressor: but he that hateth covetousness shall prolong his days.—**Proverbs 28:16**

I read about a farmer who went to visit relatives in the city. At mealtime, as was his custom he bowed his head to give thanks for his food. The sophisticated city people found that amusing and told the old farmer that they no longer observed that custom. He replied, "Well not everyone out on the farm gives thanks before eating either." "Who doesn't?" they asked. "The hogs don't," he responded.

Greed and covetousness are great plagues in our day. We live in a society that is obsessed with getting more. You've probably seen the popular bumper sticker that says, "He who dies with the most toys wins." Sadly, this materialistic pursuit has seeped into the church and impacted the way God's people view possessions. Rather than being grateful for all that God has given us, we too often fall into the trap of wishing for what others have.

Paul warns of this danger and the consequences that follow. "Covetousness, which is idolatry: For which things' sake the wrath of God cometh on the children of disobedience" (Colossians 3:5–6). Anything we covet is taking the place of God in our hearts and minds. We are promoting it to a level of worship—something that God reserves only for Himself.

God does not just command us not to covet; He also gives us the cure to guard against it—thanksgiving. Moses warned the children of Israel that when they reached the Promised Land, the bounty God had prepared for them would tempt them to ingratitude. He cautioned, "Beware lest thou forget the LORD" (Deuteronomy 6:12). Take extra time today and throughout the year to give thanks and praise to God for His great goodness to you, and the allure of covetousness will fade.

Today's Word to the Wise: When you give thanks from a grateful heart you bring glory to God and protect your life from covetousness.

A King for the Poor

The king that faithfully judgeth the poor, his throne shall be established for ever.—**Proverbs 29:14**

"Good King Wenceslas" may be the most popular Christmas carol to which the fewest people actually know the words. It has an interesting historical background. It is based on stories from the life of Wenceslas I, Duke of Bohemia in the early 900s. Revered in his day as a just and noble ruler, one biographer wrote that he rose "every night from his noble bed, with bare feet and only one chamberlain, he went around to God's churches and gave alms generously to widows, orphans, those in prison and afflicted by every difficulty, so much so that he was considered the father of all the wretched."

Regardless of how much detail has been lost through the intervening centuries, there is no doubt that when Wenceslas cared for the needs of poor widows and orphans, he was following the pattern established by Jesus. James wrote, "Pure religion and undefiled before God and the Father is this, To visit the fatherless and widows in their affliction, and to keep himself unspotted from the world" (James 1:27).

The birthplace of Jesus—in a manger for animals rather than a palace—was no accident. Nor was it an accident that His birth was announced by the angels to humble shepherds rather than to the leaders of the nation. Jesus came not to impress the high and mighty, but to rescue the perishing. In a day when the poor were often looked down on and riches were seen as a sign of God's favor, Jesus spent most of His time with simple, common people. Many of His miracles worked directly to benefit those in need. Jesus came to be a King for everyone—including those who were ignored by society.

Today's Word to the Wise: When we reach out to encourage the poor and help meet their needs, we are following in the footsteps of Jesus.

More than Just a Baby

*There be three things which go well, yea, four are comely in going: A
lion which is strongest among beasts, and turneth not away for any; A
greyhound; an he goat also; and a king, against whom there is no rising
up.*—**Proverbs 30:29–31**

When the wise men came to Jerusalem looking for Jesus, they said
something that would not normally be correct according to
human reckoning. They asked, "Where is he that is born King of the
Jews? for we have seen his star in the east, and are come to worship him"
(Matthew 2:2). When a baby boy is born into a royal family, he is called a
prince, not a king. Yet from the very moment of his human birth, Jesus
was not just a man, but also the King of kings who had come to be the
Saviour of the world.

I love thinking about Jesus lying in the manger while Mary and
Joseph watched over Him. But though that is a wonderful part of the
Christmas story, it is only a tiny part of it. Jesus was always much more
than just a baby. He came into this world on purpose, with every detail
of His birth arranged and planned by God. Paul wrote, "But when the
fulness of time was come, God sent forth his Son, made of a woman,
made under the law. To redeem them that were under the law, that we
might receive the adoption of sons" (Galatians 4:4–5).

Though Jesus was "tender and mild" as the carol "Silent Night" puts it,
when He returns, it will be as the conqueror against whom no power will
stand. In preparation for that day we should live today acknowledging
and obeying His right to rule and reign over our lives. Let us remember
that Jesus not only came to save, but that He will come again as King.

Today's Word to the Wise: As you prepare for Christmas, don't lose sight
of the power, majesty, and glory of Jesus Christ.

A WORD TO THE

WISE

THE BOOK
OF PROVERBS

DECEMBER

A Rejected Saviour

Because I have called, and ye refused; I have stretched out my hand, and no man regarded;—**Proverbs 1:24**

In 1833, the Supreme Court was called upon to decide a most unusual case. A convicted felon named George Wilson had been sentenced to death for his part in a robbery of the United States mail. Using his power under the Constitution, President Andrew Jackson issued Wilson a pardon, but the condemned man refused to accept it. Unsure how to proceed, the lower courts appealed for help in applying the law to this circumstance.

Writing for the Supreme Court in the case of *United States v. Wilson*, Chief Justice John Marshall said, "A pardon is a deed to the validity of which delivery is essential, and delivery is not complete without acceptance. It may then be rejected by the person to whom it is tendered, and if it be rejected, we have discovered no power in a court to force it on him. It may be supposed that no being condemned to death would reject a pardon, but the rule must be the same in capital cases and in misdemeanors." As a result of rejecting the pardon offered by President Jackson, George Wilson was hanged for his crimes.

Though Jesus Christ came into the world to provide God's gift of salvation and deliverance from the penalty of sin to all who believe, many people refuse to heed His offer. Isaiah foretold how the world would reject Christ: "He is despised and rejected of men; a man of sorrows, and acquainted with grief: and we hid as it were our faces from him; he was despised, and we esteemed him not" (Isaiah 53:3). This month many will celebrate the Christmas season without even realizing that they are rejecting the central purpose of the Christmas story. We must be faithful to tell them that receiving Christ removes the penalty of sin forever.

Today's Word to the Wise: This is a wonderful time of year to share the message of salvation with those who have never received it.

Walking God's Path

*Then shalt thou understand righteousness, and judgment, and equity;
yea, every good path.*—**Proverbs 2:9**

There is a European legend about a great kingdom whose roadway to the capital city was obstructed. In the middle of the road, not far from the gates of the city, was a large boulder. Travelers were forced to detour around it, and many complained that it was allowed to remain in the middle of the road. Finally, a man came along who was different. He got a long piece of wood to use as a lever, pried the boulder from its place, and rolled it out of the road. Under the boulder he found a small bag and a note from the king.

"Thank you for being a true servant of the kingdom. Many have passed this way and complained because of the state of the problem and spoken of what ought to be done. But you have taken the responsibility upon yourself to serve the kingdom instead. You are the type of citizen we need more of in this kingdom. Please accept this bag of gold that traveler after traveler walked by simply because they didn't care enough about the kingdom to serve."

When we walk in God's path we live lives of service to others and to Him. Jesus described the purpose for His coming this way: "For even the Son of man came not to be ministered unto, but to minister, and to give his life a ransom for many" (Mark 10:45). As a result He was able to say, "I do always those things that please him" (John 8:29). Jesus came and gave us an example "that ye should follow his steps" (1 Peter 2:21).

Today's Word to the Wise: Just as Jesus came to walk the path of service, we must do what we can to meet the needs of those around us.

A Lowly Saviour

Surely he scorneth the scorners: but he giveth grace unto the lowly.
—**Proverbs 3:34**

D.L. Moody was the most famous evangelist in the world in the late 1800s. People came from around the world to attend his Bible Conferences in Northfield, Massachusetts. One year a large group of pastors from Europe were among the attendees. They were given rooms in the dormitory of the Bible school. As was the custom in Europe, the men put their shoes outside the door of their room, expecting them to be cleaned and polished by servants during the night.

Of course there were no servants in the American dorm, but as Moody was walking through the halls and praying for his guests, he saw the shoes and realized what had happened. He mentioned the problem to a few of his students, but none of them offered to help. Without another word, the great evangelist gathered up the shoes and took them back to his own room where he began to clean and polish each pair. Moody told no one what he had done, but a friend who interrupted him in the middle of shining the shoes and helped him finish the task later told the story of what had happened. Despite the honor, praise, and fame he received because of God's blessing on his life and ministry, Moody remained a humble man.

Jesus Christ, the Son of God and King of Heaven, had the right to honor, praise, and worship. Yet to be our Saviour, He laid all of His privileges aside and became a lowly servant. We often hear people talk of living as Jesus lived, and while He truly is the model for us to follow, many who speak of following Him are unwilling to give up their rights and reflect His humility. We will never be like Jesus unless we are humble and lowly.

Today's Word to the Wise: As we follow Jesus in humility and lowliness, we position ourselves to receive the grace and blessing of God.

A Righteous Saviour

Ponder the path of thy feet, and let all thy ways be established.
Turn not to the right hand nor to the left: remove thy foot from evil.
—**Proverbs 4:26–27**

Since the fall in the Garden of Eden, man has needed a Saviour. None of us are able to save ourselves, because we have a sin nature and are incapable of fulfilling God's righteous demands. For us to be saved, there had to be a sinless sacrifice—and that is why there is a Christmas. Jesus came to be the righteous Saviour that we needed. He lived a sinless life, completely fulfilling the law of God. His righteousness is placed on our account to pay for our sin. Paul wrote, "For he hath made him to be sin for us, who knew no sin; that we might be made the righteousness of God in him" (2 Corinthians 5:21).

It was imperative that Jesus live a sinless life so He could be the perfect sacrifice for our sins. If His life had not been perfect, He would have had to pay for His own sin. We see this illustrated at the very beginning of Jesus' public ministry. He made the trip from Nazareth to the Jordan River where John the Baptist was baptizing people and asked John to baptize Him. John objected, pointing out that he should be baptized by Jesus instead. But because baptism was part of God's plan, Jesus insisted. "And Jesus answering said unto him, Suffer it to be so now: for thus it becometh us to fulfil all righteousness. Then he suffered him" (Matthew 3:15).

One of the greatest grounds for rejoicing as believers is the knowledge that God sees us as righteous because the righteousness of Jesus Christ has been applied to our record. As you celebrate this Christmas, give thanks to God for the provision of a righteous Saviour.

Today's Word to the Wise: Rejoice today in the righteous Saviour who in love and mercy came into the world to offer us reconciliation to God.

A Saviour for Sinners

I was almost in all evil in the midst of the congregation and assembly.
—**Proverbs 5:14**

For almost seventy years, Franz Joseph I ruled the Austro-Hungarian Empire, one of the most powerful in the world. He was feared, honored, and greatly respected. But in the end, he was a man, and, like all other men, he died. A unique part of his funeral service illustrates the sinfulness of men and our need for a Saviour.

Like his ancestors of the Hapsburg dynasty, Franz Joseph I's body was taken to the Church of the Capuchin in Vienna. When the funeral procession arrived at the doors they were closed. When they knocked on the door a voice from inside called out, "Who is there?" The leader of the funeral party answered, "His most serene majesty, the Emperor Franz Joseph I." From inside the church the answer came, "I know him not. Who is there?" The next reply was, "The Emperor of Austria and Apostolic King of Hungary." Again the words came, "I know him not. Who is there?" This time the answer was different. "A sinful man. Our brother Franz Joseph." Then the door opened, and the funeral proceeded.

When the enemies of Jesus wanted to condemn Him, they referred to Him as "a friend of publicans and sinners" (Matthew 11:19). Instead of an insult, that was actually a wonderful description of the life and ministry of Jesus. He was perfect and sinless, yet He left the perfection of Heaven for a sinful world—He walked among sinners and loved them. Even more He went to the cross where God "made him to be sin for us, who knew no sin; that we might be made the righteousness of God in him" (2 Corinthians 5:21). Christmas is not just a wonderful time of celebration and gift giving, but a remembrance of the provision of salvation.

Today's Word to the Wise: Jesus came to be a Saviour, not for the good and lovely, but for the sinful and defiled.

Guidance in the Word

When thou goest, it shall lead thee; when thou sleepest, it shall keep thee; and when thou awakest, it shall talk with thee. For the commandment is a lamp; and the law is light; and reproofs of instruction are the way of life:—**Proverbs 6:22–23**

In 1914, Ernest Shackleton and a team of explorers set out from England to do something that no one before had accomplished—cross Antarctica from one side to the other across the South Pole. Disaster struck when the team's ship, *Endurance,* became entrapped in ice and eventually sank after her hull was crushed. Marooned on nearby Elephant Island, there seemed little hope for their survival.

In a desperate effort to get help, Shackleton and five others set out in a twenty-foot lifeboat across some of the most dangerous and storm-filled waters in the world. It was an eight hundred-mile journey to South Georgia Island where help could be found. For fifteen days the men battled the treacherous seas and massive storms with waves of up to one hundred feet. Using only a compass and a sextant, Frank Worsley (who had captained the *Endurance*) navigated their course until they safely reached land and found help. Shackleton procured another ship and returned to rescue all of his men. He became a national hero in England for his courage and persistence.

All of us are making our way through a stormy world. Ever since the first sin in the Garden of Eden, mankind has struggled to make wise decisions about an uncertain future. The only way to ensure that we do not go astray is to have an objective source of truth that will guide us. Just as a compass can guide sailors through dark and uncharted waters, God's Word can guide us through uncertain and difficult circumstances. We must simply trust it—over our feelings, over our own wisdom, and over contrary advice others may give us. Because the Bible is inspired by God, it is without error, and we can always trust it.

Today's Word to the Wise: Follow the guidance of Scripture, and you will never go off course.

Keeping the Commandments

My son, keep my words, and lay up my commandments with thee. Keep my commandments, and live; and my law as the apple of thine eye.
—**Proverbs 7:1–2**

In 1896, the pastor of a small church in Topeka, Kansas, began preaching a series of sermons designed to encourage his congregation to truly live as Jesus would if He were in their situation. The next year, Charles Sheldon novelized the illustrations and stories he had used in his sermon series and published it as the book *In His Steps*. The novel became one of the best-selling books of all time with more than thirty million copies printed. Sheldon encouraged readers to make decisions based on the answer to the question, "What would Jesus do?" Many were challenged to consider their Christian walk in those pages.

People today still ask this question to help guide them in making important decisions. Sometimes people answer the question in ways that reveal they do not fully understand the principles that guided Jesus during His earthly life. With complete certainty and confidence we can say that Jesus would never do anything that violates the Word of God. He declared, "Think not that I am come to destroy the law, or the prophets: I am not come to destroy, but to fulfill" (Matthew 5:17). Part of the reason that Jesus came to Earth was to live a life in complete obedience to the laws of God.

The most important way we demonstrate our love and commitment to Christ is not through our words but through our obedient actions. Jesus said, "If ye love me, keep my commandments" (John 14:15). Some who proclaim their love for Jesus undermine the validity of their declaration by refusing to submit to His commandments. We cannot ever truly say that we are following Christ unless we are walking as He walked—in submission to the will of the Father in Heaven.

Today's Word to the Wise: Follow the example of Jesus today by keeping the commandments of the Word of God.

An Accepting Saviour

Blessed is the man that heareth me, watching daily at my gates, waiting at the posts of my doors. For whoso findeth me findeth life, and shall obtain favour of the Lord.—**Proverbs 8:34–35**

Charles Spurgeon and Joseph Parker both pastored large churches in London in the 19th century. Once someone asked Parker a question about the orphanages run by Spurgeon's church, and he responded with a statement about the urgent needs of the children who were being taken in. His remarks were reported to Spurgeon as a critique of the orphanages and their lack of care for the children. Furious, Spurgeon publicly excoriated Parker. The story even made the newspapers of London.

The next Sunday, Parker's church was even more crowded than usual as people came to see how he would respond to Spurgeon's attack. He rose to the pulpit and said, "I understand Dr. Spurgeon is not in his pulpit today, and this is the Sunday they use to take an offering for the needs of the orphanage. I suggest we take a love offering here instead." The ushers had to empty the collection plates three times before all the money could be received. That week Spurgeon came to see Parker. "You know, Parker, you have practiced grace on me. You have given me not what I deserved; you have given me what I needed."

Every one of us needs grace. We need the favor of God rather than what we deserve. Through Jesus, "the grace of God that bringeth salvation hath appeared to all men" (Titus 2:11). By our adoption into God's family through salvation, one of the benefits we receive is the same favor and approval that Jesus received from the Father. "This is my beloved Son, in whom I am well pleased" (Matthew 3:17). When God looks at us, He sees the perfect righteousness of Jesus Christ and finds us acceptable in His sight.

Today's Word to the Wise: Jesus came to offer you the only way of finding favor in the eyes of God.

Abundant Life

For by me thy days shall be multiplied, and the years of thy life shall be increased.—**Proverbs 9:11**

God's purpose is not for us to barely make it through a miserable existence. Jesus said, "The thief cometh not, but for to steal, and to kill, and to destroy: I am come that they might have life, and that they might have it more abundantly" (John 10:10). Jesus did not just come to provide us with salvation for eternity but with an overflowing life for the present. Of course that does not mean that we are all meant to be perfectly healthy and very rich—instead it means that we have the things that matter most.

There is a good illustration of this truth in the life of Adoniram Judson. The great missionary resolved to go to Burma to take the gospel to those who had never heard it. By any earthly measure the early part of his ministry was a miserable failure. Judson was brilliant and already fluent in several languages, but the Burmese language proved to be so difficult that it took him years to learn. For seven years Judson did not have a single convert. In the early years of his ministry, he endured persecution, physical suffering, and the death of his first wife and several of their young children.

Throughout that time, Judson's love for God and his faith did not waver. One man with whom Judson studied the Burmese language went home and told his family that he had met an angel. Among the people of Burma, Judson came to be known as "Mr. Glory-Face." Though he had little that the world would regard as success in those days, Judson still had an abundant life. Because his faith did not waver, he eventually saw a wonderful harvest in Burma. As we trust God regardless of our circumstances, we are prepared to live and enjoy the abundant life Jesus offers.

Today's Word to the Wise: Rejoice today in the provision through Jesus Christ of the abundance of God's blessings in the things that matter most.

A Gracious Saviour

The lips of the righteous know what is acceptable: but the mouth of the wicked speaketh frowardness.—**Proverbs 10:32**

It was the first sermon Jesus preached in His hometown. On the Sabbath day He went to the synagogue as normal. This time, however, He stood to speak the words of the prophet Isaiah—the wonderful Messianic prophecy that foretold His coming. "The Spirit of the Lord is upon me, because he hath anointed me to preach the gospel to the poor; he hath sent me to heal the brokenhearted, to preach deliverance to the captives, and recovering of sight to the blind, to set at liberty them that are bruised, To preach the acceptable year of the Lord" (Luke 4:18–19).

He announced that the Scripture was being fulfilled before their eyes. The people heard this with amazement. For them, Jesus was just "Joseph's son" (Luke 4:22)—the carpenter's boy they had watched grow up. They did not understand how He could speak such wonderful words because they did not believe that He was the Son of God.

Despite Christ's grace, they refused to receive His message. In fact, by the time the sermon was done they were trying to kill Jesus. Enraged by His message they "rose up, and thrust him out of the city, and led him unto the brow of the hill whereon their city was built, that they might cast him down headlong" (Luke 4:29). In this story we see not just the offer of a gracious Saviour but also the rejection of His offer that sin and rebellion produce. The offer of salvation is freely given, but grace is not force—God does not compel people to respond. He accepts all those who come to Him, and we should be inviting others to meet Him too.

Today's Word to the Wise: When we come to Jesus with humility and repentance, we find Him gracious and offering us acceptance.

A Delivering Saviour

Riches profit not in the day of wrath: but righteousness delivereth from death.—**Proverbs 11:4**

Arthur Hinkley was just eighteen years old that fall day in 1973. Working on a farm in Kennebec County, Maine, the teenager was startled to hear screams from a co-worker. Lloyd Bachelder who was also eighteen had been using a tractor to move an old car out of the way when it tipped over, trapping the frightened teenager beneath it. Hinkley was six feet tall and weighed two hundred pounds, but the tractor weighed a ton and a half, and the situation seemed hopeless. Fueled with adrenaline, Hinkley somehow managed to lift the tractor enough with his bare hands for his friend to crawl out. Bachelder had a hip fracture and internal injuries, but his life was saved.

Every person born into the human race since the fall has been under a death sentence. No matter how good or moral a person may be, "all have sinned, and come short of the glory of God" (Romans 3:23). And "the wages of sin is death" (Romans 6:23). It is these two truths that are at the very heart of the Christmas story. We needed deliverance from death, but our righteousness could never be equal to the task.

Jesus being perfect and sinless had nothing for which to atone, so His perfect righteousness was available to be our deliverance. In the Old Testament on the Day of Atonement, the priest would select two goats. One would be sacrificed on the altar. The other would be taken to the edge of the camp. There the priest would lay his hands on the "scapegoat" to symbolically transfer the sins of the people to it and then drive it into the wilderness. Jesus did something far greater—He did not just cover our sins but He removed them and replaced them with His righteousness so that we could be delivered from death.

Today's Word to the Wise: Rejoice in the deliverance offered to you through the righteousness of Jesus Christ.

A Saviour Who Destroyed Death

In the way of righteousness is life; and in the pathway thereof there is no death.—**Proverbs 12:28**

The brilliant poet William Cullen Bryant was just seventeen years old when he wrote what many consider to be one of the greatest poems in all of American literature—*Thanatopsis*. Many people doubted his authorship because of his youth. Though this poem, a meditation on death and the grave, is beautiful and well-written, it is filled with a sense of melancholy and futility. Bryant wrote: "Earth, that nourished thee, shall claim Thy growth, to be resolved to earth again. And lost each human trace, surrendering up Thine individual being, shalt thou go To mix forever with the elements; To be a brother to the insensible rock."

There is so much more than that to life, death, and what comes after. There is an eternity that is to come and each person will spend it in Heaven or in Hell. Apart from salvation, man has no hope for eternity. Each of us is born under the power of sin and subject to the penalty of death. Only in Christ can we find a Saviour who has already triumphed over death. John wrote of Jesus, "All things were made by him; and without him was not any thing made that was made. In him was life; and the life was the light of men" (John 1:3–4).

Life is part of the very nature of Christ. Not even death and the grave could hold Him in bondage. Once He had overcome death, there was nothing more to fear. Although each of us will face death (unless Christ returns first), we will face only a defeated foe. With Paul we can victoriously cry, "O death, where is thy sting? O grave, where is thy victory?" (1 Corinthians 15:55). This is one of the glories of Christmas.

Today's Word to the Wise: We have confident hope for the future because of our Saviour who conquered death and rose again.

A Saviour Who Made Us Rich

There is that maketh himself rich, yet hath nothing: there is that maketh himself poor, yet hath great riches.—**Proverbs 13:7**

In January of 1956, Jim Elliot and four other missionaries gave their lives in Ecuador in their effort to reach the Waodani (Auca) Indians. This fierce group was known to attack any outsiders, but the vision for reaching them with the gospel compelled these young men to take the risk. Not long after they set up camp near the Waodani village they were attacked by warriors. Refusing to defend their lives with force, the missionaries were killed. The news flashed around the world, and the story of courage and sacrifice challenged many to take up the missionary cause. Even today Elliot's words live on: "He is no fool who gives what he cannot keep to gain what he cannot lose."

In a very real sense, Jim Elliot and his missionary friends were living the spirit of Christmas. They were willing to give up the comforts of home and promising careers and to ultimately lay down their lives to take the gospel to those who had never heard. They could have fought back to defend themselves, but they chose not to.

This is what Jesus did for us in coming to Earth. Paul wrote, "For ye know the grace of our Lord Jesus Christ, that, though he was rich, yet for your sakes he became poor, that ye through his poverty might be rich" (2 Corinthians 8:9).

Nothing of lasting significance and importance for God is ever accomplished without great sacrifice. Whether it is our time, our talent, our treasure, or even our lives, we must be willing to give up what is temporary for the sake of what is eternal. When we do, we are following the example and pattern of Christ and walking in His steps.

Today's Word to the Wise: As we rejoice in the riches that were purchased for us by Christ's blood, we should share the good news with everyone we can.

A Saviour Who Will Rule

The evil bow before the good; and the wicked at the gates of the righteous.
—**Proverbs 14:19**

One of the most famous voices on radio, Paul Harvey, began his broadcast career when he was just a teenager living in Oklahoma. His personal style made him a fixture on stations across the country. One of his best known features was a series of broadcasts called "The Rest of the Story" which ran for more than thirty years. Harvey would tell part of a well-known story without revealing all of the details. Then he would fill in background information that explained what people knew and reveal whose story he was telling. "Now you know the rest of the story," he would conclude.

Christmas is like that—the parts of the story that are most familiar to people are wonderful, but they are not the full story. Jesus is more than a baby in a manger, and He is more than our Saviour. He is also coming again to rule over the entire world. Isaiah prophesied, "Of the increase of his government and peace there shall be no end, upon the throne of David, and upon his kingdom, to order it, and to establish it with judgment and with justice from henceforth even for ever. The zeal of the LORD of hosts will perform this" (Isaiah 9:7).

Many people in the world think that the Baby of the Christmas story is the One who will return. But at His Second Coming, He will return as "Lord of lords, and King of kings" (Revelation 17:14). Evil will be banished, and with perfect justice He will rule the world. There will be no question regarding His authority and right to rule. As we prepare for Christmas, we need to keep the entire story in mind and remember that Christ is King.

Today's Word to the Wise: As we live in obedience to Jesus Christ we are preparing for the day when He will rule the world.

The Way to the Gift

The way of life is above to the wise, that he may depart from hell beneath.—**Proverbs 15:24**

Walter L. Wilson was trained as a medical doctor and practiced medicine for many years, but his greatest passion was pointing people to Jesus. Dr. Wilson told the story of how he used John 3:16 to lead a young boy to Christ. Stressing the importance of receiving the gift of eternal life Wilson asked, "Does the giving of a gift make it yours?" The boy answered, "You must take it if it is to become yours." "True," said Dr. Wilson, "and so Christ must be taken as God's gift, if He is to become yours. I am a doctor," he went on, "but I am not your doctor, am I?" "No," said the boy. "Why not?" asked Wilson. "Because we never took you as our doctor," the boy replied. "Very well, then, Jesus Christ is a Saviour, but He is not your Saviour unless you take Him. Will you do so now?" The boy did.

Our society likes to view all religions and beliefs as equal. We are told there are many paths to God. But that is not the message of the Bible, nor is it the message of Jesus Himself. He came into to the world to provide the only means of salvation that is acceptable to God and available to man. "Jesus saith unto him, I am the way, the truth, and the life: no man cometh unto the Father, but by me" (John 14:6).

If Jesus is the only way to Heaven (and He is), then those of us who know this truth have a responsibility to share the good news with others and point them to the way of life. God's plan is not for us to be saved alone but to bring others with us on the way to Heaven.

Today's Word to the Wise: Never lose sight of the wonderful salvation provided for us through the birth, life, death, and Resurrection of Jesus Christ.

A Faithful Saviour

He that handleth a matter wisely shall find good: and whoso trusteth in the LORD, *happy is he.*—**Proverbs 16:20**

One of the leaders of the early church was a man named Polycarp—believed to have been a disciple of the Apostle John and appointed by him as pastor of the church at Smyrna. Polycarp was noted for his faithful witness. Late in his life (according to some accounts, he was more than one hundred years old), a wave of persecution arose and Polycarp faced martyrdom for refusing to deny Christ and burn incense to the Emperor of Rome. Asked to deny the Lord, Polycarp declared, "Eighty and six years have I served Him, and He never did me injury. How can I blaspheme my King and Saviour?"

God calls His children to be faithful to Him, even unto death if necessary. But this call is not given without an example. Set before us as a pattern to follow is the faithfulness of Jesus Christ. Though He was fully God, He was also fully human, and He lived by faith in His Father just as we are meant to do. Praying at the grave of Lazarus before raising him from the dead Jesus said, "Father, I thank thee that thou hast heard me. And I knew that thou hearest me always: but because of the people which stand by I said it, that they may believe that thou hast sent me" (John 11:41–42).

Throughout Jesus' time on Earth, He exhibited faith and confidence in the Father by living according to His will. As Jesus demonstrated, faith is not shown by having a good feeling about something but by being obedient to what God has commanded in His Word. Just as Jesus trusted the Father and fulfilled His purpose, we should be walking in faith-filled obedience. If we do not, we will miss the great blessings that come from faithful obedience.

Today's Word to the Wise: Follow the pattern of Jesus today by trusting God to do what He says He will do.

A Saviour Who Always Loves

A friend loveth at all times, and a brother is born for adversity.
—**Proverbs 17:17**

An English evangelist told the story of young Prince Edward visiting a military hospital where injured heroes of World War I received treatment. After being escorted through the cots and thanking each veteran, he turned to the nurse who led him and said, "I understood you had thirty-six patients here, but I have only seen twenty-nine."

Gently, the nurse explained that they had moved some of the more disfigured veterans so as not to disturb the prince too greatly. Prince Edward insisted on seeing them and was brought to a room where six more men lay. Once again, the prince thanked each veteran. But as he left the room, he again asked the nurse about the missing veteran. "There were twenty-nine in the first room and six here. Where is the seventh?"

The nurse hesitated. "Your Majesty, no one but those who must care for him are allowed in his room. He is very badly maimed." The prince insisted, and he was shown into the room where a blind, dismembered, and horribly disfigured soldier lay on a cot. With tears in his eyes, the prince knelt by the man and reverently kissed the cheek of the war hero.

Although perhaps not externally, you and I are far more broken even than that soldier. Our brokenness is not because of heroism, but because of the ugly sin that has stained our souls. Yet, Jesus Christ stooped low—far lower than the English prince—to love us. God's love for us is not based on our loveliness, but on His nature. Paul wrote, "But God commendeth his love toward us, in that, while we were yet sinners, Christ died for us" (Romans 5:8). Nothing that we have done or failed to do keeps God from loving us. He sent His Son as an expression of that love to provide us with a way of salvation. The love Christ has for us cannot be measured, and it will never end.

Today's Word to the Wise: Rejoice today in the great love of Jesus Christ that brought Him to Earth to be your Saviour.

An Honored Saviour

Before destruction the heart of man is haughty, and before honour is humility.—**Proverbs 18:12**

As a young man, Henry Leach answered the call of his country and served in the Army during the Korean War. When his unit came under fire, several of the soldiers were injured. Leach risked his life to help rescue them, being shot twice himself in the process. Because of a mix-up in paperwork and a records fire, he was never acknowledged or awarded for his courage. It was not until 2013 that Leach's congressman heard the story and took action. More than sixty years after he was wounded in battle, Henry Leach was finally honored and received his Purple Heart as well as other medals for bravery.

The Lord Jesus humbly came to Earth, laying aside all of the glory and honor of Heaven because of God's great love for us. Though He was despised, rejected, and crucified instead of being honored, the story does not end there. The Bible tells us that one day, in response to His humble obedience to the will of His Father, Jesus will receive the honor that He is rightfully due. "Wherefore God also hath highly exalted him, and given him a name which is above every name: That at the name of Jesus every knee should bow" (Philippians 2:9–10).

The world may not have honored Him at His first coming, and they may not be honoring Him today, but every single person will honor Him one day. Jesus is not coming the second time in the same manner as He did the first time. He is going to receive all the honor due Him at His return. Knowing that, it is important for us to honor and glorify Him with our lives today. As we glorify Jesus through our words and our actions, we are doing our part in God's plan for our world.

Today's Word to the Wise: Give praise and honor to Jesus today for the wonderful sacrifice of love that He gave for our salvation.

God's Purposes Always Stand

There are many devices in a man's heart; nevertheless the counsel of the
LORD, that shall stand.—**Proverbs 19:21**

Mary received a birth announcement unlike any other in history—
the angel Gabriel came and told her that even though she was a
virgin, she would have a son. Although this announcement was stunning,
and even impossible, she received it with faith.

Of course the birth of a baby does not happen immediately. During
the nine months before Jesus' arrival, Mary and Joseph faced many
challenges. One of the biggest was a trip that was required for the Roman
census. Because of their ancestry from David, they had to go to Bethlehem
to register, even though Mary was near her time of delivery. "And so it
was, that, while they were there, the days were accomplished that she
should be delivered" (Luke 2:6). It is important for us to remember that
none of this happened by accident or coincidence—every part of the
Christmas story was in accordance with the plan and timing of God.

The sovereignty of God is vital to our faith. When we do not see how
things can work out for the best and do not understand why our prayers
seem to go unanswered, we can be confident that God is still in control.
In the fullness of His time, the "counsel of the LORD"—His purpose and
plan for our lives—will be accomplished no matter what it takes. There
is no reason for us to fret and fear, for God is in charge.

Today's Word to the Wise: Knowing that God is fully in control of not
just the events of our lives but also their timing should encourage us to
trust Him more.

A Saviour Who Cleanses

Who can say, I have made my heart clean, I am pure from my sin?
—Proverbs 20:9

In the 1800s, childbirth was extremely dangerous. Mortality rates for both mothers and babies were high. One of the most dangerous complications of childbirth was puerperal fever, often called "childbed fever." It killed more than one in ten new mothers in many hospitals. A Hungarian obstetrician named Ignaz Semmelweis determined to find an answer to this lethal threat. After careful study and observation, he realized that puerperal fever was almost unknown among women who gave birth outside of hospitals.

As he continued his studies, Semmelweis concluded that infections were being spread by unwashed hands and medical implements. After he instituted a careful sanitation program at his clinic, cases of puerperal fever almost vanished. Rather than hail him as a life-saving hero, the medical community rejected his simple cure for the problem. Doctors refused to take part in sterilizing their hands and equipment. Semmelweis lost his position at the hospital and was eventually placed in an insane asylum where he died after being beaten by the guards.

Mankind needs cleansing, yet often we reject it. The message that we need a Saviour to take away our sins offends our pride and undermines our belief in our ability to do everything for ourselves. But sin is a disease with no human cure. No religious ritual or observance can solve the problem. The writer of Hebrews said, "For it is not possible that the blood of bulls and of goats should take away sins" (Hebrews 10:4). The only hope that we have is Someone who can cleanse us and do what we cannot do for ourselves—this person is Jesus. When John the Baptist saw Him, he cried out "Behold the Lamb of God, which taketh away the sin of the world" (John 1:29). He completely cleanses all who trust in Him.

Today's Word to the Wise: Cleansing is not just for our salvation but for our daily walk. As we confess our sins, we continue to be cleansed.

A Saviour Who Guards and Keeps

The horse is prepared against the day of battle: but safety is of the LORD.—**Proverbs 21:31**

In addition to being one of the most popular actors in America, Jimmy Stewart was an accomplished pilot. When World War II broke out, Stewart enlisted in the Army and took additional flight training at his own expense to prepare for combat. After initially being used largely for publicity purposes, Stewart was sent to Europe where he flew his B-17 in twenty combat missions. Later he was promoted to chief of staff of his combat wing of the Eighth Air Force.

All through the war, Jimmy Stewart carried with him a copy of Psalm 91, given to him by his father just before he left for the service. Stewart said, "What a promise for an airman. I placed in His hands the squadron I would be leading. And, as the psalmist promised, I felt myself borne up." Stewart remained in the Air Force Reserve after the war, eventually rising to the rank of Brigadier General.

In Jesus, we have a Saviour who offers us perfect protection and who will never leave us or fail us. There is no power that can overcome His love for us. Jesus said, "My sheep hear my voice, and I know them, and they follow me: And I give unto them eternal life; and they shall never perish, neither shall any man pluck them out of my hand" (John 10:27–28).

He is our only true source of security. Physical health can vanish overnight. Political freedom can be lost unexpectedly. Economic security can quickly be destroyed. But the security that comes from being in the very hand of Jesus can never be lost or taken away. In Him we have a Saviour who not only delivers us from sin but also ensures our security until we reach His presence in Heaven.

Today's Word to the Wise: No matter what difficulties or dangers we may face, we can be confident in the protection of our loving Saviour.

A Saviour with Answers

*Have not I written to thee excellent things in counsels and knowledge,
That I might make thee know the certainty of the words of truth; that
thou mightest answer the words of truth to them that send unto thee?*
—Proverbs 22:20–21

We are told almost nothing about the life of Jesus before He reached adulthood, but the Bible records a story about Him as a twelve-year-old boy that reveals many wonderful truths. That year, as they did every year, Mary and Joseph went to Jerusalem for the Passover. When they prepared to return home, Jesus remained behind in the temple. It took a day for them to realize that He was missing, and it was not until the third day that they found Him.

During that time, Jesus had joined the learned scholars of the Scriptures who met and discussed different points of the law and the writings of the Old Testament. Despite His young age, He displayed a depth of knowledge that those who listened found remarkable. Luke 2:47 records, "And all that heard him were astonished at his understanding and answers." Of course we know that Jesus is the very Word of God, so it comes as no surprise that He was able to speak with authority and insight concerning the inspired Word God gave to man.

There is a lesson for us in this story: Jesus has the answers for the problems and difficulties that we face. Isaiah said, "His name shall be called…Counsellor…" (Isaiah 9:6). There is wisdom and protection available if we seek wise and godly human counsel, but there is no better source of guidance and direction than that which we find in the pages of Scripture. Peter reminds us that it is in the Word of God that "His divine power hath given unto us all things that pertain unto life and godliness" (2 Peter 1:3).

Today's Word to the Wise: When you need guidance and direction, look to Jesus who is *the* Counselor.

A Saviour Who Was Obedient

Hearken unto thy father that begat thee, and despise not thy mother when she is old.—**Proverbs 23:22**

Gladys Aylward was born to a poor family in 1902. At a young age she began working as a domestic servant to help provide for her family, yet in her heart, even as a girl, she dreamed of going to the foreign mission field. Because of her lack of education, she was turned down by the China Inland Mission. Undaunted, she used her life savings to pay her own way to China where she became widely known for caring for orphans and abandoned children. During the Japanese invasion of China, she led one hundred children to safety over treacherous mountains. Asked later about her work she said, "I did not choose this. I was led into it by God. I'm not really more interested in children than I am in other people. But God gave me to understand that this is what He wanted me to do—so I did it!"

God places great value on obedience. Even Jesus demonstrated obedience throughout His life on Earth. Though He was both fully God and fully human, He did not "pull rank" on Mary and Joseph, but instead lived obediently just as God expects every child to do. The Bible says, "And he went down with them, and came to Nazareth, and was subject unto them: but his mother kept all these sayings in her heart" (Luke 2:51).

If obedience was important for the sinless Son of God, it certainly is no less important for us. Though our society often lauds rebellion and obstinate behavior, God praises those who are in submission to authority. In whatever sphere of life you find yourself, be sure that you are obeying the authorities which God has placed over you. You will find His blessing through obedience, and you will truly be following Christ.

Today's Word to the Wise: Just as Jesus did, we should devote our lives to obedience to God's will and commands.

A Saviour Who Triumphed

So shall the knowledge of wisdom be unto thy soul: when thou hast found it, then there shall be a reward, and thy expectation shall not be cut off.—**Proverbs 24:14**

In 61 BC, Gnaeus Pompeius Magnus, commonly known as Pompey the Great, returned to Rome after a startling military victory that expanded Rome's empire as far east as the Black Sea. He was honored with a "Roman triumph"—a grand festival reserved only for the most impressive of victories. The triumph lasted two full days rather than the customary one day celebration. Thousands of captured enemy soldiers and slaves were forced through the streets before Pompey's chariot, as a massive portrait of Pompey made entirely of pearls was carried overhead. A dozen years later, however, those who had once cheered him turned against him, and he was defeated in battle by Caesar. The great general died almost totally alone.

Contrast Pompey's defeat with Christ's triumph. When Christ came to Earth, He did not have an impressive reception with generals lining the streets to welcome Him. Crowds did gather throughout Jesus' ministry, but by the end of His life He was abandoned even by His closest followers. He was put to death in a barbaric and humiliating fashion. Yet in what appeared to be the moment of His defeat on the cross, Christ was actually gaining His greatest triumph over Satan, death, and the grave—and the story isn't over yet.

The final victory still remains to be accomplished when Jesus returns, not as a lowly Saviour, but as a ruling and triumphant King. Though nearly two thousand years have passed since Jesus went back to Heaven to prepare a place for us, His return is still certain. Those of us who know and love Him can be confident as we await His coming, because it is going to happen just as the Word of God tells us.

Today's Word to the Wise: As you celebrate Christmas, remember to look forward to the triumphant return of our Saviour and Lord.

A Faithful Saviour

As the cold of snow in the time of harvest, so is a faithful messenger to them that send him: for he refresheth the soul of his masters.
—**Proverbs 25:13**

In his autobiography, Charles Spurgeon described his conversion this way: "I sometimes think I might have been in darkness and despair until now had it not been for the goodness of God in sending a snowstorm, one Sunday morning, while I was going to a certain place of worship. When I could go no further, I turned down a side street, and came to a little…chapel. In that chapel there may have been a dozen or fifteen people….

"The minister did not come that morning; he was snowed up, I suppose. At last, a very thin-looking man, a shoemaker, or tailor, or something of that sort, went up into the pulpit to preach. He was obliged to stick to his text, for the simple reason that he had little else to say. The text was, 'Look unto me, and be ye saved, all the ends of the earth' (Isaiah 45:22). He did not even pronounce the words rightly, but that did not matter. There was, I thought, a glimpse of hope for me in that text."

A faithful layman opened the Scriptures, and God used his simple message to bring one of the greatest preachers in history to faith in Christ. Like the faithful messenger mentioned in Proverbs 25:13, this preacher shared the simple plan of salvation—look to Jesus alone—and it led Charles Spurgeon to trust Christ as Saviour.

The promise of God is unchanging. Through the life, death, and Resurrection of Jesus "He is able also to save them to the uttermost that come unto God by him" (Hebrews 7:25). This is the true wonder of Christmas.

Today's Word to the Wise: Rejoice today in the salvation made possible by the faithfulness of Jesus Christ.

The Wisdom of Humility

Seest thou a man wise in his own conceit? there is more hope of a fool than of him.—**Proverbs 26:12**

S amuel Morse was born into a preacher's home in New England just two years after George Washington was elected the first president of the United States. Early in his life he demonstrated two traits—a deep love for God and great skill as a painter. After finishing his education at Yale, he went to England to hone his painting skill. Upon his return to America he was recognized as a gifted artist and was soon in much demand. Morse's first wife died while he was away from home painting in Washington, D.C. He did not receive the news until it was too late. In his heartbreak he turned away from painting and began trying to develop a means of rapid communication over great distances. This eventually led to his discovery of the telegraph.

Despite his fame and the many honors that came his way, Morse wasn't proud or boastful. In a letter to his second wife he wrote, "The more I contemplate this great undertaking, the more I feel my own littleness, and the more I perceive the hand of God in it, and how He has assigned to various persons their duties, He being the great controller, all others His honored instruments. Hence our dependence first of all on God, then on each other."

When we walk in pride and are conceited regarding our talents and accomplishments, we are demonstrating that we do not understand or appreciate the role that God holds in everything we do. None of us are able to succeed in our own strength or wisdom; we should always remember it is God that makes what we do possible. As Paul put it "what hast thou that thou didst not receive?" (1 Corinthians 4:7).

Today's Word to the Wise: Pride separates us from the blessings and grace of God, and it is an expression of deep foolishness.

Be Loyal to Your Friends

Thine own friend, and thy father's friend, forsake not; neither go into thy brother's house in the day of thy calamity: for better is a neighbour that is near than a brother far off.—**Proverbs 27:10**

The 1936 Olympics were about far more than just sports. Hitler wanted to use the games to demonstrate the superiority of the German people, especially in contrast to those who "came from the jungle," as he put it to one aide. The performance of American Jesse Owens was particularly galling to the German leader. Owens would win four gold medals in track and field—a feat that had never been accomplished. The gold medal in the long jump, however, was one that Owens would not have won without help from an unlikely source.

German long jump champion Luz Long watched as Owens fouled on his first two attempts in the qualifying round. One more foul would keep Owens from even being able to compete for the medal. Long told Owens to put a mark several inches in front of the takeoff board and jump from there. Owens followed his advice and qualified. He then went on to win the gold medal with an Olympic record distance while Long settled for the silver. Luz Long would be killed during World War II, but Owens never forgot what he had done. Nearly thirty years later, Owens arranged a meeting with Long's son and told him how much his father's action had meant. Owens said, "You could melt down all the medals and cups I have and they wouldn't be a plating on the 24-carat friendship I felt for Luz Long."

A true friendship is a great treasure—and very rare. Most friendships falter when one party begins to focus only on self. Being a true friend requires a measure of loyalty and sacrifice, but the value of such a friendship is worth the investment it takes to build one.

Today's Word to the Wise: If you have a friend, cherish that friendship. More importantly, be a true friend to someone else today.

Walking in Integrity

Better is the poor that walketh in his uprightness, than he that is perverse in his ways, though he be rich.—**Proverbs 28:6**

In his best-selling autobiography, Lee Iacocca told of a painful experience from his childhood. Though people of Italian ancestry faced prejudice in his school, he decided to run for captain of the student patrol for his sixth grade class. When the election returns were counted, he lost by a vote of twenty-two to twenty. He didn't realize what had happened until the next day when a classmate pointed out that there were only thirty-eight children in the class! The teacher allowed his opponent to add extra votes to ensure he would win over Iacocca.

Our society is filled with people who try to get ahead by doing things that are not right. In sports, business, and politics the story is the same. If someone thinks he can gain an advantage, he is willing to abandon his integrity to do so. Then when the news comes out and he faces disgrace, we see tearful apologies and interviews where he explains why he made these choices. Rarely does anyone admit, "I was not a person of integrity."

Integrity is not the result of a single decision; it is the product of a day-by-day process of refusing to cut corners and do wrong just because no one will see. A life of integrity comes from a series of choices to do right because it is right. Walking uprightly demands that we do right even if no one else does. It would be nice if integrity always produced a good outcome, but sometimes there are no short-term benefits. In some cases, it even produces a negative immediate result. Even then, however, the eternal reward makes it worth any temporary hardship we may endure.

Today's Word to the Wise: When tempted to cut corners, remember the long-term benefits of a life of integrity.

The Wisdom of Silence

A fool uttereth all his mind: but a wise man keepeth it in till afterwards.
—**Proverbs 29:11**

In one of Aesop's Fables, a donkey walking through the woods finds the skin of a lion. Hunters had killed the lion and left the skin to dry in the sun. The donkey put on the lion's skin and was delighted to discover that all the other animals were terrified of him and ran away when he appeared. Rejoicing in his newfound respect, the donkey brayed his happiness—only to give himself away by his voice. The moral of the fable was clear: fine clothes may disguise, but silly words will disclose a fool.

In our day of social broadcasting it seems that anyone can become famous by disclosing every embarrassing part of his life to the world on television or the Internet. Yet what is truly gained by such "entertainment"? People may sit at home and laugh at the folly of those who hold nothing back, but they are diminished in the process. This produces a corrosive effect because it encourages people to share more and more when they have less and less to offer.

We have an epidemic of people sharing their opinions without regard to whether or not they have anything meaningful to say. Someone said, "The problem today is that those who know the least know it the loudest." Indeed much of what is promoted as wisdom is actually anything but—it is the worst of foolishness displayed publicly.

Maybe you've heard the old saying "You have two ears and one mouth—use them proportionately." Almost all of us could stand to listen more and talk less. Rather than being compelled to tell everyone we meet everything we can fit into the length of the conversation, we should remember that one of wisdom's best qualities is the ability to hold the tongue.

Today's Word to the Wise: A good goal for the New Year would be to talk less and listen more.

The Blessing of Enough

Two things have I required of thee; deny me them not before I die: Remove far from me vanity and lies: give me neither poverty nor riches; feed me with food convenient for me: Lest I be full, and deny thee, and say, Who is the LORD? or lest I be poor, and steal, and take the name of my God in vain.—**Proverbs 30:7–9**

The story is told of an early church leader who was particularly known for his display of contentment. When he was asked to explain his secret he replied, "It consists in nothing more than making a right use of my eyes. In whatever state I am, I first of all look up to Heaven and remember that my principal business here is to get there. Then I look down upon the Earth, and call to mind how small a place I shall occupy in it when I die and am buried. I then look around in the world, and observe what multitudes there are who are in many respects more unhappy than myself. Thus I learn where true happiness is placed, where all our cares must end, and what little reason I have to complain."

Every person can come up with a list of things they would like to have (and there is nothing wrong with owning things if the things don't own us). If we are honest in our assessment, however, we would have to say that we have far more than most people in the world and more than we must have to live. The reality of our lives is that we *do* have enough—we simply need to be content with what God has provided and thank Him for it.

Today's Word to the Wise: Resolve to be content with what God has given you, and you will find your gratitude to God increased.

Praiseworthy Works

Favour is deceitful, and beauty is vain: but a woman that feareth the Lord, *she shall be praised. Give her of the fruit of her hands; and let her own works praise her in the gates.*—**Proverbs 31:30–31**

Born into a wealthy family, Henry Parsons Crowell determined at a young age that he would use his resources to further the work of God. According to his biography *The Cereal Tycoon*, Crowell prayed, "God, if You will let me make money, I will use it in Your service." In addition to founding the Quaker Oats Company, he had a number of other successful businesses. He was a great personal friend and supporter of D. L. Moody and helped finance the work of the great evangelist. During the latter part of his life, Crowell regularly gave 70 percent of his income to his church and other Christian works.

As part of his vision to extend his giving beyond his lifetime, Crowell founded a trust to support evangelistic efforts around the world. The founding document he wrote stipulates that when a vacancy occurs on the board, the remaining members "shall elect a person who is an avowed disciple of Jesus Christ, as witnessed by profession and character." Though this successful businessman has been dead for decades, he continues to have an impact for the kingdom of God.

All of us are building legacies that we will leave behind. The work that we do for God establishes the testimony by which we will be remembered. The possessions we accumulate and the earthly honors we achieve will soon vanish away, but the investments that we make in God's work will last throughout eternity. If you want to look back on the coming year with joy rather than regret, make sure you take full advantage of every opportunity to serve God and others. If you do, your works will be praiseworthy.

Today's Word to the Wise: Live today in such a way that the legacy of your works will bring glory to God.

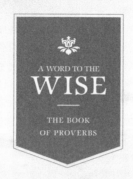

A WORD TO THE

WISE

THE BOOK
OF PROVERBS

INDEXES

Title Index

May

1 The Curse of Prosperity
2 Rejoicing in Evil
3 A Sign of God's Love
4 Staying on Course
5 The Eyes of the Lord
6 Sudden Destruction
7 A Matter of the Heart
8 Leadership and Wisdom
9 What You Do for Yourself
10 Blessing without Sorrow
11 Justice in Practice
12 The Tongue of the Wise
13 Loving the Truth
14 The Way that Seemeth Right
15 Sharing Knowledge
16 Righteous Leadership
17 Dangerous Fools
18 Take Time to Listen
19 The Protection of Obedience
20 A Faithful Man
21 Wandering from the Truth
22 Planning for the Future
23 Be an Example
24 The End of Sloth
25 The Protection of Self-Control
26 Repeating Folly
27 A Debt to Be Paid by
   Each Generation
28 Confession and Mercy
29 Pride Brings Us Low
30 The Strength of Preparation
31 Kind Words

June

1 Choosing to Fear God
2 The Paths of the Righteous
3 Incomparable Riches
4 Holding on for Dear Life
5 The Deceitfulness of Sin
6 Get Out!
7 Until the Morning
8 Our Faithful God
9 The Invitation of Wisdom
10 Missed Opportunities
11 Keep What Is Precious
12 The Triumph of Truth
13 The Company You Keep
14 Don't Buy that Bridge
15 When Less Is More
16 A Balanced Father
17 Stop Before You Start
18 The Mouth of the Fool
19 The Value of Correction
20 Known by Our Actions
21 The Poverty of Pursuing Pleasure
22 The Friendship of Angry Men
23 Hope and the Fear of the Lord
24 Standing in Adversity
25 Apples of Gold
26 Don't Grab the Dog's Ears
27 Faithful Wounds
28 The Hunger of Vain Companions
29 The Rejoicing of the Righteous
30 Hiding in the Rocks

July

August

September

October

November

December

Scripture Index

Proverbs

Ecclesiastes

Isaiah

Jeremiah

About the Author

Dr. Paul Chappell is the senior pastor of Lancaster Baptist Church and the president of West Coast Baptist College in Lancaster, California. He is a powerful communicator of God's Word and a passionate servant to God's people. He has been married to his wife, Terrie, for thirty-two years, and he has four married children who are all serving in Christian ministry. He enjoys spending time with his family, and he loves serving the Lord shoulder to shoulder with a wonderful church family.

Dr. Chappell's preaching is heard on *Daily in the Word*, a radio program that is broadcast across America. You can find a station listing at: dailyintheword.org.

You can also connect with Dr. Chappell here:

Blog: paulchappell.com
Twitter: twitter.com/paulchappell
Facebook: facebook.com/pastor.paul.chappell

Visit us online

strivingtogether.com

wcbc.edu

Other Titles for Your Daily Walk

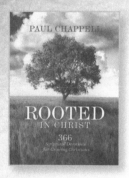

Rooted in Christ

In this power-packed daily devotional, each page beckons you to a deeper relationship with God, helping you discover for yourself the life-changing power of His unshakable love. As each brief reading draws you to the Lord, you'll be equipped to greet each day with bold faith, confident in God's faithfulness, strength, and transforming grace. (424 pages, hardback)

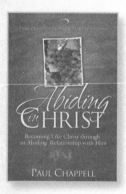

Abiding in Christ

In these pages, Dr. Paul Chappell will lead you on an exciting and encouraging journey to discover the authentic Christian life. You will learn how an intimate relationship with Christ produces a genuine heart and life change. You will find the source of true love, abundant joy, lasting fruit, spiritual maturity, emotional stability, and purpose in life. (168 pages, paperback)

Stewarding Life

God has given you one life and filled it with resources—time, health, finances, relationships, influence, and more. How you steward these resources will determine whether you successfully fulfill God's eternal purpose for your life. This book will challenge and equip you to strategically invest your most valuable resources for God's eternal purposes. (280 pages, hardcover)

strivingtogether.com

Other Titles for Your Daily Walk

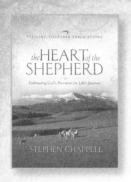

The Heart of the Shepherd

Pastor Stephen Chappell explores the twenty-third Psalm with insight that will delight, strengthen, energize, and comfort every Christian. As you draw close to the Shepherd, get a fresh glimpse of His love and see His eternal plan; your life will never be the same! (96 pages, mini hardback)

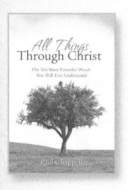

All Things Through Christ

Discover the ten words in Scripture that make the difference for those who desire to live fully for Jesus Christ. (72 pages, mini paperback)

A Maze of Grace

During a season of suffering God's amazing grace more closely resembles "a maze of grace!" If you or someone you love is enduring a season of suffering, this minibook will provide comfort and encouragement. (64 pages, mini paperback)

strivingtogether.com